ROSE MACAULAY

By the same author

The Razor Edge of Balance:
A Study of Virginia Woolf

ROSE MACAULAY

A Writer's Life

Jane Emery

JOHN MURRAY

© Jane Emery 1991

First published in 1991
by John Murray (Publishers) Ltd
50 Albemarle Street, London W1X 4BD

The moral right of the author has been asserted

British Library Cataloguing in Publication Data
Emery, Jane
Rose Macaulay: a writer's life.
1. Fiction in English. Macaulay, Rose, 1881–1958
I. Title
823.912

ISBN 0–7195–4768–7

Printed and bound in Great Britain by
Butler & Tanner Ltd, Frome
and London

To Clark and Clare

CONTENTS

ILLUSTRATIONS

29. Rose at work in her London flat
30. Gilbert Murray and Emily Penrose at Somerville
31. Father Johnson
32. Rose in Venice, 1957
33. Rose on her last cruise

The author and publishers would like to thank the following for permission to reproduce illustrations in this book: Constance Babington Smith and the Rose Macaulay Estate, Nos. 7, 13, 16, 17, 18, 20, 29, 31; Trinity College Library, Cambridge and the Rose Macaulay Estate, Nos. 1, 2, 3, 4, 5, 6, 8, 9, 19, 32; the Bettmann Archive, Nos. 12, 14, 24, 25, 28; Miss Elizabeth Godfrey, No. 10; the National Portrait Gallery, London, No. 11; Dr Mary Anne O'Donovan, No. 15; Professor Quentin Bell and the Hogarth Press, No. 21; Livia Gollancz, No. 22; Weidenfeld & Nicholson Archives, No. 23; Roland Philipps and Chatto & Windus, No. 26; the Hulton Picture Company, No. 27; Somerville College and the Bodleian Library, Oxford, No. 30; Victor Glasstone, No. 33.

ACKNOWLEDGEMENTS

All who write books belong to a society of perpetual obligation. But biographers are the most deeply in debt. They owe their survival not only to their subjects but also to archivists, reference librarians, index makers, custodians of public records, and bibliographers; they are beholden to diarists, photographers, gossips, letter writers, lawyers, and hoarders of memorabilia. Above all, they are dependent on the generosity of those, living or dead, who are willing to recount their memories – on those whose memories contradict the memories of other witnesses, on those whose memories are self-contradicting, and on those whose memories contradict the biographer.

Biographers can never pay their debts, but they can acknowledge them:

Throughout the eleven years of intermittent forays to hunt and gather evidence and during the two writing years of more intense search and discovery, I gave thanks for the inexhaustible fascination of Rose Macaulay, for the salutary influence of those who asked probing and difficult questions about her, and for the patience of those who lived in the vicinity of my obsession.

My first thanks are for the unfailing generosity of Constance Babington Smith, on behalf of the Estate of Rose Macaulay, who, despite the fact that this is not an authorized biography, made rare primary material available to me, helpfully answered many questions, and gave me permission to quote from the works and private papers of Rose Macaulay in order to write this critical biography. Secondly, I am grateful to Professor Gretchen Gerzina, who sent an early chapter of the typescript to John Murray and so initiated a happy association.

Interviews with those who knew Rose Macaulay or those with specialist knowledge of her work, friends, and milieu have been invaluable. For facts, insights, and hospitality I record thanks once more to the late

Acknowledgements

Brigid O'Donovan, Donal and Jennifer O'Donovan, Dr Mary Anne O'Donovan, Mrs Jane Redmond, John Ryan of Galway, and Mrs Muriel Thomas. I am grateful for interviews (in many instances a succession of interviews over the years) with Dr Pauline Adams, Librarian and Historian of Somerville College; Professor Quentin Bell; Lord Bonham Carter; P.N.Furbank; the Revd. Donald Harris; Professor Carolyn Heilbrun of Columbia University; the Honourable Mrs Mark Hodson; Victor Glasstone; the Revd Prebendary Gerard Irvine; the late John Lehmann; Dr C. David Ley; Paz Ley; Dr Daphne Park, former Principal of Somerville College; Mrs Elizabeth Shaw, Librarian of Oxford High School; and Dame Veronica Wedgwood.

Library personnel who have given me special assistance are Diana Chardin, Assistant Manuscript Cataloguer, Trinity College Library, Cambridge; Dr Helen Clifford, Cataloguer of the E.R.Macaulay Archive in the Wren Library of Trinity College, Cambridge; Cathy Henderson, Research Librarian, and Ellen Dunlop formerly Director of the Harry Ransom Humanities Research Center, University of Texas, Austin; Dr M.A.Halls, former Modern Archivist of King's College Library, Cambridge; Dr T.H.Hobbs, formerly Sub-librarian of the Wren Library at Trinity College, Cambridge; Sonia Moss, Interlibrary Loan Department of Green Library, Stanford University; Dr Adrian Peasgood of the University of Sussex Library; Dr Spencer Routh of the Graduate Library of the University of Queensland; the late Dr Lola Szladits, Curator of the Berg Collection, New York Public Library; Dr P.R.N.Zutschi, Keeper of Manuscripts, Cambridge University Library; and archivists of the Library of the Imperial War Museum, the National Library of Ireland, the British Library and the Department of Western Manuscripts of the Bodleian Library, Oxford.

I am grateful for a grant from the University Research Council of the University of Queensland, and for the special encouragement of two members of its Department of English, Professor P.D.Edwards and Professor K.L.Goodwin. My personal Macaulay archive was enriched by the work of Glenys Priddy, my research assistant at the University of Queensland; my ideas were stimulated by my former student, Dr Susan Thomas of the Department of English, LaTrobe University.

I profited greatly from a year as a Visiting Scholar at the Center for Research on Women, Stanford University. I have been encouraged by the Department of English at Stanford, in particular by Professor Albert Gelpi. Dr Roger Thompson of the School of English and American Studies at the University of East Anglia read and commented on *They Were Defeated*. And Modern British Literature scholars, Professor J.J.Wilson and Dr Barbara McCaffry of Sonoma State University have read and commented on passages of the manuscript.

I appreciate permission from the Rose Macaulay Estate, represented

Acknowledgements

by Constance Babington Smith and administered by Peters, Fraser and Dunlop, to publish from sources, published and unpublished, and to reproduce pictures for which the Estate holds the copyright. I gratefully acknowledge permission from the Master and Fellows of Trinity College, Cambridge; from King's College Library, Cambridge; from Harper Collins Publishers Ltd; from the Syndics of the Cambridge University Library; from the Harry Ransom Humanities Center, University of Texas, Austin; from the Henry W. and Albert A. Berg Collection of the New York Public Library; from the University of Sussex Library; and from John Murray. I acknowledge permission from the BBC to quote from the *Listener* and from their sound archives. I am grateful to Dr Mary Anne O'Donovan for permission to quote from Beryl O'Donovan's unpublished memoirs and to publish the portrait of Gerald O'Donovan.

But further thank-yous which can never be properly said remain to be said:

My editor, Ariane Goodman, has warmly encouraged me and rigorously and creatively challenged my text.

My daughter, Clare Novak, has given this book the great benefits of her professional expertise and critical distance – benefits doubled in value by her humane insight.

My husband, Professor Clark Emery, has pointed out the foggy passages of my typescript and inspired me to illuminate them. Ever the untiringly critical reader, he has also been the creator of the best of all possible worlds in which to enjoy writing and rewriting this book.

The Macaulays and the Conybeares

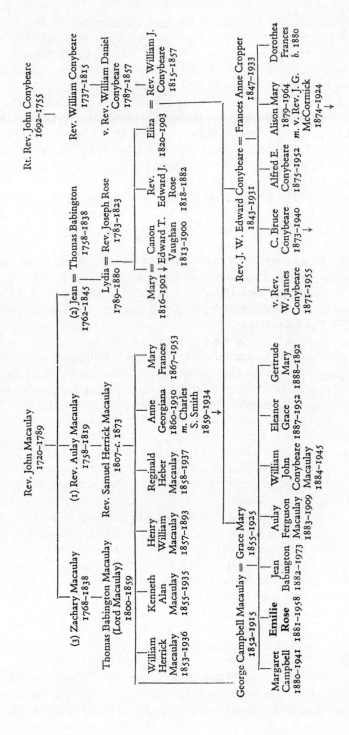

INTRODUCTION

Three Voices of Rose Macaulay

WITH ADMIRABLE CONSIDERATION and dignity, Rose Macaulay, at the age of 77, died quickly of a heart attack in her own bed in the early hours of 30 October 1958. Struck by pain, characteristically stoic, not wishing to trouble her doctor, she had telephoned, asking him to order her an analgesic from the chemist's. Instead, he came at once. But shortly after she died.

On Thursday morning, when the news spread, her many friends could not believe or accept the reality of a still and silent Rose.

Two months earlier would have found her voyaging back from Trebizond as an acclaimed but unofficial jester for an aristocratic party on an educational cruise, tracing the route of the Argonauts in their quest for the Golden Fleece. Two nights earlier would have found her in London at this Hellenic cruise's reunion, still amusing her shipboard comrades. Victor Gollancz called Rose Macaulay 'one of the best party-goers in London'.[1] She even appears unexpectedly in the middle of Christopher Isherwood's novel, *The World in the Evening*, at a lunch party in Carcassone. Nothing slowed her brisk pace. At 48, warned of her 'low-grade heart' by a cardiologist, she had written to her sister Jean, 'I shall take this as a pretext for not doing things that tire me, except when I want to. Doctors have their uses.'[2] The evening before her death, although recovering from bronchitis, she gladly responded to Robert Cecil's invitation to come round and give her lively account of the reunion gathering.

On Friday morning, 31 October, *The Times*' obituary column unreeled itself at length under a Cecil Beaton portrait of a serenely wise and secretly amused Emilie Rose Macaulay, Dame Commander of the British Empire. Describing her as a 'novelist of lively and ironic intelligence, wide scholarship, and fastidious wit' and an 'intrepid traveller', it praised her successful use of her intellectual heritage, her Oxford education, and her unmistakable talents as a woman of letters by listing her many literary accomplishments. Her honorary Cambridge Litt.D. crowned them all.

Her many friends were unconsoled by the knowledge that they still had her voice on the page. They mourned their loss of her inimitable living speech. Ivy Compton-Burnett was grieved, then aggrieved. 'A light has gone out. ... I am utterly deprived by losing Rose.'[3] From their first meeting in 1929, Ivy had regularly relished Rose's conversational company, her tough-minded, entertaining accounts of human behaviour; in Rose's late years, dismayed that her friend was no longer 'a perfectly sound agnostic like everybody else',[4] Ivy enjoyed making energetic attacks on Rose's regained Anglican faith. But their friendship remained firm.

C. V. Wedgwood recalled Rose on the telephone, sharing their mutual fascination with seventeenth-century English history, 'talking, thinking, discussing' at length, as though the issues of the English Civil War were spread out on a tea table between them. 'Who nowadays', Dame Veronica lamented in 1962, 'can so quickly spark a lagging conversation into life or prick a pretentious argument with a tart revealing comment?'[5] Rose Macaulay could imply 'Tush!' and 'Fie!' She could and did disconcert the fatuous, self-regarding, or presumptuously intimate with a few cutting words.

John Lehmann acknowledged that she had this sharp flavour, but added that she had sweetness as well. To a shy outsider at a party, as the American writer Mary Ellen Chase remembers, she could 'emanate understanding, concern, and sympathy'.[6] Alan Pryce-Jones, editor of *The Times Literary Supplement* from 1948 to 1959, remembers her, for all her astringent commentary, as a deeply understanding confidante:

> I can remember being held, late at night on a doorstep in a draughty autumn, while Rose cross-questioned me about myself. And below the surface of this firm old lady – not that anyone ever thought of her as old – little by little so much tenderness of feeling – so much comprehension – came glimmering up through her words that I felt as if she were the one person who exactly understood my own bewilderment.[7]

The memory of her high-pitched staccato voice stayed for years with old friends, and her silence struck even recent acquaintances as a melancholy void. As late as 1975 Rebecca West could hear her clearly and see her plain:

> Sometimes as I go about London I pass a house, and a name stirs in my mind, and the walls become transparent and I see a room with charming people talking and laughing, and me among them, young, and in a state of enchantment, and I relive an agreeable moment of another age. ... I see behind the front of a London house and that shows me a cocktail party dominated by Rose Macaulay, a fine comic novelist who was also a fine comic figure in her own right.[8]

Lady Diana Cooper, who met Rose for the first time on the New Argonauts' voyage, also praised her winning sallies: 'She had our ship in thrall: we gave our hearts and peals of laughter. Her manner was not gay – she threw no confetti – but her caustic flares could make us hilarious.' She concluded that by Rose's death she had been 'unkindly robbed of a new-found and still uncounted treasure'.[9] John Betjeman said she was 'the least boring of people'.[10]

Listeners who had heard her voice nimbly debating on the BBC had so enjoyed her irreverent wisdom that when her flat was destroyed in the Blitz, many sent books to replace her lost library.

That first voice – that voice of Rose Macaulay's public and social persona – was a valuable creation and was heard as the narrator of her novels. It came from an outer self which, without the disapproval of those she respected, escaped many responsibilities normally accepted by women of her class but unpalatable to her: supervising servants, entertaining at home, maintaining a fashionably chic appearance, marrying, rearing children, nursing and teaching, and living in a state of dependent domesticity. She believed this to be a cloistered life which 'damaged women's minds'. 'At the worst,' she wrote in 1925, 'a house unkept cannot be so distressing as a life unlived.'[11]

Instead, her eccentric, libertarian, anti-authoritarian public self offered laughter and social satire to her audience through her writing. She made a place for herself in a literary London dominated by men; she travelled adventurously, alone and with others (driving her car with dangerous nonchalance); she cherished family relationships (although she thought the phrase 'the sanctity of the home' sentimental cant); and she made strong, active friendships in diverse circles (swimming with Rupert Brooke, helping Elizabeth Bowen publish her first stories, attending the farewell party for Isherwood and Auden on the eve of their departure for the Spanish Civil War, trying to teach E.M.Forster to use crutches, celebrating the Christmas holidays with Vita Sackville-West and Harold Nicolson at Sissinghurst). 'Love and no ties,' she thought best for her.[12]

She neither envied nor railed against the freedom of the English bachelor; she simply pre-empted it. She had a vision of a shared human nature which could reconcile the sexes; 'women are after all people,' was her view, although she displayed the disadvantages of their lives clearly in her novels.[13] Across the span of her writing appears a range of sympathetic and extraordinary female characters, among them variations on the gamine, the waif, the poet, the quester, 'the elegant rake', and the wise auntly mentor with a sharp tongue. Her best novels bring them to life. Her own active, autonomous existence is a model of independence and individualism for women. But she did not want to be labelled 'a writer for women'.

She had been a tomboy. She understood the danger of sexual and behavioural stereotypes. As a free-spirited adult her physical and mental energies were unflagging, and they were not hampered by the conventions of gender or age. Friends recalled her climbing with agility the book ladders in the London Library, leaping from the highest diving board into the Serpentine in chill Septembers, cycling daringly through the worst of London traffic in her sixties, and at 69 spending a snowy afternoon tobogganing down Primrose Hill on a tea-tray with two little girls and their parents.

If her apparently radical claim to idiosyncratic liberty seems self-indulgent, few who knew her ever forgot that in the midst of a gregarious and roving life, she was an impressively professional and prolific writer. 'If you gave her an assignment,' said John Lehmann, 'you knew you would get a good piece and you would get it on time.'[14] Between 1906 and 1956 she published twenty-three novels, a critical biography, five books of criticism and essays, four books of history and travel, two volumes of poetry, and an anthology, as well as many uncollected book reviews, essays, and newspaper articles. Death caught her in the middle of another novel; the unfinished manuscript was titled 'Venice Besieged', and its climactic image was to have been that of the heroine seated where Rose herself had always longed to sit – astride one of the four great bronze horses of the Basilica of San Marco.

The quality of these fifty years of writing is inevitably uneven, but the minor work is still valuable as social history and the best of it is now being republished because the insight, vitality, wit, and magnanimity endure. Thirteen of her books, fiction and non-fiction, are still in print and bookshops still display fresh copies of *Non-Combatants and Others*, *Told by an Idiot*, *They Were Defeated*, *The World My Wilderness*, *The Towers of Trebizond*, *Fabled Shore*, and *Pleasure of Ruins*.

On her own compassionate terms, Rose Macaulay was a moralist for our times. Although her *joie de vivre* and humour lit up her accounts of human behaviour, experience had taught her the pathos and anxiety of the hidden life. She had a second – an inner – voice, less often heard than the first outer one. It could speak of that life with depth and feeling. And although she was a novelist of ideas and social surfaces, and a little mocking of the stream of consciousness technique, she too asked one of the major questions of the early twentieth-century modernists about the secret self. In Virginia Woolf's *To the Lighthouse*, Lily Briscoe had silently questioned, 'How then, she had asked herself, did one know one or another thing about people, sealed as they were?'[15] A diffident Macaulay character considers:

Odd how you never knew people, only on the outside ... Had everyone then some different self, that only a few people, that sometimes only they themselves knew? She had put the same question to herself the other day when reading the published diary of a man of letters, who revealed in his daily records a self strangely hidden from his friends. They had known him as one kind of person, and he was, between himself and his diary quite another. Which was the more real? Both were, but which the more? Not necessarily the secret, hidden self.[16]

These queries were critical for Rose Macaulay, for her outer life was a triumph of intelligence, humour, and courage, but her inner life required concealment and prompted self-questioning. In her essay, 'Problems of a Writer's Life', she writes, 'Readers do not know how hard even the most improbable novelist may have tried to be truthful; he has difficulties to contend with that they know not of. He no doubt knows well enough how life – some life, that is – is actually lived, but his lips are sealed: he cannot tell.'[17] 'One should consume one's own smoke,' was her stoic motto.[18] Victor Gollancz wrote that Rose, 'for all her gregariousness was "far and away" the most private person I have ever known.'[19] For twenty-four years she was in love with a married man who had been a Catholic priest; of this, and of her religion, the two deepest things in her life, she rarely spoke. The sound of her second voice was that of the inevitable inner conflict. One result of her reticence could be predicted by the most imperceptive critic; Rose herself – hardly imperceptive – observed, like others before her, that literature is most often created by concealed tensions.

But Rose Macaulay had a third voice, speaking in an inviolable world which did not include family, friends, or her 'beloved companion'. Its monologue intermittently surged up, overwhelming both her speech and the murmur of her second voice of emotion and conscience. She spoke of that third voice in a BBC broadcast near the end of her life. She began her talk by dismissing the business of life, as 'not particularly interesting, to you, nor to me' and described the 'oddly amphibious life, one foot on earth and one in misty seas, mountain slopes, or in strange secret valleys', which she thought both men and women lead – the life of the questing mind which tells itself stories of adventure, beauty, search. And that voice can speak of 'one of the age-old romances of the human race . . . the quest for a God who may be found among the queer paradoxes, anguishes and turmoils of the world.'[20]

In her first voice she narrated comic novels about those 'queer para-doxes, anguishes and turmoils'. But her last three books – *The World My Wilderness*, *Pleasure of Ruins*, and *The Towers of Trebizond* – charac-teristically diverse, together harmonized Rose Macaulay's three voices: the comic, cerebral, social voice; the private, emotional voice which could also be the biting voice of conscience; and the unifying voice of archetypal dream which linked the individual present experience with 'different epochs, different races, different sexes'. She was seeking God, but also an understanding of the turmoil – the cycles of creation, ruin, and rebuilding that make up human history and individual lives. That final harmony of her writing was a triumph, achieved after a period of loss and grief. These last, best works help us understand the days and works of Rose Macaulay, a wise and joyful woman and writer who created that rare, resilient life honoured by so many mourning friends.

PART ONE

Macaulay

I

'Does Ancestry Matter?'

IN JUNE 1928, the features editor of the *Daily Express* asked Rose Macaulay, as 'one of the most brilliant of living women writers', to write an article answering three probing questions, beginning with the unanswerable 'Who are you?'[1]

Rose Macaulay disliked such hyperbolic compliments. And as a matter of principle, she mocked headline queries concocted to generate 'human interest' features about women. She parodied them in her novel of that same year, *Keeping Up Appearances*: 'What Is the Right Age for a Woman?' 'Should Clever Men Marry Stupid Women?' 'Should Clever Women Marry Stupid Men?' 'The Post-War Girl: is she selfish, rude, clever, stupid, drunk, thin, tall, dark, fair?'[2]

But she agreed to write a brief article for the *Express* 'Who I Am' series, perhaps because, in contrast to her satirical but not too far-fetched fictional examples, the second of the autobiographical questions seemed to her to be worth considering: 'What do you owe to your forebears in the matter of attributes of mind and character?'

She entitled her light essay on this serious subject: 'Does Ancestry Matter?' This question had always been of particular interest to the gossiping relations of Rose Macaulay. It is of broader interest to such cultural historians of the nineteenth and twentieth centuries as Noel Annan, as almost every Macaulay critic has noted. In his 1955 study, 'The Intellectual Aristocracy', he uses the Macaulay family as his first example of a 'caucus of influence' which began to form in England at the beginning of the nineteenth century. He defines this group as a much intermarried clan of the educated upper middle class which both 'criticized the assumptions of the ruling class above them' and formed the opinions of its own class. And, to trace the connections between its distinguished members, he begins with Rose Macaulay's place on one of its spreading family trees because not only her parents but also their kin are conjoined in a genealogical pattern of Macaulays, Conybeares, Trevelyans, Arnolds, Huxleys, and Vaughans.[3]

It was a tree that flourished. How widely its many branches spread is demonstrated by Rose's discovery in 1952, two years after beginning the most significant correspondence of her life, that she had been writing regularly by transatlantic mail to a distant cousin. Her sympathetic epistolary confidant and informal confessor, Father Hamilton Johnson, an English Anglican priest in America, proved to be related to her through the Vaughans and the Rose family. She had been named after Emilie Rose, one of its daughters.

This was, of course, a coincidence, but Noel Annan argues that in this network of gifted related families, ancestry did often produce between its members a compatibility of temperament and interests. He shows that Rose's forebears on both sides of the family – the male clerics, dons, and writers, and the wives they chose from each other's families – were models of qualities which reappeared regularly in their descendants' minds and characters. They were intelligent, principled, tolerant, liberal, philanthropic, and literary. Devoted to literature rather than to the arts, they wrote lucid, reasoned, and graceful prose. They educated their daughters as well as their sons. Rose's great-grandmother, Lydia Babington, each morning read an Old Testament chapter in Hebrew and a New Testament chapter in Greek. Her daughter – Rose's grandmother, Eliza Conybeare – was, says her obituary, 'thrown constantly with persons of high purpose and culture'.[4] This clan of intellectual leaders took up and helped win such historically significant causes as intellectual freedom in the British university system and the creation of a public service open to talent. Even plucking a few names at random from Lord Annan's long roster of these interrelated aristocrats of the mind produces a short-list of English men and women who lived with purpose – some celebrated, others honoured on a lesser scale, but all persons of intelligence and conscience: the Revd Aulay Macaulay, tutor to Princess, later Queen Caroline; Zachary Macaulay, who agitated against slavery; Elizabeth Fry, the Quaker philanthropist; Dame Emily Penrose, who took a First in Greats and became Principal in succession of Bedford, Holloway, and Somerville Colleges. There were bishops, linguists, and scientists on the Conybeare side.

But although the Macaulay family's admirable talents and accomplishments were a matter of public record and Rose Macaulay knew them well, she chose to present a different kind of evidence in her own article. She was not a hagiographer; she believed that a family's history should show both the common humanity and the individual idiosyncrasies of its members. Her forebears had been made vivid to her through the details of their interests and tastes, their quirks and foibles, preserved in family lore, in letters and diaries. And in these records, criticism – just or jealous – had survived side by side with praise. Annan says, 'For all of them the purpose of life was to distinguish in conduct as well as in concept the sham from the genuine.'[5]

Sometimes the judgements revealed more about the critics than about the victim, but they gave credible life to both. Conceit was a favourite target. Thomas Babington Macaulay, first cousin of Rose's parental grandfather, had been the cause of laughter within the family circle because he watched himself in the drawing-room mirror while he was talking. Matthew Arnold as a young dandy was described by one diarist as 'a fashionable puppy spoiled by his father's fame'.[6]

But Rose Macaulay was not conceited. She could have subtly implied that she was like her ancestor Lord Macaulay, who, writes a former Regius Professor of Modern History at Cambridge, 'had the rare gift of awakening in others his own intense delight in the spectacle of the past'.[7] But, wonderfully skilled in distinguishing 'the sham from the genuine', she was always amused by self-importance. She first addresses the question about her eminent forebears with a brief introduction based on the editor's third query: 'What is your ancestral background in the great panorama of human life?' She gives a modest Darwinian answer. From such an absurdly grandiose perspective she sees all members of the human race as 'anonymous and approximately similar specimens of a vast simian family' and herself as 'a queer little speck in time, just appeared, so soon to go', shaped by unknown 'qualities, instincts, bodies, and minds', which link her with the 'first unconscious speck'. She, too, mocks human vanity.

Then she moves to the focused question about her unique heritage with a brief, amusing family history in which she parenthetically deduces connections between her early predecessors' lives and her individual liking for fish, islands, mutton, adventure, writing, and books. She begins:

I can meditate on that Danish Olaf who came long ago to raid the Highland coasts, settled in the Hebrides, and there bred a line of MacOlafs, or Macaulays, who doubtless lived largely on the fish they caught. (I like fish.) They developed into a warlike and turbulent little clan, with a spurred riding boot for crest and a valiant boast of intrepidity in their motto [*Dulce periculum*]. They lived largely on sheep raided from other clans: in the family records there is mention of at least one who was captured and hanged by his enemies for this theft. (I, too, like mutton.) They concurred in the slight alteration in British religion that occurred in the sixteenth century, and early in the eighteenth century one of them so far departed from the martial traditions of his family as to become a minister of the Scottish Church.

And she continues, 'Henceforth, my ancestors seem to have changed their habits and to have become addicted to preaching, reading, and writing, instead of to raiding and fighting.' She explains that after her antecedents left Scotland, they became Anglican parsons, a tradition not broken until the generation of her father, and adds that her mother's family had been

English clergymen since the sixteenth century. 'No wonder that I feel an interest in religion. ... The descendants of parsons find it hard to escape from this interest; they may believe or disbelieve in any form of religion, but they can seldom regard the subject with indifference; it is in their blood.' (She wrote this at a time when she described herself as 'an Anglo-agnostic'; one pattern of her life is the alternation of belief and disbelief.)

After disclaimers about her own erudition, she recalls that her erudite grandfather wrote 'a slight and brief novel about family life', but doubts that this similarity in their vocations 'can be twisted into heredity' because the profession of novelist is so common. So far she has been more entertaining than self-revealing. In fact, there is not one clue in the text of the article itself as to the gender of its writer. But at its close there is a sudden shift from a neutral point of view. If Rose Macaulay's name and photograph were removed from the page, the last sentence would support a wager that 'Who I Am' is written by a man: 'More citable, possibly, as heredity', she writes, 'is the great desire to enter the Navy which I had as a child, for my father's father began his career as a sailor before yielding to the hereditary impulse towards the Church'.

Like her 'addiction' to reading and writing, her boyish 'intrepidity' was a part of Rose Macaulay's ancestral tradition. She, too, in the spirit of its motto, celebrated 'sweet danger'. But both bookishness and daring were also encouraged in her early childhood by her immediate family. And so 'Does Ancestry Matter?' leads to a less historical and more personal question: 'How much does parentage matter?' Rose Macaulay comments on the influence of parents on tastes and habits. 'My mother liked reading detective and adventure stories, and wearing her oldest clothes; she disliked sewing, mustard, cats and very recently born infants. I share all these tastes and distastes. My father liked walking and disliked afternoon callers (I mean, when they called at his house), and so do I.'

Even a few vignettes of the courtship and early marriage of her parents, George Campbell Macaulay and Grace Mary Conybeare, suggest more significant clues, although certainly not all the answers, to the complex puzzle: 'Who was Rose Macaulay?'

We discover most about her father as a young man through his correspondence with Francis Jenkinson, a librarian at Cambridge. In 1877, writing as a bachelor schoolmaster at Marlborough College to his old university friend, George Macaulay created an attractive self-portrait. His letters are vivid. They testify to his intelligence, energy, imagination, candour, modesty, and humour. (Rose's many correspondents found the same appealing qualities in her letters.)[8]

Family diaries add detail to this picture and demonstrate the family closeness of both Conybeares and Macaulays. In 1874, three years before taking that first teaching post, as a Cambridge undergraduate, George and two of his four younger brothers, Will and Kenneth, had moved into the social circle of the Conybeare family by calling together regularly at the home of Grace's older brother, Edward Conybeare, vicar of the Anglican church at Barrington, and his hospitable wife Frances. As a consequence we have gossipy observations about George's appearance, behaviour, and ideas from the diaries of Frances and of his bride-to-be, his distant cousin Grace, who came from her home at Weybridge in Surrey, on extended visits.[9]

The drawing-room discourse of the young Cambridge students and the Conybeare friends and relatives (Macaulays and Roses) in Barrington was self-consciously designed to stimulate controversy. This lively salon discussed such provocative religious, literary, and social subjects as eternal damnation, Walt Whitman's poetry, and 'the caste system in England'. They debated such quandaries as 'whether riches were a blessing' and tried to define the nature of platonic friendship and love. (Rose, too, delighted in substantive, argumentative conversation.)

We know the young Grace Conybeare through many daily entries in the diaries she kept from 1867 when she was 12 until the middle years of her marriage. Those of her early years described the model life of a growing girl in mid-Victorian, upper-middle-class society. Here is a record of almost faultless behaviour: regular study, constant reading of the most approved literature, punctual daily church-going, wholesome recreation, and good deeds. She tells of taking round Christmas puddings to the poor, learning collects, trying to teach her pet dogs Gyp and Arrow not to be jealous, play-acting in amateur parlour theatricals, picking primroses, daringly galloping bareback, taking long walks, reading Shakespeare and Wordsworth aloud in the family circle, reading George Eliot or Mrs Gaskell in solitude, and admiring her widowed mother. ('Oh, mother is so very delightful!') She was not only the only girl but also the only child at home; brother Edward was twelve years older. She was both encouraged and spoiled. But her self-approbation is saved from priggishness by her high spirits. (Her daughter Rose was also active and buoyant, although not similarly indulged.)[10]

The diaries' tone of equable self-possession, however, is a little suspect. When Grace inserts comments in a private cipher, the reader infers that the accessible part of the text is for the eyes of her mother – truthful but selective. The readable entries show few emotions other than gratitude, delight, and piety, although these are youthfully intense. But when occasions for jealous or amorous feelings arise, she either shifts into her secret language, or writes circumspectly for her mother's eyes: 'Wrote to George – Mother says I may from time to time, as he evidently wishes it – and I do.'

At 19, if she spontaneously shows admiration for him ('Certainly George has a wonderful poet's face'; 'George more charming than ever'), she tries to protect the entry from any outsider's interpretation of her commitment by closing with such postscripts as 'On reading this over I think it well to add I am really still fonder of W. [Will] than of G. Macaulay.' Her feigned fickleness seems in part prompted by George's reticence. But in contrast to her tempered caution in writing, according to her sister-in-law Frances, Grace's social behaviour was dramatic and volatile. Her strong feelings about George Macaulay were transparent to everyone: 'Grace in raptures over his reading, looks, and being generally.' (Like her mother, Rose could be ebullient, but, like her father, she masked her deepest feelings.)

During the years of tentative courtship George was a student in Classics at Cambridge, undecided whether to be a barrister or a schoolmaster. But Grace was not confused about her own vocation; her days were filled with a project into which she flung herself so single-heartedly that Frances accused her of neglecting her familial and social duties. Late Victorian women undertaking worthy and demanding voluntary service were not thereby excused from family obligations.

Grace gathered a small group of village girls and formed a school, religious, academic, and practical. She rose at dawn and went to her cold little classroom, a shed in the grounds of the house, to prepare lessons – Scripture, French, History, Geography, and Needlework. She was such an inspiring and successful teacher that her 'scholars' won prizes when tested along with those from other schools in the diocese. And she makes clear in her diary that she enjoyed both the unquestioned authority over the schoolgirls and the sense of her own virtue that this volunteer teaching gave her. (Rose was both to profit from her mother's talent as a teacher and to suffer from her love of complete dominance.)

In the Victorian family style of debit-and-credit character analysis, Frances Conybeare's journal gives a mixed picture of her younger relative: 'Grace is in most things a mere child ... a wayward child.' She is passionately religious, yet in the eyes of the family, her devotion to the duty she has chosen for herself has led to self-righteousness and 'a lack of humility'. Frances praises Grace's enthusiasm and envies its driving force; she also finds her 'selfish and spoilt', possessed of 'a growing spirit of wilful independence'. (The Conybeare family atmosphere was one of earnest striving and self-examination; Frances was equally strict with herself in this exercise of spiritual accounting. Perfection was her goal.) Even though Grace was supported by her mother in her teaching project, her resistance to the wider family disapproval required self-confidence and courage. Yet her success in the atmosphere of their opposition seems to have made her a little arrogant. 'She is a strange creature,' wrote Frances, 'power and weakness interwoven to an unusual extent.'

Frances also made both positive and negative entries about the good-looking young George Macaulay, although she was biased in his favour. 'George has golden merits, but grievous faults to do battle with.' She was 'much struck' with him; she thought him 'a man with brains for anything'. She admired his quiet nature, his commitment to temperance, and his kindness. 'I am much interested in him,' she writes, 'but I am very unhappy about him. He never says the Creed. I fear his religion is utterly vague.' (The church-going George, oldest of the seven children of the rector of Hodnet, had read Darwin and suffered from Doubt. Like her father, Rose Macaulay was to question dogma.)

In April 1875, George's second year at Trinity College, Frances was troubled by the cloud that had gathered over his head. His Latin Tripos verses, in the bawdy style of Plautus, were judged 'immoral and impudent'. Ribald Tripos verses were a Cambridge tradition; in her biography of Milton, Rose Macaulay observed that as an undergraduate even that chaste young poet wrote similar vulgar rhymes for the occasion. But George's coarse mockery of an identifiable individual among the university authorities had so shocked the College community that his verses had been suppressed. Frances wrote that George was 'a black sheep in the eyes of most people, struck off from the Master's visiting list'.

His 'scurrilous' lines survive in the official records. And they were indeed disrespectful of his elders. George's Latin skit is a pun-filled comic trialogue: an undergraduate with a hangover and an aggressive prostitute are discovered together by a grey-haired senior proctor; instead of punishing the student for being in bad company, the proctor himself goes down the alley with the luscious Erotium Meretrix.[11]

The authorities were not amused. George had to sign two public apologies in the presence of witnesses. And, perhaps by official request, he stopped teaching Sunday School. This undergraduate cheekiness was seen more calmly in time, however, and a year after this ostracism, a meeting called by the Master agreed to 'forget his fault'. (Rose, too, was a parodist and a bold satirist, although not in so lusty a style. But neither she nor her father was afraid to defy officialdom.)

The same faulty estimate of his audience's sense of humour caused a lovers' quarrel between George and Grace in the second year of their friendship. It seems that in company she often made gratuitous arbitrary pronouncements about the qualities a young man must have to deserve her admiration. In August 1876, to tease her about this haughtiness, George parodied a popular poem and presented the verses to her. He at first pretended they were anonymous, but he was quickly identified as the author.

Two of the four stanzas are characteristic of the poem's list of the religious and social beliefs, habits, tastes, and talents some extraordinary young man should have to win a 'Yes' from the fastidious 'Araminta' of the poem.

If he mentions his land or his income,
If he's ever so little low Church,
If *The Rock* or *The Record* (oh, sink 'em),
Have ever engaged his research,
If he isn't both godlike and human,
If he doesn't read conics and row,
If he doesn't appreciate Newman,
My own Araminta, say NO.

He must take you to balls in the season,
He must chatter and dance like a brook,
He must read Kant's *Critique of Pure Reason*,
He must take off his hat to the cook,
Then his voice must be sweetly melodious,
He must dote upon music or go,
If his verses are perfectly odious,
My own Araminta, say, NO.[12]

(Rose, too, was to enjoy writing teasing occasional verse.)

Grace was flattered, thought Frances, but somewhat piqued as well. Was she indeed that proud adviser of Araminta? Was George initiating a courtship or, with a jest about girlish conceit, avoiding the challenge of her impossible dream? Her touchy reaction was to make too much of the joke and to behave coldly towards George as though deeply offended and angry.

Frances thought Grace hoped for an exciting scene. But to Grace's surprise George neither fell to his knees in apology nor confronted her in protest. Perhaps hurt as well, he appeared unruffled; silent, he withdrew for a time, leaving the smitten Grace 'miserable', 'wretched', and, stretched weeping upon her bed, unable to write in her diary. Even such a trivial and romantically comic incident shows the differences in emotional temperament and sense of proportion which were to affect their marriage and family life over the years. Grace was over-emotional; George's practice was to evade conflict with her. But this first disharmony was temporary; the lovers were reconciled.

In October 1876, George began teaching at Marlborough. A first-year teaching post demands much time and energy, yet in the world outside the school, following the family liberal tradition, he assumed civic duties. He gave a course that year to the workingmen of Shoreditch in London, taking the independent stand of Strafford in the Civil War for his subject. Grace attended one meeting and reported: 'The audience tremendously radical, as was George himself – They appreciated every word evidently and their enthusiasm broke out into constant demonstrations, most inspiriting – George did it *very* well. We thought Mother was a little taken aback by his "radicalism".' Grace herself was experiencing a passionate egalitarianism at the time. She refused to teach her village pupils to curtsey to ladies.

Even more courageously, George manifested his convictions in active protest; in the name of humanitarian justice he issued challenges to the ruling powers. In 1877 he organized the presentation of a Cambridge petition against war which was read in the House of Commons by Gladstone. The same year he wrote a letter to *The Times* arguing that the annexation of India obligated the Empire to feed the famine-stricken. (His daughter Rose was also to find governments and bureaucracies lacking in humanity, although she was less sanguine than he about reform.)

By 1877 George's courtship of Grace had become official. A painful event of that year, however, was to be critical to his academic and marital career: an academic disappointment burdened him with a sense of failure. (Failure was a central theme in Rose Macaulay's early novels.) Unusually intelligent, scrupulous, and hard-working, as his later scholarly work proved him to be, George Macaulay had distinguished himself as an undergraduate in 1876, tying for the fourth rank in a list of twenty-three Firsts in his Classics Tripos exams. But, surprisingly, he did not succeed in his first attempt to obtain a Cambridge Fellowship in October 1877. To his friend Francis Jenkinson he wrote, 'I did disgracefully'. He felt this 'disgrace' deeply, both then and later. Immediately after learning the results, he wrote a melancholy sonnet to Grace which began:

> I do confess I longed that this might be
> Not chiefly that the prize itself was sweet,
> But for a gift to lay before thy feet,
> Which might commend my worthless self to thee.[13]

Through the years he believed that this blot on his academic record stood in the way of his advancement and marked him as second-best. But nineteen days after he presented the apologetic verses to Grace, George placed an engagement ring on her finger. They were married on 19 December 1878 after he had become a schoolmaster at Rugby with twice the prestige and twice the pay that teaching at Marlborough had provided. By then he had made a second attempt and achieved the Fellowship, a not uncommon sequence of events. But, because the title required celibacy, he had vacated its rights and privileges and become 'a former Fellow' in order to marry. (The rule was repealed soon afterwards, allowing him as a married man to apply for a university appointment.)

How did the parentage of George and Grace Macaulay affect their second daughter Rose? What were her first years as the child of this marriage like? Several of Grace's diaries for the years between 1878 and

1887 are missing, but the remaining volumes covering the young couple's nine years at Rugby describe their happy and strenuous life as part of the school, a world into which Rose was born on 1 August 1881, and in which she lived until she was 6. Grace describes the routine as 'dear old Rugby life' – 'George always rushing in from school in cap and gown'. She enjoys the life of the young – entertaining schoolboys once a week at breakfast and encouraging her growing family in boisterous play. And she delights in the visits from George's four younger brothers; they formed a close group. But the round-the-clock daily duties and the rapid succession of Macaulay babies laid heavy burdens on both parents.

From the beginning, the conscientious George overworked himself. In his letters he good-naturedly and affectionately calls the Rugby boys 'a large assortment of idiots', but in addition to his regular duties he coached a number of them rigorously for the Trinity College Entrance Exam, attempting to replace their schoolboy fecklessness with 'a wholesome terror'. Grace tells of his giving a series of free readings to a group of workingmen at Bath. And he habitually ended the day by the fire, reading aloud to Grace such diverse classics as Plato, Dickens, Swift, and Shelley – almost invariably falling so deeply asleep that she, after retiring, must come down and arouse him by washing his face with a wet sponge.

Grace, often in a state of poor health, exhausted herself as well. After what the diary hints at as a miscarriage, she bore six children in the next eight years. Of a quick temper and determined to be in absolute control of the nursery, she had constant servant problems. (Her brother Edward's diary records in January 1884: 'Grace seeking her sixth nurse in a twelve-month!') Often with the help of her visiting mother – the strong and supportive Eliza Conybeare – Grace struggled, nursing the children through childhood diseases and accidents while she suffered herself from recurrent severe sore throats, a symptom which had first appeared in childhood. The diary was, of necessity, neglected, but its intermittent entries give the sense of a busy life and a happy marriage as well as of periods of what Grace calls 'great strain'.

The Macaulays' first child was a daughter, Margaret Campbell, born in 1880. But Grace longed for a boy and when she found herself pregnant the next year, she read 'manly' books and tried to think 'manly' thoughts. The sex of her second child, Emilie Rose, was a disappointment. Grace did not, like her daughter Rose, think it was better to be a man, but she wanted to be the mother of sons. From her youngest days, Rose was aware of her mother's dismay at her birth; she tried to be a boyish daughter. The arrival of the third girl, Jean Babington, born in 1882, was even more of a defeat to Grace's expectations, and Jean always suffered a sense of her mother's rejection. But when Aulay Ferguson Macaulay was born in 1883 Grace was jubilant: 'Our first boy born – universal joy in the household at the event which took place at 9:15 P.M.'

– 18 –

The birth of another son, Will, a year later was also cause for celebration.

In this crowded nursery, Rose could not have had a great deal of individual attention, but she made precocious progress. Although her mother's educational principles did not consider such a practice wise, Rose was reading before she was 4. The year after, she demonstrated her independence by scepticism; upon being told by her mother about the existence of God, she said, 'I don't know that'.[14] She was already imagining stories; she and Margaret as co-author invented a tale of bold adventure about two little girls and told it to Jean.

Rose's fifth year, 1886, was especially difficult for the Macaulay family. All the children weathered a grim, long winter of whooping cough and Grace was weak from nursing Aulay, who was gravely ill. Edward Conybeare commiserated with the worried and exhausted parents in his diary, 'Both George and Grace cruelly worn down with work from 5:30 A.M. to midnight daily.'[15] George, both ambitious for himself and concerned about Grace's well-being, attempted to gain a more prestigious post and a better life for his family by applying for the Clark Lectureship at Cambridge. His testimonials were in the hands of the Master of Trinity on 3 June, but on 13 June Grace tersely wrote, 'Mr. Gosse is elected to Clark Lectureship.' By the end of the summer, Grace was chronically ill; by February 1887 her throat was in a state of constant haemorrhage.

Grace was now expecting her sixth child. Relatives probably disapproved of the Macaulays' fecundity. As early as 1875, family planning had begun to be a topic of discussion among both men and women in the Conybeare circle; Frances had written in her journal, 'The responsibility of bearing children is mooted ... a child every fourteen months is not an unavoidable calamity.' Grace's health had continued to decline, and her doctors said she must live in a warmer climate and lead a less demanding life. Her father had died of tuberculosis of the throat, and, in the light of the medical knowledge of the time, the family's fears for her future were well-founded. It was around this time that George and Grace made a dramatic decision. By early summer the Macaulays' plan for a new life was forming. When a fourth girl, Eleanor Grace, was born in June, they turned their eyes away from Rugby. By September, after failing to win an appointment in Australia for which he had applied, George was busy packing the family belongings for a move to Italy.

'The Macaulays all leave September 15 for empty space,' wrote the astonished Edward Conybeare in his diary. And when the eight of them and their two servants were ready to depart, he added darkly, 'Macaulays all off to exile'. Bravely, like the adventurous MacOlafs whom Rose was to describe in 'Does Ancestry Matter?', George and Grace Macaulay voyaged out, to settle in a new world, begin a new life, and 'change their habits'.

PART TWO

Rose

2

The Island Colony

THEIR RESOLUTION TAKEN, late in September 1887, the Macaulay family left staid and conventional Rugby to begin their radically new life in Italy. Rose, 6, and Margaret, 7, bade theatrical farewells to their English days as young daughters of a schoolmaster by kissing the walls in each room of their home. However 'silly' the gesture, as younger sister Jean thought, their childish drama acted out the family's emotions about the journey ahead – excitement mingled with uncertainty as to when they would return.

Those 'silly' kisses were a true goodbye to Rose's early childhood and the beginning of what she was always to describe as an idyll. Until she was 13 she would live much of her life out of doors in a state of freedom and delight which would shape her mind and spirit, sharpen her senses, nourish her imagination, and generate an unquenchable thirst for adventure and for the means with which to capture and understand her experience. Like Wordsworth, she never forgot the glory and the dream of her active, receptive childhood; unlike him, she never lost the power to relive that joy in the radiance of its original light. Her seven happy tomboy years were to make her an original: a rebel against insincere, time-wasting social conventions and a stereotyped sexual identity; an eloquent libertarian; a lover of the landscape; and a lifelong swimmer and tree climber. In her childhood world she developed independence and resilience of mind and body.

When they began this open-ended venture, Grace and George Macaulay could not see its consequences for any member of the family; they were less ecstatic, more anxious about the outcome than their children. George was setting out for Italy with no settled position; his only prospect abroad was to produce free-lance translations of the classics and to edit school texts. Both were ill-paid tasks. Additional family income was to come chiefly from savings, Grace's inheritance, and supplementary gifts from Mrs Conybeare. In addition to slim means and Grace's illness, other worries burdened them. The parents and their six children (including the unwelcomed three-month-old Eleanor) and two English servants set out with only 'Hotel Smith, Genoa, Italy' as a forwarding address. Their Baedeker showed the daily room rate as one-fifth that of the Grand Hotel and added: 'Unpretending; English landlord; near the exchange' – a destination respectable, plain, and affordable for a brief stay, but no fixed abode for what Rose later described as the Macaulay 'wilderness of monkeys'. The noisy turmoil of the entourage would require housing at once; to find a home quickly was the parents' only firm plan for the future.

Before leaving for the Continent the large family party visited Grace's mother at Weybridge; all relatives gathered were generous with sympathy, unsolicited advice, and implied criticism. Magisterial Edward was touched by Grace's 'sweet', invalid pallor and weakness but found the liveliness of Margaret, Rose, Jean, Aulay, and Will little muted by their recent illnesses. On the dates of the Macaulay return visits to England over the next seven years, the Conybeare family diaries were punctuated by comments on the turbulence of the children's 'overwhelming', 'harum-scarum', 'tumultuous' behaviour and 'wildness'. Grace, approving high spirits, was more likely to describe this hyperactivity by recording in *her* diary: 'Children in raptures.' She believed (most of the time) that exuberance was beauty. But the journey to Genoa via Paris and Geneva did not promise to be restful.

The Macaulays' choice of Genoa as a destination was not a difficult one. Frugality was imperative and all travelling English knew that Italian living was inexpensive. More important, the chief goal of the move was Grace's recovery and 'warmth' was the doctor's prescription. Although the north of Italy could occasionally be as cold as England, the Ligurian coast had advantages in addition to its usual long season of light and heat. Compared to the south, northern Italy was more progressive economically and industrially; there were more English-speakers and English libraries there; transportation was better and 'home' more accessible; local politics were less corrupt and made life and property safer.

Whether or not the memories of the Macaulays' Italian honeymoon trip to Florence, made nine years before, included the beauty of the rocky, hilly northern Italian coast, the sight of its still loveliness was at once to confirm their choice as being aesthetically as well as practically sound. In 1891 Roger Fry visited the Macaulays under the auspices of paternal Uncle William, who was to become vice-provost of King's College, Cambridge. (Years later Rose remembered, 'We adored him.') He wrote to G. Lowes Dickinson, who was then his tutor, 'The journey from Genoa to Rome was most exciting all along the Mediterranean, which looked like Shelley's poetry. It was very calm and quite unlike any sea I've ever seen before.'[1]

The child Rose sensed this calm excitement, too. At 10, cherishing her own illustrated *Complete Shelley* ('an intoxicant'), she waded along this shore alone chanting his poetry. Again and again in novels, poems, essays, and letters she would describe this sea she loved, her prelapsarian playground, 'stretching level and limpid, blue as evening ... the still, clear, tideless edge, that was as a lake's margin, lifted by no ripple, but having for waves a soft, soundless sway to and fro.'[2]

But although a beautiful and advantageous site, Genoa provided no reward for the Macaulays' diligent house-hunt. After several days, advised by a railway official, Grace and George began searching in Varazze, a small fishing village between the sea and the hills, twenty miles to the south-east along the coast, easily reached by train. There, in the centre of the mile-long town whose deep, stony streets smelled, as the adult Rose recalled, of 'fish, drains, and roasting coffee', they found a large upper-level apartment with a romantically painted drawing-room ceiling, a wide balcony facing the bay, and an orange-treed terrace. The rent was £6 a month. In two days the Macaulay household was installed, awaiting the arrival from England of their stored boxes, packed with such familiar objects as would make the children feel at home – carpets, pictures, books, and 160 pots of jam.

In a 1932 memoir Rose offered what seems at first an odd rationale for the choice of Varazze: 'My intelligent parents, compelled by my mother's health to live in Italy, had selected a place devoid of English visitors, churches, doctors and consumptives.'[3] Given Grace Macaulay's passionate High Church Anglicanism and the fear that she suffered from the early stages of tuberculosis, the churches and doctors of Genoa might be thought to have been considered assets. But this mixed list – creating a vignette of the expatriates, tourists, and invalids to be found huddled in English compounds in all the larger Italian cities – does signal a major reason for Rose's own happiness in Varazze. She continues her description triumphantly with the most significant fact of their distinctive location: 'We were, in fact, the only foreigners there.'

Their seven years of living outside any institutions, English or Italian, except the family, offered more immediate prizes than penalties. First, the Macaulays lived unbullied by local social conventions. Neither George, a hard-working scholar who became absorbed in his studies, nor later the adult writer Rose, liked the chatty interruptions of unexpected afternoon callers. And as for church, although the family were friendly with the benign local *parocco*, as outsiders and heretics they incurred no parish obligations. Grace, as an inspiring Sunday School teacher, needed no churchman to take over the religious teaching of her children, and as for formal church services, with some *sotto voce* complaints about the Italian

habit of spitting on floors, she had to substitute Roman Catholic Bene-
diction for Anglican Evensong and often knelt with the children in what
Rose remembered as the 'dusky, incensy' twelfth-century church of San
Ambrogio, as Christians but not Papists.

When the Macaulays arrived, the ministrations of doctors were not
required. What Grace needed most was rest – rather hard to enjoy, even
with servants, in the midst of a large family – but surely less likely a
condition of her regimen if complicated by a demanding life of calls and
entertaining like that of busy Rugby or a leisured English colony in
Genoa. And as for Rose's rather hard-hearted joke about shunning the
company of consumptives, convalescents would certainly have talked of
illness, conversation which Rose was to detest all her life. In short, to
their delight, in the absence of school, church, and polite society, the free-
spirited children of the small Macaulay world outnumbered the adults.
The oldest formed a children's clan, self-named 'The Five'.

The Macaulays did have English visitors, but they were from 'home',
chiefly their invited favourite family members: a cousin, Daisy Smith,
who gave the children some drawing lessons, their vivacious grandmother
Eliza Conybeare, and the four jolly child-loving bachelor Macaulay
uncles. They were to be close to each other and to George's children all
their lives. Uncle Willy, the distinguished mathematician and Fellow of
King's College, and Uncle Kenneth, a successful Birmingham business-
man, were not above playing children's games, and Uncle Harry, whose
feckless ways were to bring him to grief, sang them music-hall songs. Best
loved was Uncle Regi Macaulay, Rose's godfather, already at 32 a partner
in Wallace & Co., a major mercantile firm in Bombay; he tipped the
children generously, built castles of blocks with them, and gave them a
pony. He had early opportunities to assess Rose's intelligence; his favourable judgement of her quick mind was to be critical for her future.

For the children another advantage of the family's cultural isolation
was that, except for six months in 1892 when the three older girls attended
convent classes, their schooling was tailor-made and their teachers were
superior. 'We did lessons with our parents: Latin, Italian, mathematics
etc. with our father, other subjects with our mother,' wrote Rose.[4] Daily
lessons were adjusted to the young Macaulays' individual talents and
abilities and were more devoted to questions than to rote learning,
stimulating their curiosity and intellectual independence. Brothers and
sisters often worked together at the same tasks; Uncle Edward, following
a Conybeare parlour-game tradition in which he conducted oral quizzes
on family reading, forwarded from England examinations on the books
they read together.

The children had the advantage of their father's intellectual supervision
and interest. Their mother taught them reading, writing, literature; there
was some needlework instruction for the girls, but more imaginatively,

Grace organized poetry contests and set all the children to imitating the styles of favourite writers. Rose, being, as she remembered in late life, 'poetry-drunk', excelled in her attempts at pastiche.

For Rose, the best of all aspects of their new life was the sense of the family's making up an island colony, living in a world of their own; she always delighted in the isolation, interdependence, and resourcefulness of the members of the Swiss Family Robinson. Islands became her symbol of Eden. Relations with the town were cordial but not intimate. 'From the time we first went there, we were among friends,' Rose wrote years later.[5] But in spite of the warm generosity of the Varazze shopkeepers (whom Rose always remembered as 'kind and charming'), some brief formal social exchanges with the local upper classes (whom the Macaulay children found gushing and boring), and dependence upon Italian maids-of-all-work, the Macaulay life in Varazze was self-centered and self-sufficient. It had all the advantages and disadvantages of insularity; the problems created by that isolation would not emerge until they returned to England.

But the young Macaulays emphatically did not mind being castaways from the mainland of upper-middle-class academic etiquette and decorum. Their English milieu as the children of a Cambridge don would have been that described in Gwen Raverat's memoirs of her childhood, *Period Piece*, published in 1952. She was born four years after Rose, but the period she describes parallels the Macaulays' years in Varazze. All university children were fenced in by genteel and over-protective rules; Gwen, the oldest of the four Darwin children, remembers sympathetically those more restricted than she: 'There were some children who might not ride bicycles, and others who were forbidden to go in boats; some who were forced to play the violin, and others who always had to wear mufflers; some who might not eat currant buns, and others who were obliged to have cold baths.' Even though the less regimented Darwin brothers and sisters and their male cousins played the same dangerous games of adventure along the Cam as the Macaulays acted out on the verge of the Mediterranean, and walked, like the young Rose, in daring terror along the top of nine-foot walls, Gwen Raverat concluded about her upbringing: 'But when all is said and done, our liberty was only relative; we were only just a little more free than some of our contemporaries. I have no hesitation in saying that all our generation was much too carefully brought up.'[6] For girls in Cambridge the customs were especially stifling; to live there as a boy, as Rose did in the Varazze world, would have been a much more difficult enterprise.

Nor did Rose and her siblings during their Italian days suffer from criticisms of their behaviour which strict housekeeping laws are bound to hand down. A family anecdote contrasts Varazze and Cambridge judgements of child conduct. In 1960 Dorothea Conybeare, Rose's cousin of her own age, daughter of autocratic Uncle Edward and critical Aunt Frances, still recalled with some astonishment small Rose's aplomb in the face of what to Dorothea would have been an occasion for shame and punishment. She writes of an early Macaulay visit to England from Italy:

> Rose was always adventurous. Once, at Barrington [the Conybeares' home near Cambridge until 1901], doing something over-adventurous in our brook, she fell in the Cam (which ran past our garden) and came out in a muddy mess. My mother was vexed; it gave trouble, and Rose didn't seem a bit sorry. (*We* should have felt terribly guilty!) Mother told our grandmother she thought Rose a selfish inconsiderate child, and Grandmother replied, 'Grace says the reverse. She says she is a *very* good child. The cry of the whole family is "If only we were as good as Rose!"' Later on I told Rose this. 'Oh dear', she exclaimed. 'I *am* thankful the boys didn't hear that.'[7]

Rose knew, of course, that the boys' cries had been tongue-in-cheek.

Rose's accounts of Varazze in print and in letters are romantically joyful, but they are always realistic in their description of the nature and behaviour of children. Rousseau and original sin are paradoxically mingled. In an essay called 'Fraternal' (1935), she speaks to her adult brothers and sisters, remembering them as children, 'my savage kind':

> What undignified compromising situations have I seen you all in, brothers and sisters! Suspended head downward from the knees from trees, like monkeys by their tails; rolling like barrels down green slopes to lie at the bottom and vomit; crawling along the top of a high wall to inhale the drain-trap placed (surely oddly) thereon; sitting astride on an overturned canoe at sea; slithering bare-legged up and down a rope; prone in impassioned sobbing on the floor; rolling over and over in angry wrestling; pulling hair, pinching, fisticuffing, hiding books under chair-cushions, as a dog buries bones, that no other may have a turn at them.[8]

One of Rose's best vignettes of the Macaulays' family life describes both its emotional vortex and the common interest that kept it whirling as a unit: 'In our home, which looking back, I see as passionate and ecstatic, like a wilderness of monkeys, pleasure and pain being, both by children and parents, very sharply felt as ecstasy and anguish – in our home, which was a largish, self-sufficing, and somewhat neurotic community herded together on a Mediterranean shore, bibliomania obtained and bibliomachy intermittently raged. Our library seemed so large; our parents were great readers; we had the free run of it.'[9] ('Bibliomachy' was Rose's invented term for 'book-making'.)

Grace's diaries, George's letters, and Rose's memories confirm that books dominated their Varazze lives, from George's hours of translation and editing to the forms of the children's play in and out of the sea. Only the younger brother Will was not a true bookworm; he excelled at games. At an early age, jealously feeling that Rose neglected him by reading too much, he had several times thrown her most enthralling books into the well or the sea.

In the early Varazze days a pleasant rhythm between living and literature developed: after the family breakfast (which was not attended by the rejected baby Eleanor), Grace and the five older children – or a chosen few – did the shopping in the village where merchants often gave them toys and sweets. Then there were lessons for several hours, followed by basking or bathing on the shore and dinner at 1.30. The afternoon was free for outdoor play and private reading. ('One hid', Rose writes, 'under tables and sofas, in the tops of orange trees, in the ivy clumps on high walls, to be out of reach.')[10] The children also gathered wild flowers on hill walks with Grace and George; their father, as they climbed, shared his translations by telling stories from Froissart, the *Odyssey*, and Dante. The young Macaulays had nursery tea at five; Benediction often followed.

Then, in true Victorian family style, George read aloud to all. The day ended for each child with a private talk with Grace, *The Book of Common Prayer* and hymn book in her hand. She enlisted the young Macaulays in the exciting war between Good and Evil, taught them the collects, and vividly called up the dangers of hell-fire, stimulating in Rose both a passionate desire 'to be good', and a lifelong love of the liturgical language of the Anglican prayer book. 'Religion', Rose later wrote, 'was what was taught by my mother.' 'We were never', she went on, 'brought up in a Church or Vicarage atmosphere; but we did have those collect lessons, and I remember them still and the excitement and inspiration they caused.'[11] At 8.15 the parents had their own evening meal – presumably exhausted.

The difference between the minds and temperaments of Grace and George was as critical to Rose's learning as the teaching, reading, and story-telling. George was always to be Rose's model of the intelligent, knowledgeable, sceptical, painstaking searcher and critic. In her 'Who I Am' article, she identified him as a Cambridge don who 'pursued literary research along paths of scholarship which I can never hope to tread'. Present-day scholars still respect his major four-volume edition of John Gower's English, Latin, and French works (annotated and translated). To read his preface on selected poems of Matthew Arnold or his contributions to the *Cambridge History of English Literature* is to admire his comparative scholarship, his critical thoroughness, and his intellectual rigour and honesty. Although his field was English Literature, he was what would today be called an interdisciplinary scholar, often editing historical texts of literary interest. The entry beside his name in the 1915 *Who's Who* includes his identification as 'the editor of *The Modern*

Language Review' and a respectable list of academic publications.

In her 1924 novel, *Orphan Island*, Rose had a little affectionate fun creating Mr Thinkwell, the Cambridge don: 'His manner, though kind, was a little alarming to persons of a muddled and incoherent speech; he seemed to take them up rather too precisely and thoroughly, and continually to be assuming that their remarks meant more than was the case, which, though flattering, was confusing.'[12] Thinkwell was perhaps a blend of her father and Uncle Willy, well-known at King's, Cambridge, for his astringent insistence on precision of expression. As a translator, George also pursued the exact word and as exact an imitation of the original style as possible. Rose had even more fun in creating Mr Thinkwell's dreamy daughter Rosamund, a part of herself, who was interested in nothing quite so much as her one great obsessive fantasy – life on desert islands.

But for all the novelist's good-natured teasing about Mr Thinkwell, he ended up as the admirable philosopher-king, accepting the task of reforming the social injustices of the imaginary antipodean *Orphan Island*. George Macaulay was one of Rose's intellectual heroes; any doubts as to his perfection as a human being were suppressed except in her fiction. In a difficult period of her young womanhood, he was a companion in escape and as a child she believed, like the Macaulays' Italian cook, that he knew everything, *'tutto, tutto'*. He was careful to correct the children regularly on this point.

Her autobiographical essay 'Astronomy', dramatizing a night lesson on the beach (telescope set in the sand, children and fireflies swarming about the lecturer) contrasts scholarly father and inspirational mother as teachers. One child asks, 'Father, what would you do if you saw a quite new star?' The narrator continues, 'But my father, a modest man, whose profession is not astronomy, says that he would not know it for a new star.' A few paragraphs on, the children get no reply to their question about what would happen if a star hit the earth. But, writes Rose, 'My mother told us very wonderful and interesting things.... If we were to ask *her* what would happen if a whole star hit the earth, we should have a tremendous blaze and conflagration in a minute.'[13]

Rose described her mother's enthusiasms as infectious, but came later, even in childhood, to find Grace's 'facts' sometimes invented (she told the children that the hills east of Genoa were 'marble mountains') and her emotions often inflated (she 'was vexed when defeated at cards'). In *Catchwords and Claptrap* (1926), an attack on careless language, much in her father's spirit, Rose writes that exaggeration 'may be called a primary human need, which should be placed by psychologists with the desire for nourishment, for safety, for sense-gratification, and for appreciation, as one of the elemental lusts of man.'[14] In short, exaggeration is at best primitive, at worst childish. In contrast, Rose's own adult wit was largely based on irony; she understated the case with dry humour. (Her admired Uncle Regi was a master of meiosis.) But she also was a talented fantasist and a poet *manquée*. Rose's vivacious mother told her 'entrancing stories out of her head' and read her poems and Shakespeare's plays, intensifying her imaginative powers and her love of strange or musical language. And there were temperamental affinities between mother and daughter. Grace had a theatrical flair; Rose's emotional, verbal, and physical energy were to create an attractive social personality.

Rose Macaulay's adult writing often explodes into images of mesmerized pleasure. Her description in a personal essay of a quite ordinary event shows that she enjoyed playfully practising her mother's arts of ebullience and surfeit, even though her prose is characteristically distinguished by the balance, rhythm, and economy of her father's style:

> Does the dandled brain itself dream harmony, drowned in warm sweetness like a tropicked ship? The waters lap gently about the almost submerged island; sirens sing, the lotus flower opens, naiads move in rhythm, genius flows like wine, poems, tales, and pictures create themselves, swim in heavenly brightness, and dissolve. I am in the Golden Age; in Paradise; in the Fortunate Isles; in the Gardens of the Hesperides and Alcinous; in the floating gardens of Montezuma.... So, lulled in these flowers with dances and delight, I drowse entranced.[15]

Rose Macaulay is taking a hot bath.

As a character and as a writer Rose reflected the best qualities of each parent. But as a child she seems to have increasingly not only identified with her father but also loved him at her mother's expense. This pattern of thought and feeling was more complicated than the classic Freudian family romance. In daily life she trusted George Macaulay's reason and judgement; she mistrusted Grace Macaulay's emotionalism and inconsistency. She could see and feel at an early age that her mother's life of serial child-bearing was debilitating; Grace's loss of health and free time seemed to her daughter an unappealing sacrifice. In the last year of her life Rose Macaulay said in an interview, 'I think on the whole men have a better time. I'd prefer to be a man. When I was a child I thought I would like to be a boy.'[16] And when, as a very young child, Rose exultantly printed 'I CAN WRITE' on every available surface, she may have aspired unconsciously (although she planned to be a sailor) to live her father's kind of life – as a maker of books.

Certainly George's evening reading aloud made 'bibliomachy' the art most glamorous to them all. Book illustrations were their paintings; music other than hymns played almost no part in their lives. From those dramatized literary hours together at the end of the day the sprawling,

lounging, listening children created their play and daydream identities–
'a glittering galaxy of heroes, villains and adventurers who set one's life
marching and swaggering as if to trumpets and drums.'[17] The cast of
characters is too long a roll to call, but among Rose's favourites were
Masterman Ready, the Little Duke, Sydney Carton, Rudolf Rassendyll,
Jason with centaur and the ship *Argo*, Jack, Ralph, and Peterkin from
The Coral Island, Jules Verne and Sherlock Holmes, and above all, never
unseated from her heart, the hot-tempered, proud Sir Guy Morville of
Charlotte Yonge's *The Heir of Redclyffe*. (*Ivanhoe*'s Rebecca and Rowena
are not mentioned; the villain Brian de Bois Gilbert was preferred. All
the alter egos, heroic or wicked, are male.)

Over the years, as the children grew, George read *Robinson Crusoe*, all
of Dickens and Scott, selections from *The Origin of Species* (to which
they were inattentive listeners), *Lorna Doone*, Shakespeare, 'a lot of
poetry', Jane Austen, Meredith, and maternally censored versions of *Tom
Jones* and *The Three Musketeers*. (Grace had pasted together many pages
of the Dumas.) 'My mother thought the coarseness of the bedroom scenes
might displease us,' wrote Rose, who believed the assumption mistaken.
'I don't think we should have been more than bored; children, anyhow
in our innocent and sheltered income-group attach no meaning to companionship in bedrooms.'[18] Grace firmly 'sheltered' them; Rose's sense
of gender was formed by observing the better opportunities for freedom
and fun enjoyed by boys. Her explicit sex knowledge came painfully in
adolescence. For a very long time her self-image was firmly linked to her
wish to live as a pre-pubescent boy.

Apolitical as the list of books might seem, the children's best-loved
adventure stories were the very stuff of Victorian Empire, inspiring young
lads to sail off from home in a spirit of gallant, exalted self-sacrifice,
nobly and courageously to plant the Union Jack abroad, exemplifying
the manly British virtues to lesser breeds without the law. Many Victorian
hymns Grace taught them were in the language of the Church Militant
and the Church Regnant, recruiting and commanding: 'Onward Christian
Soldiers'; 'Stand Up, Stand Up for Jesus, the strife will not be long'; 'The
Son of God goes forth to war/ A kingly crown to gain/ His blood-red
banner streams afar,/ Who follows in his train?' Any list of warlike and
regal metaphors in mid- and late-Victorian hymns would be long.

The purpose of the family reading was mutual pleasure and its hidden
persuasion was to instil virtue itself rather than to enlist the listeners in
the service of the Establishment, but the futures of these children prove
that the emotional messages held lingering power. Five of the six young
Macaulays who survived to adulthood became adventurous servants of
Church or State throughout the Empire. Rose neither ignored nor joined
the imperial system, although her longing for the naval life died hard and
once in a fit of grief and penitence she unsuccessfully applied for mission-

ary duty. Instead, she studied history, escaped institutions and officialdom (except for her service in the two World Wars), and found adventure as a jousting social critic and an intrepid traveller. She had fallen in love with action as well as literature. The boys' adventure stories never lost their attraction (their plots surface suddenly in her novels) nor did she lose her concern for the ethical questions they simplify and dramatize, but she scoffed at British jingoism, opposed war, and transformed her love of plots of conquest into a love of travel, the exploration of ideas, and a lifelong wandering, questioning religious search.

In Varazze, the Five's rapturous identification with those stories of struggle and quest was realized in rough-and-tumble play, bold battles acted out on the seashore with their canoe, the *Argo*. 'There was no dull moment,' Rose remembered. The scenarios, probably devised by the girls, Margaret and Rose, as the oldest and strongest, were perilous. In Rose's telling these dramas took place in a child's world. Can these voyages and wars have been as unchaperoned as Rose remembers? The sloping beach at Varazze drops off sharply into deep water about eighty yards out, but the Five were in and out of the sea in an exuberant, risky amphibious life. Their father, a fine athlete, could and did swim the three miles across the Varazze bay; he must have taught them to be young dolphin-children. They seem to have had free range of the beach as well as the library. 'The great thing', she remembers, 'was to be as far out to sea as possible when one was summoned in, so as to have a long swim back.'[19] Rose recalls a twilight canoe trip alone far out beyond her swimming range, memorable for the near-swamping of her craft by a passing steamer. She was greeted on return, not by anxious parents or a scolding nurse, but by brothers and sisters protesting that she had pre-empted the *Argo*. They had wanted to play pirates on a jut of rocks half a mile up the shore.

All of the Five aspired to dauntlessness. For their mother the most admired virtue was courage; she wanted all of her girls and boys to be brave sons. Her dream was a boon to Rose. At 67 she wrote with some scorn, 'Henry James and Stevenson told one another that girls do not play at pirates; neither had daughters; as to Alice James, the only sister they had between them, probably neither she nor Henry was ever a child.'[20] That same year (1948) in a *New Statesman* review of *Peter Pan* she took fierce issue with the casting and characterization of Wendy: 'What age did Barrie mean this intolerable child to be? Young enough, apparently to sleep in the nursery with her brothers. But this year's Wendy can scarcely, from her appearance, be under seventeen. Young children are not bothered by this; they accept Wendy as a little girl; but they do not understand why she was such an odd little girl, with such an improbable taste for mending other people's clothes instead of tearing her own. It seems possible that Barrie knew no little girls.' Two of the little girls who were her guests at the 'sickly' panto thought Wendy 'very strange, and, I think, something of a class traitor, quite unnecessarily putting into grown-up minds the notion that little girls might be thus profitably and horribly employed.'[21]

However privileged the children were to have more time with their parents than they would have had in England, perhaps these outdoor escapes and the clan's resulting solidarity, which was to be lifelong, were even greater advantages. Though bonded, they were five quite different personalities: Margaret, bearing the burdens of the oldest child, was sometimes her mother's chosen companion, required to be stately and dignified. But she was also 'nervy', and had a high temper, a kind of triggering symptom of the involuntary, unpredictable spasms and grimaces of chorea from which she suffered. Rose in some adult letters called her 'my favourite sister'; they wrote poems and stories together. Yet Rose slept with and was close to her unconfident younger sister Jean. All the available evidence points to Rose being the brightest child and the most attractive girl. Pictures of her in childhod have a delicate charm. Yet she did not seem to sense these distinctions; at all ages of her life she was modest, uncomfortable when she found herself the subject of the conversation. Aulay was the family prince, though not the automatic leader among the egalitarian Five; he was an open, confident, likeable, intelligent, mathematically talented boy. Young Will was the appealing, philistine family clown, particularly fond of Rose.

They *were* unalike, but with a great instinct for self-preservation the Five supported each other against the sudden shifts of their mother's emotional volatility and the insecurities of her open favouritism. The brothers and sisters in Rose Macaulay's fiction do compete and tease, but they are united against the adult world. Forced to hide their fears from the mother who wanted them to be round-the-clock Spartans, the Five shared and joked away their anxieties.

Rose's early novels often show the pain caused by mistakes in parenting and the solace of close brother-sister pacts; the loyalty of the Macaulay clan ran deep. In the last scenes of Rose's second novel, *The Furnace* (1907), the careless near-twins Betty and Tommy Crevequeur, after suffering sobering vicissitudes and disappointments, conclude that their treasure is their mutual understanding. 'We can help each other,' says Betty, 'and no one else in the world can help us. Because we know each other so awfully well.'[22]

And in her essay, 'Fraternal', Rose writes to the surviving adult brothers and sisters: 'We have been banded together under pack codes and tribal laws. The remembered jungle is behind us, with its pleasures and pains, follies, adventures and jests.' Rose, as a jester, knew how important were 'the clan jokes' which distinguish the pleasures of fraternal association from any other. They are a defence against adults; they are exclusive. Later in life her popularity as a dinner guest depended in part on her ability to bring the company together in shared laughter; to create such momentary delight was one of her gifts, an art of mockery and healing learned in childhood. But party jokes are not the same as 'the uncontrollable mirth' of the Five, 'deep in the common stock of memory'. The members of the clan were allies, held togeher by the passwords of a unique pack humour.[23]

The close brother-sister combinations in her novels represent the heterogeneous and symbiotic Five; there are sibling or sibling-like pairs in seven of her novels, and one in the last unfinished manuscript. Each pair is distinctive, yet there is an interesting similarity in all: the sister is usually the older and the braver of the two. Often the boy is timorous and dependent on her support. This may be a reflection of Rose's relationship to Will, but just as likely the twinning is also an ingenious fictional way of dividing her own two selves, unconventionally attributing fragility to the imagined boy-Rose and strength to the real female identity. These images of androgyny reinforce her persistent rejection of sexual stereotypes and her empathy with those who do not fit them.

To read Rose Macaulay's memories of those Mediterranean years is to believe that she had lived in Eden. Chronology seems non-existent; Rose's Varazze was a timeless land. Her generalization was that the Macaulays were 'a large and cheerful family'.[24] And for the most part, during those Italian years, the statement was true. But the darker recollections of her younger sister Jean and a reprise of the major events of those seemingly timeless sunny years show that the child Rose had good grounds for anxieties: some misfortunes did befall the Macaulays. And for an account of them we are indebted to Rose's third cousin, Constance Babington Smith. Her interviews and correspondence with Jean Macaulay in Jean's last years produced a less sanguine narrative than Rose's cheery public memoirs.

Rose was too sensitive not to be shaken by the instabilities, but too intelligent not to discover enduring strategies of burying, escaping, and transcending worries. The thrust of her life was against melancholy. Both the joys and the sorrows of Varazze are re-experienced and transformed in her early novels.

One misfortune, however, did lead to better things: while the family were on their annual trip to England in the summer of 1890 when Rose was 9, George stayed behind at Varazze. He fell critically ill from typhoid caused by the bad drains in their rented apartment; his condition was then complicated by pneumonia. When Grace returned she found him in a state that brought about the summoning of four doctors and his brothers from England, followed by Grace's nursing, Grace's collapse, and George's long convalescence.

To enable them to escape from the danger of the village apartment's pollution, Mrs Conybeare presented the family with £1,000 to buy a handsome villa on the beach. The Macaulays installed English drains in their new home and took possession. It became the Villa Macolai, or as it was known in Varazze, the Villa Inglese. The photographs show a large two-storey stuccoed villa with verandas and tiled roof, but Rose's fond description, not surprisingly, is of its grounds and the landscape around it. 'On either side of the house was an orto, full of oranges and lemons, eucalyptus and figs, and behind rose steep terraced hills, clad with pines, olives, myrtle and juniper, with stony paths winding up them.' As it 'stood so near the waves' that a high sea would occasionally rush into the garden and through the basement windows, 'making a subterranean ocean that could be pleasurably navigated on boards', the children were 'in raptures.'[25]

But typhoid fever was not George Macaulay's only trial in Varazze. He was the exception to the family's instant acclimatization. In addition to his worry about Grace's health, he was depressed by the exile from his profession and from England and by the extended family's judgement (and his own) that he was a failure; he was never to believe himself otherwise. There was another cause for his melancholy: Grace became pregnant again three months after their arrival, a further threat to her recovery and a condition that recommended frustrating marital chastity. George's undergraduate Tripos verses at Cambridge imply that he was a young man who understood sexual desire. The last lines of his short comedy explain why an unmarried college Fellow went off with a pros-titute: *'Hoc inde fit quia Sociis nondum licet/ Uxoris habere.'* ('This all comes to pass because Fellows can't have wives.')[26] Perhaps as a form of birth control, Margaret, Aulay, and Will had slept in cots in their parents' bedroom in their first home in Varazze.

The children sensed their father's occasional dispirited moods but could not understand why he did not want them to celebrate his thirty-sixth birthday. Perhaps he did not feel himself in Varazze. George Campbell Macaulay's name on the title page of the Herodotus he trans-lated there was followed by an indication of his sense of self – 'Former Fellow of Trinity College, Cambridge', an English scholar exiled in Italy. A minor incident reported amusingly by Rose years later implies that he was troubled that his British family might merge too easily and completely with the Varazze folk ways, losing what he believed, like a true English gentleman, son of Eton and Cambridge, to be their superior heritage:

The *parocco* wanted one of my brothers [Will], a beautiful child with curly hair and large, thoughtful, misleadingly innocent blue eyes, to be little St. John the Baptist and lead an unruly lamb in the annual procession of Santa Caterina de Siena, the town's patron saint. My brother, I think, was for doing this; he thought it would be fun to lead the lamb. His brother and sisters were certainly for it; we thought it would be fun to see the lamb leading him. Our mother was for it; she thought it would be friendly to accept. Our nurse was for it; she thought it would look sweet. But my father, the only member of the household who had been to a public school was not for it; he thought it would look silly, and vetoed it.[27]

Cultural snobbery, but understandable. Like many late Victorians George Macaulay supported Christianity for its moral power but found no comfort in personal faith. Yet the severe dignity of Anglican forms was important to him; he was the oldest son of an English clergyman who took the service in a plain black gown. He himself had declined the priest's invitation to carry a taper in the Varazze Candlemas celebration. The spectacle of the colour-splashed *festa* – the banners, the flowers, the candles, and the happy disorder and emotional symbolism of the half-pagan Italian Catholic procession beloved by his frolicking children – was a world away from the dignified choir processions he remembered in Eton Chapel.

But their kind and reticent father's silences were not as troubling to the children as their mother's favouritism and unpredictability. Freedom was exciting, but Jean Macaulay said, looking back at the age of 81, 'You never knew whether to expect kindness or a scolding.'[28] The individual standing of any child could suddenly tumble. Rose wrote, 'Temperamental she certainly was!'[29] The rough everyday rule of thumb for precedence did not follow the birth order; Grace preferred the boys. Aulay was her darling, closely followed by Will and Margaret, the oldest. Rose came next in the pecking order, then, rather farther below, the insecure Jean. The scapegoat was Eleanor. Grace's diary shows that some children were taken for treats, others left at home, and that the extravagant Christmas gifts sent by the uncles were sometimes divided rather unevenly. Neglected Eleanor was given money for Christmas one year, though the other children had splendid presents; one summer the entire family went to England leaving her behind.

Eleanor's story, in fact, cannot be confidently or fully told. One would never know from Rose's published memories of Varazze that this young sister had been part of the family. Jean's language in recalling Eleanor's life must be carefully quoted; her words are at once vague and disturbing. She said that at first Eleanor suffered from 'open neglect' from her mother and then 'savage punishments'. Although Eleanor was only three years younger than Will, she was completely excluded from the clan's play and she seems not to have accompanied them on expeditions to the village.

Why this maternal rejection? Constance Babington Smith writes that Eleanor was an 'ill-favoured' child. No baby pictures and only two informal adult pictures of her survive in the archival family photographs. Perhaps Grace's severe illness and exhaustion during her pregnancy with Eleanor had prenatally disadvantaged this daughter in mind or body.

And as an infant, she, along with the five others, had suffered measles shortly after their arrival in Varazze. She may have been less physically attractive than her brothers and sisters, although she is a pleasant-faced petite young woman in the surviving photographs. In her isolation she may have developed habits, speech, or mannerisms Grace found annoying. But whatever the reasons, she was kept out of the public eye. Italian servants, who probably treated her kindly, cared for her as a small child. Her life story has a positive ending: she became a beloved missionary teacher with the Society for the Propagation of the Gospel in Ramchi, India. But in Varazze she must have suffered great loneliness in the midst of the riotous fun of the other children. Rose, at Eleanor's death in 1952, felt remorse: 'I feel now that I should have put more in our relationship.' And learning about her sister's life of devoted service, she wrote in a letter, 'I feel she was far more than we knew.'[30]

Certainly Eleanor's position was worsened both by the birth of the beautiful and precocious baby Gertrude when Eleanor was little over a year old, and the family's shock at Gertrude's sudden death at $3\frac{1}{2}$ from meningitis. George had written Francis Jenkinson a few weeks after Gertrude's birth: 'The baby is thought to be very good-looking, more so than our other children at her age.'[31] The photograph of Gertrude in her coffin shows an exquisite doll-like brunette. From the day of Gertrude's birth, Grace described this fairy child as unusually beautiful and gifted, perhaps to emphasize the contrast with Eleanor. Shortly after Gertrude's funeral Mrs Conybeare took Grace and the three older girls to Venice to divert them. Leaving behind the youngest child, the closest in age to Gertrude, after such a bewildering loss seems to fit Jean's description of Grace's 'open neglect'. (Somewhat later her grandmother arranged for a young child near her age to visit from England to give Eleanor some companionship, but this was not a permanent arrangement.)

After Gertrude's death, Eleanor, then 5, began to steal sweets and money from the cupboards, the predictable behaviour of an unloved child snatching at comforting substitutes for affection. Earlier, when Eleanor was 3, Grace had written a poignant description in her diary: 'E. keeps watch over the coming of food with the eyes of a little dog.'[32] Grace's punishments of her unloved child for the pitiable stealing, Jean says, became 'savage'.

How can we understand the maternal ferocity which deeply and permanently troubled Rose? She wrote to Jean in another connection during the war in 1939 that cruelty 'is the quality that is hardest to get over in anyone.' 'We were afraid of my mother,' said Jean.[33] Grace had lost the more loved of her two youngest daughters; she made Eleanor the hapless victim of her grief. The Five dared not interfere or protest.

Eleanor had been born at a difficult time; even with the help of servants, care of very small children wearied Grace. 'Heavy day with the babies,' she writes in her diary more than once. Often she was not well: 'My throat bad.' George was kind and helpful, but his work secluded him for part of each day. Like many women, Grace preferred the role of the mother-teacher of school-age children to that of the caretaker of small, demanding dependants; she was a happy parent of the more independent Five. Her 1880 diary entry on the day of her first child's birth shows that she began motherhood with little experience or understanding of the nature and needs of infants; motherhood seemed to her a battle of wills. Of her newborn daughter Grace writes: 'Baby obstinate and perverse,' and that (at the age of three days) she 'will do nothing she is told'. Grace adds later that the 'yelling' baby had become 'submissive'. But on Margaret's birthday in 1889 she exulted, 'It is delightful to have a child of nine.' However sympathetically we speculate, the truth, sadly enough, is that Grace's treatment of Eleanor in her early childhood was abusive.

Why did not the just George intervene? His obituary in the *Cambridge Chronicle and University Journal* characterizes him as 'especially fearless and outspoken in his denunciation of wrong and oppression wherever he found it.'[34] He may well have been shut up with his work when Eleanor was punished; he seems to have withdrawn, leaving discipline to Grace, who was wilful, fatigued, and impulsive. George Macaulay's 'unselfishness', always praised by Rose, may have sometimes harmfully manifested itself by allowing the domineering Grace to rule the household.

We suspect that a sensitive Rose was for years troubled by Eleanor's childhood misery. Throughout her revealing early novel, *The Valley Captives* (1911), a bullying stepbrother cruelly torments young Tudor Vallon and his older sister John (Joanna). The children's father, a crippled, unsuccessful scholar busy in his study and intimidated by his second wife, does not investigate. The boy Tudor becomes more and more fearful; his uncontrollable fright irritates the bully, causing him often to shut up his weeping, pleading victim in the dark. The sister, John, bravely suffering the same blows, loves and comforts her brother. The novel's minor plot has a vivid scene of sadism and one of violent attack. Although the novel ends with Tudor's courageous, self-sacrificing death, what remains in the reader's memory is the troubling, wasted short life of a child who is permanently scarred in mind and body. Rose as a young writer had a need, it seems, to embody this theme of cruelty in a melodramatic plot and to imagine as a compensation for parental neglect a sisterly support which was not given to Eleanor. Rose dedicated the book 'To My Father'.

In addition to these suppressed anxieties about the life of the immediate family, discussion of the Macaulay family difficulties in England echoed in Varazze. One of George's younger brothers, Henry William Macaulay, died suddenly of fever in India at 35 when Rose was 12. Whatever the Macaulay children knew of the scrapes of young, amusing Uncle Harry who, disgraced by unpaid debts at Oxford, fled to America and was then employed in Bombay through Uncle Regi's influence, we know that Rose felt conflict; how should she feel about a much criticized and condemned family member who had done her no harm and whom she loved? (Was her distress about his rejection connected to the outlawed Eleanor?) This ethical and emotional question of loyalty to and justice for the ostracized was central in her first novel, *Abbots Verney* (1906), and persisted in later novels as well.

In addition, Margaret, Rose, and Jean had a troubling new experience of their own to understand and adjust to. Prospects for scholarly work were opening for George in England; the family began to think of returning. George prepared the boys more intensively in Maths and Latin, readying them for English schools. Perhaps the father thought his harum-scarum, boyish daughters should also prepare for the routine of school, and Grace may have been too devastated by the loss of her youngest child to continue daily tutoring. As a result, shortly after Gertrude's death, the three oldest children were enrolled as day pupils in a Varazze convent school. This turned out to be as much of a fiasco as an earlier experiment, the unmusical Rose's brief spell of guitar lessons, terminated by mutual consent of pupil and teacher.

Rose's reminiscences of the convent interval are blithe and amusing; she said it was 'rather boring' and the nuns seemed 'silly'. From the distance of maturity she transforms her account of what may have seemed at the time to be persecution and rejection into an essay on the Macaulay girls' naïve puzzlement at cultural differences. But the three found themselves alien outsiders, jeered at for the knee-length sailor dresses that gave them physical freedom, scolded for bringing a Bible to school, forbidden, as heretics, to kneel and pray with the other girls, and worst of all, assigned to pages of rote learning in Italian about which critical discussions were not permitted.

What mystified them most was the nuns' assumption that their worst danger lay in any association with males. Rose, looking back, could see from a distance that their teachers were 'merely actuated by the charming prudery peculiar to nuns. On the very few occasions when we joined in a school walk, the nun in charge, when men came in sight, would modestly turn down her eyes and say to her flock: *"Abbasso gli ochi."* I do not remember if the little Italians lowered their eyes, but the little English certainly did not. I remember, too, my oldest sister, aged thirteen or fourteen, strolling to the window during a lesson to throw out some pencil shavings, and being asked, surprisingly, if she was throwing a note to a man in the street.'[35]

They were not happy at the convent, but clan solidarity and perhaps clan jokes preserved them. Nor were their parents happy with the arrangement; George disliked the Genoese accents which began to distort the

girls' Italian and French. Although in 1888, George had written Francis
Jenkinson, 'I am quite fixed here,' in 1894 family plans to return to
England began to mature and at the end of six months, the Macaulays
withdrew their daughters from the school. This period had been a trial
for all: the Reverend Mother had frequently cast her eyes to heaven and
muttered, *'Pazienza! Pazienza!'* when faced with their disruptive curiosity;
the ideal Italian convent maiden did not ask probing questions. And
Rose's happy associations with the Roman Catholic Church had become
mingled with an unpleasant sense of being judged against an antipathetic
sexual model. But her essay on 'Church-going: Roman Catholic' in
Personal Pleasures (1935) is a love song to the ambience of San Ambrogio:

> From whatever cause, when I think 'church,' I am back in a great cool, dim,
> pillared interior, shut from a sunlit piazza by heavy leather door-curtains,
> clouded with drifts of that agreeable smoke which, while it ascends to heaven,
> fortunately perfumes all about it, and which we have always so rightly and
> wisely offered to our gods. Indeed those churches which do not do so probably
> make a tactical error which no audible or visual beauty can redeem.[36]

She goes on to praise the processions which to her father had seemed
garish and vulgar: 'A church, like a monarchy, must be potentially and
occasionally processional, must show itself for worship and jubilee in the
open, must at times be peregrinating and agoral, and wind, in rich pomps
and gauds, through market-place, street, and town.'[37] Later, as something
of a theologian and church historian, she came to challenge some tenets
of Catholicism as she understood them, yet no happy memory of Varazze
and the church of San Ambrogio seems ever to have faded.

The time for departure from Italy was near. The farewell was to be
wrenching for Rose, impossible to soothe by kissing the walls of the
Villa Macolai. But Varazze had marked Rose Macaulay and her writing
forever. And in addition to the tumbling fun of the Five she had discovered four private joys which were to last her for life: the rewards of
solitude, the love of landscape (especially the Mediterranean coast), the
escape of narrative daydreaming, and the delight of life in the water.

One of Rose's 'patterns of memory' from 'the wild stuff of that tranquil
time, childhood' recreates in a brief space three of those charms: 'sitting
alone in an olive tree up the hill or in an ivy clump on the top of the orto
wall, reading or writing poetry or stories ... or spinning one's private
interminable tales of perilous and heroic adventure by land and by sea,
while the mule carts jingled along the shore road, and the fishermen
hauled in their heavy nets with loud cries of expectation and hope, and
the hot sweet tang of the hillside above mingled with that of the sea
below.'[38]

Rose, who was gregarious, also valued the concentration of the senses sharpened in such solitude. In 1935 she wrote to her sister Jean, 'I don't agree about human nature being the most delightful thing we know. I think many things are more so. Think of a lovely mountain side, smelling of lemons and silver with olives, and the sea below. Or a coral lagoon with fishes swimming in it. I won't mention poetry because you'll say it is by human beings.'[39] In the same year she wrote a forgivably purple paean to 'Solitude' and with nice balance wound it up with an aphorism: 'How rich, how sharply hued, how pregnant with meaning does the universe appear, where but an hour since it was a wild and wandering globe lost in chaos and the chattering of voices. I am alone. I can look, listen, feel, apprehend without muffling presences to bound imagination's flight. . . . Good company is delightful bondage; to be alone is to be free.'[40] In such freedom and solitude she escaped the busy family life and focused on the world around her.

The descriptions of landscape in her novels are an escape for the reader. She has the power to outline a panoramic scene and to fill it with sharp detail – sound, shape, colour, movement, light, texture, contrast, smell – placing even her fantasies and satires in a living reality. The terrain is important in children's stories of chase and flight; its well-managed description grounds the action in belief. Rose always loved maps and records of voyages.

The natural world in her novels is not a mother, a god, a miracle of divine creation, only rarely a fecund power, never red in tooth and claw. Mystery, sometimes threatening, surrounds and infuses it; yet its beauty is rendered as richly sensory experience, providing unsentimentalized joy. When it has a symbolic function in a novel, that suggestion is perfectly fused with the actual. (Her third novel, *The Secret River* (1909), is an exception; in its sacramental world the mystical vision is more vivid than the shadowy mundane.) Our imaginative pleasure in her descriptions depends on the accuracy of her eye – its sense of proportion and scope, yet its attention to significant, selected detail. She became an accomplished travel writer.

'To be alone is to be free.' She used the freedom of solitude to enjoy the natural world, but the greatest freedom nature offered Rose Macaulay was her life-in-water, for no other phrase will describe her lifelong, world-wide Swim. An anthology could be compiled of her bathing essays and her bathing adventures from 'In the Cam' to 'Off the Florida Coast'. Streams, pools, rivers, seas play important parts in her novels. Floating in the calm, warm, erotic Mediterranean water, simultaneously feeling a sense of boundlessness, of bodily delight, and of the guiltless safety of the womb, contributed to her idyllic memory of Varazze: 'Such felicity seems to know no limit; measureless to man, it seems the pleasure of some celestial state in which we swim and sport in the blue and heavenly inane, like the *putti* that leap through wreaths of flowers upon a painted ceiling.'[41] All her life, wherever Rose Macaulay travelled, she swam.

But there was one more powerful and seductive means of escape for Rose which began in childhood – that daylight dreaming in an olive tree which captures the high spirits of her expanding consciousness, her imaginative use of her experience, her sense of herself, and her identity as a writer and an independent woman. That dreaming was the continuous inner tale of a child's secret life, continuously related: 'The dream', she says, 'of an ordinary little girl, nourished largely on literature, going about her ordinary way, playing, doing lessons, climbing trees, bathing, canoeing, quarrelling' who lives as the young hero of the adventure stories; she is a knight, a sailor or soldier, an explorer, or Perseus with winged heels, always a male. She bravely fights the battle of Good against Evil, the struggle which is the action of epic and legend. She is surrounded by 'some kind of mysterious world, interpenetrating this world, in and out of it and all around its margins'.[42] And as she begins to tell her story to herself, she says, her palpable, familiar surroundings are suddenly 'magicked':

> I ran with Mowgli's wolf pack, leaped across great ravines, plunged into rivers pursued by wild dogs, rode my pony into battle against enemy spears. Needless to say, I showed on all occasions, great courage and resource; I was praised for these qualities by captains and kings.[43]

Such inner routes of escape and strategies of adaptation strengthened her in the painful changes ahead, yet held her in the idyllic past. The Macaulays' seven years of freedom from etiquette and criticism, from shoes and neatness and nosy neighbours, were not without price for each of them: Grace and George had lived as the rulers of a kingdom of children, without the challenge, support, and intellectual company of other adults; both their marriage and their minds suffered. George became more withdrawn; he was never again to engage in vigorous political activity or protest. Grace became more dominating; she had neither the criticism nor the advice of peers. The happy monkey children, educationally precocious, socially retarded, and sexually ignorant, were to be faced with difficult adjustments upon returning at last to England. But for Rose Macaulay, in the end, the joys offered and the strength earned by the island colony life were rich compensation. She never lost touch with it.

3

Landlocked

R OSE CLOSED HER memoir of the Villa Macolai with a self-mocking anti-climax:

> Later they took us to England and school, and we lived in a University town, where we wore shoes and stockings all day, and where, did we lapse (and we did) in the streets from respectable behaviour, a schoolfellow from the girls' High School or the boys' Preparatory was sure to pass and put us to shame. We could, and we did, be Sherlock Holmes and track criminals unobtrusively (or so we hoped) in the streets, but it was a poor kind of life.

Summer visits to relatives in England had not foreshadowed this 'poor kind of life'. Before the move to Oxford, one or both parents and, as Rose phrases it, 'about five children' (the trips did not always include the whole family) had annually returned 'home' from Italy, so England's cold rain, paved footpaths, and dignified, disapproving pedestrians were not unknown to the Five. The clan had managed, however, while visiting their grandmother's summer residence in Gordon Place, Kensington, to move about London with what seems today amazingly unsupervised freedom. (Rose's cousin Dorothea Conybeare said she and her brothers and sisters were never allowed such liberty.) George Macaulay disappeared daily into the British Museum to hunt for lost manuscripts, 'so he could not take us about London much', Rose continues. (On one such library hunt he did indeed discover one of the two original French manuscripts of *The Ancren Riwle* of 1250, long believed to have been destroyed in the Cotton Library fire in 1731.) And so each morning, says Rose, their grandmother Eliza Conybeare would say to them, 'Now children go and play in the streets while your mother and I talk.'[1]

The once-upon-a-time tone of the practised storyteller arouses disbelief, but in the essay 'Coming to London' (1957) Rose continues with convincing details: the Macaulay children visited Theobald's in Clerkenwell Road, a shop now long gone, to buy (with their 'noble-hearted uncles' tips') 'ships, magnets, pistols, cannons, knives and other tools, roller-skates, mercury, lead for melting and other very useful things.' And they kept happy walking on stilts, playing hide-and-seek, and roller-skating in a passage running by St Mary Abbotts' Church, riding up and down the lifts in a department store on Kensington High Street until routed by the staff, and travelling, on one-stop tickets, all around the sooty Underground's Circle Line with a fine sense of 'having swindled the Railway Company'. They even went to Baker Street on the inevitably fruitless search for 221A. They ventured as far as Earls Court and Olympia 'for the scenic railway' and other delights. Although they were sometimes taken by a parent or an uncle to the Tower or the Zoo, on the whole, in Varazze style, they made their own fun. The family did not fret, Rose reports; 'no one seemed to mind our behaving like street arabs in London, and we had a very good time there.'

But settling down in Oxford in 1894 was no game. Their new home offered neither big city adventures nor seashore delights. The Macaulays moved into a large gabled, brick, Tudor-like house with a small garden; it was in Summertown, today a suburb of Oxford, but then a village, and so distant from the centre of things that the family named the house 'Thule'. The Five were now physically divided: Margaret, Rose, and Jean went to Oxford High School for Girls; Aulay and Will went as day boys to Mr Lynam's Preparatory School. Rose was no longer to be 'Rosie', but the more dignified 'Emily', her first name – sometimes altered from its christening form 'Emilie'. (Oxford High School records show both spellings.) Her mother discouraged any further play with dolls, which Rose had begun late. Quite possibly Grace knew that Rose and Jean had a game called 'Families' in which they ranked 'the children' periodically on 'Charm Lists', demoting favourites arbitrarily at frequent intervals in their mother's changeable mode. Their play does not seem to have been an admiring imitation of motherhood. In any case, Grace was encouraging the renunciation of dolls according to a new maxim: 'Girls will be young ladies.' 'Girls will be boys' was no longer the family wisdom.

Most sobering dictum of all, George Macaulay firmly told the 13-year-old Emily Rose that she must give up talking about being a boy and announcing that she was going to join the Navy when she was a man. And to darken the bleakness of this pronouncement he became less comfortingly accessible, for he worked daily in the Bodleian Library, endlessly copying in the cottage industry scholarship of the day, editing Middle English poetry texts, and later accepting a commission from the Clarendon Press for the excellent and massive edition of John Gower's works which occupied him for six years.

The sudden condemnation of Rose's boyish role and the loss of the free air of Varazze were painful blows. To please and compensate the mother who was disappointed at the birth of a second girl, Rose had begun very early 'being a boy'. And she had discovered that the spontaneous, active life open to her brothers suited her. Now, suddenly, at an age of inner change and in a changed world, her myth of a male self was disapproved by both parents. Her task was to devise a happy alternative.

She had learned to accommodate her mother's shifting levels of approval; her father was her rock, her model of steadfast justice. 'I always feel like M. Aurelius about the example of my father,' she wrote years later.[2] (All her adult life she sought the company of older male mentors, although usually she was the stronger of the pair and came to know this.) As a former schoolmaster, knowing she might be ridiculed, George Macaulay was attempting to protect her, but to Rose his rebuke must have seemed a cruel rejection, a support of her mother's distressing reversal of direction. Rose suppressed, hid, even from herself, whatever hurt or anger against him she might have felt; her direct words about her father were always to be praise, although her fiction implicitly and explicitly condemned blind or absent fathers. So, during the ensuing five years in an incompatible environment she imitated the silent stoicism of George Macaulay (and Marcus Aurelius) about her deepest feelings. The boy-self lived on but in a hidden world. Close friends of the adult Rose often remarked that the seemingly candid talker was always secretive about what most keenly touched her. 'People don't think I'm shy', she wrote in 1951, 'because I gabble away to anyone about anything or nothing.'[3]

That dream of naval service her father ordered her to abandon does not seem so foolish today when we think of the men's work women performed in 1914, gladly and well, but in 1894 Rose's deeply internalized fancies of bold masculine life exposed her to mockery outside her own home, certainly among maternal relatives. Years later her cousin Dorothea described Rose's early sense of herself as the result of 'a queer sexual kink', possibly a phrase for Rose's behaviour used by the extended family. The whole George Macaulay household was vulnerable to Conybeare criticism. Fond as they were, Uncle Edward, his wife, and his children were so much in the habit of coolly analysing their relatives, as their diaries show, that on returning to England Grace had refused to settle in Cambridge, a location too close to the Conybeare home in Barrington.

The paternal attempt to alter Rose's strong self-image by defining it as outworn childishness did not succeed, but although resilient, she was shaken. True, she still had her strategic defences: her books, her imaginative scenarios, and the adventurous play with her sister and brothers and with cousins. And the Five enjoyed summers outdoors at Uncle Kenneth Macaulay's country home, Walton House, half a mile from the village of Clent and ten miles from Birmingham where Kenneth Macaulay worked in the firm of Chance Brothers, a glass manufacturer. His younger sister, the alarming Aunt Mary, kept house for him, but her thorny personality does not seem to have spoiled the children's fun. They played rounders and cricket (although Rose thought the sport 'too tame') and rode ponies in a beautiful landscape.

Rose worshipped the athletic young son of the local squire as a hero to emulate. But Margaret, Rose, and Jean were uncomfortable with the neighbouring girls of their age. One of them remembers, 'I don't know how long they had been living in Italy, but they felt strange among our local people, and it made them even more shy.' She goes on to say, 'My vision of them [at 13, 14, and 15] is three sisters together, walking side by side, skirts rather longer than mine, and wearing enormous hats edged with falling lace. "The garden tents" my schoolboy brother called them, and he was terrified of them.'[4] And she sketched the trio.

The children had other escapes from Oxford – until 1903, the year of her death, they continued visiting their delightful grandmother. (Frances Conybeare's diary refers to her lovingly as 'mirthful Eliza'.) The family even made some trips back to Varazze; Grace's semi-invalidism sent her back to Italy for two winters and on each occasion Rose was one of the children chosen to accompany her.

In Oxford Rose still contrived her solitude and secretly composed poetry. Poetry, she wrote in old age, 'meant more than anything to me.'[5] Her verses chiefly reflected her homesickness for the old active, amphibious life. Her first publication was in *The Oxford High School Magazine* when she was 17 – a prize-winning poem entitled 'The Sea'. (It is the only writing signed by her to be found in the magazine.) The four stanzas are a characteristically Romantic lyric of varying line lengths with repetition and refrain. The speaker apostrophizes the personified sea in archaic diction, describing its darkening moods – initially 'Sunny and calm and bright' – as it ruffles an 'angry brow', and becomes an ocean haunted by 'wild dreams' of wreckage and defeat:

Rose

Fair vessels won and lost,
And ships gone down by yonder rocky coast,
Ocean,
By yonder wind-swept coast.[6]

Even in her late school years Rose could still escape into her childhood daydreams and later find their realization in writing: 'This other world went on; it didn't fade away with childhood, or even with adolescence, though school life did interfere with it rather.' She describes the entrancement of imagination: 'It was more than a life; it was a world; a magic world; a key turned ... sudden beauty ... Its ecstasy possessed me utterly; after I had recovered my senses a little, I wrote poetry, the only vent for such dreams.'[7]

A faded portrait of Rose in 1895 at 14 is more poetic than playful, solemn rather than vivacious. Admittedly, because of the still primitive technique of photography, we rarely see any smiling or animated sitters from the turn of the century; poses had to be held stiffly for minutes and under the strain gravity was more naturally maintained than spontaneous joy. Yet Rose's face here is more than serious; it is vulnerable. (She was never at ease before a camera. Her adult portraits are stiff and forbidding.) Slight, wistful, pretty, a little shy, the would-be dauntless hero is in this picture a questioning child. There is nothing manly, or even boyish, about the young face or figure.

A number of her novels give us day-dreaming young girl characters who suffer nostalgia for their tomboy days and are sometimes unhappily trapped by physical maturity and sexual passion. As an adult in whom self-pity was almost non-existent, she wrote that she had identified with the adolescent heroine of *The Constant Nymph*, 'a happy child who had grown up to find that everything hurts.'[8] None of her characters, of course, are pure self-portraits, but all the skilfully varied characterizations make use – comic or pathetic, sometimes even tragic in the modern sense – of a longing to arrest the change from childhood to adulthood, from sexlessness and play to puberty and responsibility. One of these aspiring adventurers, 8-year-old Imogen Garden (from *Told by an Idiot*, 1923) watches the sailors march past in Victoria's 1900 Jubilee parade (Dorothea Conybeare says Rose was much like her and cherished the same fantasies):

Imogen, who had always meant to be a sailor, and who even now blindly hoped that somehow, before she reached the age for Osborne [the preparatory school for the Royal Navy] a way would be made for her (either she would become a boy, or dress up as a boy, or the rule excluding girls from the senior service would be relaxed) gasped and screwed her hands tightly together against her palpitating breast. Here were sailors. Straight from the tossing blue sea; straight from pacing the quarter-deck spy-glass in hand, spying for enemy craft, climbing the rigging, setting her hard-aport, manning the guns, raking the enemy amidships, holding up slavers, receiving surrendered swords.... Rule Britannia, Britannia rules the waves. The moment was almost too excessive for a budding sailor, with wet eyes and lips pressed tight together to keep the lips steady.[9]

Later, at 18, Imogen, her recreational tastes only a little changed, is still playing Indians in the woods, and, when her relatives think her mad, mutters angrily: 'Rotten it was being grown up. Simply rotten. Because you weren't really grown up. You knew some more, and you cared for a lot of fresh books, but you liked doing all the things you had liked before you grew up. Climbing, and playing red Indians, and playing with soldiers, and walking on stilts. But when you grew up you had to hide all sorts of things away, like a guilty secret.'[10] She says she could not compensate by marrying a sailor; she would be too jealous. Her dream was to be a naval officer who secretly published poetry. (For Imogen to show her verses to her brothers and sisters would have been against their code; it would have been 'swank'.) At 18 Imogen 'was at this time as sexless as any girl or boy might be. She was still, in all her imaginings, her continuous, unwritten stories about herself, a young man.'[11]

The last we see of her at the end of the novel, although she is headed for the delights of a year on a coral island among palms and parakeets, map-making for the government with her younger brother Hugh (a practical fellow, much like Aulay), is her vision blurred by tears. She is fleeing from an entangled, impossible love affair. Becoming a woman had not proved a satisfactory fate for Imogen.

There were no blue lagoons in the landscape of Oxford. And the duties of young ladies were not defined by sea captains, although they were as strictly codified. The stated threefold goal of the headmistress, Lucy Soulsby, of Oxford High School was not only the same as that of Thomas Arnold of Rugby, but was also ranged in the same moral hierarchy: the instillation of 'true religion, good manners, and sound learning, *in that order* [her italics].'[12] To understand her is to understand the school, and to understand the school is to understand Rose Macaulay's shy adolescence.

Although Lucy Soulsby left Oxford High School before Rose's last year, she moulded its spirit and the life of its pupils for years to come. She became a leading figure in girls' and women's education in England, ascending to successively more influential posts of command in women's colleges. After a long life of admirable service she left a weighty legacy: a complete, even redundant, compendium citing her moral, social, and intellectual ideals for educated young women. Thirty-eight books, including those devoted to advice, warning, and commands to teachers, parents, and young ladies survive today on obscure library shelves. The recurring text of their sermons is that all studies must be viewed in a moral light;

Miss Soulsby had uncompromising faith in the inspirational power of such a system. 'I am inclined to think that if Lady Macbeth had had better influences around her in early life, she might have been fit for "the constellation of fair women".'[13] This delightfully humourless observation exemplifies the high-minded tone of Emily Rose's school.

Decrying mental sloth, Miss Soulsby writes joylessly in *Stray Thoughts on Reading* (dedicated to the girls of Oxford High School) of 'the duty, not the pleasure, of reading'.[14] (She would have defined Rose as a 'Real Reader' for whom such counsel was unnecessary.) While she approved of Jane Austen and Charlotte Yonge, she believed in putting *contemporary* fiction on an Index and, indeed, said she would prefer a girl not to know how to read at all rather than to read French novels. She approved of some – but not too much – reading of poetry: 'Poetry can narcotize our moral sense.' Most dangerous of all to young girls, in her opinion, were novels which 'tamper with religious faith'. (Mrs Humphry Ward's sensationally popular *Robert Elsmere* would have fallen under this ban.) Her argument ran: 'It seems to me most crudely unintellectual to imagine oneself qualified to pronounce original opinion, without theological and evidential training which only the most exceptional woman possesses.'

But judging Lucy Soulsby by these words alone is unfair. Her heartfelt moral convictions were characteristic of those held by the headmistresses of girls' public schools in her day; they reassured the mothers of the respectable middle-class young ladies who attended them. (Daughters of the aristocracy were rarely enrolled in the relatively new girls' public schools; parents feared they might pick up impure accents and unsuitable friends.) The girls' innocence was to be protected, their emotions kept in check, and their minds not so enlightened as to make them unmarriageable.

On the whole Lucy Soulsby supported maternal wisdom, but she had higher intellectual aspirations for her charges than did their parents. She herself was that 'exceptional', well-educated woman she describes; she had passed the Cambridge Higher Exams; her reading list was formidable and broad; she wanted girls to study more mathematics, literature, languages, and history. Nor was health neglected; against opposition, Miss Soulsby succeeded in replacing the 'exercise' of the traditional decorous crocodile walk with games. 'I want more physical exercise brought into the curriculum, but I find a good many parents and doctors are afraid of the possible "strain".'[15]

The Macaulay girls, therefore, studied in a respectably rigorous academic atmosphere; future intellectual distinction was open to them. Rose's schoolmate Helen Darbishire was awarded a scholarship to Somerville College, Oxford, became an honoured Wordsworth scholar, and was in 1931 appointed the Principal of the College. In 1902 *The Oxford High School Magazine* lists graduates taking both First and Second Class

Honours examination places at Oxford. Miss Soulsby's high standards were effectively implemented.

There is still more to be said of Lucy Soulsby after acknowledging her reputation as a noble moralist and 'brilliant headmistress' of national renown. Parents praised her for the attention and sympathy she extended to each young charge. In her *Times* obituary she was justly recognized as a leader; the eulogy describes her as 'an arresting figure' and goes on to honour her androgynous qualities in stereotypical Victorian terms: 'a man's power of grasping essentials and a woman's greatness of heart'.[16]

In Lucy Soulsby Rose could observe the model of an educated woman in command of her life who could stand beside the intelligent, educated male figures she admired. Miss Soulsby had had a free-ranging childhood in New Zealand, was well educated at home, had wanted to be a boy, and had, like Rose, studied her lessons perched in the tops of trees. As an adult she was described by her colleagues as having 'a grand commanding eye and countenance'. One would imagine her to be a perfectly sympathetic character for Rose's emulation. But Rose could see, too, that the future of the girls whom Lucy Soulsby guided was envisaged by the headmistress and her staff as that of model wives or self-sacrificing junior teachers, vocations which did not attract a would-be naval lieutenant cum poet. For Lucy Soulsby, though a leader, was not a revolutionary. According to Oxford High School's official history, she believed that while Chemistry must be introduced into the curriculum, Needlework should not be neglected and that participation in such Lady Bountiful organizations as the school's Guild of Charity, 'helping the poor by sacrifices of money and time, pleasures and luxuries', was of major importance. (The signatures of both Rose and Jean appear on the membership list.) In short, the message was clear: Oxford High School girls should prepare for marriage and charitable community service.

In 1896, during the heated controversy in Oxford as to whether degrees should be granted to women, Miss Soulsby, although strongly for 'female education', was nevertheless of the opposing party. And as late as 1913, pleading for an end to 'Woman's Unrest' (her phrase for the Women's Movement), she was still describing the role of a woman, married or unmarried, as the Mother of all 'her men-kind' and of all children. Woman's 'one Right is Service,' she insisted, 'working through man and with man, not separately or against him.'[17] The spirit of 'Individualism' was, in her eyes, a dangerous force in young women's lives.

Rose, the Individualist, whose strategy of survival at school consisted of silence, neither openly rebelled nor verbally assented. Her name is surprisingly rare in the school's annals, not even appearing on class athletic teams. The official life view, mental and physical, of Oxford High School was too claustrophobic to accommodate her visions of freedom. George Macaulay's humour, scepticism, and broad tolerance were missing within its walls and a student essay on the school image in *The Oxford High School Magazine* frowns on 'rough play' for 'young ladies'.

The spirit and rules of the school were late Victorian; Miss Soulsby reprimanded one young lady for walking on the High Street with her brother, unchaperoned. 'Remember,' she said, 'everyone does not know he is your brother.' The codes of moral rectitude sometimes seemed to be confused with appearances, etiquette, punctuality, and tidiness. Rose believed that the eternal pursuit of neatness was a trivial and hopeless quest. In 'Problems of a Woman's Life' (1925) she wrote of the overwhelming duties of homemaking: 'And ever at your back you hear Time's winged chariot hurrying near ... and so the grave yawns, and at the end you will be able to say, not "I have warmed both hands before the fire of life," but "I have Kept House"'[18] ... Better a house unkept than a life unlived. She did not change her slap-dash ways; she wanted time for action. In Rose's dreams the battle of Invincible Good against Almost Unconquerable Evil was excitingly carried on in a more daring and less self-consciously genteel world than that of Oxford High School. She was a partisan of the cause of virtue, but she did not accept for herself the ideal of the Magna Mater.

The Macaulay girls shyly conformed at school, clung together, and after hours, with their brothers reverted (unchaperoned) to street games, detective scenarios, and practical jokes. (They were, of course, heavily frowned upon in Oxford for such pranks as taking their tortoise to church.) The 'good manners' of the system and of their schoolmates froze them into social shyness. Margaret, Rose, and Jean could not be wooed into conversation by C.L.Dodgson as a family dinner guest, although they liked him. As the High School Logic teacher and idol, Lewis Carroll must have been shocked by this defeat of his charm. For him such a family dinner party was usually the prelude to gaining maternal permission to have a friendship and tête-à-tête luncheons and teas with one of the schoolgirl daughters; he called these interludes 'the sweet relief of girl-society'. But although he was a friend of George Macaulay and Margaret was in his Symbolic Logic class (as he notes in his diary of 1896) he did not, Jean reports, accept another invitation to dine with the speechless Macaulay sisters.

The three began awkwardly in the school's social world. Grace, as an act of economy, had bought brown corduroy outfits in working-class south Oxford for her daughters' school clothes. Jean recalls that they were jeered at by cads and urchins as the three girls passed on their long walk to school: 'Corduroy breeches.' That garment was the Oxford labourer's uniform. Their more fashionable schoolmates may have giggled and sniffed. In the early teens such snubbing is nearly mortal to self-esteem; for the three it was far more painful than being called 'Long Legs' by the Italian convent girls to whom, even in their disapproved

short dresses, they had felt superior. As an adult satirist Rose more than
once mocked the tyranny of passing female fashions: 'Sometimes I think
I will give them all up, and just be dowdy.'[19] She wrote to Jean in 1957,
'Dress has never been a gift in our family; neither father nor mother had
it.... Looking back, I see we were dressed most eccentrically.'[20]

In the classroom she was also the odd girl out. Rose was better read
than her peers, but her shyness put her at a disadvantage. Jean says
Rose's work was 'about average'. This memory may have underestimated
her somewhat, for in 1951 Rose wrote in a letter to Father Johnson, 'I
did aspire to being top of my form as a rule.'[21] But the records show her
in that leader's role only in her last year, and in any case, she left no vivid
impressions of brilliance. Fortunately, Rose greatly admired her young
History mistress, Bertha Browne, whom one of her pupils praised for
'her vigorous mind and fine, clear teaching'.[22] Miss Browne must have
accurately assessed Rose's intelligence, range of knowledge, and budding
understanding of historical methods and given her the kind of encouragement she had received from her father.

In part because her father had prepared her by his intelligently sceptical
methods and his humane interpretation of historical texts, History was
Rose's best subject. She was to write of historical events with scholarly
accuracy and humanistic understanding, not only because of her pleasure
in painstaking research but also because of her amusement at human
error. From George Macaulay she had absorbed the humane lettrist-
historian's point of view: while as a young child in Varazze she was
enjoying his rendition of Froissart's action-filled chronicles of contemporary wars and his descriptions of Herodotus in search of the
legendary monsters of *Terrae Incognitae*, she was also being exposed to
her father's careful weighing and testing of the facts known to nineteenth-
century scholars against accounts of more gullible and more poorly
informed historians of the past. Herodotus himself, as George Macaulay
pointed out, was sceptical of some unlikely tales he could not verify and
separated what he had seen from what he had heard.

As a mature historian Rose Macaulay continued to explore and evalu-
ate ancient ignorance and modern discoveries, the superstition of the past
and the scepticism of the present. She enjoyed balancing oppositions. In
her collected essays, *Personal Pleasures* (1935), she includes two short
pieces on the delights and dangers of 'Believing' and 'Disbelieving':

I believe ... that Diogenes lived in a tub, St. Simon Stylites on a pillar,
chameleons on air, salamanders in fire, mermen in the sea; that corpses bleed
when their murderer approaches; that what I read in the newspapers is true
... I can be everyman's gull, and am infinitely persuadable. For to believe is
to enlarge life's oddity ... The clear and garish lucence of the sceptical spirit
I utterly reject; it is so dull.[23]

But, after a curious list of 'ridiculous tales' which demonstrate both human credulity and Rose's pleasure in collecting legend, rumour, and pre-scientific explanations, she later turns to the pleasures and pitfalls of disbelief:

> I believe very little.... It makes me feel agreeably aloof not to be imposed upon by all these strident, thundering events of which I hear, not to be taken in by rumour-mongers, magicians, gossips, quacks, moon's men, old wives' tales, ... But sometimes a thought troubles me, and I ask myself, should I, many centuries back have been numbered among those who denied ... the rotundity of the earth? ... I must beware then of too wide and deep an incredulity, and remember that there are many things yet hid from us, and that really everything is extremely peculiar.[24]

As a schoolgirl her strength was chiefly an excellent memory for what interested her; she could not then have been as articulate, facetious, or wise as she was in these essays of her adult years. But the interplay of both wonder and scepticism, those ideal intellectual and emotional qualities for a scholar, was already central to her temperament. *Told by an Idiot* gives us not only the naïve, dreaming Imogen Garden but her sister, another Rose Macaulay alter ego, the cool, disbelieving Rome, 'a woman of the world' with 'ironic blue-green eyes and mocking lips a little compressed at the corners'.[25] And still another aspect of the complex Rose is embodied in a third sister, young Stanley Garden, the religious seeker.

A blend of Imogen and Stanley at an emotionally and physically immature 13, Rose Macaulay was struggling on her own with formative inner experiences. A deep distress seems to have been generated by her discovery of the physiological facts of sex; from behavioural evidence and from cautious inference from her fiction we can be fairly sure that this knowledge came to her early in school at a stage when she was resisting her own future as a female and in a home where such concealed matters and the inner turmoil they released could not be recognized or discussed, even by the clan. The knowledge compounded her emotional confusion. (Jean said Grace attempted to frighten the children when any mention or hint of sex arose, but gave them no information except that sex was sin.) Five children were born at home before Rose was 9, but she must have suppressed her natural curiosity about their origin as did her character Imogen who, the narrator says, was at 13 in the ignorance her mother 'thought suitable to her years'. Imogen's boy cousin attempts to inform her:

> 'I know something you don't. I know how babies come.'
> 'Don't care how they come,' Imogen returned, astride on a higher bough

on the aspen tree than her cousin could attain to. 'They're no use anyhow, the little fools. Who wants babies?'[26]

We do not know how Rose was simultaneously informed and disturbed, whether by books or by an aggressive playmate, but we do know that the new knowledge fascinated and repelled her. She may have been fighting off her painful thoughts by what Jean called her 'craze' at this time for the ascetic Thomas à Kempis's meditations and rule of conduct, *On The Imitation of Christ*, which her godmother gave her when she was 13. 'I was, I suppose,' she writes to Father Johnson in 1951, 'in some ways, an odd child, for I fell for this book.'[27] She remembers sitting 'in the top branches of trees' reading it. In her authorial voice Macaulay says of her character Stanley's troubled reaching out to works of the spirit, 'Of the many impulsions that drive human beings to one form or another of religion, the strongest perhaps is pain.'[28]

There is, of course, both naïvety and risk in taking her fiction as autobiographical truth, but *Keeping Up Appearances* (1928) presents a believable story of the 12-year-old Anglican Cary Folyot's 'hidden life' in which she 'alternately sickened herself with reading hints of a life so disgusting that it kept her awake with nightmares, and sought emotional and spiritual outlet in secret religious practices'. And the story of Cary's anxiety is surrounded by the comments of Daisy, a compassionate young adult who echoes much that Rose Macaulay wrote in her own voice about sex and love. In any case the anecdote of Cary's agitation as she secretly reads Freud's *The Interpretation of Dreams* and her ensuing clandestine visits to the 'incensy' High Church Anglican confessional for comfort (as Cary 'had seen people do' in Italy) helps toward an understanding of Rose's developing sexual and religious emotions.

The fictional anecdote, obviously, is not an exact account of Rose's own girlhood experience. The first version of Freud's monograph on dreams as manifestations of sexual repression was not published until 1900 and not translated into English until much later. But Rose Macaulay's touching description of Cary's hidden torment could be an echo of her own experience. Cary reluctantly reveals her fears to Daisy, the young woman protagonist of the novel:

'I think perhaps when I grow up I may be a nun, and write my books in a convent, and not have any name on them, just "By a Nun." '

'Why should you be a nun? I don't suppose you'd be at all a very good one. I don't believe you're a bit religious really.'

'No,' Cary considered it honestly. 'I'm not really very religious. Only interested in religion. But I think I shall be a nun. Then I needn't marry.'

'You needn't marry in any case. Lots of people don't. But I thought you wanted thirteen or fourteen children.'

'I don't now.' The child seemed suddenly, standing in the tube entrance, to shrink and become frightened and babyish. Her eyes were on her muddy little shoes.

'I don't like the way they come.' . . . 'Beastly.'[29]

'Desiring to shield and guard her', Daisy comforts Cary, rejects Freud's 'pretty nasty book', and tries to dispel 'the sinister shadow' of her troubled imaginings. Daisy sees Cary as 'small, frail, spindly, and young . . . a child who had scared herself in the dark'. And walking on, musing on 'the oddness of life',[30] Daisy envies the unselfconscious animals: 'What a perverse anomaly, that we should revolt in displeasure from the methods of our own origin. . . . How fortunate are the animals, arriving into this world without the sense of fastidiousness that so deranges and dualises the mind of man.'[31] ('Fastidious' was one of Macaulay's epithets for a delicately discriminating intellect.)

This described distress is not necessarily a universal one (although it bears a strong resemblance to that of Rachel Vinrace in Virginia Woolf's first novel, *The Voyage Out*), but the narrator implies that all young humans are frightened and repelled by their first knowledge of sex. Daisy goes on to dismiss Cary's dark state of mind as 'an impermanent shadow', 'a little passing revulsion', and reassures herself: 'Cary had brains, and Daisy believed, perhaps erroneously, that brains are apt to pull people through.'[32] Yet Rose Macaulay knew that intelligence was not enough to guard the young from the dangerous vulnerability of sexual ignorance. The central young girl characters in two of her major novels, *They Were Defeated* and *The World My Wilderness*, are damaged or destroyed by adult failure to provide them with sexual knowledge and by adult carelessness in putting them at risk in situations where they become victims of seduction and rape.

But however passing their fear and disgust were, it seems that both the fictional child Cary and the adolescent Rose also wanted to escape the thought of sex in the repulsive and dominating form in which it had initially possessed their minds and emotions. Rose's own 'secret religious practices' to combat her night horrors seem to have been in part rooted in an intense concentration on à Kempis's religious meditations, which fixed attention on a spiritual world, rejecting the flesh. She seems to have longed for the relief of the sexless state of mind his words promised her.

Thomas à Kempis does not appear as an author in the list of books, essays, and sermons Lucy Soulsby recommended to young women for 'Sunday reading'. And although Grace preached hell-fire to the children, *The Imitation*'s denial of life is uncharacteristic of her life-affirming enthusiasm. In fact, Rose wrote that her mother 'threw cold water' on à Kempis's precept that 'one should withdraw the heart from the love of visible things.'[33] But his spiritual instructions promised that 'Inward Peace' Rose was seeking.

The ten books, a collage of closely knit biblical quotations, are compiled and written in the faith and spiritual abjection of fifteenth-century ascetic Catholicism. They urge contempt for all the vanities of the world, the practice of obedience and humility, the subjection of the will, a mean conceit of ourselves, the rejection of sensory pleasures, the preference for a good conscience over knowledge, and the acceptance of inescapable temptation and of our own insurmountable imperfections. These meditations are not mystic; they are an other-worldly monastic rule of life. Imperative, final, they form an unshakeably consistent *modus vivendi*, promising not earthly happiness but divine love as compensation for an unremitting acknowledgement of imperfection and a life of inevitable tribulation.

The first four books of *The Imitation* have been described as the most used collection of Christian meditations after the Bible. They promise a way to the 'cleanness of heart', which both the immature and innocent fictional character Cary and young Rose longed for. The life described requires an unending struggle against the appeals of the senses and affections. Rose may have taken to fasting; her frugal eating habits were one way of keeping her undeveloped pre-pubescent body from assuming sexuality. In any case, at about the time of reading à Kempis's 'Meditation on Death' she filled out a renunciatory (but not suicidal) legal Last Will and Testament form. The forty-two bequests she made were the possessions of a child – among them 'My dog Fido to Will', 'all my dolls' to Eleanor, stilts and skates, knives, trinkets and books to immediate family members. Constance Babington Smith observes that Rose must have felt friendless except for her sisters and brothers; no schoolmate was named as a beneficiary. It is, of course, unwise to take such self-dramatizing gestures too seriously; most adolescents make them at some time.

In the end, however, at the age of 70, Rose wrote to her friend Father Johnson that conformity to the role of self-sacrifice was 'quite impossible'; to attempt death-in-life was at odds with her temperament. And when she was 14 she discovered two writers more compatible with her buoyant spirit; they restored her well-being, affirmed the virtue of intellectual freedom, and simultaneously undermined her faith in orthodox Christianity. In later life, she attributed her adolescent lapse of faith to her out-of-school reading, particularly of John Stuart Mill. The problem of her denial of her sexual nature was not worked out, but a new preoccupation took its place.

She read Renan's *Life of Jesus*, which had proved so critical to George Eliot's substitution of Duty for God. As a corollary text, Rose discovered the rousing, hopeful words of Mill who argued for the sacredness of her larger duty to herself. (Like à Kempis, Mill was not a choice directed by school; while Lucy Soulsby mentions reading him in her student days, she omits his stirring work from her reading list for girls.)

Which of Mill's many writings awakened Rose's resistance to asceticism as an obligatory spiritual state? It seems a fair guess that his widely circulated 'On Liberty' was available to her; his three posthumous essays on religion are long, difficult, contradictory, less emotionally powerful and less relevant to her situation. We can hardly alight categorically on any exact passage to explain her release from fear, but Mill's message can be seen in a paragraph which challenged an uncritical acceptance of the obedience of à Kempis. Mill begins by defining 'the pinched and hidebound type of human character' as 'Calvinist', an anachronistic adjective for à Kempis, but ideologically a sound one. And he goes on to say:

> According to that [the Calvinistic theory], the great offence of man is self-will. ... [This] is held, in a mitigated form, by many who do not consider themselves Calvinists: ... [It teaches that] all the good of which humanity is capable is comprised in obedience.... Many persons, no doubt, sincerely think that human beings thus cramped and dwarfed are as their Maker designed them to be, just as many have thought that trees are a much finer thing when clipped into pollards, or cut out into the shapes of animals than as nature made them. But if it be any part of religion to believe that man was made by a Good Being, it is more consistent with that faith to believe that that Being gave all human faculties that they might be cultivated and unfolded, not rooted out and consumed.[34]

Mill's praise of freedom and growth throughout his work describes that Edenic Varazze where Rose *was* obedient, yet had space and private time in which to escape cramping authority. And in reading *The Life of Jesus* she exercised the freedom of intellectual curiosity that the author of 'On Liberty' urged on his audience. Renan contends throughout the carefully argued biography that Christ was all human, although 'among the sons of men there is none born greater than Jesus.'[35] Rose turned away from the misery of ascetic self-examination, finding Renan's portrait of a human Jesus far more attractive than the icon of the thwarted self urged by à Kempis. Her lifelong opposition to Puritanism took root; her faith in the miraculous powers of divinity wilted, as she herself explains.

In her letter to Father Johnson (24 April 1951), describing her private interview with the Anglican rector of SS Philip and James, Oxford as she prepared for confirmation, she says she would have liked to ask, 'As I really can't believe all this as I should, ought I to be confirmed?' But, she goes on, 'being a shy child of 14 (nearly 15, I suppose) I could say nothing at all. I remember I had been reading John Stuart Mill and rather absorbed his views. (The Thomas à Kempis period was then over.)'[36] Probably she was not prepared to face her High Church mother with this resistance to the sacrament. Although Grace had taught her children what her daughter called 'a liberal kind of theology', she was capable of making scenes and creating guilt about some acts of nonconformity.

In this same letter Rose goes on to 'suppose that most young creatures pass, each in his or her own way, through some such stages, *cuiusmodi.*' And her account of Imogen's similar experience at 14 in *Told By an Idiot* makes the same assumption that this compromise was common:

She then said to her brother Hugh, now in the fifth at Rugby: what did one do about confirmation if one believed Nothing? Hugh did not think it mattered particularly what one believed. One was confirmed; it did no harm; it was done; it saved argument. Himself, he believed very little of All That, but he had suffered confirmation, saying nothing. No good making fusses, and worrying mother. Jennie [Imogen] had much better go through with it, like other people.

'Well ... of course *I* don't care ... if it's not cheating...'

'Course it isn't. Cheating who? *They* don't care what we believe, they're not such sops. They want us to do the ordinary things, like other people, and save bother. And, of course' – Hugh was a very fair-minded boy and no bigot – 'there may be something in it after all. Lots of people, quite brainy, sensible chaps, think there is. Anyhow it can't hurt.'

So Imogen was confirmed.[37]

Rose was rescued from the misery of sexual nightmares by her brains, not because she had been able to dissipate her 'fastidiousness' about sex through logic, but because she had first sought an escape into other-worldly religious belief and then discovered greater emotional comfort in an intellectual freedom and emphasis on humanity that undermined supernatural faith and placed her solidly on earth. But she had not definitively worked through the inherent confusions. 'Perhaps I shall be full of the Holy Ghost,' thought Imogen. ... 'Perhaps ... but more prob'ly not.'[38] After all, Imogen and Rose were only 15. Until a family tragedy that lay ahead, Rose's interests in the Church remained chiefly historical, literary, and ethical; for a decade she was to be like her father, as she described herself, an intermittent church-goer, an Anglo-agnostic.

What was the family life of these high school years during which Rose's inner life was so intense? George Macaulay's days were spent in conscientious toil on what he described as the 'very large piece of work' of editing Gower, a task for which he had talent and interest, but which was narrowly focused. His work was lonely and, as he wrote to Francis Jenkinson, 'not likely to be at all remunerative.'[39] He had less time with his children than in the past, but to the best of his ability he showed his family the unselfishness and integrity for which Rose praised him. His financial worries were ever-present; family reserves and family generosity must have been required to shore up the household. Responsibility for

Aulay's and Will's school fees loomed ahead. Grace was never completely well.

It is unlikely that the Macaulays had much contact with university society; George was not attached to a college and their means were limited. But intermittently during the next five years Grace tried to launch the girls in a social world for which Rose and Jean had neither interest nor skills. After high school Margaret went, docile and apparently happy, to a succession of Cambridge balls with her mother, but later Rose and Jean were so unnerved by the strain of being assessed by Aulay's friends at a Woolwich dance that, in spite of their brother's assurance that they had passed muster after the painful scrutiny and that he had received compliments on their appearance, they never attended another.

The Five tried to maintain their solidarity but were at last to be permanently divided. The boys were to go off to school; the girls were to remain at home awaiting suitors. Margaret, who finished at Oxford High School in 1896, was a companion to her mother and immersed herself in church work. Grace's diary records the serial departure of her sons. Aulay, choosing an Army career, left for Woolwich in 1897, when Rose was 16. In 1898 Will, never a keen student, went off to Marlborough where his father had once taught, with plans for later attendance at an agricultural college and a rural life. Jean attended school alone the first term of that year; then Grace took all three girls to Varazze for the winter, leaving George at home alone to proofread his Gower galleys. Perhaps the staggering of Rose's and Jean's last school years was an economic decision; no English family would have been likely to allow the sons' education to be interrupted by money problems if this could be avoided. But leaving the somewhat uncongenial school for a year in Italy was scarcely a great disappointment to Rose and her sisters who, even in the absence of their brothers, could play at being the Five.

Emily Rose finished the Sixth Form in 1899 and the following year, at 18, the openly defiant Jean left school determined to become a nurse. Her mother responded to her ambition with horror. (One thinks of Florence Nightingale's account of her own mother's reaction: 'It was as if I had wanted to be a kitchenmaid.')[40] If George supported Jean's bid for independence at this time, we have no record of it. Money could not have been a central issue; after probation nurses in training earned their keep. But contemporary records show that the newly instituted hospital nursing courses were flooded with applications and their administrators strongly advised young women to defer undertaking this rigorous physical and emotional regimen until they were 22. Grace's reaction to Jean's ambition may have been in part conditioned by social snobbery and was certainly another manifestation of her belief that unmarried daughters should live at home, but whatever Grace's reasons, her objection *was* supported by practical contemporary advice.

Eleanor, financially supported by her grandmother, attended a series of unsatisfactory boarding schools, and was, at last, in 1901 to be placed in a school where a sympathetic mistress transformed her life by giving her the attention and affection for which she hungered. Not surprisingly Eleanor's goal was to be a teacher.

As for Emily Rose Macaulay, she had left Oxford High School and put up her hair in 1899, shortly before she turned 18. She spent a second winter with her mother in Varazze, a happy return into the past, but not a forward step. Jean says that in 1900 Rose had no plan for the future. But Uncle Regi descended as a *deus ex machina* and provided a brilliant one. On graduating, Rose had taken the obligatory external Oxford and Cambridge Higher Certificate Local Examination. She had satisfied the requirements in French, German, and Elementary Mathematics, but in addition had been awarded a Distinction in History; this academic success qualified her for a place at either university.[41]

For Rose, competing for this opportunity had been an exercise without hope of reward; although the expense of a university woman's education was considerably less than that of a man's, the family could not afford to continue her education and also pay for Aulay's and Will's schools. But Uncle Reginald offered to send her to Oxford; he had seen the waste of her fertile mind lying fallow. He also saw that Rose needed to get away from home, for he made it financially possible for her to be a resident student at Somerville College rather than to make economies by being one of the Home Girls who attended Oxford lectures under the aegis of the local Association for the Education of Women Students.

This act of a fairy godfather was characteristic of Regi; whatever the objections felt by either the immediate or the extended family, they could not stand against him. And it was not to be his last rescue of Rose from domestic dullness. His obituary noted that 'his wisdom and influence affected very many of his juniors, both in his own business and elsewhere, whose careers he watched and guided till the last days of his life.'

Rose admired and loved him, but not because Reginald Heber Macaulay was publicly acknowledged as 'a man of many gifts – a scholar of Eton and King's, a famous athlete and sportsman, and a successful India merchant.' She enjoyed and benefited from what others praised: his hospitality, his kindness to children, and his fund of friendship and generosity. And though she rarely showed her deepest feelings in public she wrote a published tribute, a postscript to his obituary in *The Times*:

He was, at his best, the most entertaining company in the world. His brilliant gifts as a raconteur of odd and amusing happenings in all parts of the world, his *meiosis*, his slight stammer, that preluded infallible alighting on the precise and telling word, his felicity in apt illustrative quotation from English and classic literature, his crisp and comic summing-up of personalities, both public and private, his concise and spontaneous epigrams, his rich laughter, made him an incomparable companion.... One could say an infinity of things in his praise; what I prefer to select from them is that no one in his company can ever have had a dull moment, which seems among the more important epitaphs that a human being can have.[42]

Except for the lifelong stammer, the Rose of 1932 might have been describing herself; uncle and niece were a matched pair.

And because Reginald Macaulay was, as she said, 'a fine uncle and friend', the young Rose was, in 1900, to step out of a confined household into a new world and a new century – through the gate of the young Somerville College to read Modern History.

4

A New Island

I<small>T WAS NOT</small> the shy, silent Emily of Oxford High School who enrolled at Somerville College. Instead, the voice of a very voluble Rose Macaulay was soon to be heard in its College Meeting Room. Her university friend, Olive Willis, said Rose's speech as a first-year student was 'an almost unintelligible torrent of words'.[1] The discovery of her extra-familial voice was a turning point. (Rose had taken part in only one school debate; her adversary had been her sister Margaret.) In the first years of the twentieth century, Somerville proved to be a milieu which released, stimulated, and challenged Rose Macaulay's pent-up opinions, a small world which nurtured the gestation of the mature writer's critical but compassionate view of life among the English.

She had come to the right community for self-discovery. Vera Brittain was to observe of a more established Somerville in the Twenties that it was 'very mixed'. 'In such a community with its large choice of companions and its wide range of ideas, the inquiring, unconventional mind of the creative writer finds ample opportunity for unrestricted development along its own lines.'[2] In 1900 both the college and unorthodox Rose Macaulay were in the early stages of imagining and creating a new, free identity.

But from the first opening of Somerville's wisteria-draped door, the policy of encouraging strong individualism had been clearly stated. Founded in 1879, along with Lady Margaret Hall, it was, unlike that Anglican-supported women's college, non-denominational. To reassure parents, Lady Margaret Hall described its atmosphere as 'Christian'; Somerville's self-definition of its own aura was 'English'. The two institutions complemented each other; over the years Somerville enrolled students from a wider spectrum of national, religious, economic, political, and class backgrounds than the consistently conservative, clerical Lady Margaret Hall. Both Margaret Thatcher and Indira Gandhi were Somervillians. Vera Farnell, retiring as Somerville's Vice-Principal, Dean, and French Tutor in 1947, introduces her published talks by explaining that the College's statutes were 'based on an idea of intellectual integrity and independence, of a wide tolerance and of a liberal attitude to innovation'. She adds, 'A certain tendency to eccentricity may sometimes accompany these admirable qualities.' And she illustrates by quoting what she describes as a university tag, current some years before – 'Somerville for *Brains*,' and adds 'sometimes unkindly translated – Somerville for *Freaks*.'[3] Was not the college named for Mary Somerville, a brilliant nineteenth-century mathematician and astronomer who wrote formulae on the back of her fan to be studied when she was bored with genteel conversation? And was not such a female scholar like the monster apparition of a woman in academic regalia who appeared in a troubled don's nightmare?

As a consequence of this scorn the Somerville individualists had to cultivate self-sufficiency, self-esteem, and humour. They had been labelled by the male students as frumps, prudes, and earnest bores, yet had been chaperoned as though they were flirts or sirens. Fear of their disrupting, damaging influence was strong; they had dared to knock at the gates of a securely exclusive all-male preserve. The famous Dr Pusey had described the establishment of women's halls as 'one of the greatest misfortunes that have happened even in our own time in Oxford'.[4] One anecdote appears frequently in university histories: Dean John Burgon, preaching in New College Chapel on Trinity Sunday, 1884, addressed the women present, 'Inferior to us God made you, and inferior to the end of time you will remain. But you are none the worse for that.' Vera Brittain tells us: 'Contemporary records report that the congregation laughed aloud.'[5]

The angry opposition did not halt the steady progress of Somerville toward excellence and recognition. When Rose joined its seventy-five other students in 1900, the college was defining its intellectual standards and entering a new phase of its history; symbolically, that year Somerville replaced its oil lamps with electricity. The college aimed to instil in women what Vera Brittain defines as the core of university teaching: 'The integrity, as scholarship understands it, of the facts, and the knowledge and perception which put facts into perspective.'[6] This teaching aimed to help women achieve the dignity of 'a right judgement in all things', the quality Rose Macaulay saw as central to her father's character and habits of mind.

Improvement in the university's perception of the women's colleges – won by academic success, tenacity, patience, and tact – had been gradual. In 1893 a humiliating and absurd requirement had been dropped: professors no longer insisted that chaperones accompany women students to lectures in case a female fainting fit should embarrass the lecturer. (Not once had the services of the bored, knitting chaperones been called upon.) Since 1894 women students had been allowed to sit for and be ranked on all examinations leading to the BA degree; their performance had been impressive. In 1894, Somerville raised its status from that of a residence hall to that of a college.

Nevertheless, when Rose enrolled six years later none of the women's college administrators, tutors, or students were allowed to wear academic gowns or were, indeed, by any definition, members of the university. Their position was anomalous. Yet in spite of the 1896 defeat in Congregation of a strong bid for women's right to take degrees, the quietly pertinacious Principal, Agnes Maitland, was confident of eventual success. She gathered a group of brilliant tutors around her and effectively began to build the college's resources: the library, the treasury, and the support of former students. Precedents had been set. Could not women at that time earn degrees at the universities of London and Edinburgh? Were not opportunities of social roles other than wife and mother, schoolmistress, or governess now conceivable for upper-middle-class women? (One of Rose's Somerville contemporaries became HM Deputy Inspector of Factories.) At this transitional moment, the college's students had the constant responsibility of proving to Oxford University, of which they formed no official part, the capacity of women for serious intellectual work.

Other demands on the young in this milestone year were, as always, exhilarating and daunting, particularly for thoughtful young women. Rebecca West wrote in her retrospective album *1900*: 'We were all facing the dilemma which confronts every generation. We had to recast our impression of the world as it had been altered by the work done by the last generation in the way of thinking and feeling, and once we had done that we had to work out what our place was in this new world.'[7] Later, Rose as a social critic was to be consistently wary of making portentous pronouncements about radical changes in historical cycles; in 1925 she wrote wryly of cultural egocentricity: 'An important time: that is what the times we live in have always been.'[8] But England was changing; Rose Macaulay went up to Oxford during the first year of the Boer War and came down in the year of Queen Victoria's death. And for her private history, the first three years of the twentieth century, organized around life in a large altered grey stone house on Woodstock Road, were to be critical for the successful invention of an idiosyncratic place for herself in what must be accounted an altered world.

However fortunate her choice of college, Rose, like all freshers, had some difficulty in adjusting in her first year. She was certainly not troubled by those unaesthetic, Spartan living conditions of unendowed Somerville which in 1906 offended the gently reared Margaret Haig Thomas, Viscountess Rhondda-to-be. That feminist leader of the future abandoned Somerville in a mood of accumulated distaste after two terms of residence as a first-year student. She disliked both its social and its physical atmosphere. 'Somerville smelt frousty to me,' she wrote.[9] She turned her back on the food, the ugly crockery, limited service, makeshift decor, scarcity of hot water, bathrooms, and living space, the lecture-room-and-hall-as-library. These were not deficiencies which mattered much to Rose, although Somerville's necessary frugality was in harsh contrast to the plush amenities of the wealthy men's colleges.

Perhaps, however, official dining and the indifferent food contributed to Rose's bad eating habits. Olive Willis reports that she 'was entirely obstinate about college meals and would go without food rather than sit through a college dinner.'[10] Rose could write eloquently of the pleasures of tasting gourmet dishes but found long meals a bore and the preparation of food an even greater one; later she was to say that one of the great pleasures of travel is to consume delicious food and drink without having had the trouble of preparing it. What Olive Willis's remark implies is that the constraint and tedium of having to dawdle and fidget, long after the bread pudding and custard had been consumed, until the Principal rose from the Head Table, gave the dismissing benediction, and led the procession from the hall, was as annoying to her as the uninspired menu.

Olive, who was four years older and had come up two years ahead of Rose, continued to fret about her. Rose would not, sensibly and gratefully, accept Olive's offer to bring her bread and milk. She *hated* bread and milk. Her college friends were distressed by her self-neglect and though she seemed indefatigable, the older Olive said maternally, 'She looked like an unfledged bird, a young eaglet perhaps, but in that thin, defenceless form, it wasn't easy to recognize future development.'[11] To Olive, a physical breakdown for Rose seemed probable.

There is not enough evidence to diagnose Rose's behaviour as a pathological eating disorder; habitually as an adult she would become too preoccupied with telephoning, reading, and writing to bother about eating. Indeed, she recommended that those living alone should survive by foraging at odd hours on tinned food, bacon and eggs, and biscuits. Ruth Gollancz, calling on an ill Rose in London years later, wondered if Rose lived mostly on tea; she counted nine dirty teapots in her flat. Mark Bonham Carter speculates that, too engaged with her writing to cook, Rose subsisted on the fine food of parties, which she enjoyed. At Somerville, however, she might still have been unconsciously resisting achieving the curves of sexual maturity. But Rose was congenitally epicene and, in her energetic old age, as more than one friend says, lean as a rake and almost as transparent as alabaster. She was 5 feet 8 inches tall and weighed 112 pounds. Her description of the naked body of the 43-year-old Neville Bendish, mother of two, swimming alone in the dawn hours (*Dangerous Ages*, 1921), is of the slight, androgynous female figure that was chic in the Twenties (rather like Rose herself): 'long in the leg, finely and supply knit, with light flexible muscles – a body built for swiftness, grace and wiry strength.'[12]

Other constraints irritating to fellow students did not seem to trouble her. The unwritten rule, usually conveyed when necessary from Principal to student via a tactful emissary, was that the women permitted to attend lectures at Oxford and to read at the Ladies' Table in the Radcliffe Camera should dress in drab clothes, neither dressy nor odd, lest they distract the young gentlemen; the official hint – *Somervilliae semper subfusc*. One young student was gently dissuaded by the first principal from wearing a hat that was 'too becoming'.[13] On the other hand, aggressive mannishness was also discouraged. Such limitations did not arouse in Rose the later rebellious flamboyance of Dorothy Sayers, notorious for her three-inch scarlet headband and shoulder-length caged-parrot earrings. The students knew, of course, that the recommended inconspicuous appearance did not represent Somerville's aesthetic taste, but was an aspect of its official strategy to convince the high authorities that the presence of young women was not necessarily an incongruous feature of Oxford's grey monastic landscape. If the women would be Oxonians, was the counsel, they had best adopt camouflage. The men's university publications, however, habitually described them as dowdy bluestockings.

In contrast to the competition in dress practised at Oxford High School, Somerville's sartorial restrictions suited Rose exactly; she wanted only to be comfortable in conformable clothes that allowed for playing vigorous hockey and tennis, for boating, and for climbing roofs and trees. Tomboy Varazze freedom was still her style. Her impatience with fashion was lifelong; friends of her middle years described her wardrobe as 'sparrowgarb', or, with eloquent brevity, 'brownish'. One kind friend said, 'She had her own style.' At 47 she wrote, 'Why do I not like clothes? Chiefly because they have been made into gods, demanding time, money, and intelligence which can ill be spared from more entertaining subjects. ... I dislike skirts because, however brief they may be, they are hampering in human activities. I dislike evening clothes because they are chilly in damp weather; hats because it is more comfortable without a hat; stockings because they get splashed with mud; fur because it has an unpleasing and barbaric appearance, comes off my fellow animals, and is soon devoured by moths.'[14] Writing about Second World War clothing shortages in 1942 Rose said, 'Standards of smartness depreciated, to the relief of those who had always found them tedious or inaccessible.'[15] At Oxford she did not even follow Professor Mark Pattison's suggestion to the Principal of the Home Students that the college women be neat and tidy. A classmate harshly described Rose in her first year as 'slovenly'.

What pleased Rose most was the pursuit of 'the right judgement in all things' and the talk, talk, talk that explored its nature. Ethical quandaries always fascinated her and she found examining spiritual questions one of the high adventures of student dialogue. As a non-denominational college Somerville was not non-Christian; rather, it was committed to the inclusion of a variety of dissenting beliefs. The First Rules of Somerville suggested to its students regular attendance at the church of their choice; Rose did not attend often. College prayers were said daily, and although there was no chapel building in Rose's day, chapel addresses, largely morally uplifting, were delivered each Sunday evening in the dining hall. However, she persisted in her religious scepticism; as Alan Pryce-Jones said of her, 'She disliked things to be finally settled.'[16]

As a passionate college debater, torn between the old shyness and the new compulsion toward self-expression, she sometimes stammered like Uncle Regi. Her wild-rose English complexion would become suffused with a blush. Olive Willis, who became a lifelong friend, later wrote of her: 'Perhaps the most curious trait in her character when she was young was her great diffidence, a sense of failure and inadequacy, combined with a confidence in her own opinion. ... As she became famous, this diffidence left her and she spoke deliberately and firmly, without that engaging hesitation which used to trip her up in her most vehement and absurd argument.'[17] Yet in the midst of the new life of lively intellectual interchange, the old, escaping, fantasizing self survived. Olive remembered that 'her strange eyes never altered, grey as glass and often unseeing as though she realized the world through other senses and other ways.'[18]

However diffident, she was remembered for exercising freedom of behaviour, writes Vera Brittain, recounting the legends that lingered behind Rose at Somerville ten years after she had gone down and had begun her career as a successful author. Brittain's stories were gathered from the memories of a college servant by aspiring undergraduates who later came to be members of what is known as the Somerville School of Novelists; the details of Rose's oddity collected by her admirers may well be slightly exaggerated. 'On a cold winter's night, we are told, she would write her weekly essay on the lawn with a lighted candle flickering beside her.'[19] (Perhaps she did this once or twice; the 'weekly' is a little suspect. Rose always described herself as 'a heat glutton'.) The tale goes on to say that Rose, 'attended by two or three devoted friends', would spend several days lying in bed, 'interminably scribbling on loose sheets of paper, which she would leave lying about the floor or push into her dressing table until the doors refused to close.'[20] But although onlookers were sometimes startled by the mature Rose's short-cut solutions to practical problems or by her intrepidity, Rose was never an exhibitionist. She did not, however, mind being found comic.

The 'devoted friends' were particularly important because not only did the Five no longer gather, but after her first year she was three counties away from the Macaulay home. In 1901 her father failed in his application for a post in Australia but succeeded in being appointed Professor of English Language and Literature at University College, Aberystwyth, and the family moved to 'Ty-issa', 160 miles from Oxford as the crow flies. For the first time Rose was at ease with a range of congenial companions outside the extended family.

Somerville students enjoyed the same close bonding as the Macaulay clan and in part for a similar reason – to weather criticism. Miss Maitland held together this heterogeneous community of students by developing in them an intense personal loyalty to the college. The women were willing to forego 'the advanced behaviour' which would bring opprobrium on their joint enterprise, for they, like their Principal, had unbounded ambition for its future. Yet within the democratic college they enjoyed and valued the intoxicating pleasure of intellectual disagreement. The original vision and a strong *esprit de corps* remain; Somerville is still a single-sex college, and a thumbnail description from a recent issue of *The Times* closes with the statement that Somerville 'actively encourages application from a wide variety of backgrounds. ... its students have a reputation of enthusiasm for their college.'

Rose Macaulay never wrote a university novel, but her *Spectator* column of 5 April 1935, challenging the male reviewer of such a fiction, calls up her happy memory of that communal life. (Years later she wrote of it to Father Johnson, 'I enjoyed myself hugely.')

> Why do male reviewers believe that life in a woman's college is gruesome? Or even 'thin and self-conscious' (to quote this recent reviewer further)? There is, of course, the natural masculine inclination to disbelieve that a community of young women can enjoy as vivid and full a life together as a community of young men.... Many young girls are bores but many are not. And there are among those sent to a university, enough amusing, intelligent, vivacious, high-spirited, intellectual or otherwise pleasing young women to make one another good company.... You may see them, any night, gathered around a fire and arguing on all manner of topics, with the zeal and satisfaction proper to their years.... Friends, work, games, the river, rooms of their own, comparative grown-up freedom, the University atmosphere – those who enjoy none of those things should not have come up, but have come out instead.[21]

This description of daily pleasure and challenging liberty is nothing like the diary entries of a young woman living at home; those last items on Rose's list of satisfactions could be the details of a young man's Oxford journal. Their own good company, indeed, proved so enjoyable for many women students that one of the men's magazines which had regularly produced columns of print caricaturing their man-chasing empty-headedness, one day printed the astonished, shocked, and injured male observation, 'They are combined. There is union. They do not want us.'[22]

The portraits and vignettes of young university-educated women in her fiction show that Rose observed and prized the differences between the argumentative young women of that united group. Two characters from *Told by an Idiot* are representative: Miss Stanley Garden – who, in 1879, was fresh from her first term at Oxford – is an emotional, attractive Christian Socialist, planning to work in a settlement, excited by Ruskin, Morris, and the Labour Movement; her sister Rome is an anti-enthusiast, an urbane commentator, *au courant* but jaded.

Rose often described women in terms of the proportion of intelligence, humour, and imagination in their temperaments; she usually presented their points of view on politics and religion as well. As she did the former perceptively, she did the latter even-handedly. In *The Making of a Bigot* (1914) we are helped to understand and to like both the Dean's daughter, Daphne, 'an ardent and potentially militant suffragist', and her mother, Mrs Oliver, a 'calm but earnest member of the National Union for Women's Suffrage, who went to meetings'.[23]

Such understanding, inclusiveness, and avoidance of confrontation in spite of frank intellectual disagreement were characteristics of personal relationships in Somerville; its university politics were practised on the same principles. And when Rose Macaulay ten years later moved successfully into the mysogynist world of literary London she made use of, consciously or no, a variation of the tactics by which the Somerville Council established a women's college on the periphery of Oxford and brought it into the male university. The poised avoidance of open protest, divisiveness, and of humourless misanthropy suited her own style and temperament.

Though 'torrents of words' poured out by intellectually provocative friends came high on Rose's list of university pleasures, 'work' followed closely. She elected to do Modern History Honours, a popular subject at Somerville both for students interested in history and students interested in literature because it did not require competence in Latin and Greek, a competence acquired by few young women. But Rose's choice was in part the fruit of her already discovered enthusiasm for the past. Her Special Subject was the same as that on which she had written her High Distinction paper in the Oxford and Cambridge Schools Examination – English History from 1509 to 1688; her Special Foreign Period was also the seventeenth century. Religious and political clashes were always to fascinate her. She was required, as well, to study all of English History and to take courses in Political Science and Political Economy; the latter two interested her less.

Remembering her omnivorous curiosity and examining the meticulous notes from the research in progress which survived her death, we know she read widely, deeply, and with delight on any subject she decided to explore. Like her father she did not seem to know when to stop. Both her life of Milton (1934) and her 1946 book on the English travellers who went to Portugal in the last eight centuries had to be cut by half before publication. To prepare for writing *Milton* she had read *all* of his prose, both Latin and English, both literary and official, discovering aspects of his character less attractive than those of the creator of the poetry.

As a history student at Oxford she would, of course, have concentrated on primary documents – contemporary records and letters, proclamations, legal papers, tracts, broadsides, and satirical verse – examining all sides of the debate of the Civil War period. She was always, as she impersonally describes herself in her 'Auto-Obituary' (1936), 'much interested in religions; the voluminous calf-bound theological works of the past centuries were among her reading, and no curious heresy, or antique doctrinal squabble failed to intrigue her fancy'.[24] The official records of her Somerville years have not survived, but it is no risk to conclude that she was busy for nine terms with work which absorbed her.

This happy life went on for Rose and her friends in a small autonomous community situated rather like an island off the shore of a continent ruled by a largely hostile or dismissive male hegemony. Officially the college had both to solve its own internal problems and to accommodate the greater power which could determine its fate. But, as always, oversimplifying factionalism is dangerous. To be fair, the women's colleges could not have been even tentatively established without the stout, sustained support of such influential and generous men (to name but a few) as Professor Henry Pelham, Professor T. H. Green, and Dr John Percival, President of Trinity. In opposition to its male friends, it had female critics; despite the advocacy of such Somerville pioneers as the irreproachable novelist Mrs Humphry Ward and that formidable scholar of Latin, Greek, and Ancient History and invaluable legal authority on the University Statutes, Annie M. A. H. Rogers, the daring experiment had met with opposition from women who believed only harm could be done by the expectations aroused in young ladies by higher education and their consequent unfitness for matrimony.

Even in 1900, twenty-one years after Somerville's founding, Rose Macaulay as a first-year student witnessed the politics of the four parties which had developed: two, formed by men *inside* the university, acting *for* and *against* the intellectual development of women; and two, formed by women *outside* the university, acting *for* and *against* the practical realization of the same goal. In the struggle Rose could see both the value of quiet, intelligent tenacity and the cost of loud, aggressive partisanship. Though she was fascinated by intellectual controversy she was disturbed by the emotional extremes of fanaticism; as a friend of long standing said of her, 'Rose loved debate. She didn't like a row.'[25]

The leadership of the women's colleges, thinking along similar pacific and strategic lines, had, for example, determined, whatever their private views, to ignore the inflammatory question of Votes for Women for two reasons: first, Oxford University had officially declared Women's Suffrage an issue that was 'political', not to be introduced into university deliberations. And, second, there would be a split in the women's ranks if the issue was publicly debated among them. Such Somerville supporters as Mrs Humphry Ward and such prominent social critics as Beatrice Webb had taken a public stand against the vote for women. Indeed, Mrs Ward was the organizer and spearhead of the anti-suffrage movement. Official Somerville could not afford division; solidarity was necessary for success. All shades of opinion co-existed within the college walls, although the overall tendency was overwhelmingly pro-suffrage. But the governing council, with practical wisdom, focused only on its chief aim – to achieve the granting of degrees to the women students who were doing with distinction the same intellectual work as the men.

Rose, too, avoided the suffrage campaign because it was divisive and potentially violent. But she also thought it politically futile. In 1957 she commented on the issue rather breezily in her memoir about cultured London life just before the First World War. 'Behind all the talking and writing and the ballet and the theatres and the poetry, there were a few quite uncivilized noises off, from Ireland, and from the Balkans, and from strikers and suffragettes. Not being politically minded, I do not think that I attended very closely. Naturally I knew it was ridiculous to deprive half the people of the country of any voice in the laws they had to live under, merely on account of a trifling difference in sex, but I did not think anything I could do about it was likely to be helpful.'[26]

This light-hearted statement illuminates some of her methods as a novelist of ideas; she was engaged in advancing what she believed was a unifying and reconciling vision of human nature; she believed that gaining the vote for women was a relatively minor victory. In 1925 she wrote that suffrage 'does not seem to amount to very much; the Government seems to go along its own way without much reference to public opinion.'[27] In 1950 she wrote, 'After all, the British constitution has never been in any sense a democracy; those we vote into Parliament escape thereafter completely from our control and pass any laws they like without consulting us further, so having a vote is no great catch.'[28]

Her claim of 'not being politically minded' defines her ignorance and dislike of party politics at the time, but both her interest in and distrust of the dynamics of power grew with the years. Her dislike of extremes and violence, however, is clear; Rose Macaulay understood the Pankhursts but did not march beside them. The empathetic male protagonist of *The Making of a Bigot* (1914) defends a young woman who has 'jabbed her umbrella into a lot of Post-Impressionists in the Grafton Galleries': 'I do see what they mean, all right. They smash and spoil and hurt things and people and causes because they are stupid with anger; but they've got things to be angry about, after all.'[29] In her highly successful novel of 1920, *Potterism*, the narrative voice says ruefully of 1914, 'The conversation turned tediously on militant suffragists, Irish rebels and strikers. It was the beginning of an age of decision by physical action which has lasted ever since and shows no signs of passing.'[30] Looking back, in a Third Programme BBC broadcast (3 April 1950) she said, 'I disliked the noisy fuss the suffragettes made.'[31] Such consistent opposition to force throughout Rose Macaulay's life and work is like the Somerville leadership's careful avoidance of divisive conflict – a caution considered craven and ineffectual by the militants.

To avoid as a matter of policy what she saw as the limiting label, not only of 'suffragette', but also of 'a writer for women', was important to Rose Macaulay's purposes, just as avoiding the label of 'suffragist' was important to the Somerville Council. She muted and qualified her feminist sympathies in her writing to emphasize a wider theme and reach a wider audience. She said, 'All right-minded men and women object to being catered for collectively as a sex, their common humanity ignored.'[32] She made constant disclaimers that she was a fighter for the Cause; in her 'Auto-Obituary', that essay of mingled self-deprecation, jest, fantasy, evasion, and biographical fact, she says of herself disingenuously, 'She never had any strong link with her age, or was much interested in social questions, such as the position of women, and so forth.'[33]

Her advocacy was broader; she might best be called, in Judith Moore's apt phrase, a 'humanist with a brief for women'.[34] She freely and often acknowledged that women were disadvantaged; if she felt anger about this truth she transformed it into cooler responses of satire, irony, and compassion, and into persuasive examples in her novels. She frequently filtered the feminist view through her characters; Jane Potter in *Potterism*, comparing her career prospects with those of her twin brother who got a less distinguished First than hers at Oxford, thinks: 'Though she might be one up on Johnny as regards Oxford, owing to her slightly superior brain power, he was one up on her as regards Life, owing to that awful business, sex. Women were handicapped; they had to fight much harder to achieve equal results.'[35]

If we use the opening words of one of Carolyn Heilbrun's definitions of a feminist – one who 'questions the gender arrangements in society and cultures' – then Rose Macaulay is a feminist; her novels expand the possibilities of active lives for women. But if we take her corollary – 'For to be a feminist, I would suggest, is to be where women are and to value the presence of women there' – the description fits her less well.[36] She greatly enjoyed the community of women at Somerville, but she did not seek out communities of women. She never privileged women as a sex over men; she believed it was as wicked to hang a man as to hang a woman. She helped novice writers of both sexes publish and move into her world. Her exposure of human cruelty throughout history did not blame its effects upon the male power structure but on some flaw in humanity's moral nature. She had many close and long-lasting friendships with women, but her closest friends over a lifetime were men.

The brilliant young Julian Conybeare of the seventeenth-century world of *They Were Defeated* (1932) is destroyed by political, religious, and sexist intolerance, but for the most part she suffers silently; the reader's indignation is aroused by her acceptance of her fate. Not until Macaulay's last triumphant novel did she create a declared feminist – the dauntless Aunt Dot who set out for Turkey to investigate 'the position of women, that sad and well-nigh universal blot on civilization'.[37] If we trust the tale and not the teller, we see Rose Macaulay's deep sympathy with women's handicaps throughout her writing and see it becoming more intense after the First World War. But the injustice of sexual inequality was not the central circumstance she consciously aimed to portray.

She attempted to enlarge the understanding of human difficulties by depicting the many ways in which men and women of the world she knew were more alike than different. Attempting to diffuse the impression that she was partisan, she wrote, 'Let us spare pity for both sexes, and not spend it all on women, for after all, in most respects, men and women have always been in the same boat, suffering from *mal de mer* together on the rough seas of this troublesome world.'[38] She suggested shifting the focus from gender differences to a consideration of the range of the shared identity of both sexes. Sitting down to write a satirical essay on 'Problems of Women', she wrote a satirical companion piece on 'Problems of Men'. Precociously, she had come to understand in childhood the male elements in herself and the female elements in her brothers; 'androgyny' was not then an intellectually fashionable term, but it was hardly a new concept.

Rose believed our better understanding of the sexual spectrum would make for more harmony between the sexes – at least for more compatible coupling. She considers some androgynous social behaviour of upper-middle-class 'neutrals' in her novel, *Mystery at Geneva* (1922): 'It may be observed that there are in this world mental females, mental males, and mental neutrals. You may know them by their conversation.'[39] She characterizes the mental females and mental males as apt to talk about subjects that fall in their gender spheres – the women about children and clothes, for instance, the men about such matters as sport and finance. They are, in their interests at least, 'more fully sexed' than those who live between these polarities. She goes on to describe the middle-range interests:

In between these is the No-Man's Land, filled with mental neutrals of both sexes. They talk about all the other things, such as books, jokes, politics, love (as distinct from love affairs), people, places, religion (in which, though they talk more about it, they do not, as a rule believe so unquestioningly, as do the males and the females, who have never thought about it and are rather shocked if it is mentioned), plays, music, current fads and scandals, public persons and events, newspapers, life, and anything else which turns up.[40]

Such categories cannot be drawn arbitrarily; 'womanly women' do talk of music, plays, and current scandals; 'manly men' do discuss public events, jokes, and newspapers. Sharp distinctions cannot always be clearly perceived. The detective 'hero' of *Mystery at Geneva* is at its climax unmasked; 'he' is a woman. From her first novel Rose played many variations on the concept of a spectrum of sexuality; all Macaulay readers know that most of her central female characters either have masculine names or names which are appropriate for either gender. From the earliest reviews of her work most Macaulay critics have noted the theme of male and female likeness and reversal of stereotypes as her hallmark.

In fact, on the much discussed subject of sexual differences and rights Rose Macaulay did not follow any party line; she went her individualistic way. And she was not always consistent. She wrote for Lady Rhondda's feminist periodical *Time and Tide*, but one of her book reviews elicited an angry letter from a reader; Rose had spoken of 'the intellectual superiority of most men' as 'an obvious fact'.[41] Her assumption was made on the outmoded Darwinian grounds of comparative physical size, strength, and stamina in a species as indicators of intelligence. As an established writer she wrote in the essay 'What I Believe' (1931), 'After all, women are physically less and frailer in every capacity, and it is not likely that the brain should be excepted. Let it be admitted that the female sex in humanity is the less rough and robust, mentally, nervously, and physically.' And she adds controversially, 'the less fitted to endure strain and hardness, to create, to initiate, to organize, and to perform.' With a touch of élitism in her argument for women's education, she continues, 'the stupidity of such women as have received little learning is a heavy retarding weight on the world's progress.'[42] She had lived and worked among and was the descendant of exceptionally intelligent women, yet she saw them as exceptions. She viewed women as disadvantaged by nature as well as by nurture. In a review of *The English Miss Today and Yesterday* (1939), called 'Onward from Noodledom', she wrote:

What to put into the vacant and ill-regulated minds of young females – here is a problem that has not always exercised their guardians as it should. The vacant and ill-regulated minds of young males have, until lately, received more attention, which is probably a mistake, since nature would seem to have made these on the whole more efficient, needing, therefore, rather less training to bring them to a standard which should not greatly harm society.[43]

Rose Macaulay's conception of the female mind and the destructive effect of years of domesticity on its powers made her a pessimistic and mistaken prophet about the future of mature women re-entering professions. The last half of the twentieth century has disproved her certainty that middle-aged women who might attempt to return to serious study and work when their children leave home would inevitably fail, but she did not in 1925 have many models for a character like Neville Bendish of her *Dangerous Ages*.

Neville, once a brilliant medical student, discovers at 43 that an intellectually undemanding although socially active life as wife and mother has withered her ability to concentrate and to grasp her subject; reluctantly she concludes that her brain has atrophied and her will has become soft. She has found study 'difficult beyond belief; it made her head ache.'[44] True, her feminist husband and sympathetic doctor brother contradict their principles and make a few discouraging judgements of her ambitions, but it is she herself who acknowledges her inability to prepare for examinations. She suffers 'a nervous breakdown' under the strain of two tasks – light nursing care for a grown daughter with a mending broken leg and studying for qualifying medical exams. She gives up her hopes of doing the serious 'work' she craves.

Perhaps Rose Macaulay made some negative generalizations about women to demonstrate her fair-mindedness in the War Between the Sexes which the press had, in her opinion, inflated as a New Phenomenon. Her bald statements of anti- or non-feminism were more likely to appear in journalism and radio talks than in the novels, where as a discriminating observer of human nature, she had more room to display her characters' individual differences and show their double-sexed natures. Is it an unconscious contradiction or merely an intelligent corollary to her claims for male mental superiority that in fiction she would insist, as a character says in *Mystery at Geneva*, that 'Women are so different from one another. So are men. That's all I can see, when people talk of the sexes.'?[45]

The daughter of a former Fellow of Trinity College had no understanding of (and little opportunity to understand) the problems of working-class women who came to want not political equality but economic independence. Her imaginative boundaries were set by her class and education and her belief in the importance of intellectual superiority. Her vision was limited but within its class limitations it was reasonable and generous.

Rose Macaulay always greatly enjoyed intelligent male company; she frequently said men were better talkers than women. Good talk was her food, and her mind was bonded to the male world. (Virginia Woolf said Rose had 'a donnish mind'.) And she entered the society of male writers in London in the early twentieth century attempting a role as nearly neutral and sexless as possible. She had lived at Oxford with women who successfully competed intellectually with men, yet knew they had a hard road to travel in the outside world. She was prepared by the university for the prejudices which could work against a woman's inclusion in a male-dominated profession and was aware of more than one way to circumvent or diffuse them.

Besides avoiding confrontation she used another tactic of the eventual Oxford victory for women as people: the art of gradually disarming the enemy. Somerville's opening strategy in 1879 was Victorian; to diminish the perceived threat of the monstrous regiment of women as scholars, the Founders appointed as its first Principal, Miss Madeleine Shaw Lefevre, on the basis of 'her wide experience of life, of her attractive personality, and her devoted character.'[46] She was well established in Oxford society and more interested in art, travel, and charitable enterprises than in scholarship; by the ancient method of pleasant social subversion she began undermining the fearful conviction that the women were a threat to the university's masculine citadel.

Although Somerville's students were forbidden to cultivate attractiveness to the male undergraduates, one much repeated story is enough to characterize the gracious guile of Miss Shaw Lefevre's political success: John Ruskin had categorically refused to 'let the bonnets in' to his lectures on the grounds that they would only suffer from 'disappointed puzzlement'.[47] One Somerville history tells of his recantation: 'It is no secret that at first the idea of a Women's College was repugnant to him. But Miss Shaw Lefevre persuaded him to come to Somerville to meet the students. He capitulated at once, and not only presented the College with some of his own paintings and books, and the beautiful sapphires and rubies now set in the pendant worn by the Principal, but wrote after his name in the birthday book which he gave to the College, "So glad to be old enough to be let come and have tea at Somerville Hall ..."' This early Somerville history of the occasion does not quote his closing, patronizing words of gratitude: ' ... and to watch the girlies play at ball [tennis]'.[48]

Feminists will rightly groan at Miss Lefevre's manipulative use of sexism, but by such disingenuous manoeuvres and by her intellectual modesty she won influential friends in Somerville's early days. As opposition eased somewhat she was followed by the more aggressive Miss Maitland, seen as a 'woman' rather than as a 'lady', and one with business capacity and administrative talent. After Rose's time Somerville was reigned over by the statesman-like sphinx, Miss Emily Penrose (a distant relation of Rose and later Dame Emily) who, because she was the first woman to receive a First in Greats, and because she would not accept a permanent marginality for Somerville, was called 'masculine' by some (an intended compliment) and by others 'a great person', a phrase without gender. Each inch of high ground won by persistence and dignity was steadily secured. The infiltration began on a social level in 1879 and ended with the achievement in 1920 of equal rights in the university.

Rose must have heard stories of Miss Shaw Lefevre's tactful reign, but she had no desire to call attention to her own sex or to employ such winning ways. She had her own methods of disarming and derailing Establishment resistance. Like Miss Shaw Lefevre she had a genuine and appealing modesty, but she could not and did not attempt to conceal her intelligence and formidable wit. She was more like Miss Elizabeth Wordsworth (later Dame Elizabeth), Principal of Lady Margaret Hall, who, having proved herself 'a brilliant, caustic talker who never bored others', breached the barriers of Oxford male society as a scintillating dinner guest.[49]

Rose's spontaneous and apt use of comic devices in conversational debate – the sudden reversal of a *non sequitur* or a *reductio ad absurdum* and the ambush of an irreverent and illuminating question or a perfectly timed epigram – both made her point and kept her adversaries in good humour. As a young woman in London she became, like her character Rome Garden, 'a known diner out, a good talker, something of a wit, so that her presence was sought by hostesses as that of an amusing bachelor is sought.'[50]

She went her own way without a supportive party, like the lone young adventurers in the childhood stories she loved. Her critical attacks were masked by comedy; like Rome, by 'her light and cool touch' in deflating authority, she gained the freedom to speak candidly. She made use of Somervillian 'eccentricity' and perhaps the example of Uncle Regi. She developed a successful social persona; that 'known diner out' was the narrative voice of her most popular novels. This strategy meant she had strong friendships in a variety of London literary circles but was identified with none. In the competitive literary world authorial vanity, one of her favourite targets of mockery, made such loyalty as that between the Macaulay brothers and sisters unlikely. But although she was aware of professional jealousies she was for the most part unthreatened by them and did not give up the cultivation of personal affections with other writers.

Whether or not she absorbed Somerville strategy, its methods of avoiding rejection were compatible with her own. She enjoyed the self-sufficient women's community of Somerville, but sensing the excitement of the lively mental life of London, she wanted to share it too. There was no reason for men to have all the fun. The boy's adventure story of achieving victory had to be modified; she did not storm the castle but entered it as a privileged court jester. She was fortunate enough, writes A. N. Wilson, 'by reason of breeding, intelligence, and financial security, to be able to mix on equal terms with men all her life.'[51]

But to envisage her dining out triumphantly as a published author is to leap an intervening decade between her going down to Aberystwyth in 1903 and coming to London in her '*Annus Mirabilis*', 1912–13. For before her days of increasing professional and social success in a man's world she lived out a ten-year trial of her courage and resilience during which she struggled to overcome the humiliation of her last days at Somerville and to escape a home where she had limited control over her own life.

In June 1903 she sat for Schools – her final examinations in Modern History Honours. In the preceding weeks she had had influenza; after reading the questions, she abandoned the task. Her father intervened with the examiners on the grounds of her physical state and Rose was awarded an Aegrotat, a special ranking signifying that the candidate would have received at least a good Second but was, because of illness, unable to sit for the examinations. (Though not granted degrees, the women did receive the traditional Class rankings on their examinations.) The examiner would unquestionably have had the last word, but might have consulted her tutor, the respected scholar Miss Beatrice Lees, who would not have concurred in this decision to award her an Aegrotat had Rose been judged guilty either of malingering or deficient preparation.

This fiasco was inevitably a keen disappointment. It need not have been felt as a disgrace, but Rose suffered deep shame. Some of the confidence instilled by Somerville was damaged. Her sense of failure, like that of her father, was intense and profoundly affected her life and work. But in the end, with characteristic stoicism, she made use of its pain. As a novelist she examined the theme of failure again and again.

For years Rose suffered a sense of defeat because she believed that greater disabilities than convalescence had kept her from attempting her examination. She confessed her self-doubt to Olive Willis, and again and again in her writing she subtly analyses the emotions and the rationale of her refusal to continue the examination, although she never does so explicitly. Her resulting misery is clear.

Her self-blame may have motivated her decision not to collect a degree in 1920 when, in a historic ceremony in the Sheldonian, Oxford at last awarded degrees and university membership retroactively to the women who had met the requirements. Even though Rose, when a resident student, had not taken all the minor qualifying examinations, she could, like some others with deficiencies in their credentials, have sat for them belatedly by special dispensation. Vera Brittain reports that more than one grey-haired candidate did so. Rose may have feared another fiasco or simply believed she did not deserve a degree.

Rose Macaulay to some extent faded from the Somerville scene. Mention of her Aegrotat is sometimes omitted in reference books; she did not reunite with her old comrades at the annual Gaudies and, although she gladly helped with such fund-raising efforts as London book-sales, spoke of her fondness for Oxford, and in 1921 wrote an article for the women's magazine, *The Fritillary*, she willed no money to her college. But she did not turn her back on the university world; she attached herself instead to her father's university, Cambridge.

Why did she falter on the threshold of success? The award of the Aegrotat shows that she had earned the high opinion of those whose judgements were rigorous. And she had done exceptionally well in History in the Oxford and Cambridge Schools Examination in 1899; then as a schoolgirl examinee her major question had been to 'outline the events in English History between 1509 and 1688'. Her success on that occasion was chiefly dependent on a good memory, a knowledge of chronology, and a sense of the relative importance of historical events. But as a Schools candidate she would undoubtedly have been presented with essay topics requiring succinct comparison, causal reasoning, analysis, and final evaluation of the facts at her disposal after three years of study.

The subject was congenial; her reading had been voluminous. Certainly, well or ill, she would have had the details of the Civil War at her mind's beck. Her wide-ranging knowledge may have been a burden, but her eager identification with all sides of all questions, while up to a point a great merit in a historian, may have been her true nemesis under exam conditions. Essay topics to be finished at a given hour demand the prompt organization of conclusions that Rose believed at the time she could not produce. Afterwards she told Olive Willis, 'I cannot answer such questions to order.'

She herself suggests an explanation of her sudden balking in an essay, 'On Taking Sides' (*Spectator*, 17 November 1933). The self-description shows how both the extent of her knowledge and the pressure of her sympathies worked against her powers of instant organization.

> I myself do not find it [taking sides] always easy, so great is my pleasure in the antics of both armies in most battles. I could not, for instance, be *either* a Roundhead or a Cavalier: I must be both. After all both Crown and Parliament were striving for a great end – more power, money, and liberty for themselves, and our sympathies must needs go out to them.[52]

Here she is only manifesting the strengths and weaknesses of the academic mind, described by her friend E.M.Forster upon being faulted for the overuse of the word 'but': 'I have had a university education, you see, and it disposes one to overwork that particular conjunction.'[53]

Rose goes on to demonstrate how her processes of judgement can be temporarily abandoned as she brings to life the actors in the historical drama of the Civil War:

> Besides I must admire the animated, strutting figures on each side of the stage. Regard the sad, unsmiling little King, with his unhappy prawn's eyes, his

faintly Chaplinesque air and walk, his immense conviction of his own Divine Right, his thick, impeded Scotch speech, trying so hard to convince his subjects of their duty, with how small success. Observe his smart and ingenious friend, Buckingham, and the bustling, red-faced plebeian little Archbishop, his eyebrows two perpetual arcs of astonished displeasure at what he saw, his mind so busily and so rightfully bent on being Protestant High Church and having off the ears of Puritans. And here, one on each side, stand those two great black-shirt Fascists, Lord Strafford and Oliver P., both so hampered and impeded in their duties by troublesome factions, so that one lost his head, and the other, though he could expel parliaments and take away their baubles, never dared be king, because of his disagreeable, suspicious army. Behind these march, in the bull-dog mood that has been theirs for twelve centuries of king-baiting, the obstinate, legally-minded, close-fisted squirearchy of England, so set on the privilege and power of that great club of theirs, Parliament, so determined that King or not, Britons never should be slaves to a Single Person Government. And then come the Puritans, those wild, frenetic moon-men, with their fierce terror of surplices, altars and the stage, imported from the so wicked Abroad. To watch an argument between Laud and a Puritan – how much one would pay for a seat! But one must leave before the end, for the end shows the Puritan in the pillory, branded and slit. It does not do to pursue our ancestors too far in their activities; at some point or other, one has to quail and flee ...

But there it is: I cannot even, like Lord Falkland, ingeminate, 'Peace, peace,' nor echo the Somerset farmer's impartial grumble against both the plundering armies. I cannot say, 'A plague on both your houses,' for I love to see them at wrig-wrag: it makes half their charm. ... After all, does not the blood of ancestors on both sides stir in us yet, moving us to impartial affection? Though I must admit that several recent (and less recent) writers on this period have, if they feel thus moved, managed to conceal it. But then, they are all male.[54]

Although she wrote history, 'I cannot, could not,' she is declaring, 'be an unengaged, unmoved male historian.' She was demonstrably capable of logic and evaluation, of 'putting the facts in perspective', but she characteristically writes in a mode which combines history with biography, drama, satire, and the familiar essay. In the article above she shows how initially her objectivity and reasoning are interrupted by the voice of her subjectivity and humour; her power of sympathetic imagination delays her judgement. But the virtuosity found in this tableau scene suggests why Rose Macaulay succeeded as a novelist, although not as a Schools examinee in History in the spring of 1903.

With some embarrassment she explains her choice in her comic novel, *The Making of a Bigot* (1914): its hero, Eddy Oliver, is a pleasant and affirmative young man who sees some good in every religious and political cause and sympathetically joins a great number of them, half of which square off in sharp disagreement with the other half. *The Making of a Bigot* is a one-joke novel, sustained by the amusement provided by its wide and diverse cast of attractive, though prejudiced, characters. In the end, Eddy, about to lose his fiancée and most of his friends, concludes that nothing can be accomplished in life without passionate commitment. He cuts cards to decide what his prejudices will be. And he ruefully considers his future:

> In these dark hours of self-disgust, Eddy half-thought of becoming a novelist, that last resort of the spiritually destitute. For novels are not life, that immeasurably important thing that has to be so sternly approached; in novels one may take as many points of view as one likes, all at the same time; instead of working for life, one can survey it from all angles simultaneously. It is only when one starts walking on a road that one finds it excludes the other roads. Yes; probably he would be a novelist. An ignoble, perhaps even a fatuous career; but it is, after all, one way through this chaos of unanswerable riddles.[55]

But in writing one of her finest novels, *They Were Defeated*, in 1952, Rose Macaulay did sit for the abandoned final examination in her own way and did achieve a redemptive triumph. It is the story of the English Civil War in which a seventeenth-century anomaly, a very young girl who is a promising thinker and poet, is destroyed between the warring male factions. And the novel does, for all its general human sympathy, in the end take sides and make a major statement about the course of English history and culture as well as about the waste of female intelligence and talent. In the introduction to a 1960 reissue of *They Were Defeated*, Dame Veronica Wedgwood writes of Rose Macaulay's final judgement, 'While she was never sure she liked their politics, she preferred the minds, and the company, of the Cavaliers. Her sympathies were with the clerics and poets and scholars whose harmless lives were disrupted by the Civil War.'[56] Rose did come to a conclusion: that their downfall was a great loss to England. She said that *They Were Defeated* was the novel she most enjoyed writing.

All this speculation about the movement of her mind, emotions, and imagination can be illustrated; the evidence can be evaluated. That she, unlike many fellow women candidates, had no experience of sitting for university examinations is a matter of record. But one can supplement the theory that Rose was overwhelmed by an avalanche of facts and emotional responses with a tentative insight. Ever since she could understand such things, she had known that her father's 'disgraceful' results (as he described them) on his first Fellowship examinations had been a shadow on the family life and fortunes. The posts he had applied for had fallen to others with higher credentials; despite admirable accomplishments he saw himself as a failure in academia. When the time came, could it have been possible that the unsatisfactory first Fellowship results of her father, a scholar she admired, discouraged her? Or that subconsciously the opportunity to surpass the father she so respected was not an appealing one?

The accomplishments which would compensate Rose Macaulay for her sense of defeat in 1903 were far in the future. She went to her going-down party in a spirit of gallows humour, costumed as a pale green caterpillar, a witty allusion both to her unhatched stage and to the women's literary magazine *The Fritillary*. She kept a stoic face, but the burden of believing that she had failed Uncle Regi, her family, Somerville, and herself was heavy. And she left her liberating college life with no clear plan for the future to return to a claustrophobic, isolated family life, no longer a happy island but a valley of entrapment.

5

The Valley

HUMILIATED BY HER sense of failure, temperamentally modest, Rose Macaulay did not, at 22, announce any ambitious goal for her future. But, in the major woman character of her first novel, *Abbots Verney,* published three years after leaving Oxford, she embodied her vision of success – to be an intelligent human being with an independent point of view, living courageously, sanely, generously, and joyfully.

The hero and central character of her *Bildungsroman,* Verney Ruth, is an appealing and foolishly proud young man with embryonic artistic talent. He stumbles awkwardly toward maturity. His sturdy maleness is convincing, so is his 'feminine' hypersensitivity. But it is a young woman in the novel who captures our interest. Verney's acquaintance, Rosamund Ilbert – lively, nonchalant, perceptive – boldly questions his decisions and actions. She takes the risk of presumption: one ethical quandary of *Abbots Verney* is whether friends have the right to offer unsolicited advice. Rosamund's probing queries become a catalyst in Verney Ruth's maturing and help bring about his graceful acceptance of two grave defeats.

Rosamund is witty, whimsical, amused, mocking, spontaneous, candid; her briskness verges on rudeness. Gender stereotypes do not hold; she is the more tough-minded of the two. Rosamund is also disinterested and without flirtatiousness; she is a free spirit and the novel does not close with wedding bells. The hero realizes on the penultimate page, 'He had desired love, and had accepted instead friendship.'[1] Rose's publisher, unhappy with this dénouement, requested 'a gleam of light'. A neophyte as an author, she wrote to a friend that she sat down 'with set teeth' and added an epilogue to the original manuscript which only tentatively hints that 'the delicate flame of friendship' might, in years to come, flicker to fire.[2]

Rosamund is not a completely original female character; the reader is unsurprised to find *Pride and Prejudice* on Verney's bookshelves. But neither is she a mere Jane Austen imitation; she is the prototype of a persistent Macaulay character, the girl with 'the quizzical, comprehending eyes'.[3] She foreshadows the author's narrative voice and her adult self. But months of ennui and periods of trial and grief were yet to be endured before Rose Macaulay could achieve Rosamund Ilbert's freedom and insouciance.

Coming unconfidently down from Oxford, Rose had not recorded the ambition to be a writer; without much hope of publication she simply began to write. Had the disaster of the examination interfered with her plans? What were her choices? Marriage was considered by her college contemporaries to be a poor second best; there is evidence that such a possibility did not loom large in Rose's dreams. Although romances with happy endings were popular fiction, *Abbots Verney*'s open ending was not idiosyncratic for the times; the first novels of both E.M.Forster, *Where Angels Fear to Tread* (1905), and Virginia Woolf, *The Voyage Out* (then in progress), also abort an anticipated matrimonial conclusion.

In 1914, ten years after Rose's return from Oxford, her sister Margaret Macaulay published her only novel. In *The Sentence Absolute,* two sisters debate the importance of marriage. The leading character, Peggy, a young woman much like Margaret, speculates that married life may be 'completion'. But her sister Gwen (who incidentally loves to swim) unequivocally rejects the possibility for herself: 'Nature intends all sorts of queer things, and by no means are all of them desirable; and though marriage is no doubt desirable for a great many people, it isn't for everybody. We've all got to develop along our own lines, it seems to me, and some of us can work out our salvation best by ourselves, in freedom and independence. It's a splendid thing to share and hand on your gift of life if you can be a cheerful giver, but I couldn't, I know.'[4]

Later in their dialogue Gwen says with laughter, 'Haven't you yet grasped the fact that I don't want to marry anybody, however attractive? I tell you no marriage in the world could make me half so happy as I am at the present with my freedom.' And the chapter ends with Gwen's diving 'cleanly from a sun-warmed boulder into the living depths of the pool nearby ... rejoicing in the cool embrace of the water'.[5]

The Rose character is useful to Margaret Macaulay as a devil's advocate in her novel's argument for marriage, but if Gwen seems to protest too much, hers remains the more forceful and interesting voice in this debate. Margaret may not be quoting her sister verbatim, but Rose did deny that being an 'eligible' young woman completely determined her destiny. She still wanted male freedom for herself. And in her early twenties she still 'fastidiously', and perhaps fearfully, preferred 'the cool embrace of the water' to the 'completion' of marriage. Gwen does ultimately accept a proposal, but in the course of the novel she has become more like the romantic author Margaret than like the rebellious model Rose.

Rose's anti-matrimonial views were not uncommon. A wedding was not, at Somerville, as it was at Oxford High School, elevated as the great happy ending. Rose's fellow students were encouraged and aided by Miss Maitland to make plans for careers; graduates of Rose's decade became librarians, tutors, research fellows, professors, administrators, barristers, MPs, civil servants, ordained ministers. More than one profession was open to her. For example, Rose's Aegrotat need not have barred her from teaching; Olive Willis had secured a desirable teaching post through her tutors' supportive references, sent out before the examinations, and her disappointing Third did nothing to change the position. In fact, she went on to found and direct Downe House, an excellent girls' school. But Rose had never wanted to teach and had a fine scorn of bureaucratic procedure and government service.

Twenty-two years later she published *A Casual Commentary,* a volume of mildly satirical essays which included several on the problem of choosing a career. The book is dedicated 'To R.H.M.' – Uncle Regi. Its jesting is based on the flippant assertions that all work is dull, that in the end most of it is unimportant, and that few workers will achieve worldly success, but that unfortunately a choice of career is necessary. (The laziness is a pose; Rose's friends noted that had she not secretly over-worked she would not have been so prolific.) Her half-serious, half-jocular advice about careers is, 'Personally I regard teaching the young and nursing the sick as the two hardest and most disagreeable. Sick persons and young children demand altogether too much output of exertion and trouble. They are, I imagine the two noblest careers in the world. ... Someone (I have always felt) must teach, someone must nurse, but let it be others, not I. Both these professions are among the very few in which it seriously matters whether they are carried on well or ill, so my advice to young men and women is to avoid them.'[6] Although all of her sisters practised these professions, neither teachers nor professional nurses are major characters in any of her novels. Rose Macaulay's life was to be radically different from the lives of Margaret, Jean, and Eleanor.

A Casual Commentary does include two amusing essays on the careers of writers and journalists, but in 1903 she had not the financial inde-pendence to set herself up in London as an aspiring poet, historian, novelist, or journalist. Her own situation upon returning to Aberystwyth is ironically, and a little bitterly, described in those essays published two decades later:

> But women who are not married must do something else. If they are very much disinclined or inapt for physical exertion, and very fortunately situated, they can perhaps prevail on a parent or parents to maintain them in idleness

in the parents' home. Their career is then that of the parasitic loafer or daughter-at-home. If they choose this career they must endeavour to make themselves as agreeable as may be to their maintainers, or they may lose their position. They should affect to tolerate their parents' follies and reactionary obscurantisms, and refrain from mocking the bread of their support. They may even, with advantage, render little services, such as informing their mother what is in the newspapers, or their father what the village is saying about this or that. Having performed a few such filial acts, they may have the rest of the day for their own amusement, and can play games, walk, talk, write poetry, drama, or unsaleable novels to their heart's content. This career may be called the primrose path.[7]

Rose's career as a daughter-at-home for the next ten years was no primrose path. Not only did she return from Oxford to a household of more tension than harmony, but she was expected to remain there. The immediate and the extended family took the stand that a social, even moral, stigma was attached to an unmarried young woman living away from home who did not have a vocation requiring such liberty. According to this principle, for example, no objections were later made to Eleanor's acceptance of a teaching position in London, or to her going to Lahore as a teacher, and finally remaining in India for her lifetime as a missionary, devoted to – a poignant choice – teaching 'untouchables'.

Jean and Margaret escaped an increasingly possessive mother by undertaking vocations of commitment which justified their departure. But the Macaulays believed that only by living at home could an unemployed single woman claim respectability. Writing, the family and the relatives agreed, could be practised at home. Much later, after the death of her father, Rose published several attacks on what she termed a cant phrase about family life. Her 1925 essay, an inquiry 'Into the Sanctity of the Home', unsuccessfully attempted to clarify its cloudy meaning; finding only one aspect of the phrase clear, she defined that one: the concept 'allowed no sanctity to the homes of the celibate'. (She always used this word in its correct sense as 'unmarried' rather than 'virgin'.) As an unmarried woman living alone in London she queried, 'Does my home have sanctities? Do I occupy myself with them? Do I, in short, complete my destiny?' She exposes the phrase as humbug.[8]

In a 1932 *Spectator* column, 'On Family Life', she examines a questionnaire on that subject sent out to the British public by the Director of the London School of Economics and the BBC. She despairs of their getting many helpful answers and observes that there is too little space allowed for answering questions about its inevitable irritations and conflicts. After a grimly funny account of the violence of family life in the Old Testament, on Mt. Olympus, in Greek tragedy, and in Shakespearean plays, she decides that 'for all ages it [adult family life] has been a disease troublesome, dangerous, and frequently fatal'.[9] She is playing the clown, but her point that family life is not intrinsically virtuous is serious, and she adds that assumptions of its inherent morality are hypocritical.

In 1942, she wrote:

> What is quite certain is that the family, that essentially like-it-or-leave-it natural relationship, is not 'a Christian institution'; it is something far more primitive and less civilized. We all accept the family, (we had better, as Carlyle said about the universe); but there seems to be rather an exaggerated fuss about it in some quarters, and to hear it exalted by Christian Fascists such as Pétain and Franco as a kind of sacred substitute for the liberty they reject is to feel there must be something wrong with it.[10]

On the other hand, the interplay of families, their mutual support, their efforts to inculcate principle and stimulate the mind, the enjoyments of sibling affection, and familial private joking are important actions in the novels. In *Dangerous Ages* (1921), Neville Bendish and her daughter Gerda have an eloquent disagreement about the relative merits, personal and social, of marriage and co-habitation; the strongest arguments are for marriage as a civilizing institution. But unmarried Nan Hilary, Neville's sister and a writer, 'had a good time socially and intellectually'. Celibacy and the 'free union' that she finally settles for are not categorically damned.

In Rose Macaulay's novels happy family life is sometimes darkened by the selfishness or blind error through which the older generation inflicts damage on the rising young. After the publication of Samuel Butler's *The Way of All Flesh* (1903), that landmark attack on the parental hypocrisy of Victorianism, fictional portraits of self-righteously tyrannous English parents were frequently painted. Sir Thomas Browne's 'Frustrate not the opportunity of once living,' is the first epigraph for Rose's novel of domestic tyranny, *The Valley Captives* (1911).[11]

In 1903 the disadvantages of being an unemployed daughter down from Oxford were at once clear to the author-to-be. She was financially dependent; she no longer had the exciting university talk and work, a room of her own, or the 'comparative grown-up adult freedom' of Somerville. Opportunities to meet intellectually compatible friends were unlikely to occur. In *Abbots Verney* she writes, 'From London to the country is a wide step, yet a bridge may cross the chasm; between country and University there is a great gulf fixed, and no bridge will cross it, for on neither side will a bridge be sought.'[12]

After Somerville's mental stimulation she may have felt a kind of intellectual distance from her mother and her home-bound sisters, although she was always to be emotionally close to Margaret and Jean. Later as a successful writer she developed a touch of impatience with less sophisticated minds. Once established in the London literary world after her father's death, with the exception of a few close friends who visited her mother with her, she rarely introduced her family to her professional colleagues.

There were, however, compensations to the tedium of Wales. The rugged, romantic setting of the new Macaulay home, Ty-issa (The Lower House), might have been expected to delight her; set in a wooded valley four miles from Aberystwyth and near the sea, it was to Uncle Edward's eye 'an extraordinarily out of the world but very pleasing abode in a hillside clearing, overhung by dense woods ... [with] a fairyland ravine hard by.'[13] Grace was content with the slow pace and was at first in rather better health than usual. She liked moving house. To Professor George Macaulay, Ty-issa's inaccessibility was less attractive, adding effort and time to the pressure of a new career. He had written to Francis Jenkinson, shortly after settling in Wales, 'I have now to be prepared to teach almost anything – much more than I know, at any rate, and have to spend my time in learning.' He drily described commuting to the university at Aberystwyth by pony trap, bicycle, or train as 'quite an adventure'.[14]

Rose, alive with characteristic energy, explored the countryside, hiking and bicycling alone or with Margaret for miles in the larch woods and along the cliffs. *The Valley Captives* has some rather over-written passages describing the landscape of western Wales. But the mountainous beauty only intensifies the pain of the sensitive hero, Tudor, a young man with artistic talent, tormented by his stepbrother and unhappily trapped in the provincial valley:

> Beneath the hillside the shining river ran and sang, limpid and translucent and pretty like glass, and the sun glittered on it and set it dancing with diamonds. Tudor looked down on it from the wood path above, and between him and it the white masses of the hawthorn climbed. The earth was a glory of pure and fragrant white. Above the muddy path the Scotch firs stood blue against the tender larch-green, and sang in the breeze and smelt of resin. Everything smelt poignantly of itself today.[15]

The lyrical tone rises, but crashes down with a chord of dissonance as Tudor thinks of the evil in his private world: 'It was not beautiful; it was a prison where walls shut one perpetually from the fulfilment of desire, shut one into that blind place of unfulfilment which has been called the only hell.' Tudor is a defeatist; Rose experienced less self-pity and had more than one imaginative resource for escape. (She had become entranced with the automobile, which was later to play such a liberating role in her life.) Yet she chafed; the second epigraph for *The Valley Captives* is from Charles Lamb and protests, 'Give me old London at Fire and Plague times, rather than these tepid gales, healthy country air, and purposeless exercise.'[16] Even visits to Uncle Regi's Scottish home,

Kirnan, a large, winged former farmhouse, beautifully set among lakes, streams, and the broad moors, did not dispel her sense of entrapment.

And the ambience of Ty-issa within doors did not hearten her. Once more George was consumed by his work. Grace was increasingly distressed by the loss of her sons. Her diary had diminished to a datebook of her children's arrivals and departures. The boys' triumphs were carefully recorded: 'Will starts at Birley as Captain of the Marlborough VIII'; in 1901 Aulay excels at Classics, Electricity and Tactics on Prize Day. On 5 June 1903 he is designated 'one of the six best at Chatham' and selected for 'important work' with the Royal Engineers in India; he leaves for his assignment at the age of 20 on 1 December 1903. (Grace did not make a note of Rose's Aegrotat.) Will prepares for a life of farming in Canada by making an overseas tour of inspection, finally settling at Gibbons, Alberta. Through the years he was to come and go across the Atlantic; each winter after 1909 a return engagement of his good-natured clowning revivified the household.

The three daughters now at home were all seeking escape from the monotony of a routine which required attendance on the ever more emotional and possessive Grace. Margaret, closest to her mother, was subject to her greatest attention, including matchmaking; Grace encouraged the frequent visits of Dick Brooke, Rupert's older brother, a family friend of Rose's age from Rugby days. Margaret, too, tried the vocation of authorship; her version of Chaucer's *Canterbury Tales* for children, to be published in 1910, eventually sold 5,000 copies. She immersed herself as well in church duties. Her Aberystwyth diary, sporadically kept for a few months, tells of walks with Rose, afternoons at the tennis club, visits to relatives. It shows a more socially engaged life for the two older sisters than Rose presents for the characters in her novel of bitter parochial isolation in Wales.

Jean, still set on becoming a nurse, was bored by social courtesies with the neighbouring English-speaking gentry whose company her mother now enjoyed; deliberately out of step with life at home, she studied Welsh and developed relationships with rural Welsh families. Determined to achieve freedom, she was to be the first of the three sisters at Ty-issa to break away. The nursing profession had steadily gained status and was no longer seen as either menial or potentially immoral; in January 1905, at 23, Jean was at last permitted to become a probationer at Guy's Hospital in London on a training course for upper-middle-class 'ladies'. The regimen was a little less physically strenuous than the standard course of work and study, but still had a discipline as professionally strict as the military.

For the exuberant Rose, life in rural Wales was dull, even dreary; the isolated Ty-issa was not the romantic 'island' of Varazze. Although in Wales she had the six blessings of her Italian childhood – natural beauty, a place to swim, the company of brothers and sisters, occasional solitude, books, and the pleasures of fantasy – she had no sense of living in a free world, the indispensable quality that had made those gifts precious. And there were no more chances to live as a young man. At Ty-issa the only 'games' the daughter-at-home might play were croquet matches on the front lawn with her father and sister or tame tennis at a genteel club.

There was very little reciprocal entertaining with the Welsh university community; in any case the distance to Aberystwyth worked against such exchanges. The days began with family prayers, accompanied ludicrously by the tone-deaf Grace inaccurately thumping the piano and the tone-deaf family clumping through a hymn. Rose attended, but persisted openly in her agnosticism, one way of defining herself in opposition to her mother.

She devised a private study and began to write; by 1905 her parodies, pastiches, and poems written for contests on the 'Problems Page' of the *Saturday Westminster Gazette* in London were winning encouragement, publication, and prizes of a guinea or two. (Its editor, Naomi Royde-Smith, was to become an important friend in 1912.) Rose's humour had not deserted her. Nor her imagination. Although, oddly, she had not mentioned reading as one of the occupations open to the 'parasitic loafer' she could hardly have given up that compulsive pleasure.

Her reading can be surmised from her 1938 critical monograph on *The Writings of E. M. Forster,* one year older than herself, and from a donnish-clerical, university-educated ancestry like her own. In it she lists what she imagined his reading must have been at the turn of the century – a 'rich and exciting choice of field for the young rider into fiction'.[17] In a non-stop sentence of eighteen lines she moves from H. G. Wells to Saki, from Kipling to Pierre Loti, from Arnold Bennett to Gide; she displays her own knowledge of a range of contemporary choices. As before, she wrote much poetry, and to judge from the epigraphs and allusions in her published work, she read much verse from the sixteenth and seventeenth centuries. But however dismissive she was always to be of the novel form, it is reasonable to assume that she began early to experiment with fiction; her first novel has the merits of a carefully imagined, explored, and polished creation. *Abbots Verney* has a strong structure and plot, an even narrative pace, an attractive narrative voice, clearly realized characters, lucid style, and lively, credible dialogue.

Rarely jealous, Rose nevertheless complained to Margaret that their mother's interest was directed solely to the older sister's doings. Jean remembers that Rose became 'restless, argumentative and very critical, especially of her mother'. A symptom of irritated ennui – pacific Rose, who 'hated a row', now sometimes began one. There was more than one reason for the bickering between Rose and Grace. Rose had spent three years learning the integrity of facts and the dignity of reason; she was open to differing opinions but was accustomed to rational debate. Not only was Grace poorly informed after being out of England for years, but she also habitually rejected evidence and logic, oscillating between highs and lows of emotion; at best she was rather like Lady Bunter of Rose's *Views and Vagabonds* who 'had flashes of accuracy'.

The arguments were often petty, the outward and visible sign of Rose's discontent with her intellectual confinement. Margaret's diary refers to a heated discussion between mother and daughter as to whether larches were more beautiful crooked or straight. Two of Rose Macaulay's chief targets as a critic were to be muddled thinking and imprecision of language, the very faults she found characteristic of her mother's conversation. She admired those who brought their minds to bear on a significant matter at hand.

Grace was surely passing through a change of life which intensified all strains; she would no doubt have benefited from the medical and therapeutic help nowadays available to menopausal women. As a young girl she had been an intelligent reader, but now her occupation was her feelings. She had few interests outside the family and only minimal duties within the home. The household was run by two or more servants in spite of the critical, even quarrelsome, supervision of its mistress; in more than one novel and essay Rose ridiculed such self-important exercise of domestic command as a waste of time. Grace was by no means an impeccable housekeeper, but she relished dominance. 'For God's sake,' Rose wrote in *A Casual Commentary,* 'let the cook cook, the housemaid housemaid, the laundress launder, the dustman remove his dust, without interference. There is no reason why all this interference should be one of the problems of a woman's life.'[18]

Undoubtedly Grace's tendencies toward easy tears, hysterics, and clinging demands on her daughters were exacerbated by the departure of her sons and, in 1903, the death of her mother. Eliza Conybeare had been a steadying influence through the years. Indeed, the whole family suffered a loss at her death at 82. Rose's life was to bear some likeness to hers; her grandmother's obituary noted Mrs Conybeare's courageous creation of a useful and zestful life after her husband's early death, her cultivation of intellectual and spiritual interests, and 'her power to make life brisk and interesting, her elastic step and upright carriage, which did not fail even in old age.'[19] She had been a powerful support during Grace's worst illnesses and a dependable source of financial aid; she had, on the other hand, contributed to Grace's childishness by unfailingly cosseting her daughter.

Eliza Conybeare left over £7,000 to Grace, a considerable sum in those days, sufficient to give Grace the means to help her family greatly. An upper-middle-class single person could live respectably at this period on £150 a year. (Mrs Conybeare left nothing in her will to her son Edward, who, to his credit, nevertheless assisted in administering the estate and remained close to the Macaulays.) We do not know what use Grace made of her mother's bequest, but with George's steady income and the completion of the boys' education, the family was now without doubt relieved of their former financial anxiety by the dividends it produced. George and Grace had the opportunity to give each daughter some financial independence, yet the dispersal of capital was considered unthinkable by this class and generation; the custom was to invest it. Rose's correspondence shows she had no personal financial resources; to a friend she laments her inability to 'earn her salt'. 'I spend a pound a week, which is fearful,' she adds.[20]

Grace's arbitrary prejudices triggered Rose's greatest irritation. And while the daughter expressed her counter-arguments regularly – and regularly suffered guilt for doing so – she was less forthcoming about what was perhaps another thorn in her side – her father's patient tolerance of Grace's increasingly difficult temperament. George was that 'cheerful giver' who the anti-marriage character Gwen in Margaret's novel said she could not be. There is some evidence in Rose's fiction that she resentfully longed for her father to be less passive, to create intellectual order, and to disapprove of his wife's emotional excesses. Yet, admiring him, she directed the resulting double anger solely against her mother. 'I doted on my father,' she wrote to Father Johnson.[21] There is proof of his importance to her. After she left home, three intelligent men in succession, each considerably older than herself in years or self-image, were in turn to be her closest confidants.

Twenty years later, six years after her father's death, in her prize-winning *Dangerous Ages* (1921), Rose Macaulay portrays an ageing widow, clutching her adult children, foolishly and falsely pretending to an intellectual and social superiority she does not possess, announcing ignorant opinion as truth, favouring her sons, and suffering jealousy of her daughters' affection for each other. The novel illustrates those 'follies' and 'reactionary obscurantisms' – pronouncements about unionism, social change, feminism, literature – which Rose had in *A Casual Commentary* somewhat cynically advised a daughter-at-home to 'affect to tolerate':

'Those lazy men, all they want is to get a lot of money for doing no work.'
'I like the poor well enough in their places, but I cannot abide them when they step into ours.'
'Let women mind their proper business and leave men's alone.'
'I'm certainly not going to be on calling terms with my grocer's wife.'
'I hate these affected, posing, would-be clever books. Why can't people write in good plain English?'[22]

The narrator describes the effect of such repeated banalities on domestic discourse:

> And so on and so on and so on. Richard Hilary, a scholar and a patient man, blinded by conjugal love, had met futilities with arguments, expressions of emotional distaste with facts, trying to lift each absurd wrangle to the level of a discussion; and at last had died, leaving his wife with the conviction that she had been the equal mate of an able man. His children had to face and conquer, with varying degrees of success, the temptation to undeceive her.[23]

Although this characterization comes close to cruel caricature, it is justified. There are resemblances to Grace in Mrs Hilary. Nan, the novelist daughter of *Dangerous Ages,* is, of all the family, the most critical of her mother. She sees her as 'a mind fuddled with sentiment and emotion as if with drink, a soft, ignorant brain which cared about nothing except people,' but, conscience-stricken, suffers the nightmare that, being emotional herself, she may in old age become like her mother.[24] Rose believed that women who lost touch with their early intellectual and social interests deteriorated irrevocably.

Grace Macaulay, discovering the contents of the *Dangerous Ages* manuscript and recognizing a similarity to herself in this unattractive yet pathetic character, begged Margaret to ask Rose to modify 'Mrs Hilary'. There is no evidence that Rose altered the novel. Her concession was to dedicate the book 'To My Mother Driving Gaily Through the Adventurous Middle Years'. The verb has a double meaning, literal and metaphoric. The literal image is not a true one; although Grace owned a car when *Dangerous Ages* was being written and briefly attempted to learn to drive, after a mishap or two she was in the end dependent on a chauffeur. And her life itself cannot be called adventurous.

The family at large were not unaware of the limited life Margaret and Rose were obliged to lead attending to Grace's wants; the bachelor Macaulay uncles may have (and should have) felt somewhat responsible for the girls' frustration in purdah, for, as important figures in the closely knit Macaulay family, they helped enforce the ideal of filial piety and respectability which kept the daughters tied at home. So in the spring of 1905, after Jean's departure and before Eleanor came home from school, bachelor uncles Willy and Kenneth took Margaret and Rose on a trip to Italy, visiting Naples and Rome. The two captives' flight from the valley was inspiring to Rose; we can see this in the accomplished rendition of the backgrounds of her first two novels: *Abbots Verney* takes place chiefly in Rome, and *The Furnace* is a Neapolitan story. Immediately upon her return, she began working on that first novel, which initially she called 'The Aftermath'.

In it she captures not only the Holy City's guidebook wonders, and the skyline, the chiaroscuro, the street sounds and smells but also the atmosphere of the English colony, the gossip and speculation, the after-noon calls, the dinner parties, the Playing-at-Art of the young English students. And she succeeds at an even more difficult scene for the outsider to realize – a glimpse of the life of the very poor in the back streets of Rome. Writing to her Oxford friend Margerie Venables Taylor after the book was published, she accuses herself of self-indulgence in developing the descriptive passages: 'I suppose it was such fun writing it that I went on and on and couldn't bear to condense. Specially the Roman part I loved doing; it was just like being there again, you know, and walking about the streets – but it's rather alarmingly expanded.'[25]

The main action turns upon an upright but unjust grandfather's nar-rowness of vision. In spite of years of contrary evidence, he assumes that his grandson, Verney, is cast in the image of his dishonest, charming father, Meyrick, the family remittance man. Stubborn and blind to the last, the ironically named Colonel Ruth disinherits the straightforward young Verney, chiefly because, too loyal and too proud, the young man will not turn his back on his caddish father. Verney fails to become the heir to Abbots Verney and fails to capture the elusive Rosamund.

Rose deliberately attempted to avoid writing the transparent auto-biography of most apprentice novelists. She convincingly wrote the story of a young man in a foreign milieu, imaginatively transforming and extending her own experience. Identifying the source of the novel's details is less important than analysing her talent as a beginner. But Colonel Ruth's damaging flaw is close to one of Grace Macaulay's faults as described by Rose in a letter to Father Johnson: 'My mother, too, was prejudiced, both about ideas and about people; certain people she could not and would not like. This often made life difficult, as she couldn't hide it. She was so charming and friendly and expansive to those she did like, that the difference was painfully obvious.'[26]

The rigid Colonel Ruth, from the first chapter, is patently biased in his harsh treatment of Verney and in his indulgence toward his three other less gifted and less honest grandsons. The old man is not a villain; he is single-mindedly concerned with the family honour. But he 'could not and would not like' his grandson Verney. And there are other similarities to the Macaulay family, which had its own version of the novel's scapegrace Meyrick, the Uncle Harry whose charm Rose had felt in childhood and whom the family, like the Ruths of the novel, had both exiled and supported. Her feelings about Uncle Harry in her girlhood may have been as confused as Verney's about his father.

The main plot of *Abbots Verney* is Victorian in its ethical search: indeed Verney's struggle with pride and his painful journey through poverty and illness to self-sufficiency is a psychological rendition of a public-school *Boy's Own* adventure, but without the victorious climax. Yet Rose's power to see both sides avoids the black-and-white moral structure of nineteenth-century children's fiction.

Moreover, Rosamund's irreverent catechizing adds a fresh touch to what is a rather conventional *Bildungsroman* plot; she foreshadows the strong and elegant Shavian female questers of the twentieth century. Rosamund's boldness was apparently not excessively threatening to the conservative reader, however, for the conservative Lucy Soulsby herself graciously took time to write to John Murray, her friend and Rose's publisher, to praise her former pupil for her insight and her sympathy with the young:

> I believe you have hit on a new writer which I very seldom think when I read young women's novels!! The feminist movement of today is not conducive to a knowledge of human nature as it really is. I was amused to find in her a piece of wisdom which I never found before except in my own dealings with girls who find their elders difficult – therefore, I think it very wise. I mean that it is so much harder for old people to behave nicely than for young ones. It is absolutely true – but something still remains in the air (at all events with preachers and elders) of the old belief that elders are always good and nice.[27]

There is another character, a minor one, in *Abbots Verney* whose features were drawn from Rose's experience. Years after the novel was published she confessed to Olive Willis in a letter: 'I tried to put some of you, very clumsily, into my first novel (I expect you never guessed) but I'd sooner have died than tell you. ... I sincerely hoped you'd never detect anything, in fact. And of course one doesn't put people whole into books – one alters and twists to suit the emergencies of the story – at least I do. And often mix up two people together, or invent half and copy half.'[28] One 'half' of Rosamond's confidante Jane Gerard was Olive Willis. But Olive's biographer Anne Ridler says something more interesting about the transformation of Rose's friend into a fictional character: 'Possibly there may also be something of Olive in the heroine herself, whose affectionate but unromantic interest in people leads her to try to arrange their lives for them – did Rose remember the unwanted bread-and-milk?'[29]

Rose had been in correspondence with Olive in 1905 and 1906, and her old friend, troubled at the thought of Rose wasted in Wales, attempted once more 'to arrange her life', although Rose's days in Ty-issa had become more hopeful. Rose was working steadily at her novel and was elated in the process by the news, on 5 December 1905, that her father had been appointed to a Lectureship in English at Cambridge and that the family was to move back to a university town. But seven months were to pass before they were settled in their new home at Great Shelford.

We do not know when she finished the manuscript or when she submitted it to her father's old Eton friend, John Murray. But she so enjoyed writing it that it is unlikely that she would have broken off before its completion to act on Olive's suggested project of settlement work, toward which she was lukewarm. However, there was an inevitable nervous hiatus after the last word was written while she awaited the publisher's verdict; she would understandably have felt vulnerable and at a loose end at home watching for the post. Consequently, during the early months of 1906, she accepted her friend's rescue plan.

Elsie Willis, Olive's sister, was Warden of the Chesterfield Settlement House in Derbyshire; Olive persuaded an unenthusiastic Rose to go there on 12 May 1906 as a volunteer helper. Olive later believed that the experience had helped Rose over a bad time before her work reached publication. But for Rose the Chesterfield experiment was not a practical or psychological success, although her view of some of the settlement's principles and practices was to play a role in two of her novels, *Views and Vagabonds* (1912) and *The Making of a Bigot* (1914).

The women's crusade for which the reluctant Rose was recruited had been in train for four years. At the turn of the century, Chesterfield was a coal and iron town of 13,000, medieval, dank, dirty, unhealthy, and populated chiefly by the exhausted and underpaid working poor. In 1901 one of its citizens, Violet Markham, the 30-year-old daughter of a wealthy local industrial family, inherited enough money from a friend of her dead father to look about for a way to speed 'social betterment'. Unwilling to be a young lady of leisure, she had served as a school manager under the Chesterfield School Board and on achieving financial independence she chose home ground for a social experiment. Having discovered by experience, and with some satisfaction, the truth of the fine Fabian principle that 'education is a disruptive social force', she believed that civic education would be a good means of changing the system which produced and maintained the wretched living conditions of the town. She dreamed that a settlement house, modelled after Toynbee Hall in London and run by and for women, could educate them in maternal and child health, improve the town's disgraceful insanitary conditions, and make inroads on the patronizing system of 'charity' which had subsidized and perpetuated 'bad health, bad housing, and bad wages'.[30]

Another principle lay behind the plan: Violet Markham at this time was an active anti-suffragist (although she changed her convictions in 1918). Part of her rationale for believing that women did not deserve the national vote was that 'they made little use of the municipal vote and the municipal opportunities open to them.' She determined that the Chesterfield Settlement House should be a civic association, a joint effort made by its women citizens, from all ranks, a model of how to initiate effective, class-blind, feminine influence in government. Chesterfield House was to have 'no atmosphere of doles and of the odious spirit of patronage that aims at "doing good to the poor". Citizenship, not charity, was our watchword – the sharing of things and ideas; the promotion of the good life.' Ruskin was a guiding spirit.

She bought an old house in a back street and in 1902 began the project. Looking back in 1953, when the house was still in operation, Miss Markham was most proud of two accomplishments: founding a School for Mothers long before government Child Welfare Clinics came into existence and offering classes for 'crippled and defective children', who were not at that time admitted to the city schools. Chesterfield House also started classes to encourage the local factory girls in amateur efforts in music and art.

In a number of ways Rose proved unsuited as a volunteer there. The major work involved forms of teaching and nursing at which she was inept. She was at all ages a great favourite with children – but as a playful comrade in collusion against authority rather than as a disciplinarian and leader. She was, as she admitted, a failure as a nurse; courageous, even foolhardy, and always stoic about her own pain and fatigue, she experienced nausea at the sight of the physical pain of others. On this score she was the exception in the family; Margaret, Jean, and Eleanor, all equally compassionate, were able to follow professions in which they were bound to witness suffering. And her brothers were cheerfully thick-skinned. In a letter to his father from Clifton (12 March 1899), 16-year-old Aulay describes with objective interest the reported appearance of his drill sergeant's body after he had shot off the top of his head; it is unlikely the letter was passed to his sympathetic, queasy sister.

But Rose Macaulay believed her own distress in the face of pain was characteristically feminine. In her comic detective novel, *Mystery at Geneva* (1922), the young woman posing as a male detective is unmasked because she is daunted by the sight of a cat devouring a live goldfish. The impostor, Miss Montana, is overcome by nausea. 'It was a feeling to which he [she] was unfortunately subject when he saw the smaller of God's creatures suffering these mischances at the hands of their larger brethren.'[31]

The story is a satire and a farce, defensively subtitled 'An Improbable Book of Singular Happenings', but the unmasker generalizes axiomatically about the real world: 'Never yet have I seen boys disturbed by such episodes. Masculine nerves are, as a rule, more robust.'[32] The androgynous Miss Montana had been able to be a convincing male journalist in every other situation in the novel's dangerous detective chase. This 'trifle' of a fish's pain undid her.

Rose was not prepared for the everyday misery of many citizens of Chesterfield nor the particular pain of the disadvantaged children. She knew there were pain and cruelty in the world and that to react so strongly or to protect oneself against them so effectively as to be unable to help the victims was cowardly and sentimental. But she found it difficult to witness the physical suffering of others. Her work protests against the world's cruelty, but sometimes she tries to shut off her power to imagine the pain of others' suffering by accepting with a jocular pessimism the philosophical view that an individual's fate is relatively unimportant in the great scheme of things.

Her ideal of balance was that expressed by Anatole France, whom she quoted as offering the right epigraph for Forster's novels: 'Irony and Pity should be the witnesses and judges of human life.'[33] To wring one's hands and wipe one's tears are futile acts. But to watch life, like Rome Garden of *Told by an Idiot,* 'from her seat in the stalls as a curious and entertaining show' is to risk a cold cynicism.[34] Rose balanced precariously between stoic detachment and generous empathy. The balance shifted from novel to novel, from decade to decade. She called life a paradox, 'a tragic farce', and in her best books she allowed equal roles to humour (her first voice) and compassion (her second).

Her hypersensitivity must have been discovered early at Chesterfield; Rose was enlisted in the teaching of the factory 'girls' rather than of the disabled children. And here, too, she failed. The Chesterfield young women could not understand her sophisticated enthusiasms and ideas. (She came to believe that to try to change the taste of others is patronizing and presumptuous.) And they could not understand her rapid, high-pitched speech. To hear a recording of her voice is to understand why she in particular would have had difficulties in communicating. And the Derbyshire working-class accent must have been a block to Rose's powers of understanding as well. This impasse was not a drama of class snobbery but a scene of social comedy. The situation was not, however, amusing at the time. Rose was unhappy there; she was doing no good.

Sometime before the end of July, less than three months after her arrival, she went back to Ty-issa to help with the move to Cambridge. Here thoughts of her failure in Chesterfield were nearly erased by good news: the word came that John Murray would publish her first novel. She modified but did not radically change its ending at his suggestion. By November it was being favourably reviewed. The blurbs quoted in the final pages of her second book praised a variety of strengths. 'Far above the common run of novels.' 'A notably sound, original, and well-constructed story.' 'A clever book – unusually so; a thoughtful, judicious, well-developed book, full of interesting people.'[35] *The Times Literary Supplement* was more cautious but predicted a bright future: 'It is undoubtedly a very able and interesting piece of work, and the failures are of a kind that promise success.'[36] And her publisher, sending the final royalty cheque, wrote, to her surprise, that 'it is a good deal more than what is earned by a large majority of first novels'.[37]

A long letter to friend Margerie expressed her reaction to the novel's publication: its appearance initially struck her as a sudden embarrassing exposure. (Rose had wanted to publish the book anonymously, but agreed to sign it 'R. Macaulay', hoping to be known as '*Mr* R. Macaulay'.) She was astonished, pleased, amused, and shy. But, diffident or no, she was already eager 'to keep Mr Murray in a sweet temper, against another time' and began her life in Cambridge at work on a second novel, a professional writer at last.

6

Journey Through Pain

R. MACAULAY, NOVELIST, was now living in a community abounding with libraries and bookshops, with opportunity for good talk and compatible young friends – a bright contrast to rural Wales. The family had settled in what the dramatic Uncle Edward described as 'a castellated mansion' in Great Shelford, four miles from Cambridge. To Rose's surprise, however, in the flat landscape of Cambridgeshire she missed the rugged beauty of Ty-issa. 'But why complain?' she writes to a friend. 'There are three mountains in our neighbourhood at least six feet high.'[1] Complaints would have been ungrateful; the change was inspiriting. Rose's sense of lost liberty was now lessened; in 1900 she had been elevated to the freedom and status of a symbolic son by going up to university; then in 1903 she had been cast in the cloistered role of a female dependant; but now, three years later, as a writer, to be published like her father, with a small earned income in addition, she was moving forward again toward that ideal identity – the unhampered Individual of *On Liberty*.

She had begun to travel the road to a success in London which would earn her mature work such reviewers' epithets as 'Wise. Civilized. Wholly entertaining'. Yet in each of her next quite varied novels – a 'realistic' plot stripped almost to allegory, a visionary cosmology, a melodrama of sadism, a satiric comedy, another plot of gracefully accepted failure in contemporary life – the imaginative source was pain, and at the time of writing, pain not wholly overcome. In fact, in the midst of their creation was to come family tragedy, checking Rose's progress. The distress was transformed by fiction but was discernible enough to trouble the reticent Rose Macaulay in middle life when her narrative voice had become that of the stoic comedienne with a long view. At that time she attempted to withdraw her early works from the public eye; as early as 1912 she did not wish them to be republished, dramatized, filmed, or even preserved.

Some officials of the London Library feared at one time that this respected (and eccentric) member might secretly remove her first novels from the shelves after the head librarian had refused to do so. She attempted to purchase the remaining stock of them from her publisher in 1921 because, she said, they were an embarrassment – they were 'jejune'.

Her modesty about her writing was genuine, but her argument in favour of its erasure is perhaps not wholly candid. Personal revelation, not insipidity, characterizes these five early novels. Embedded in their pages are the private griefs of her girlhood and youth: the shock of the move from Varazze to Oxford; the humiliation of the Aegrotat; the misery of Aberystwyth; the random evil of a murder; the tensions of claustrophobic adult family life; the hurt of an unequal, ultimately diminished friendship with Rupert Brooke; and her persistent consciousness of cruelty in human behaviour.

These novels are not confessional, but they do reflect her experience, even though Rose advised critics that they should look not to lives but to literature for sources that influence a writer's work. (This counsel is much like Eliot's magisterial prescription that the poet was never to be found in his poems.) Rose Macaulay's books are indeed bookish, and, of course, biographical criticism as a method of reading fiction has serious limitations; it offers little insight into artifice and fails to explain why we are not all novelists. But because Rose Macaulay's early books enact her strategies for recovering from pain and regaining her temperamental *joie de vivre*, one of their subtexts is emotional autobiography. They are, in addition, explorations of belief and of sexual identity. Writing them was her life itself for a time.

Although the climaxes of all five plots are painful discoveries, in three of them the dénouements are achieved by the tough-minded acceptance of a limited reconciliation of desire and disappointment. *The Furnace* (1907), *Views and Vagabonds* (1912), and *The Lee Shore* (1912) show life as a bearable compromise; in these novels without victory, good humour flickers throughout, and at the close, its warmth survives. Departing from Rome, the disappointed Verney Ruth of her first novel had come to a new understanding of his hopes and ambitions: 'One did not get one's ideal in life. Most of it was a sort of *pis-aller* – making the best of things. But it was a good *pis-aller* after all.'[2] This wisdom, expressed more gaily, was to be one of Rose Macaulay's abiding themes.

In another mode, the darker novels, *The Secret River* (1909) and *The Valley Captives* (1911), close with the escape by honourable death; the effect of the former is melancholy, of the latter a sense of waste. But the narrator ensures that we close each book with a recognition of the hero's dignity. These novels, her third and fourth, are revealing exceptions in her work; until her last two novels she never again wrote as openly about the dark night of the soul.

All five works, even the prize-winner, *The Lee Shore*, are minor. Of each it might be said, as her Murray reader reported of *The Furnace*, 'The story is clever and it has distinction.... There is a limited cultured public to which it would appeal.... It is too good [for great general popularity], yet not supremely good.'[3] But the five early variations which follow the more conventional *Abbots Verney* reflect Rose Macaulay's intelligence, courage, and sensitivity. As a writer, she was experimenting with plots, characters, and themes she would later use with more artful and ironic distancing.

Although she had now established herself as a professional writer with work to do, her new home life in 'Southernwood' was still controlled by her mother's desire to be read to or to be waited on. She had not quite escaped the bondage of being a companion. And her father, always conscientious but now less pressed and more content with his work, also made a companion of Rose. On the surface this was a happy relationship. In a rare public word of support for adult family life, Rose Macaulay wrote in 1942 that parental affection was 'a not unwholesome ingredient – a kind of mental vitamin'.[4]

But in its own way this father-daughter friendship was another kind of imposition; George enjoyed Rose's power to compensate for the dull monologues of his wife, whom he still indulged at the expense of his daughter's freedom. Rosamond Ilbert of *Abbots Verney* had lightly accused her mother of having too much petting by her parents, husband, and children; the authorial voice adds that Mr Ilbert, 'while making of his daughter a friend and comrade, gave to his wife a delicate, affectionate deference.'[5] A similar pattern in the Macaulay household gradually altered, according to Jean, from George's patient reasoning with Grace to his increasing practice of silence. He had Rose to talk with.

When he wrote to Francis Jenkinson in 1902, congratulating him on his engagement, he spoke of 'the blessing of being able to turn to my home for sympathy and help when things are unsatisfactory.... No doubt we give hostages to fortune, rather lavishly in cases like mine, but the joys are more happily felt than the fears.'[6] He seems to be giving thanks in part for the company of his daughters, hostages to respectability. Jean had said, 'My mother kept me at home.' But George Macaulay had not overruled the restriction. In Rose's 1950 novel, *The World My Wilderness*, Rickie Gulliver, a young man whose credentials for intelligence, maturity, and a civilized point of view have been well established, generalizes about parents:

Parents are untamed, excessive, potentially troublesome creatures; charming to be with for a time, in the main they must lead their own lives, independent and self-employed, with companions of their own age and selection, not with those planted on them by the inscrutable and capricious workings of nature and divided from them by a gulf of years. . . . Parents, unfortunately, sometimes had charm, and held sons and daughters (or was it only daughters, those unbalanced, prodigal beings?) in a net, like leaping fishes, gasping in an alien air.[7]

Mercifully for Rose, unfortunately for Margaret, the older sister was still at hand and was Grace's preferred servant. Rose was not ungrateful; the nostalgic central theme of her next novel, *The Furnace* (1907), was not paternal intellectual stimulation but the value of sibling under-standing. The book was dedicated to the dispersed Macaulay Five:

To the Other Citizens of Santa Caterina, Varazze, who, at present scattered laboriously over three continents, intend, in the spacious days of leisure that age shall bring, to inhabit again the red house beyond the town and navigate the white canoe.[8]

Rose began *The Furnace* in a state of gratitude and subservience to her publisher, determined to listen to his advice and to learn from her own experience as an author. Her letter to her Somerville friend, Margerie, about her reluctant addition of an Epilogue to *Abbots Verney* described her sense of the writer's powerlessness: 'Publishers of course have you altogether in their grip; if they say you must do a thing you have jolly well got to do it.'[9]

But John Murray was no bully; he was exceptionally supportive, and later, making suggestions about *The Valley Captives*, he wrote to Rose, 'I do not believe any change can be made in a work of fiction against the grain, and so I never recommend, but only suggest such changes.'[10] Murray praised Rose's novels to his influential friends and consistently wrote reassuring answers to her apologetic letters. He believed in her future. Nevertheless, in a pre-publication letter to Murray about *The Furnace*, Rose Macaulay describes her unconfident attempts to anticipate his response and her reluctant compromise with popular taste:

I did my best to make it appeal to the general public by filling it with what I gather is liked – it is in fact practically a love story, so if after making it into that they still do not like it, it will be rather hard. If I had been pleasing myself with it, it would have been quite differently worked out. I am afraid as it stands it leaves a good deal to be desired.[11]

Such modest defeatism can be read as special pleading, a ploy uncharac-teristic of Rose Macaulay. But the candid expression of her conflict is not disingenuous. There *is* a conflict: her imagination is not in harmony with 'what is liked', but she wants to continue with what she told Margerie was a 'fearfully amusing occupation'. Women writers, she rightly inferred, were expected by the male publishing world of London to write romances for women readers. (Her publisher's reader for her novels was, she knew, a woman, but as she discovered, an extraordinary one – Lady Robert Cecil. Her judgements in retrospect seem sounder than those of the reviewers. It was John Murray who hoped for happy endings.) R. Macaulay would, to a slight degree, adjust. But once more she refused to end her novel with an engagement.

The ironic twist: what Rose believed to be 'practically a love story' not only fails of consummation, but is, in fact, only the subplot. The true love story of *The Furnace* is the symbiosis between the expatriate English brother and sister, Betty and Tom Crevequer, who retreat to Santa Caterina (Varazze) from Naples in the last chapter. Their slovenly, hedonistic way of living as urban gypsies cannot, after the unspoken criticism of English visitors, either remain a happy life without responsibilities or be adapted to make possible successful marriages to proper British ladies and gentlemen. (In fact, they are misfits – like the Macaulay children in Oxford.)

The main action illustrates a Macaulayan proverb: if we submit what we value to the consuming fire of life, its dross will be burned away and a small lump of pure gold will be left in our painfully scarred hands. The literal consuming fire of the novel, the *deus ex machina*, is an eruption of Vesuvius, perfectly credible at that uneasy period of its threatening activity. Debris from the disaster strikes down Tommy Crevequer in a narrow Naples street. Finding her brother unconscious, Betty realizes that their priceless treasure is their intuitive mutual understanding. The painful cost of the revelation is that she cannot marry the self-regarding Englishman Warren Venables, and Tommy cannot woo Warren's cousin, the cool Puritan, Prudence Varley. The Crevequers must go on together in humorous harmony – reading each other's thoughts, teasing, tiffing, finishing each other's sentences. They must retain their spirit of playful freedom, but they must live more responsibly.

While writing, Rose was reading Henry James, but she uses quite a different tone from James in developing the plot of contrasting cultures and values. Except for the climax, *The Furnace* is lightly comic. But the mood of the dénouement shifts to pathos; the Crevequers' resolve to make a fresh start is a necessary compromise between their present Italian hedonism and a rediscovered English morality. But their solution is not a return to England. Betty explains, 'We came to England when we were about thirteen or fourteen; we hated it; the beastly weather and all our relations.'[12] They will return to Santa Caterina, look for work in nearby Genoa, and continue enjoying their interdependence – the Good Life.

The Furnace is not as fully developed a novel as *Abbots Verney*, nor, in spite of Rose's hope, as general in its appeal. John Murray's reader, who recommended publication with the caution that the book would not sell well, speaks to the point in noting its weak popular appeal: 'It is too delicate and fine for the average novel devourer. It lacks "the grip" that the confirmed fiction-reader likes; nor has it the dare-devil cruelty or incisiveness of *Where Angels Fear to Tread*.'[13]

The comparison with Forster's first novel, which had been published in 1905, is apropos. (Rose read him with admiration from his first book on, and later became a close friend. In 1938 for the Hogarth Press, she wrote the first full-length critical work on his canon, *The Writings of E. M. Forster*.) The action of both novels is the effect of English trippers invading Italy. In Forster's book the priggish suburban English are either humanized or painfully shaken by Italy; in Macaulay's novel the young English exiles, afflicted with what Rose diagnosed as 'the amorous disease of falling in love with Italy', are put on the road to recovery from their irresponsibility by their exposure to English ethical values. In one way the books are alike, however: in *The Furnace*, Macaulay, like Forster, boldly gives us what she describes as the 'enchanting, unaffected, cynical, callous, gay and somewhat barbaric Latin people'.[14]

As the *Times Literary Supplement* reviewer observed, both the main characters and the form of the novel are hybrids. Betty and Tommy are the Macaulay clan rolled into two, but they also have some traits of the black sheep Meyrick Ruth of *Abbots Verney*. And the novel's mixed form – comedy and novel of ideas – anticipates Macaulay's novels written between 1918 and 1950, which were increasingly structured by point of view and thought rather than by conventional plots. She was experimentally creating a form unified by her unique authorial voice; she was learning to use dialogue to move the story on and epigrammatic, tolerant authorial observations to provide insight. Except for her detour in *The Secret River*, her course through the Twenties and Thirties was not that of the modernists. They were trying to create intricately unified fictional forms in which the narrator disappears, but she was experimenting with the comic novel of ideas with an omniscient point of view.

Certain of her ideas continue to recur. Macaulay's belief in the broad common ground upon which both genders exist is advanced more clearly in *The Furnace* than in *Abbots Verney*. The Crevequer boy and girl are mirror reflections of each other, yet there is one telling difference between them. Betty is the wiser, stronger, more accepting of the two in their moments of painful discovery.

The Furnace differs from *Abbots Verney* in another way; the second novel shows a greater awareness of sex. In one way it is like *Daisy Miller*; Betty's freedom of movement, night and day, damages her reputation with the English. And both the Crevequers discover that the casual, open love-making of their Italian friends further tarnishes their social credentials in the eyes of the Venables. But the questions raised concern propriety, not carnal knowledge. Betty and Tommy remain childlike throughout; their innocence makes their habitual caddish dishonesty tolerable. In the dénouement they flee from sexual choice; they progress as moral beings but refuse adulthood.

Although less successful than *Abbots Verney*, *The Furnace* represents improvements in Rose's technique and explores new themes. Having listened to the reviewer who had suggested that her first book needed pruning, Macaulay presents the local colour more economically in this novel, using the Italian background to develop character and action rather than for ornament. She creates the Neapolitan life in effective vignettes. And she finds targets for satire which will reappear in various guises throughout her fiction – the inanities of the popular press and the insensitive, intrusive curiosity of newspaper interviewers and popular novelists.

But while awaiting the London reviewers' critical acclaim or blame, Rose continued her everyday life in Great Shelford, making new friends through hockey, tennis, and cycling. And seven days before her nostalgic second novel was published, on Tuesday, 29 October 1907, she kept a trivial social engagement in Cambridge. Rupert Brooke recorded the occasion in a letter to his mother, testimony to an old friendship which was to be increasingly important to Rose Macaulay, woman and writer: 'Today, Mrs., Margaret, and Rose Macaulay are coming to tea, and bringing a friend! So I am busy tidying up.'[15] The dutiful son is honouring an old family relationship from Rugby days and soliciting approval from his mother by making his digs respectable for the genteel, chaperoned afternoon tea-party. As a college host, however, he preferred panache to neatness; Rupert's new sitting-room was on this day decorated by lighted paper Japanese lanterns.

At 20 Rupert was, when he chose to be, an accomplished entertainer and diplomat. He was returning Macaulay family invitations of the previous year; he had learned the value of a welcoming Cambridge home to a young man weary of his university routine. After being the golden-haired Prize Day pupil and athlete at Rugby, he had found himself during his first term at King's in 1906 a little deflated, even depressed. The competition was unnerving. He was a supernumerary, not the leading man on this new stage. The Macaulays were very kind to him, offering him tennis, the company of ladies, boating on the river, and perhaps honey for tea. And after his older brother Dick, who had courted Margaret, died suddenly of pneumonia on 13 December 1906, they gave Rupert all possible comfort.

Rupert Brooke's friendship with Rose was to pass through three phases: his undergraduate years; his life at Grantchester; and – the most important time for Rose's future – a period when both Rose and Rupert were commuting between lives in Cambridge and in London, the hub of the English literary world. At first Rupert viewed Margaret and Rose as girls of his brother's generation; Rupert said he was rather in awe of them. Rose and his brother Dick were six years older than he. Rupert was an infant when the Macaulays left Rugby for Italy and 7 when Rose entered Oxford High School. Before 30 such an age difference seems very wide. No matter how young Rose seemed, and was, for her age, it is probable that Rupert did not see her as a peer or a possible lover. Noël Olivier, the young woman he pined for longest among the many competing loves of his short life, was five years younger than he – in fact, only 15 when he fell in love with her in May 1908.

Rupert never invited Rose to become part of his young Neo-pagan coterie, and she appears in only three of his published letters – each to his mother. She is only briefly mentioned in the three Rupert Brooke biographies; she appears in none of the jolly photographs of the magical picnics and camping trips near Grantchester over which Rupert presided between 1909 and 1911 like an Ariel-Puck. Correspondence between them has not survived.

But she and Rupert did see each other with regular irregularity for eight years. The age gap between them, together with his distaste for women or men who made brash sexual overtures to him, does in part account for Rose's attraction as a perfect asexual comrade at times when his complex sexual network was not buzzing with the intrigues he initiated and so enjoyed. Rose had a code of behaviour with young men which she took to be the norm. She recalled it in a letter to Father Johnson in 1952:

> I used to go bathing at Grantchester with Rupert Brooke (a family friend from our childhood). So I mean, friendships and outings with young men were common form. What *has* increased out of all knowledge is the further intimacies, which we (in my generation and class) never even conceived of, as far as I know. We should have thought such a notion excessively 'low'.[16]

Most of Rupert's Neo-pagan women friends were unconventional, free in their manners, rude to the chaperoning older generation, but chaste. Rupert said they shocked the kindly woman who let rooms to him at Grantchester by going barefoot; she did not know that they were all fond of bathing together in the nude. The four Olivier sisters' sexual roles seemed to be formed, not in order to avoid the appearance of 'low' manners offensive to Mrs Grundy, but to avoid pregnancy and the consequent loss of Perpetual Youth. Rose might have been shocked at the sexual candour of their conversation, but perhaps she, too, like Virginia Stephen in 1911, the year before she became Mrs Woolf, was persuaded in the name of pagan freedom to enjoy 'child of nature' nude bathing in the Granta with Rupert.

Rose did enjoy and write about swimming in the nude; in 1936 she published an article on swimming in *The Listener*'s 'The Spice of Life' section, and after describing bathing in Cambridgeshire rivers, she adds, 'Which reminds me that if one is so fortunate as to find a place and time when one can bathe without a bathing suit, it enormously increases the pleasure of the bathe. The feeling of water, even river water, against one's skin is delightful.'[17]

Rupert enjoyed mixed bathing for yet another sensation: the exciting tension between innocent childlike pleasure and suppressed adolescent titillation. For, simultaneously puritanical and sensual, he was persistently torn between love for a very young, beautiful, elusive dryad type and for an emotionally and sometimes sexually generous partner of either gender – whom he subsequently devalued. In 1913 he described his long-term dilemma to Elisabeth van Rysselburgh: 'I'm in love, in different ways, with two or three people. I always am. You probably know this. I'm not married to anybody nor likely to be.'[18] He was probably glad of the restful escape offered by the company of the older but naïve Rose. Being in love with several people, he was wont to say, was not all jam.

Rose was an undemanding, delightful comrade for the quiet times, the best of all compatible companions for a tramp or a swim. She was fit and adventurous, and, like Rupert, her senses were keen. Both loved poetry and language and relished serious and lighthearted discussion; both were publishing prize-winning pastiche and parody in the *Westminster Gazette*. There were other sympathies, for in their jaunts together they were both reliving childhood: Rupert had loved his Rugby days; Rose wanted to recover her boyish Varazze life. Both were critical of marriage: Rupert thought domestication brought the inevitable, sad death of youth; Rose thought marriage a choice that could be refused. And both had domineering mothers and donnish fathers.

Perhaps most important of all, however, Rose was amusing; she and Rupert were both jesters. Rupert's stunning bisexual beauty attracted such attention that he might have been intolerably vain had he not had a saving, self-mocking sense of humour. Rose was never a bore. Bathing in Byron's pool, bicycling, or punting on the Cam together – such activity must have recreated for her the fraternal, unselfconscious camaraderie of Varazze. The two seem a genderless, congenial, easy pair. And Rose's constant presence in Cambridge was, to be a bit cynical, a great convenience to sociable Rupert. In contrast to Rose's description of the casual contemporary social style, women students at Newnham and Girton were not supposed to go about the vicinity of Cambridge unchaperoned; Rupert's bold, beautiful, and financially independent women friends from outside the university were not always at hand.

He craved company. According to Paul Delany, his most recent biographer, he was an 'incurable poseur', or in kinder terms, a mercurial, theatrical, and over-admired young man who cultivated his talent for making those who seemed worth his attention feel an instant intimacy.[19]

His self-conscious and confessedly hypocritical plan for making his mark in Cambridge during his second year was confided to Geoffrey Keynes:

> I shall be rather witty and rather clever & I shall spend my time pretending to admire what I think humorous or impressive in me to admire. Even more than yourself I attempt to be 'all things to all men'; rather cultured among the cultured; faintly athletic among the athletes, a little blasphemous among blasphemers, slightly insincere to myself.[20]

Of course, this self-portrait is playful, but it is no surprise that Rupert should confess to Julian Strachey, later, perhaps more sincerely, that solitude was his one unbearable fear. Although both Rose's father and Uncle Willy in the role of his tutorial advisers at King's had officially counselled him in 1910 to get away from distracting company and move out of college to study for his fellowship, he retreated only a few miles from the university to a beautiful spot where he had frequent visitors. He claimed to be 'enamoured of solitude' only in order to say no to a friend who wanted to share his rooms there. He was an actor who needed an audience and was, when he wished to be, a charming performer.

It was possible that he did not want to know he was arousing deep emotions in his refreshing tomboy comrade. And if he suspected their existence, he was unlikely to have felt guilty. Both E.M.Forster and Leonard Woolf, excellent judges of character who had many opportunities to observe him and his relationships, thought Rupert was fundamentally ruthless. Yet, for all the comradely tone of their friendship, even before he took his degree and in 1909 moved to nearby Grantchester, he had affected Rose's feelings and her creative imagination. She was not wholly uncritical; some of the imperfectly concealed patronizing conceit of the Englishman Warren Venables in *The Furnace* might well be a joke at Rupert's expense. He enjoyed and tormented himself with the company of women friends, but he became increasingly anti-feminist; he adjured women to be women and not feminists.

It is not straining the point to see a hint of Rupert in the beauty-struck lover and poet of Rose Macaulay's third novel, *The Secret River*, written in 1908, or to glimpse him as a major influence in the creation of important male characters in four other novels. From Rose's fiction we can infer that Rupert stirred her far more deeply than she touched him and that she had reason to be pained by his intermittent neglect of her.

But Rose was not dependent on Rupert's company for diversion. In the summer of 1907 Uncle Kenneth, Margaret, and Rose went to Venice where the gondolier, Rose wrote her father, allowed her to 'gondole' delightedly. And in the summer of 1909 Rose, her father, Margaret, and 'my uncle' (probably Willy) went on a bicycle tour in Italy. She writes to Margerie:

We had a glorious time – down the Riviera and about Tuscany. Isn't Siena splendid? I'm sorry we hadn't time for Cansontino, or for a hundred other things we wanted to do; but we did a great deal in the time we had & did it so cheaply my uncle was almost shocked! However, we warned him what to expect if he came with us, & is quite an adaptable person really & I'm sure it was educating for him.[21]

Rose had a glorious time, indeed, and once more George Macaulay escaped in the pleasant company of his daughters. Like many parents he was simultaneously doing both good and harm; Rose enjoyed his companionship but was tied by it.

That early summer trip was a brief mid-year holiday from Rose's writing; she had been at work since the publication of *The Furnace* the previous autumn. On 23 November 1907, eighteen days after the tea with Rupert, she was back to planning her career. Still diffident, she wrote to John Murray that she wished to offer him her next novel 'when – or if – it is written (perhaps by next summer)', but that another publisher had written asking for the opportunity to consider it. 'I did not wish to answer before finding out whether you would care about seeing it. If you would, I could tell him so.'[22] Murray responded at once, 'Most certainly I would like to see your next novel. As you know, I do not rate *The Furnace* as high as its predecessor ... but I hope that number three will more than carry out the promise of *Abbots Verney*.... I have felt all along that you and your public would discover each other.'[23]

Perhaps self-conscious about the identifiably autobiographical basis of *The Furnace*, Rose turned her mind and emotions in another direction. She wrote a short lyric novel on three levels: a skeletal account of the real-life events of a young poet's worldly defeat and triumphant death; a lyrical imitation of his moments of mystic revelation and his days and nights of suffering; and an overarching non-Christian myth of both immanence and transcendence. *The Secret River* provides a mystic world-order which accounts for the indifference of nature, the presence of injustice and evil, and the accessibility (to the fit few) of a healing vision of unifying Beauty. Like Yeats, Rose Macaulay is inventing – or assembling – her own cosmology.

Despite her instruction about the public's hunger for romantic novels, Rose Macaulay defied this prescription for popularity. If she could not succeed by bending her creations slightly to fit a formula, she would please herself. An imp of the perverse emerged more and more frequently in her work and personality; in *The Secret River* Rose is a trifle cheeky to her publisher. The hero Michael Travis refuses to write the nice money-making book his wife Cecilia suggests – 'a really popular novel ... a novel with lots of love in it and people coming together at the end.'[24] Instead he gives up the poorly rewarded vocation of poet and becomes an apprentice in the firm of Cecilia's uncle. His sacrifice satisfies her wish for more income.

The Secret River is not a happily concluded love story designed for the novel-devourer; it is the opposite – the account of a friend's betrayal of a friend and of a fatal marriage which destroys the hero's poetic gifts, his happiness, and his life – a plot, as more than one critic has observed, with parallels to Forster's *The Longest Journey*. But although not a love story, *The Secret River* does have a characteristic which satisfied contemporary literary taste – fascination with mysticism. Some of the chapter epigraphs allude to other writings, both antique and contemporary, which probe the unseen. And in this aspect of the novel there is a further likeness to Forster: Rose, his critic, knew his way of introducing what she called those 'primeval strays from a pagan world' who invade his socially realistic plots. In a time of failing Christian belief, a longing to imagine and explore alternative supernatural systems permeated much poetry and fiction, and in 1908 Rose was in tune with the time. Virginia Woolf, like Olive Willis, saw this other-worldly consciousness in Rose Macaulay's gaze: 'Might be religious though: mystical perhaps . . . Clear pale mystical eyes.'[25]

Almost four decades later, in a BBC discussion with John Lehmann, P. H. Newby, and L. P. Hartley on 'The Modern English Novel', Rose Macaulay said, 'I want the sense of the background of poetry brought out more in novels. We're living in a world which is, in itself, an immensely beautiful and rather sinister poem which we've hardly begun to explore, like some vast, nebulous plain, that we see in the distance, with a forest on one side and a great river running down it. That is poetry itself, you see.'[26] John Lehmann responded drily, 'It would be rather difficult to make a novel out of that.' (Surprisingly, this former member of the Hogarth Press had forgotten Virginia Woolf's *The Waves*.) As early as 1908 Rose Macaulay was preparing to make just such a poetic exploration into a beautiful and sinister landscape, with a great river running down it, developing an avant-garde modernistic lyric form she was never to use again. But its plot of spiritual search was to persist in her fiction.

The epigraphs of *The Secret River* come from the wide and deep reading that always enthralled her – poetry and tomes of theology, philosophy, mysticism, and early psychology. There is an intellectual structure behind this drama of released emotion. We can speculate that through the winter she did much seeking, thinking, and fantasizing before the book was finished in a rush of creative pleasure during the summer and early autumn of 1908. ('I loved writing it,' she wrote to Margerie.) John Murray's reader praised the unity and clarity of the cosmological scheme, the absence of 'the muddled thinking and vagueness of expression that makes so many books of this kind so tiresome. The author seems to know what she means and mean what she says.'[27]

Rose's preparatory discipline of study was like her religious quest in adolescence. That search had led from belief to disbelief. But because of the family tragedy which lay ahead in 1909, this journey was to take her from agnosticism through depression to tentative faith. In 1908 she chose for her novel's epigraphs describing its system of belief a variety of eight symbolic mythic landscapes, benign and malign, Christian and non-Christian – from Plato to Yeats, Sir Thomas Browne to Verlaine.

The universe of *The Secret River* is both sensory and visionary. The book's frontispiece is a photograph of a riverscape overhung with willows; a small porched hut can be seen on the bank. This is the actual site of the book's composition. Uncle Willy had given the George Macaulays this boathouse in September 1906. But it is also the central symbolic scene of the novel, recorded by the camera and transformed by imagination.

Rose wrote to Margerie on 2 June 1909 in thanks for her praise of the book:

> It kept me amused through last summer when I was playing down by the river and sleeping out – it is so nice down there, & we have a nice little hut to play in & it's so far away from everything that you can pretend you don't hear the bell for meals.[28]

Here is her old escape to nature, play, privacy, and fantasy, and – to include the mundane – escape from obligatory family dining as well. She 'played' happily, but she wrote of rejected love, solitary suffering, and the infatuation of a young poet for a crass and stupid, although beautiful, young woman. Her cosmological creation is intellectual; the novel's action is emotional.

On returning from the Italian trip in the early summer Rose spent as much time as possible by the Cam; Rupert was also sleeping out on the Backs. He was busy with his friends in Cambridge putting on *Comus* between May and mid-July; she saw him only now and then. But he spent some time with her when left alone between the co-educational Fabian workshops, reunions of Apostles, mixed walking parties, and productions of amateur theatricals with his friends.

All around her isolated hut on the river were the outward and visible signs of the visionary world of her novel's hero, Michael. The natural beauty of the scene in the early pages is erotic, perhaps even more so than the virginal Rose realized, although to underestimate her intelligence and her conscious symbolic imagination is presumptuous. She aspired to be a poet.

The river scene of the novel creates and reveals intense emotion. The description of Michael's dawn hours is lyrical, the imagery is sexual and fertile: the water gently caresses his body and the sunlight mixes with the vegetation – 'the gold and white cups of singing delight' blend with the juicy waving stalks and wands. A newly hatched brood of water birds launches itself. And when the world becomes 'a spreading and blossoming rose, in whose heart of sweetness he lay and worshipped, drinking the wine that was so eagerly poured for him', the effect of the scene and the meaning behind it upon Michael is orgasmic. 'The thin intense sweetness of it shivered through him, like a silver wire wind-twanged.'[29] The moment is only exceeded in intensity by the post-climactic vision of unity and *jouissance* – the highest level of the book's mystic order: Michael lies 'at the heart of the Rose at the World's End.... its petals flamed and covered him, and he had no more need of music.' He thought: 'Love, for instance, was: and possessing it one possessed the universe: giving it, one gave a golden cup, light-brimmed; and receiving it, one received the mystery of the Rose.'[30] The Rose is in the midst of all.

Was that symbol of love and beauty the idealized Rose herself? Wanting to be male and to be a poet, she created Michael Travis as her hero and alter ego; but Michael Travis is also a young male poet like Rupert Brooke, and he is in danger of being entrapped by a woman who is unworthy of him. Michael is now Rose, now Rupert. The male-female imagery in the bathing scene almost necessitates Freudian analysis, but when it became the literary critical fashion in the Twenties, Rose Macaulay rejected its focus as too narrow to take in the whole of human experience. She must have appreciated Virginia Woolf's derisive, phallic metaphor which defines the Freudianism of contemporary fiction and criticism as 'a patent key which opens every door'.[31] *The Secret River* clearly reflects Rose Macaulay's sexual attraction to Rupert Brooke. But the sacramental world of the novel encompasses a great deal more than an evocation of the joy of sexual love. The secret river is life itself; the symbols of the amoral natural world, the powers of Evil, and the Rose of Beauty are the elements of an imagined universe. The novel is a religious as well as a sexual dream.

Almost every morning that summer of 1908 Rose herself was waking early, bathing, and writing. Her own aspiration to translate the morning beauty into words is that of Michael, trying to catch what is 'high and far and sweet'. He is a mystic, or a visionary, or a romancer, whom the purblind humans or 'new people' might call 'madman or liar'. The grey veils of everyday life slip from his eyes, and he sees the lowest order of the 'real' unseen world – the river people, 'the old people' who dwell in natural things and are untouched by love, death, or the moral law. They counsel him: 'Love is the delight of the eyes,' but they warn him that Beauty is not enough. Love is also 'a common harmony that would make one sentiently receptive to what the other would impart.'[32] Michael hears the first axiom gladly but closes his ears to the corollary. His downfall begins.

The worship of the crass Cecilia for her beauty alone brings doom on

Michael's head. She betrays him by leaving with his best friend on the day she is to marry Michael. His grief and murderous anger almost destroy him. First we come to understand his poetic powers, his naïvety, and his capacity for violence; next we see him deep in hell in the grip of demons who inhabit the novel's universe on a plane between the earthy, amoral river people and the spiritual perfection of the Rose vision. The nightmare of his flight at the mercy of his three blind guides, Hate, Pain, and Ugliness, brings him 'to the very edge of the pit, and there sets him down'.[33] He burns his poetry; the riverbed dries into slime. Yet from these Evil Lands, Michael sees again the Way of the Rose; he knows it now for a sacramental vision, more powerful than his former joy of the senses. But he is barred from the Rose by his anger and hate.

He struggles out of his slough of despond, however, to 'a detachment, a self-possessing liberty ... a new vitality, a new rejoicing exuberance.'[34] Then Cecilia returns, and this second event is more damaging than her departure. He is free of the fetters of infatuation, but out of a false chivalry he marries her, to their mutual disadvantage. The rest of his life is a cruel punishment. He lives in the world of shadows, becoming as blind to the three Platonic realities as his wife. Conventional gender roles have been reversed: Michael, the sensitive and frail, is undone by the hard, materialistic Cecilia. But he is at last released and dies experiencing a mystical return to the river.

Anticipating objections to the novel's brevity, Rose wrote to Murray on 15 October 1908, with a sure confidence in its poetic unity, 'I am afraid that this particular book could not possibly have been longer.'[35] The Murray reader praised it warmly: 'The river's hidden aspect is extremely well done.... The work seems to me to have unusual interest and charm – some people will not look at it, but it would please others very much.' The *Times Literary Supplement* reviewer, dropping the review into the Brief Notices corner, writes that the book has 'the one great merit of being out of the common, a novel not so much of events (which are rather shadowy), but the mental history of a Sacramentalist who sees visions beyond material life.'[36] The reviewer goes on to say, however, that the book has a limited audience.

By the time reviews appeared in late March, Rose had little interest in them. The whole Macaulay family had been struck down by a cable from the North-West Frontier of India; on 11 February 1909, Lieutenant A. F. Macaulay of the Royal Engineers had been murdered at the age of 26 after five years' overseas service. He was to have come home in the spring. The loss was the harder to bear because Aulay's sense of justice had placed him in the path of danger and the cruelty of coincidence had caused his murder.

He had supervised a number of building projects throughout the district with extraordinary conscientiousness. His obituary in the *Civil and*

Military Gazette of India described his work, which included the care of many isolated posts and the roads connecting them:

> His energy was boundless, and to see that his gangs were at work he would undertake frequently on foot the longest and most trying journeys often in the middle of the hot weather and over rough and inhospitable country; then after a day which would have prostrated with fatigue any ordinary man, he was ready to plunge into calculations and figures for future projects and to sit over them late into the night.... The sight of his red, sunburnt face and hardy figure dressed in khaki coat and shorts was a familiar one in the district, and it is hard even now to realize that his activity has ceased forever.[37]

He was a modest, happy, intelligent, hard-working, and well-liked junior officer. His letters home are cheerful and matter-of-fact; the photographs he encloses are of the construction he was supervising; his own figure in these scenes is but a minor detail. He was wholeheartedly committed to his duties. He took the trouble to learn the Pathan language, and though he was clearly a firm task-master to the Indian work gangs, he came to his death out of concern for their welfare.

After discovering that the Indian officers, to whom the crews' wages were issued, kept a large portion of the sum for themselves, he began delivering the payroll to each worker individually. His system was both moral and practical; he demonstrated British justice and he ensured the labourers' loyalty and their interest in following his personal orders. He had assigned himself a risky task, but he was good-naturedly sanguine, even foolhardy. A friend wrote to the Macaulays that he never carried a revolver, although he was on dangerous duty.

The Brevet-Colonel of the Kohat District described the day of his death:

> He was bicycling along the main road, up the Miranzi Valley, about 3 or 4 o'clock, when he was stopped by 3 or 4 men, bound, and a cloth tied tightly over his head and face, and taken away from the road some 150 yards, to a little watercourse in a depression between two hills, and then shot dead with one bullet through the heart.... From what has happened since, there seems reason to think that the motive was robbery only, and that they might not have murdered him if they had not been disturbed, as they were, before they could get away into the hills.[38]

His commanding officer praised him highly as a valued colleague; the letters of condolence from his fellow officers show that each writer believed himself to be Aulay's special friend. At a loss for eloquence, each offered the highest compliments in his soldier's vocabulary: typical comments were 'an exceptionally good chap in every way you could name'; 'an English gentleman'; 'a good sportsman, a cheery companion, and a true and most reliable friend'. And there was a letter from an Indian worker, praising Aulay as 'a good master'.[39] Regi made the inquiry into the circumstances of Aulay's death in the name of the family and wrote to Grace, 'He was like George in his capacity for thorough, sound, and whole-hearted work.'[40]

Grace collapsed completely at the news; she had lost her favourite child and made this distinction clear to all. Turning away from her writing, Rose, too, fell into a state of lasting shock and grief. *The Secret River* was in the press, and she telegraphed directions to Murray to insert a dedication to her mother and not to send copies to any of her friends or relatives. One thought only dominated the family consciousness: Aulay had died like a hero from one of the Five's childhood stories – a brave and just young man, bent on an errand for the Empire beyond the call of duty. Five minutes, more or less, allowing the robbers' escape, might have saved him. His death must have seemed to Rose to be the work of the random Evil of which she had vividly written in *The Secret River* – a permanent, inescapable aspect of the universe, not to be redeemed by a momentary vision of Beauty.

Four months later, she was still suffering from a paralysing depression. As a child she had tried to be a son, but she could not then or now take a son's place. She not only felt the survivor's guilt, but guilt for the apathy that the guilt brought about, a treadmill of misery. In June she wrote to Margerie Taylor:

> I have come to the conclusion that my besetting sin is Accidie – do you know Paget's sermon on it? – Consequently I sit at home & feel like a toad under a stone. I'm afraid I don't do anything these days, which is very feeble. I don't even write books.... I am so stodgy these days. I haven't an idea in my head or a word to bestow on anyone – total vacuousness and inertia.
>
> Thank you very much for your sympathy. One of the minor troubles of a thing like this is that it seems to take all the object out of life & makes it difficult to do anything of any sort – but that again is Accidie, I feel sure, & should be discouraged.[41]

Both her parents were crushed; Grace had no strength or will to help any other family member bear this grief; sorrowing George bent his sympathetic eye on his wife. Rose, her Uncle Edward wrote in his diary, was 'sadly broken'. Her reaction seems a shade deeper than mourning; the limbo of depression she describes to Margerie left its victim without energy, appetite, or restful sleep. Worst of all, life seemed void; shock and despair erased colour, hope, appetite, and purpose, making the most ordinary task both wearying and absurd.

Rose's grief for Aulay was deep and genuine; he was the ideal young man she had longed to be; he was not only her brother but also the model hero of her childhood's happy story. But she also must have felt some rage at the prospect of her further entrapment by his death and at her own helplessness in the face of it. Grace was more of a psychological invalid than ever; she saw herself as the most wronged of the family, the chief mourner, and began to have tantrums when her needs were not instantly met. Margaret and Rose were even more firmly tied to her service.

The combination of survivor's guilt and a desire to escape seems to have brought about Rose's rash application for service with the Universities' Mission to Central Africa. She was rejected on the very sensible grounds that she was not 'balanced' enough at the time of the offer to be considered as a missionary.

Her advance to control and freedom was intermittent. But she began to progress by means of three healing strategies: by releasing her guilt and renewing her sense of her own worth through the Church; by writing a novel which discharged her suppressed anger; and by making an actual and psychological journey from Great Shelford toward London – a change of worlds made possible in part by a liberating intellectual challenge to Rupert Brooke.

The last three novels of the sextet, *The Valley Captives*, *Views and Vagabonds*, and *The Lee Shore*, were to bring Rose Macaulay closer to the 'detachment and self-possessing liberty ... new vitality and rejoicing exuberance' which Michael Travis enjoyed when he emerged from hell.

7

The Road to London

AT 28, SLOWLY emerging from despondency, Rose Macaulay began to manifest her gift of strategic buoyancy. Day by day she called on her talent for finding and using sources of strength, discovered and developed years before by a child who could not be unfailingly confident of her mother's love.

The first process of her recovery was gradual. Her church attendance began to change from a dutiful but privately sceptical act of familial piety to a search within the range of the Anglican ritual, liturgy, and sacraments for some means of regaining her power of joy and hope of freedom. She did not abandon her intellectual questioning or her humanistic individualism; she believed, she said in old age, 'that the Church is a framework for the aspirations of man ... that people are always seeing different facets of religion' and that this diversity was 'a good thing'.[1]

Although, because of her family history, her practice was Anglican (and sometimes Anglo-agnostic), she saw religious life ideally as ecumenical and evolving; her own creed was always selective. (At 70 she said her mind could not yet 'quite take certain things – such as the physical Resurrection.')[2] Perhaps this selectivity is true of most seekers and Rose was only more analytical and more honest than many about her own mixture of belief and disbelief. But at this time she earnestly sought in the Anglo-Catholic Church a source of deliverance from hell more dependable than the intermittent epiphanies of Eternal Beauty that released the suffering Michael in *The Secret River*.

For Rose did have a hell to escape from. Paget's *The Spirit of Discipline*, which provided the definition of accidie that she used in her letter to Margerie, is a Victorian echo of Carlyle's 'The Everlasting Yea'; the preacher begins by urging 'the spiritually slothful sinner' to make a heroic effort of will – to act, to work. Yet any such counsellor commanding the exercise of self-discipline is blind to the sufferer's real state: a sense of powerlessness is the essential symptom of depression. Toward the close of Paget's sermon he shows some understanding that persisting melancholy is both a malady and a 'dismal, bitter rebellion', a condition of repressed anger. Modern psychiatry defines depression as anger against the sufferer's plight, against the forces and persons held responsible, and against the self for helplessness. Depression can be, as Rose Macaulay shows in *The Secret River*, anger at being unloved. The most helpful advice in the sermon is not a peremptory call to action, but the recommendation of fortitude, a patient courage which understands that a long war, not a battle, lies ahead. The sufferer must in the end take action; it cannot be commanded or forced from the outside.

Rose's mental and emotional condition at this point is not difficult to deduce: she was in a seemingly inescapable maze of grief, anger, and guilt. But despite her lassitude she began the attempt to purge these debilitating emotions by going to a church retreat where meditation, private confession, and the receiving of absolution were central actions. The essential religious act for Rose at this time was to make a new beginning by receiving forgiveness for her despair; for over a decade such regular experiences of renewal were to be vital to her. She also performed a kind of self-imposed penance by taking on church duties: acting as a parish visitor, teaching in Sunday School, participating in a plan to befriend orphans and locate them in foster homes. She was not aiming at heaven but at a good life on this earth; in her late years she named her realistic goals – to be 'strong, intelligent, and moderately good'.[3]

But in addition to sacraments and good works she found other resources for recovery in church life. She still believed that beauty had benign power; she often attended Evensong in King's College Chapel in Cambridge and she described its aesthetic delights in *Personal Pleasures*:

> How dignified, how stately, how elegant, with ranks of tapers wavering gold against a dim background, while boys' voices lift the psalm *Audite haec, omnes* high above the pealing organ to the high embowered roof, to linger and wander there among ten thousand cells. Through the windows richly dight, slant crimson, violet and deep blue rays of October evening sunshine; it touches the round heads and white surplices of little singing boys; it glints on the altar, dimming the tall, flickering flames, gleaming on the heads of thoughtful clergymen who listen to the quire's chant.[4]

The incense, candles, chanting, and formal ritual of the High Church service at Sawston which the family attended reminded her happily of Varazze. And she always praised the language of the Anglican liturgy, 'long since so gracefully adapted, so fitly, beautifully, and ceremoniously assembled.'[5]

She went in search of guides who could instruct and inspire her, and her criteria for the clergy were demanding. Not only did she want intelligent sermons about contemporary ethics, she also wanted them preached well and wittily. At a later date she wrote admiringly to Father Johnson of Father Waggett, the Cowley father who was preaching at St Giles in Cambridge in 1909: 'He was the most brilliant and enchanting person. ... he could, by the turn of a phrase, set the whole congregation laughing (which he once said he deplored, but I think can't have).'[6]

Twenty years later, during a period when she was not a communicant, she still went to services occasionally for ethical counsel and described what was for her the ideal church experience. She wrote that a congregation should be 'attracted, stimulated, or disturbed' by preaching, 'but never bored'; that the preacher should be trained in 'the avoidance of cant and clichés and the right instinct as to the moment to stop'.[7] (In later years she departed in the middle of a dull sermon muttering, 'Nonsense, nonsense'.)[8] The preacher should leave his hearers 'with an increased regard for his finer virtues: courage, honesty, friendship, unselfishness, tolerance, and well-bred indifference to their neighbours' private concerns'. Recalling her childhood, she wrote, 'The sermons addressed to children [should] contain exciting moral stories of daring and adventure.'[9]

She made friends with the clergymen she admired. But a quest for virtue through pastoral friendships with such mentors as Father Waggett and F.H.A. Williams, the High Church vicar of Sawston, was only one of her self-prescriptions for recovery. She was working in a quite different way in the secular world of her writing to exorcise the dark demons that seemed to hold her powerless.

Writing was a second life and her novels reflect her slow return to health. The creation of her fourth novel, *The Valley Captives*, was cathartic. It portrayed lives so wretched or perverse that Murray's reader wrote, 'Miss Macaulay is a little hard on her readers in this novel. ... All the incidents must be called more or less melancholy or painful.'[10] She herself was surprised upon receiving her first copy when it was published in 1911: 'It seems to have a sort of dejected tone about it. I was rather shocked to find it so dreary.'[11] Uncle Edward called it 'sad'. Its relationship to old griefs – Eleanor's childhood punishments and her own unhappy claustrophobia in Wales – has already been remarked. But *The Valley Captives* contains elements which reveal and release more pressing and also more deeply repressed miseries.

The early chapters describe realities as mundane as muddy boots and rural pubs and shrewish stepmothers. But different as the novel's everyday Welsh landscape is from that of the poetic *Secret River*, the two books have significant similarities. The powers of Good and Evil that war within its everyday world are very like the Platonic Realities and demonic forces of the poet Michael's universe.

In *The Valley Captives* the young Tudor Vallon's talents as a painter
are warped and rusted by his confinement in a rural valley, and his body,
mind, and spirit are tormented by his cruel stepbrother, Phil Bodger.
Like Michael Travis, the poet of *The Secret River*, Tudor feels intensely
the lack of love, the indifferent beauty of nature, and the inescapable
presence of evil spirits – Ugliness, Fear, Hate, and Cruelty. He consistently behaves with cowardice, hates himself, and takes to drink. And,
like Michael, he experiences a rose vision in a river pool:

> Into the pool full rain waters swirled down over rocks, and the pool was the
> colour now of a pink rose, since in the west pale yellow had blossomed to a
> ruddy glow. Beneath the quiet evening light, the riverpool circled, smooth and
> still, a lovely rose of dreams.[12]

When Tudor Vallon steps naked out of the woods and slips into the
'cool swirl' and lets it hurry him 'down into the still dreaming rose'

> then for him, was all ugliness sloughed; slipping from him like a garment, it
> left only the vision of a glowing river running softly from him between golden
> hills to a sunset sky, and when he turned to the green east, a river coming to
> him dimly blue like evening, cool from the height of twilight hills far off.
> Between these two rivers was set the cool rose of peace.[13]

Later Rose wrote to Father Johnson, 'I like those pagan religions
which include a bathe in sea or pool as part of their initiation.'[14] But here
the rose pool offers Tudor only fleeting respite from a despairing existence
and destructive self-contempt. The peace of this moment is a temporary
aesthetic absolution rather than a climax of love. All ugliness is for the
moment washed away, but he must climb the hills back to the house of
hatred. A greater force than Beauty is needed to free him permanently.

In 1909 Rose's dark state, like Tudor's, could not be dissolved in rose-
coloured waters. If she was seeking forgiveness, she was not yet quite
ready to forgive. In the novel, Christianity's redemptive power does at
long last appear in Tudor's heroic self-sacrifice and in the consciousness
of his strong and loving sister John (Joanna), who believes that Tudor
lives after death through her. But such love does not operate in this valley
world until hell is fully experienced and irrevocable damage is done.
Although one reviewer called its narrative 'morose', *The Valley Captives*
was for the saddened Rose Macaulay an effort, conscious or unconscious,
to create a fiction which released anger and made a place for joy.

For her as a writer, it was but a first step out of her depression. The
next step, a novel she began and temporarily abandoned (eventually *The
Lee Shore*), was more hopeful; it celebrates a man, somewhat like her
father and very much like Father Waggett, temperamentally fated to

worldly defeat, who transcends his losses by developing 'the gaiety of the saints'.

But for the time being, the plot and subplot of *The Valley Captives*, as well as the characterization of Tudor's father, Oliver Vallon, seem to have been a means for Rose to discharge resentment against her own father's equable passivity, a resentment always suppressed by love and respect. The book is dedicated to him. This apparent tribute might have called to his attention his own harmful preoccupation with his research. Vallon is a cynical, crippled scholar who sequesters himself from the woes of his children; they are the victims of the unrelievedly wicked and stupid stepchildren, Philip and Cecily Bodger. Oliver Vallon is bullied by his vulgar second wife, who holds the purse-strings; he hides his weakness by 'screens' – irony and withdrawal. This is hardly a portrait of George Macaulay's genial temperament, but some of its features suggest his parental myopia as he buried himself in his work and fled from Grace's complaining monologues.

But there is a character in the novel whose nature does bear a resemblance to George Macaulay – young, likeable Laurie Rennel, who has the attractive characteristics Rose always attributed to her father but who, through lack of forcefulness and control, loses his chance for love and success. John (Joanna) sees these virtues and also sees their limitations: Laurie's 'gentleness, his ready sympathy, the temperate pleasantness of outlook that endeared, yet failed to carry liberation with them. He had the gift of shedding laughter over life, yet he remained essentially a dweller in the valley of defeat'.[15] He could never be, John thought to herself, 'a door-opener'. Laurie's fate in the novel is to receive a sadistic beating and maiming (probably sexual) by religious fanatics, a shockingly violent event unlike any other in Rose's fiction. Some of the cruellest episodes in the story judge or punish both Laurie Rennel and Oliver Vallon for not being 'door-openers'.

For John's word 'liberation', always crucial to Rose Macaulay, is central to the plot. Tudor, having nearly murdered his stepbrother in a long-suppressed fury, flees, but he must free himself more truly by returning to face the consequences. Setting out for Italy, he has a paradisal dream of a small sunny village there, although he has never been out of gloomy Wales. So close to freedom, he turns back along the road to home and sacrifices his life. His chief motive for returning is 'that before one began to live one must kill fear'.[16] On the way home, in a violent climax, he dies saving both his loving sister and his spiteful stepsister who careen toward him in a runaway cart.

Tudor's heroic redemption is predictable old-time melodrama, hardly Rose Macaulay's forte, but the novel offers other examples of liberation. The narrator suggests that the religious fervour burning across the countryside, though anti-intellectual and crude, has the power of genuine feeling, illuminating some brutish lives and creating breaches in the walls surrounding the provincial valley. The story also offers as an exemplar of courageous escape from the tyranny of public opinion the decision of the conventional, worldly, middle-class Dorothy Wynne to marry an impassioned young evangelist who is the son of a blacksmith. He is a 'door-opener'. And the freed survivors of the novel are female – John and Dorothy; they are stronger than the central male characters.

It is always a mistake, however, to categorize Rose Macaulay's characters as masculine or feminine too quickly. Her pattern of mixing attributes from people in her own experience is nowhere more apparent than in her sister-brother pairs; she often splits her own or her family members' characteristics between the two, disregarding gender. The sturdy, pragmatic, tough-minded John who mourns her brother's death at the end of the novel is eerily like Aulay, and also, in her love of farming, like Will; Tudor, like Rose herself, responds sensitively to the world's beauty, has artistic talent, shrinks from pain and cruelty, and feels miserably trapped in the valley. Yet *both* brother and sister have characteristics of the author; like John, Rose too could be stoic and resilient. Upsetting traditional gender stereotypes and intermingling characteristics of people whom she knew was often Rose Macaulay's method and a way in which to protest against the stereotyping of herself.

Even this brief summary explains why *The Valley Captives* was not a popular success. The novel depresses its reader by dramatizing injustices that, like the murder of Lieutenant Aulay Macaulay, can never be rectified. In fact, John Murray did not immediately accept the manuscript when he received it in the early summer of 1910. His reader suggested that it was not publishable without some revision.

Although Rose had gone her own way in writing this novel, she was not at this dark time sufficiently confident of the book's worth to demur. Uncharacteristically, she rather humbly made the suggested changes and her contract was signed in late August. The hopeful, sermonizing ending, which the reviewers criticized, may have been what the publisher called for. The novel was published on 2 November 1910, her first to come out in both England and the United States, but, as might be anticipated, it was coolly reviewed and did not sell. In fact, *The Valley Captives* lost money for John Murray. On 6 August 1911, Rose attempted to repay the firm's loss on her advance, a rare gesture from an author. In astonished gratitude Murray refused to accept her offer and once again voiced his faith in her future.

In the didactic last pages of *The Valley Captives* the young girl John realizes that life cries out, 'Live me, love me, enjoy me ... look at the way earth things die and are renewed.'[17] In the summer of 1911 Rose herself began renewal, leading three lives each more forward-looking than the last. Later she spoke of this period as an increasingly happy time: 'I was absorbed in writing, both poetry and prose; and a small branch of the Cam flowed past a field beyond our garden, where we boated and bathed and slept out, and I played a lot of tennis and read a lot of books.'[18] She continued to be an active player for the Great Shelford Hockey Club, to participate in their theatricals, and to share the company of mutual friends with Margaret. But at the close of her account of this time, she adds the key to her third life: 'But London always beckoned.'[19]

From 1912 she was a frequent traveller from domestic Cambridge to literary London, her journeys bringing her to the world for which Oxford life had prepared her. The brilliant intellectual and artistic excitement of London just before the war, the pleasure of Rupert's occasional company, her success, and the acquisition of a London *pied-à-terre* were to make 1913 a year to remember, a year she called her *Annus Mirabilis*.

But in 1910 she was still shackled at home. In the mid-summer of that year, probably soon after she had sent off the manuscript of *The Valley Captives*, Rose had a painful disagreement with her father; her response to it reveals the ambivalence of her feelings toward him and toward the home ties which still bound her to respond as a child. The conflict was caused by an invitation to Rose from Rupert Brooke to make a short *tête-à-tête* caravan holiday trip with him.

The invitation formed a part of one of Rupert's many complicated plans; its details are central to *Views and Vagabonds*, Rose's fifth novel, to be published in 1912. Although he had begun in 1909 to establish literary friendships in London which did not include his Grantchester crew, Rupert was back at The Orchard among those friends that summer, intermittently studying for his fellowship. It is likely that the intriguer Rupert did not invite Rose to join this group because of the Macaulays' friendship with his mother. After a disastrous weekend party at which Mrs Brooke took a strong dislike to the Neo-pagans for their lack of courtesy and consideration to her as the hostess, Rupert may not have wanted to include Rose in the group because word might get back to Mrs Brooke that her son was continuing to see the disapproved Olivier sisters. But he had more than weekend parties on his mind.

During term he had been active in national politics at Cambridge; he was by now committed to Socialism, although he judged the utopias of Shaw and the Webbs too arid and neglectful of the arts. He was, however, prepared to play a noble role in public conversion to greater social justice. He and his friend Dudley Ward had planned to travel through the villages of southern England in a caravan, making speeches explaining and supporting the Webbs' 'Minority Report on the Poor Law' to any audiences they could lure to the public squares. Rupert took this question seriously enough to make a careful study of the issues, political and moral, which the arbitrary Webbs had so meticulously and unanswerably argued. He prepared a well-documented, rousing, and rhetorically persuasive speech supporting a complete revision of the antiquated Poor Law. Whether or not the poor wanted to be cured of what the Webbs called 'the social disease of poverty' by being continuously classified and dealt with under the rigour and efficiency of the Webbs' new system, Paul Delany writes, 'was irrelevant' to the Fabians, but it was important to the libertarian Rose and to her next novel.[20]

Rupert's trip with Dudley was to be more than a lark. The twelve-day journey in July is easy to satirize as quixotic, adolescent, and futile, but it was part of a nationally organized Fabian effort of public education, and Rupert took it as seriously as a young man of 23 with an excellent sense of the ridiculous could. He claimed in a letter, 'As a public orator, I am a great success.'[21] The mundane facts of the trip are farcical: it rained every day, their cat was run over, the horse Guy ran away. But when all seemed a fiasco, Dudley and Rupert retired to enjoy a lobster tea and warm, dry beds in a country inn.

This anecdote of literary and political history led to Rose's next novel: Rupert's convictions involved her over the next year in fruitful debate with him on both Anglicanism and Socialism. Their disagreement became so lively that she laid aside *The Lee Shore*, the novel she was beginning to write in the summer of 1910. To write *Views and Vagabonds*, a novel challenging Rupert's convictions, was a more exciting venture. This new novel was a sign both of emancipation from Rupert's ideas and of her desire to catch his attention.

The seed of *Views and Vagabonds* was planted in Rose's mind in July 1910 when Rupert's political evangelism had caused him to rent the caravan and to make his somewhat unconventional invitation to her. He and Rose could have had a pleasant jaunt *à deux* either before or after the lecturing trip while he had the caravan in his possession. Rose was nearly 29. One might think she would have been free to accept or refuse, but she deferred to her father's veto. There was probably more than one reason for George's disapproval. He knew Rupert as an old family friend, as his family's frequent guest, and as one of his university wards. George was aware of Rupert's failure to prepare well for his Tripos, and of the Cambridge community's disapproval of the unchaperoned parties at The Orchard. Although George Macaulay had been a political radical in his own youth, his sense of decorum and concern for his own reputation at the university were conservative checks in 1910. He probably did not wish his daughter to become associated with Rupert as a subject of college gossip. And there was always the family jury of the uncles to consider. But he also cared for Rose's happiness and had doubtless sensed the discrepancy between the intensity of Rupert's and Rose's interest in each other. Perhaps, without knowing it, he was also jealous of Rupert. He said no.

Rose found her father's refusal an indignity, an expression of distrust in her judgement, and one more reason to resent his failure to be 'a door-opener'. It was also a bitter reminder of the lesser freedom enjoyed by women. She was keenly disappointed; she was chagrined. But she valued her father's respect and she did not defy him.

This incident does not seem to have caused any ill-feeling between Rose and Rupert. He himself constantly defied convention but also took elaborate precautions to conceal his behaviour from his puritanical mother, on whom he was financially dependent. Macaulay-Brooke relations remained friendly; on 16 August 1910, Rupert writes to Mrs Brooke of meeting Rose on the street in Cambridge and inviting her and 'Mr. M.' to attend the Marlowe *Faustus* that he and his friends were producing the next night.

But we know that the embarrassment rankled in Rose's mind. She eventually found her own means of salving her hurt pride and hidden resentment by openly rebuking her father in this passage from *Views and Vagabonds* (1912), Chapter X, 'A Conscientious Bohemian':

> One understands that it is rather *outré* to travel alone with a cousin of the opposite sex in a van, even with the most fraternal feelings. Whoever lays down the law on these and similar principles of conduct would appear to have laid down that one quite firmly. Of course the sensible plan is tranquilly to ignore the law, if one wishes to do so; the best people always do that with laws. ... Benjie didn't mind Cecil [his female cousin] coming, if she wanted to. He had a genuine contempt for social conventions, and knew that she had. It was probably a good plan for sensible people like them to set an example of freedom. Besides Cecil and he were practically brother and sister.[22]

The reader cannot miss Rose's careful insistence on their fraternal feelings. Cecil joins Benjie on the caravan trip; they plan to give talks on beauty in the home to the villagers the next day, but at nightfall she leaves the caravan to sleep in the inn. 'It was rather dull, but more correct.'[23] Cecil had dependable judgement, the story shows, as did its author.

But the restricted existence against which Rose was protesting was to be suddenly enlarged: on 17 March 1911, Margaret sent her mother an unheralded announcement from London, where she was carrying out her regular volunteer duties at a mission conducted by Anglican deaconesses in the East End. The news: she had entered herself as a postulant in that religious order 'for a year at least'; she was not committed to remaining. She did not explain, but her attempt to make a career as a writer had collapsed and she could no longer tolerate her mother's emotional demands. (A long history of headaches testifies to her general misery at home.)

Jean said Margaret was not sure that she would be happy as a member of a religious community, but to Margaret getting to a nunnery seemed preferable to life at Southernwood. Knowing Grace's predictable reaction (she fainted), Margaret sent the news from a safe distance, leaving Rose to announce what was to Grace a sudden calamity. Although Margaret, like Jean, was eventually forgiven and even praised, Grace made such hysterical objections at the time that her daughter was permitted frequent visits home.

Margaret, Jean, and Eleanor were to live lives in radical contrast to Rose's worldly, intellectual, creative, and adventurous career. All three committed themselves to sacrifice, unrelenting hard work, and spiritual devotion; all were to know at first hand the problems of the disadvantaged. Although Rose, too, was using her talents appropriately, she sometimes faulted herself. In 1926 she wrote Jean with comic ruefulness, 'I feel I always decide on the selfish side. It is very bad; I feel rather like St. Augustine, that perhaps I shall be better when it matters less, at some future date, perhaps when I am too old to go about etc.'[24]

After her two years as a novice, Margaret Macaulay took a vow of celibacy and became the serene Sister Margaret; her former temper and nervousness disappeared. Unlike Rose, she was not opposed to marriage; for her this choice of a religious life was initially a second best.

But in her non-fictional *The Deaconess* (1919), written to recruit women to this service, Margaret describes her eventual happiness in her vocation. Deaconesses lived a life of regular prayer and served the community in both practical and spiritual ways; Margaret tells a vivid story of days spent going between 'the joyous, squalid turmoil' of Bethnal Green and 'the ordered tranquility' of the chapter house. The book describes the smell of the fish and chip stands, the roistering of the pubs, the swarms of children in the streets, and the calm of All Saints' House where the day began with Nones and ended with Compline. The deaconesses – 'everybody's sisters' – prayed and busied themselves with endless good deeds. They visited the isolated sick and the overburdened mothers of many children, gave tea-parties for families in the beautiful garden of the chapter house, helped teach Sunday School kindergarten classes of 200, fed the hungry, assisted the clergy, listened to people to whom no one else listened, lived and taught Christianity. They were respected and loved.[25]

This chaste and charitable ministry was a life from the past, accepting the material status quo. It changed individual lives but not society. Unlike the Fabians, the female Anglican diaconate made no attempt to reform the political or economic structure in order to benefit the poor. Nor did these women aspire to become priests. They were set apart; male deacons did not vow celibacy. The sisters' work was conversion. Their educational tasks and the concepts behind then were solely religious; they aided their indigent neighbours as struggling individual souls rather than as the victims of social problems. Although the sisters lived frugally themselves,

such reformers as Violet Markham of Chesterfield House, charged with
the desire to raise the level of education and social responsibility in
working-class women, disapproved of such charitable service. To her it
was the old-fashioned 'odious patronage' of the poor.

Rose applauded Margaret's escape from domestic misery. As a result
of her sister's brave flight, Rose's obligations to Grace increased, but so
did her sense of obligation to herself; Margaret's boldness inspired her.
She may, like her character John at the close of *The Valley Captives*, have
wondered whether she had not exaggerated the power of those who
blocked escape from an unhappy home. Rose began to travel down to
London to make new literary friendships, signalling her rising spirits and
sense of confidence.

And out of her new confidence of the summer of 1911 emerged the
first of the good-humoured satirical comic novels of ideas which were to
create Rose Macaulay's popularity and literary identity in the Twenties.
No change of tone could have been more striking. If one were to say of
the author of *The Valley Captives*, 'Blessed are they that mourn,' the new
beatitude for the writer of *Views and Vagabonds* would have to be 'Blessed
are the debonair.' She had at this moment found her voice, her unique
first voice – ironic, satirical, questioning – just as she had as a fresher at
Oxford, and with it she was to challenge Rupert.

In May 1911 Rupert had just returned from three months of desultory
study in Munich to spend a heavenly summer at Grantchester. But he
was also making frequent trips to London where he was an ever-welcome
house-guest of the generous patron of the arts, Edward Marsh, at that
time private secretary to Winston Churchill. Rupert often invited Rose
down to London to literary lunches or the theatre; she regularly received
letters and postcards from him written at Marsh's flat. ('Vast networks
of his minute [social] arrangements survive on postcards,' wrote Edward
Marsh in his memoir of Rupert. 'He was always a great fitter-in of things
and people.')[26]

According to Marsh, Rupert saw the Ballet Russe perform fifteen times
that year; he took along many different companions to marvel at the
thrilling leaps of Nijinsky which caused Queen Alexandra to have her
seat changed from the royal box to the theatre's front row. At 76,
looking back, Rose remembered these occasions happily – 'those pre-war
confections of Diaghileff and Massine and Nijinsky and Pavlova and
Lopokova and Karsavina' – and she told of going about London with
Rupert in a state of breathless enchantment: 'I was envious of Rupert,
who walked about the streets without a map, often with a plaid rug over
his shoulders, as if he was Tennyson, which seemed to me a very good
idea and gave him prestige and people turned to look at him as he strolled
through Soho with his golden hair and his rug, and I was proud to be
with him.'[27] But she was aware of Rupert's knowing theatricality, and in

her broadcast about those happy days described this behaviour with affectionate amusement as one of his 'occasional poses' and 'affect-ations'.[28]

She went with him at least once to see the musical *Hello, Ragtime*, for which, as Marsh says, 'he had conceived a passion' and which he saw ten times. She uses the experience in *Views and Vagabonds* to describe just such a revue of mindless ebullience; the Crevequer pair (who reappear from *The Furnace*), in a period of low fortunes, are engaged as members of its chorus. And later, in her wartime novel, *What Not*, Rose introduces a delightful musical comedy star, Pansy Ponsonby. She is 'lazy, sweet, and extraordinarily supple', and a smashing success in *Hello, Peace*.

Russian ballet and ragtime were, of course, not the only new art forms that stirred London. Rose Macaulay was one of many contemporaries who described it as 'a time of literary ferment'. And it was a time of ferment in political and scientific thought too. Given their interests and their voluble natures, Rupert and Rose must have debated the questions of poetry, religion, and politics that swirled about them. And as a part of their dialogue, *Views and Vagabonds*, which she was writing in the summer of 1911, offers a direct counter-argument to the Fabianism of Rupert's caravan evangelism, a challenge both to his political reformism and his long-standing related opposition to the Anglican Church.

As early as 1907 Rupert had written a letter to a friend expressing his anti-Anglican views:

> I used to be cynical about the C. of E. when I went every Sunday but didn't care (or think) twopence. ... Now I'm no longer cynical about it. I hate it; and work against it; because I think it teaches untrue things; and that it is bad for people to believe untrue things. It leads to misery; on the whole. Also I think it has a bad influence. A very small part of this may be seen, very clearly, if you and the other Liberal members of your family will get a book and see exactly how the Bishops in the House of Lords have voted for the last twenty years.[29]

There are no bishops in Rose's *Views and Vagabonds*, but the narrator works to make the reader (and Rupert) believe that the three rep-resentatives of the Anglican and Catholic Churches in the novel say true things about political systems and the individual. The Christian Socialist curate says: 'Once you make it [the political system] a limiting or cramping of character, it's precious little use.'[30]

Rupert is not directly attacked – in fact, his talent and wisdom are flattered. The poet in the book is only partly modelled on him: Jerry Bunter, a minor character, is an attractive young man who lives at Cambridge; has Aubrey Beardsley drawings in his room (a room like Rupert's as a freshman); takes his brother, the book's main character, to

The Orchard for tea; and represents the ideal artist by Rose's values. He is no arbitrary theoretical reformer; 'his dreams are of things as he found them'.[31] Anne Vickery, the most dependable witness in the novel, says of him, 'He's a reasonable, sane, young man with a truthful imagination and sees straight. Poets and artists do.'[32]

Benjamin Bunter is not at all like Rupert, but the anti-Anglican and pro-Socialist views of the fictional Benjie and the real-life Rupert are identical; these views are the subjects of the novel's many-sided inquiry. One shrewd stroke in Rose's attack on them is the use of Goldsworthy Lowes Dickinson's words from *A Modern Symposium* for the epigraph. Dickinson was, of course, the guru for the Apostles, that sacred Cambridge society of metaphysical debate and male pleasures to which Rupert had been elected. And Dickinson had some misgivings about Fabianism. Rose took her quotation from the *Symposium's* dramatization of an all-night debate. One speaker argues against the Socialist's intellectual devitalization of life: 'This kind of attitude is bound up with the idea of progress. It comes of taking all the value out of the past and present, in order to put it into the future. And then you *don't* put it there. You can't! It evaporates somehow, in the process. Where is it then? ... Life itself is the interest.'[33]

Views and Vagabonds itself is a continuing argument, often amusingly expressed, but serious in examining its thesis: namely, that political evangelists like the Webbs, who believe they have 'the *one* right answer' to social problems at the expense of citizens' individualism and freedom, are blind. Diplomatically, Rose has the poet Jerry (Rupert) oppose Fabianism. He muses critically: 'Was the effect of Cambridge to merge personalities in causes? ... People opened doors into ideas; that was certain. But did the ideas matter because of the people or the people because of the ideas?'[34]

Benjamin is a young Cambridge graduate from a wealthy upper-middle-class family who becomes a blacksmith out of Socialist principle. 'Loving' the working class, he lovelessly marries Louie, a gentle, hard-working, inarticulate young millhand; the plot is the story of this mismatch. Benjie is earnest and (unlike Rupert) devoid of humour and imagination; in terms of the novel's values he is guilty of turning the person Louie into a class symbol. And his kind but patronizing family see her as a *tabula rasa* to be inscribed with their intellectual and cultural biases.

During the newlyweds' visit to London, the warm, enthusiastic Cousin Cecil plans to take the intimidated Louie to the Post-Impressionist Exhibition, *Major Barbara*, and down to Chelsea 'to get an Arthur Rackham view'. And she adds, 'You ought to know French, Louie; I think I'll teach you, shall I? There are such heaps of ripping things you could read if you knew it. Though of course you really ought to begin with Latin.'[35]

A much quoted sentence from the novel is Louie's wise and sad observation as they trot her around London's improving sights: 'Wi'out I was pore, they's none of 'em care. Not one.'[36]

Rose's disapproving view of 'the cult of the poor' was conditioned in part by her disapproval of the attempts at cultural uplift at the Chesterfield Settlement House. While at Chesterfield Rose met young women like her fictional millhand Louie who were indifferent to the literature and the ideas Rose talked about. An intellectual élitist, Rose believed that trying to 'raise' the aesthetic taste of other groups is arrogance. One of the 'views' of the novel is like that of Forster who believed that we cannot know, help, or love classes of people – only individuals. The Bunters did not see Louie as an individual. They were 'interested' in her 'working-class' reactions. Although Rose saw the limitations of Sister Margaret's outlook, she saw her as an individual helping individuals. The vicar, the Christian Socialist curate, and the Catholic priest in *Views and Vagabonds* all represent a belief in the dignity of the free individual, a Christian belief central to the novel's case against attempts at patronizing and homogenizing reform. (Here Rose Macaulay and E.M.Forster parted ways; although Forster shared Miss Macaulay's nineteenth-century individualism, he was as hostile to Christianity as Rupert Brooke.)

To confuse the multiple political, social, and religious positions represented by the whole cast of characters, the happy, hedonistic Crevequers from *The Furnace* reappear in a donkey cart, improbably inherit and then lose wealth, upsetting both the class system and the work ethic of the community by their childlike playfulness, affectionate egalitarianism, and reckless sharing of their bounty. Splashing in the sea, they provide the novel with a variation of the inevitable Macaulay bathing scene, for which the narrator makes more modest claims than usual: 'You are not the same after a bathe as before. You return to the dusty world either braced, or enervated, or with a slightly shifted scale of values, or with some quite new vision. The water vision may or may not work on dry land; but it is, anyhow, interesting.'[37]

Rose Macaulay's satirical method poses a problem regularly observed by her critics: the difficulty of balancing irony and pity. Her comedy is cerebral; her characters are, in Forster's terms, chiefly flat, yet sympathetically as well as wittily observed. Louie's sorrows, although lightly touched upon, threaten the novel's equilibrium; she loses her baby, realizes Benjie does not understand love, parts from him, and is a figure of genuine pathos. But she is also exceptionally colourless. And because she is a silent sufferer, she does not greatly darken the novel's light tone.

The narrator herself defines the problem common to both the social theorist and the satirist:

What would be the result if a chess-player's pawns up and said they were alive, and must count as players, not as pawns at all? The player must return imploringly, 'Can't you be both, then?' and they would probably say they couldn't, and so either the game or the pawns would abruptly cease to be.[38]

'The poor' cannot be both the objects of rigid social planning and free individuals; the novel's characters cannot both stand primarily for ideas and have experiences which deeply move the reader. Rose, attempting cool distance, chooses for the most part (like Shaw) to create pawns and play the comic game, although, paradoxically, this method contradicts the novel's thesis that their individuality is what matters.

The ideas and the humanity of the characters compete for the reader's interest throughout. Benjie's own sudden conversion to humanity occurs when he bravely enters the shiftless Crevequers' burning house to save these 'vagabonds' because he realizes suddenly that he cares for them, although he despises their 'views'. He is pulled out of the flames but badly burned. However, he has not been made sympathetic enough for us to feel his pain; what we respond to is the moral of the tale. To the readers his sacrifice becomes almost comic when we discover that the happy 'twins' were not at home but out sailing.

In an improbable final reconciliation, a Macaulay *pis aller* is reached. Benjie stops 'straining after coherence' and so does the author. He gives up the idea of creating an idyllic artisan's life (*à la* William Morris) in which he would arrange all the simple, picturesque details; he and Louie settle down in one of the villas of 'respectable vulgarity' he had formerly scorned; they hang both Coronation portraits and Augustus John paintings over their horsehair sofa. Cecil cannot believe the Cambridge-educated Benjie is happy with this muddled compromise of ideas, manners, and taste, but Jerry, the poet, who has the last word, believes 'Benjie has a pretty good time. I believe he's learnt how, you see' – a characteristic Macaulay compromise.[39]

Murray's reader called it 'a clever book and a very pleasant one, and both in subject and treatment much in point at the present moment. I think it is a stronger piece of work than *The Valley Captives*.'[40] (This comedy was the first of her books Rose directed Murray to send to Uncle Regi.)

When the book came out in February 1912, Rupert had suffered a breakdown, had joined his mother in Cannes, and then had fled to Munich to meet one of his current loves, Ka Cox. If, in the midst of this self-centered turmoil, he made any response to *Views and Vagabonds*, there is no record of it. In any case, Rose had made a positive stride towards independence by thinking out her opposition to his Fabian commitment and independently defending a Christian point of view that was not intellectually chic in his Neo-pagan world.

Her novel does not pretend to solve or even to define the grave social problems of the period; she makes no mention of the large economic questions which preoccupied the Socialists. She does, however, offer a way to live as a humane being in a mixed society; tolerance, generosity, vitality, humour, and respect for the individual are some of the keys. And through the curate's uncontradicted argument the novel accepts the inevitability of what the Webb Poor Law Report opposed – characteristic English piecemeal reform.

But if we do not know the response of Rupert Brooke, a 19-year-old Fabian who was later an admirer of Rose Macaulay *did* counterattack vigorously. Rebecca West, beginning her career as a hot-blooded Socialist and feminist, reviewed the book scathingly in *The Freewoman*.[41] Acknowledging that *Views and Vagabonds* is written 'exquisitely', she rips into what she sees as the conception of Louie as an anaemic near 'imbecile', and scoffs at the implication that Louie's 'weak grip on life' is representative of the working class. She is especially critical of Louie's failure 'to set out the whole force of her vitality to a fair fight' for the man she loves, as the vital West herself was to do the following September in pursuit of H.G. Wells. (He is fleetingly represented in *Views and Vagabonds* as the thinly disguised Alec Potts.)

But Louie is not meant, as Rebecca West assumed, to be the Working Class; she is as much an idiosyncratic individual as was the working-class Wells. The reformist characters of the novel who err are those who make West's generalization that Louie is a symbolic millhand. Yet Rose may have damaged her case by making Louie so pale, patient, and passive and her family so stupid and unattractive. Nevertheless, West warps the novel's view when she takes its argument to be 'forgive the poor their vulgarities because of their weakness'. The story shows that Louie, with her capacity for love, is stronger than the unfeeling Benjie.

Well before the novel was published in February 1912, Rose took up the manuscript she had earlier impulsively set aside, *The Lee Shore*, turning away from comedy to tell the story of a young man's worldly failure – a return to the subject and manner of *Abbots Verney*, her first novel. Emotionally, however, *The Lee Shore*, an anatomy of love, is closely linked to her fourth novel, *The Valley Captives*, an anatomy of hate.

In the year of her death, Rose Macaulay was asked by a BBC interviewer, 'What starts you off writing a novel?' She answered that she was 'not a true novelist' because she began, not with characters or a story, but with 'an inchoate idea. And then a framework arises.' In sitting down to write *Views and Vagabonds* she had clearly begun with an idea.[42]

But *The Valley Captives* had not begun with an intellectual thesis; its epigraph is an angry commandment: 'Frustrate not [with cruelty, blindness, and hate] the opportunity of once living.' The novel's major characters are defined by dark emotions, by the destructive bitterness they cause or experience. The idea behind the complementary *Lee Shore* also has emotional power: the inequities of human existence are fundamental and inevitable, but the Have Nots can transcend their worldly losses by their power of loving and their capacity for delight.

Instead of judging as weak its anti-hero Peter Margerison, who accepts exploitation and injustice, the novel gradually reveals his *caritas, claritas, hilaritas*, and *humanitas*. He ends as a 'merry unfortunate', a destitute St Francis, 'having nothing yet possessing all things'.[43] In the last chapters he travels along the Ligurian shore of Italy with his very young son and a dog in a caravan (Rose's symbol of freedom and pleasure), selling his beautiful embroideries. 'Blessed are the meek, for they shall inherit Varazze.'

As the protagonist of *The Lee Shore*, Peter loses Denis, the friend he most loves; Lucy, the woman with whom he enjoys perfect understanding; his much-enjoyed profession; his reputation for integrity; and Rhoda, the wife whom he marries out of pity and who deserts him to run off with a stage villain. All are lost to him through the unlovingness of others whom he freely forgives. Such saintliness would be intolerably sentimental were Peter not blessed with the complete understanding of his own plight, with laughing self-mockery, and with a compensatory gift for enjoying the world's beauty.

Creating a holy fool who is an attractive character is difficult. Gentle Father Waggett, whom Uncle Edward's critical diary entry described as 'silly', was probably in part the inspiration for the abused Peter. Rose quotes him in her epigraph. But George Macaulay, in his quiet and frank acceptance of his lack of worldly success in comparison to his eminent, well-to-do brothers, is also like Peter. This novel offers a reversal of Rose's earlier condemnation of 'the pleasant temperateness of outlook' that she saw as defeatist weakness in *The Valley Captives*. In *The Lee Shore* a character like George Macaulay who has 'the ready sympathy ... that endeared' is sainted. These two novels which she was 'absorbed' in writing in 1911 illuminate her progress from anger to understanding. As *The Valley Captives* is a novel about failure and punishment, so *The Lee Shore* is a story about failure and forgiveness.

Peter has qualities ordinarily assigned to admirable women characters – tenderness, sensitivity, and the habit of selflessness. To achieve his worldly happiness, he would have had to hurt Denis Urquhart, his great love. (The love in the novel is almost devoid of sex although not of physicality; Peter loves what is beautiful, both Denis and *objets d'art*.) *The Lee Shore*'s 'idea' of utter self-denial is old-fashioned, but the novel's imaginative characterization surprises us: not only does it reverse sexual roles, but also its Irish earth-mother, Hilary, is lazy and selfish; its gentleman 'hero', Denis, has a heart of stone; Peter, the man who has lost the loves of his life, in forgiving proves to be the happiest character left on the stage.

On 30 July 1912, *The Lee Shore* made the young author who wrote of failure a professional success. Having been judged the best of 140 entries, the novel won the first prize of £600 offered in a competition organized by Hodder & Stoughton. The publisher's archives were destroyed in the Blitz, so we know little about the rules, but the contest was open to amateurs and professionals alike. We do know that Rose entered it on her own. She had embarrassed apologies to make afterwards when she was magnanimously congratulated by John Murray, who had so long supported her. She wrote him,

> The book isn't a very good one, as a matter of fact, but fortunately the taste of the judges can't be very good either, so all was well. Perhaps it may make my future books sell better than the past ones – Hodder and Stoughton seemed to think it probably would, so I hope it will. Though I don't believe my books will ever sell really well. The results of this competition surprised me very much. I sent in mine because I thought it was more fun to, but I never thought it had a chance and was contemplating approaching you with it in the autumn after I got it back rejected![44]

Praising its originality, the critic from the *Spectator* wrote, '*The Lee Shore* is emphatically not the sort of book that any well-conducted competitor would write who wanted to win the prize. . . . in an age when the worship of success is perhaps more pronounced than it has ever been before, it is unusual to find a book succeeding by its exceptionally sympathetic treatment of unsuccess.'[45] (Olive Willis thought that Rose's repeated use of failure as a theme was the result of her distress about the Aegrotat.) Quite probably most of the manuscripts that were passed over were formula romances; Rose Macaulay's novel is a love story with a difference.

On 10 February 1912, before the triumph of the prize, *Views and Vagabonds* had been published. It was immediately well received, both by the critics and by the public. In celebration of Rose's success father and daughter set off in early April on a two-week Hellenic cruise. Rose wrote of this: 'In the spring I went to Greece with my father, the best of companions and a brilliant classical scholar; that alone would have made for me an *annus mirabilis*.'[46]

She described the ship as 'laden with Eton masters and Oxford and Cambridge dons, who knew what all the islands were, but couldn't talk modern Greek.'[47] Logan Pearsall Smith was there, and Jane Harrison. George may not have had as much of Rose's conversation on the voyage as he anticipated. The 30-year-old Rose and another passenger, the 23-year-old Ronald Ross, struck up a friendship, although their interests and backgrounds were different. Ronnie was reading for the Bar; he was a young sportsman from an Irish county family. He and his father, the hearty Lord Ross, contrasted with the academic party.

Rose and Ronnie got on well, exploring the Greek islands together in high spirits. Rose won the father's approval as well as that of his son, for in August she was invited to join a small house-party at Dunmoyle, the charming, well-wooded Ross estate in Northern Ireland. Rose, the successful novelist, must have been feeling confident and happy. But the visit ended in embarrassment for her, although in later life she was to be in friendly touch with Ronnie and his wife.

Before Rose's departure for Ireland, Jean remembered, Grace's match-making propensity was stimulated. Although she did not make the mistake of discussing matrimony with Rose, she hinted to Jean of an engagement to come. Ronnie's mother also wondered about the possi-bility of romance between these two unselfconsciously carefree com-panions; with no personal animus against Rose, Lady Ross saw the bookish young woman as a less than suitable mate for the much younger only son and family heir. Intentionally or not, she commented during the visit, within earshot of Rose, that their Cambridge guest seemed to be setting her cap at Ronnie.

Stung and humiliated, Rose lost her spontaneity. She announced the next day that she had received an urgent letter summoning her home to an ill mother. She departed in haste. Apparently, a young unmarried woman could only be seen as a creature hunting a husband, although there is no hint that either she or the congenial Ronnie had romance in mind. In Rose Macaulay's 1914 novel, *The Making of a Bigot*, the Irish Eileen Le Moine says, 'I wonder will the time ever come when two friends can go about together the way no harm will be said.'[48]

But Rose once more had the published writer's last word. Fiction is not fact, but soon afterward she wrote a short story about a Hellenic cruise, setting sail in April, packed with schoolmasters and their families. All its outer details fit the cruise the Macaulays had enjoyed. 'The Empty Berth', published in the *Cornhill Magazine* the next year, is a Forster-like ghost story; in fact, it contains an allusion to Forster's 'The Road from Colonus' (1911). 'The Empty Berth' introduces a socially ill-matched young couple – Classics schoolmaster Shipley and enthusiastic, untaught Miss Nancy Brown, who meet on board ship. Although only acquaint-ances, they get to know each other through their mutual consciousness of a ghost passenger who acts as a guide to Greece. He tutors them separately, and both 'come to see the world and its radiance with new eyes'. Shipley acquires some of Nancy Brown's candour and enthusiasm and she gains some of his intellectual knowledge and understanding of Greece.

As a consequence of Shipley's heightened sensitivity, he abandons his plan of proposing to the headmaster's daughter, a conventional 'Nice Girl'. But the narrator says to the reader: 'In case anyone thinks he proposed instead to Miss Brown, I hasten to add that he did not.'[49] The story insists that no observer can accurately assess the degree of intimacy between shipboard acquaintances. Shipley and Miss Brown have merely enjoyed a pleasant, enlightening two-week companionship, thanks to the ghost of the Hellenic spirit. Their parting is happy and casual: 'Shipley said, "So it's over," and she nodded, turning her pale face and shining wide eyes on him in the starlight. "It's been ... *jolly*," she said.'[50] So much, Rose is saying publicly, for shipboard romance.

The Hellenic cruise *had* been jolly. And Rose had much to divert her from long thoughts about the misunderstanding and rejection at Dunmoyle. She had money of her own to give her freedom of movement. She had invitations from Rupert asking her down to London. She had new friends there.

By 1912 the social circle of the Macaulay home had diminished. Grace was not well and her children were unable to visit frequently. Margaret was preparing to take her final vows as a deaconess the following year. Jean was working in a King's Lynn nursing home with Nancy Willetts, who was to be her lifelong professional and personal partner. Will was in Canada; Eleanor was in India.

Rose was ever more independent; she managed to leave Cambridge alone regularly. The annual autumn trip with her father was shortened to a two-day bicycle ride in the New Forest. At last, some enlargement of her liberty had begun, although the change was gradual. But as far as we know there were no dramatic maternal fainting fits as Rose was drawn more and more to her new friends in London. Years later she described their magnetism: 'Altogether these people seemed to me to be the people I felt at home with and liked to know, and I wished that I, too, lived in London, with whose inhabitants I had fallen collectively in love.'[51]

At first she spent her London weekends with friends or at Uncle Regi's town quarters. But Reginald Macaulay, himself an appreciated wit, seeing Rose's need to be in the centre of things, appeared again as a good genie and gave her a flat in Chancery Lane. 'For the first time in my life', Rose wrote, 'I had a home of my own, where I used to spend part of every week.'[52] She called that period her *Annus Mirabilis* and until 'the world went up in flames' in August 1914, she found London life 'gay and amusing and civilized'.

PART III

Miss Macaulay

8

Flight and Fall

IN 1928 ROSE MACAULAY, always fascinated by arcane words, used the heraldic term 'essorant' in a popular novel. It is a rare reader who does not need to consult an unabridged dictionary for its definition – 'poised for flight, ready to soar'. But it is small wonder that she absorbed it into her vocabulary; the image catches her spirit and catches it most precisely as she launched into London literary life in 1913. Although she was still officially living in Great Shelford, she was dining and talking regularly with those 'young or youngish London inhabitants' with whom she felt at home – novelists, poets, civil servants, editors – widening her horizons and stretching her wings.

Her love affair with the world of writers had begun when Rupert Brooke introduced her to his friends, whom the two would join at lunch, 'usually at the Moulin d'Or'. They 'were apt to be poets, Ralph Hodgson or Wilfred Gibson,' Rose later reminisced.[1] Rupert had discovered that Rose was not only a stimulating companion for evenings of drama, ballet, and music – Shaw, Chaliapin, Caruso, *The Rite of Spring,* Granville-Barker productions of Shakespeare – but also an excellent guest to bring along to the frequent luncheon parties. She was a better conversationalist than most of his Cambridge friends, from whom he was deliberately estranging himself. He made an opening for her, but she quickly created her own place. No longer 'Rose' except to her closest friends, she was now the welcomed 'Miss Macaulay'.

Professionally, however, Rupert was not a dependable ally. He did not, for example, introduce her into the world to which Edward Marsh had secured him an entrée – that of the major artists and aristocrats entertained by Ottoline Morrell and Violet Asquith, social leaders in the world of power. Nor when Brooke and the anti-feminist Marsh brought out the *Georgian Poetry* anthology of 1913 did these two co-editors include Rose Macaulay's work. Her collected verse, first published in

May the following year as *Two Blind Countries,* is neither markedly superior nor inferior to most of the poetry selected; they included *no* woman poet. Although Edward Marsh was willing to include 'a poetess' if one could be found to meet his standards, Rupert did not believe that a woman could be a poet. (But Rupert was aware of Rose's keen interest in *his* work; the only two women to whom he asked Marsh to send presentation copies of *Georgian Poetry* were Rose Macaulay and Virginia Woolf.)

Rose knew that Rupert's invitations to her were limited to certain types of occasions; now his indifference to her aspirations might have reminded her that, for all his camaraderie, he showed little interest in her writing. She began to go about more and more on her own, for in May 1913 Rupert left for America on a trip that was ultimately to take him to the South Seas. He did not return until June of the following year.

But she did not lack social opportunities and admiration. Through its literary editor, Naomi Royde-Smith, she met fellow contributors to the *Westminster Gazette* – Walter de la Mare, Katherine Mansfield, John Middleton Murry, Hugh Walpole, Wyndham Lewis, Gilbert Cannan. She also met a less prominent figure, the unsuccessful minor poet and Deputy Secretary of the Ministry of Labour, Humbert Wolfe, who was to be one of her lifelong admiring friends. She regularly enjoyed candlelit verse readings at Harold Monro's Poetry Bookshop in Devonshire Street, intoxicated by the poetry of de la Mare, which had, she said, 'a magical, sad, unearthly quality which no other poet, writing then or since, has approached.' She thought him 'very beautiful', a man with 'a fantastic wit and funniness'.[2]

She described herself, at 32, as an 'innocent from the Cam', 'a provincial', wide-eyed and bedazzled among the sophisticates.[3] But when Royde-Smith, as a celebrity-hunting hostess, looked back in 1920 on her friend's London début, she saw the role Macaulay had come to play in literary society not as that of a gauche onlooker but as that of a magnetic gamine. Oxford had prepared Miss Macaulay for this part. Royde-Smith described her discovery as 'the golden talker':

> Those of us who have outgrown the age of despair know that every now and then along the current of boredom there floats a golden talker. . . . In modern society these rare and gifted beings take the place of the jongleur and the troubadour. Their antics are intellectual, their *lais* and *gestes* are of contemporary foolishness, they are welcome at any dinner-table, invaluable for week-ends.[4]

Although she is specifically referring to Rose throughout an extended passage about the attributes of the scintillating talker, it is no accident that the entertainer's gender is nowhere given. Like the Oxford women fighting for degrees, Rose Macaulay avoided calling attention to her sex. She succeeded on her intellectual merits. In contrast to Naomi's kittenish coquetry, Rose's attractions were her cool intelligence and her *élan vital*. In her critic's role she praised Margaret Schlegel of *Howards End* because 'beauty, merely feminine charm, single-track emotion, biological urge, so confusing and swamping to personality and character, so much the stock-in-trade of the heroine-maker ... scarcely exist' in her.[5]

Years later, trying to sum up Rose Macaulay's appearance and manner, Frank Swinnerton found it hard to pinpoint their effect. After admiringly listing her energetic 'boyish traits', he insisted at once, as though he had maligned her, 'On the contrary, she was in no sense a masculine woman.'[6] David Wright, meeting her when she was 69, said she was female, not feminine, and called her 'a combination of tomboy and perfect lady'.[7] Attempting to picture her, each portrait painter found he must redraw the stereotypes. She was *sui generis*.

Over the years it was her 'incorruptible youth' by which friends most often characterized Rose Macaulay. In fact, they were generally likely to sketch her in action, in the words with which she sketched her character Ellen Le Moine: 'a vivid, impatient, alive person, full of quips and cranks and quiddities and a constant flow of words.'[8] Where and how did she absorb the fascinating matter for that golden talk? There are clues in her seventh novel, *The Making of a Bigot*.

At the time of its writing Macaulay could probably still imagine herself in the role of that upwardly mobile young man – Dick Whittington. The main character of the novel she was working on at her London flat in Chancery Lane and at home in Great Shelford was Edward Oliver, just down from Cambridge and setting out for London from a deanery in a cathedral town to discover his vocation. He is neither markedly male nor female. Like Rose Macaulay, he is travelling the road to London life, but he and his friends are ten years younger than she, still aspiring amateurs; their friendships are primarily those made at university. One reviewer praised the novel for the rare feat of having caught 'the air of youth'.[9]

The Making of a Bigot gives us both the contours of Macaulay's contemporary worlds and her perceptive, amused way of surveying their surfaces. Like her, once in the city, Eddy is bombarded by political, religious, ethical, aesthetic, literary, and social topics of discussion. But he is a far less complex character than his creator. Eager, curious, and generous, a twentieth-century Candide, Eddy is all-inclusive in his sympathies and interests. Ingenuously, he believes there is good in all points of view and that people ought to be able to disagree agreeably. He is the opposite of that obstinate, single-minded champion of one idea, Benjamin Bunter of *Views and Vagabonds*; malleable, open-minded Edward Oliver likes all people and makes no distinctions among the causes they favour. But Benjie and Eddy journey from different directions toward the same end. Each must modify his ideal – Benjie his cool-hearted principle and Eddy his warm-hearted tolerance. Rose Macaulay, too, was trying to strike this balance.

In a constant exchange of ideas Eddy finds himself at odds with friends and family who think him naïve, insincere, or simply stupid. He attempts to reconcile social debates about such divisive current topics as Readiness for Invasion, Home Rule, Women's Suffrage, Revision of the Prayer Book, Socialism, Post-Impressionism, Modern Poetry. To mark the path of his journey, Macaulay creates a map of educated upper-middle-class English provinces of opinion just before the First World War.

With the author, we go about urban and suburban England, listening to the large cast of quickly described, amusing characters chatting amiably or disagreeing on a variety of occasions in a variety of settings – a supper party in the bedsitter of two young women artists, a New Year's weekend at the deanery, tea in a Cambridge professor's garden, a censored Sunday drama performance, leisure hours in a county family's home, a weekend walking party, a 'little' literary magazine's offices, a busy publishing firm, and two settlement houses, one Christian, one radical-agnostic. (Some characters are adapted from life: there is a Rupert-type poet and a young Irishman much like Ronnie Ross.)

Eddy, unwilling to exclude or reject, tries and fails at one job after another in London circles, from social worker to editor. His failures are predictable; an undiscriminating enthusiast incapable of hurting anyone's feelings cannot, God knows, succeed as a book-reviewer. His own 'little magazine', *Unity,* which includes articles of varying quality and of even more varying opinions, pleases no subscriber and not unexpectedly fails.

The authorial voice of *The Making of a Bigot* is tolerant, but she is not the blithely undiscriminating Eddy; she is the attentive spectator. Royde-Smith said Macaulay was a gifted talker; she was also, like E. M. Forster, a talented listener. In this novel we learn where she has been, who has been talking, and what has been said. Her touch is sure. She took notes for her novels in the small loose-leaf notebooks she carried everywhere in her handbag. But she does not use these jottings to produce a documentary. Comedy is selective. And Rose Macaulay sees what Edward Oliver does not – the humour inherent in the clash of differing tastes and opinions when each is claimed to be Truth.

Every page is filled with unconsciously self-descriptive talk, laced with topical references to what is *au courant* with the post-university crowd: Aubrey Beardsley is out; Duncan Grant is in. A circle is drawn around this little world of the young and their parents. They are would-be highbrows, upper-middle-brows, and middle-brows; such innovative or iconoclastic outsiders as Proust and Lawrence do not enter, although the more sophisticated Macaulay knew of their significant new literary presence.

Eddy comes of age through instructive failure. He persists in bringing together pleasant but intellectually incompatible friends. The occasions are often marked by strain. Even his well-read, broad-minded parents could run out of patience; they 'liked to hear two sides (but not more) of a question'.[10] His only epiphany of universal harmony occurs on a lonely night walk: 'He had a keen sense of unity, of the coherence of all beauty and good; in a sense he really did transcend the barriers recognized by less shallow people.'[11] But his vision is not shared in a world of factions; the novel shows his dream to be unworkable in practice.

None of the novel's controversial intellectual and political questions could have been new to Rose Macaulay, because she had heard them posed during her many forays from Great Shelford into Cambridge, which was, she wrote, 'conscious of the world's complexities and imminent problems and questionable destinies'. But her daily life was lived in Great Shelford – a community which she described, a little wryly, as intellectually docile, a village 'that means well; many of its inhabitants are leisured, and will readily, if advised, form study circles, and read recommended literature'.[12] In contrast, London was alive with spontaneous debate.

In this novel, however, Rose Macaulay introduces an experience new to her fiction and prophetic of her future – an irreconcilable conflict on a question of conduct, the quandary which threatens Eddy's happiness. For the first time Macaulay the novelist writes of an illicit passion. Two of Eddy's friends, married, but not to each other, believe adultery to be 'uncivilized' and 'wrong' but at last find life apart intolerable. The love affair of Ralph Datcherd and Ellen Le Moine is presented chastely, entirely off-stage and from the outside. They are high-minded people, both separated from destructive spouses; divorce is impossible. Datcherd is critically ill. In the end the hitherto frustrated pair go off and spend his few last days together. Even in the relative freedom of post-Edwardian society Ellen thereafter becomes a pariah.

Eddy and his fiancée Molly see this situation quite differently. Their disagreement about the propriety of Eddy's maintaining a friendship with Ellen threatens to wreck their plans for marriage. The narrator is just; Molly's sincerity in believing that she is upholding the structure of society by breaking the engagement is accorded as much respect as Eddy's magnanimity.

In the end the novel, by a trick, evades settling the issues. As in a Shaw play, all sides have had a fair chance to speak eloquently, but unlike Shaw, Macaulay does not deftly unravel the tangled problems. Instead, she cuts the Gordian knot. When the isolation of his own position of 'omni-acceptance' becomes intolerable, Eddy bows to Molly and to social convention. And, as earlier described, on the dawn of his wedding morning he light-heartedly cuts cards to determine the prejudices by which he will live, concluding regretfully that in a state of even-handed-ness (like that of the novelist), one can take no significant action. Complete commitment is necessary, the narrator argues, for a life of achievement, although she equates commitment with bigotry, and adds with Macaulayan irony, that to become a respectable bigot 'takes energy and will'.

The comic ending, a never-to-be-repeated jolly dinner party for all Eddy's incompatible friends, holds in brief abeyance the inescapable conflicts of intellectual-political life. The novel itself is free to report those quarrels without taking sides. The muddled, soft-hearted Eddy, a likeable young man, but no social and ethical pathfinder, will sacrifice his intel-lectual freedom and some of his friends, and will live a good, happy, and narrowed life with Molly.

For all the calm amusement of the last scene, however, disturbing problems of conscience for Rose Macaulay herself remained. Delighted by the intellectual fun of London life and enjoying her liberty, she was yet secretly troubled by the conflict between the sexual freedom of her new artist friends and the unbending shalt-nots of her father, Great Shelford, and the Church. In later years she described the literary world rather airily as 'a coterie' – 'a law unto itself conceivably ... rather less conventional than what's usually called, I believe, the society set. ... very independent and amusing people.'[13] And looking back to 1913 she confidently identified herself with that freedom: 'We certainly, in the circles in which I moved, never thought of ourselves as convention-ridden or enslaved.'[14]

But although she was at last a *de facto* libertarian, she was to write to Father Johnson in 1951 that immediately before, during, and after the First World War she had been 'rather in the middle of counter-pulls.'[15] Among her friends there were arrangements of double lives which she had never before witnessed. The unmarried Naomi Royde-Smith and the married Walter de la Mare, a glittering pair with whose glamour Macau-lay had 'fallen in love', spent much time together in London and exchanged intimate letters twice and thrice daily when he was at home with his wife and children in Dorking. Constance Babington Smith describes de la Mare as Royde-Smith's 'devoted admirer'.

Rose Macaulay, too, had a secret life at this time – regular pilgrimages to St Edward's House, headquarters of the Cowley Fathers. She depended on the London retreats and confessions to Father Lucius Cary to maintain her faith even as she was enchanted by this worldly society. During her depression after Aulay's death she had chiefly sought assurance that an underlying and overarching benign power existed; from 1912 to 1922 she wanted from the Church clear answers to murky ethical problems. Her dilemma at first was not precisely a sexual question, but one of balancing duty and independence. Although she was less naïve than her character

Eddy Oliver, she was as hopeful as he that a way to live as a unified, although illogical, self, could be found. But she was never tempted into the complacency of bigotry as a solution.

The Making of a Bigot was, like *Views and Vagabonds,* a novel inconclusively exploring systems of belief and conduct. Macaulay's 'cross-pulls' created its even-handedness. But in accepting the moral insouciance of the London literary coterie while privately maintaining her allegiance to the Church, she was, as a writer, led more and more to choose comedy, satire, and detachment and to combine a certain disingenuousness with a touch of rueful pessimism about human nature.

As for sexual mores, she was to conclude in 1918, the year she fell in love, that when desire for 'one person out of all the world' asserts itself, then 'principle, chivalry, common sense, intellect, humour, culture, sweetness and light, might crumple up like matchboard so this one overwhelming desire, shared by all the animal creation, might be satisfied.'[16] In the light of this assessment of the irresistible drive of sex – even when opposed by the values she most honoured – and her increasing belief that vanity determined human behaviour even more frequently than sex, she perfected the role of a jesting, compassionate, and somewhat fatalistic commentator on human folly. This speaker became her social and her authorial self.

The Making of a Bigot was not as didactically Christian as the prize-winning *Lee Shore* of 1912. Nor was it quite as well-received. After mentioning its 'caricature' and the 'charming absurdity' of 'the artless plot', the reviewer of the *Englishwoman* became rather helplessly equivocal in judgement – it 'is not a really good novel, but we should be sorry to exchange it even for a good one'.[17] (This verdict would have been applauded by kindly book-reviewer Eddy Oliver.) Here is a humourless, lame acknowledgement that Macaulay had established a form of her own – a contemporary comedy of ideas that gave pleasure – but also that such a novel could not be taken seriously by a reviewer.

Even without a conspicuous critical success, however, the summer of 1914 began propitiously for Miss Macaulay. She was still poised for flight. On 30 June she gave 'a flat-warming party'. As she had taken possession of her London flat late in 1913, Rupert Brooke's return on 5 June seems to have been the real occasion for the celebration. His letters show that he may have been rather hard to catch as a guest. For reasons she does not explain, Rose's somewhat confusing party invitation asks her guests for alternative dates. Rupert was spending much time with the beautiful actress Cathleen Nesbitt whom he had met through Edward Marsh several months before he left for America. So sought after a guest was he that he sometimes waited until the last minute to choose among his social opportunities. But he did come to the party. He must have made a memorable entrance, for since Rupert's return passers-by had turned to stare at him on the street. His beauty had become spectacular; after his hedonistic basking in Tahiti his hair was bleached to pale gold and his skin was tawny.

Rose's guest-list was made up from the London world known to them both – among them were Rupert's favourite of this group, de la Mare, and 'some other poets', Royde-Smith, Iolo Williams of the *London Mercury,* and Frank Sidgwick, publisher of Rupert's poetry and of hers. Macaulay remembered the occasion with a kind of innocent delight: 'It wasn't an ambitious party, there wasn't much to eat or drink, so far as I remember, but we played paper games and it was great fun at the time, and part of the sociable London life which seemed so happy, clever, exciting, and good.'[18]

The strong bond with her father had been stretched but not severed by this happy, clever, new life. A month later on 17 July, to round off her *Annus Mirabilis* which had begun with the cruise to Greece, Rose and George sailed for Canada on the *Megantic* to visit Will Macaulay in the clapboard house he himself had built on his farming property in Gibbons, Alberta.

The snapshots Will had mailed back to Great Shelford are of his crude home, of himself on horseback, of his dogs, of friendly, rural neighbours and their children, with whom he was a favourite – all showing a rough, hard-working, but apparently happy life. His mother urged Will to find a bride, even suggesting (with great lack of sensitivity) Jean's flat-mate, Nancy Willetts, as a candidate. Will demurred, arguing that sharing his primitive life would be too hard for an English girl. Of his decision, Jean commented that all the Macaulay children were fearful of marriage.

We are indebted to Constance Babington Smith for this account and for other family lore about the trip's mingled pleasures and excitements: Rose's love of 'sweet danger' must have been fully satisfied by a hair-raising race for safety from an oncoming train steaming down a narrow culvert along which she and her father were hiking. But their adventuring in Alberta ended abruptly on 14 August 1914.

England declared war on Germany.

The two Macaulays booked passage for the return journey at once on the *Laconia,* a British liner disguised as a Dutch ship. They arrived in Great Shelford on 25 September. Jean had returned home nine days after war was declared to prepare for overseas duty with the French Red Cross; Will followed George and Rose across the Atlantic to enlist as an officer in the King's Royal Rifles.

Rose's first soaring flight was ended.

The year ahead, 1915, the year of the devastating Battle of the Somme, was to be one of sorrow for England. Rose Macaulay, too, was to suffer the loss of men who were dear to her. Earlier than most of those on the home front, she apprehended the madness and waste of the war, although through voluntary war work she grimly engaged in the battle she increasingly hated.

Within that same painful period, she began the slow work of recovery from crushing personal grief by writing her war novel, *Non-Combatants and Others* (1916). She created a surrogate mourner – Alix Sandomir – a young painter who is redeemed from despair by a *dea ex machina* who combines the most admirable qualities attributed to both man and woman. The 'nervy' Alix speaks with Rose's second voice, her most private self during the early war years.

But Rose Macaulay initially reacted to the war by seeing it as high adventure in the spirit of Rupert Brooke's war sonnets. Back in England in camp after a brief naval foray to Belgium under fire, he writes to his Cambridge friend Frances Cornford, 'Rain, rain, rain. But it's all great fun.'[19] And a week later from the Royal Naval Barracks to another friend, 'Camp is all right; there's Romance in it; it's rather like "camping-out".'[20] After the terrible casualties of the Somme both his euphoric poetic image of soldiers going to war like 'swimmers into cleanness leaping' and Macaulay's poem 'Many Sisters to Many Brothers' were to seem obscenely inappropriate.

> Oh, it's you that have the luck, out there in blood and muck:
>   You were born beneath a kindly star;
> All we dreamt, I and you, you can really go and do,
>   And I can't, the way things are.
> In a trench you are sitting, while I am knitting
>   A hopeless sock that never gets done.
> Well, here's luck, my dear – and you've got it, no fear.
>   But for me . . . a war is poor fun.[21]

Significantly, she did not address this poem to Jean, who had arrived to serve in the war zone under dangerous and miserable conditions months before Will Macaulay had even left England. Rose did not identify adventure with a nurse's service at the front.

Rose's romantic blindness about war was brief. And in 1950 she looked back and said she was confident that Rupert Brooke, too, would very quickly have begun to respond to the war's reality; 'the content of Rupert Brooke's war poetry would have changed utterly. It would have become all that is most disgusted and disillusioned.'[22] She even came to imagine her own worst fate at the front as a man: in her novel, Alix's brilliant and sensitive 18-year-old brother Paul kills himself in the trenches because of the suffering of his comrades. He 'couldn't stand the noise and the horror and the wounds and the men getting smashed up all around him.'[23]

Non-Combatants and Others was, in its consciousness of suffering and human waste, far ahead of the popular press, which repeated chivalric accounts of Hunnish atrocities being revenged by cheerful Tommies and their gallant gentlemen officers in the trenches. In the early months of the war, however, Macaulay's feelings were irrationally split. Alix Sandomir says, 'I can't bear the sight of khaki; and I don't know whether it's most because the war's so beastly or because I want to be in it.... It's both.'[24]

Rose, like Alix, felt 'the bitterness that eats the souls of so many of the medically and sexually unfit'. There was to be no more playing imaginatively at being a young naval lieutenant; the war forced her to accept her womanhood. After the war she began to write more about the range and complexity of women's choices. Although she did not want to be seen as 'a writer *for* women', she was to write only one more major novel with a man as the central figure. Her romantic vision of a female soldier died hard, however. A minor character, Meg Yorke – a brash, ginger-headed, long-limbed girl in her English Civil War novel *They Were Defeated* (1932) – boldly dons her brother's clothes and arms and rides out secretly to join the troops that fight Fairfax around Ashburton. But she is killed in the first skirmish.

Initially, Rose found ways to block out her bitterness. London's literary life went on at the beginning of the war in almost unruffled self-absorption. During the Second World War Mary Agnes Hamilton recalled, 'Existence was not then as now, subdued to and at every point conditioned by the war. Then, as not now, daily life for a good many of us still went on in normal channels. We continued to meet socially.'[25] For over eight months, Rose Macaulay was much like the unhappy Alix, who continues to go to her art lessons at the Slade and to see friends throughout the novel. Alix was like the hidden, anguished self in Rose who went on writing; her central quality is what Rose thought most feminine – the capacity to experience pain vicariously. Alix is ill and lame, the sign of her emotional vulnerability, just as it was for the Vallons in *The Valley Captives*. In describing the character of the lame Rickie in Forster's *The Longest Journey,* Rose says he is a 'delicate, civilized, amiable, unlucky, perceptive creature ... one of those with whom the readers naturally identify with themselves (it is always the weak and sensitive characters in fiction who are thus identified, since practically every reader knows himself to be sensitive and weak)'.[26]

Rose did not in the first ten months volunteer for any war work, although Hamilton says she was not a pacifist. But a personal shock that spring jolted her out of her attempted retreat from the sight of khaki. Unbelievable news came without warning: on 23 April 1915, only a few days after developing septicaemia, Rupert Brooke died and was buried on a hill at Skyros. The hurried funeral service was read at night, just before the saddened Cambridge friends who carried his body up the steep hill in the dark sailed to Gallipoli. Many of those mourners were soon to be wounded or killed.

Within days of the death, Walter de la Mare published a eulogy, and Macaulay, in sorrow, wrote to him on 7 May, thanking him for his portrait of her friend: 'It is so entirely himself. . . . It seems all alive with his humour and aliveness, and the most inside self that I should not think very many people even who knew him well understood.'[27] She describes for him a scene of herself and Rupert boating: 'a day in May three or four years ago, when he and I were paddling in the Grantchester meadows', happily singing de la Mare's praises together, 'rather like versicle and response.' In a poignant use of the present tense she continues, 'My only excuse for writing is that I am so fond of Rupert – we've known each other since we were children – and that I do like your article so much.'

'I am so fond of Rupert.' Although dead for two weeks, he is, for the moment, still 'all alive' to her. Grieving, she seems able to feel or to imply that their friendship had been equally significant to both. Rupert courted admiration and, as she wrote, was always 'charming and amiable' in her company. But she had seen him rarely between the flat-warming and his departure for war; he spent much of his time with Cathleen Nesbitt.

The sub-plot of *Non-Combatants* is a one-sided love affair; its hero is a young artist in uniform. Although the climactic scene may or may not be based on a conversation with Rupert, its emotional conviction shows that Rose understood the pain of unrequited 'fondness'.

In the novel the young painter-soldier Basil Doye is about to return to the war zone. Alix has seen him kissing her cousin, the lovely Evie, for whose flirtatious company he has suddenly and totally neglected her. Explaining to himself his present preference for the shallowness of Evie, Basil considers his former attachment to Alix: 'Before the war one had wanted a rather different type of person, of course, from now; more of a companion to discuss things with, more of a stimulant, rather, and less of a rest.'[28] (As in *The Secret River*, Macaulay shows an artist in love with a beautiful woman unworthy of him.)

In a critical scene of the novel Alix and Basil are alone in her brother's flat after a chance meeting has brought them together. It is to be their last. Basil speaks suddenly of Evie:

> 'She doesn't care a hang.' . . .
> 'She doesn't care a hang.' She repeated his phrase, mechanically, sitting very still. 'But I do.'
> Then she leant towards him, putting out her hands and a sob caught in her throat.
> 'Oh, Basil, I do.'
> For a moment the silence was only broken by the leaping, stirring fire.

Basil looked swiftly at Alix, and Alix saw horror in his eyes before he veiled it. The next moment it was veiled: veiled by his quick friendly smile. He leant forward and took her outstretched hands in his, and spoke lightly, easily. He did it well; few people could have attained at once to such ease, such spontaneous naturalness of affection.

'Why, of course – I know. The way you and I care for each other is one of the best things I've got in my life. It lasts, too, when the other sorts of caring go phut ...'

'Yes,' said Alix faintly. The raft of that small word drifted back to her, and she climbed on to it out of the engulfing sea. She took her hands from his and lay back in her chair, impassive and still.[29]

(Rose was 'horrified', Uncle Edward wrote in his diary, that someone who knew her interpreted scenes of the novel as autobiographical.)

The humiliation of this impulsive confession and Basil's tactful, but unmistakable, rejection overwhelms Alix. Her jealousy of Evie, which shames her also, seems to her to be one more example of the general spiritual deterioration caused by the war.

After Rupert's death Rose Macaulay was less often in her London flat. She signed up in June as a member of the Voluntary Aid Detachment at a military convalescent hospital which had been established the month before in a large modern home, Mount Blow near Great Shelford. She was living at home again. She worked as a 'scrubber'; perhaps some sensible matron was attempting to distance this hypersensitive volunteer from the wounds which physically sickened her. But as basic domestic help Rose was hopelessly and clownishly inept – dragging her skirts in the suds by scrubbing forwards across the floor, scrubbing carefully *around* the men's boots which stood at the foot of the beds, and making foolish mistakes in the kitchen.

Such a sympathetic observer in such a small institution could hardly fail to respond to the pain around her. In Rose's novel Alix Sandomir is not a VAD, but her cousin Dorothy is, and when Alix breaks down after witnessing the tormented, weeping sleepwalking of her cousin John, wounded and on leave, Dorothy counsels her, 'After all, what they can bear to go through, we ought to be able to hear about.' Alix lies awake: 'What they can bear to go through ... But they can't, they can't ... they can't ... we can bear to hear about ... but we can't, we can't ...'[30]

Macaulay's poem 'Picnic, July 1917' has the same theme. The speaker lies 'in the bracken of Hurt-Wood', 'eating sweet hurt berries' and listening to the big guns firing across the Channel. Its final verses describe her attempt to shut out her nightmares of the battlefields:

And far and far are Flanders mud
And the pains of Picardy,

And the blood that runs there runs beyond
   The wide waste sea.

We are shut about by guarding walls;
   (We have built them lest we run
Mad from dreaming of naked fear
   And of black things done.)[31]

Another of Alix's recurring griefs is the war's destruction of irreplace-able minds and talents. In the middle of *Non-Combatants and Others* she visits the convalescing Basil in a London hospital. They avoid mentioning that the impending amputation of a finger will end his career as a painter. His wound has been interpreted psychologically as Rose's punishment of Rupert-as-Basil, but it should also be seen as her appropriate symbol for the war's crippling of all artists, 'smashed and lost to the world'.[32]

This hospital visit gives Macaulay another scene in which to show the derangement and pain of the wounded and the exhaustion of the nurses, who are not allowed to sit at any time while on duty. Vera Brittain wrote that 'the endless series of special traditions and the nagging instructions' in voluntary civilian institutions were harder to bear than nursing conditions at the front.[33] Rose's own unhappy stint of hospital work made clear her unfitness to observe at close range the fighting which she had romantically aspired to join. Constance Babington Smith effectively captures an image of Rose's predictable wretchedness as a VAD: 'In a wintertime photograph of staff and patients on the Mount Blow terrace she is just recognizable as she sits hunched and miserable in her thin uniform, a starched cap pulled down over her head.'[34]

Rupert's death had stunned her; a second loss staggered her. On 3 July 1915 George Campbell Macaulay, at 63, suffered a stroke shortly before he was to retire from his Cambridge lectureship. He had been anticipating the completion of a task dear to his heart – the editing of his important discovery, the manuscript of *The Ancren Riwle*. But on 6 July he died.

Jean rushed back from France to share the family's mourning, but of the immediate family only she and Margaret attended George Macaulay's funeral. Will was in Salonika and Eleanor was in India. Both Grace and Rose were too stricken by shock and sorrow to appear in church.

Rose Macaulay's grief was deep, but there is no evidence that guilt for whatever anger she had felt against her father was part of its burden. She cherished and spoke of her memories of George Macaulay's teaching and companionship. He had nourished her mind and was a model of intelligence, honesty, modesty, and selflessness. She honoured his scholarship and intellectual integrity. Father and daughter were alike, especially in their humour and in the lifelong childlike qualities for which Francis Jenkinson praised George Macaulay in his obituary.

After the first keen anguish of this loss, what prevented another period of accidie, another paralysis like that which had seized her following Aulay's death? Rose seems to have come to understand and to some degree forgive, in terms of his nature and the nature of his marriage, her father's inability to open the door which would have made possible her escape from home. She still believed the domestic cloistering of daughters to be wrong and continued to show it to be so in her novels. But she seems to have found a way to discharge her ill-will against inadequate fathers by realizing them as characters in her fiction and by judging, punishing, and forgiving them within those created worlds. In life, she understood George Macaulay's failure to confront Grace; she diverted resentment to her mother. She did not allow anger at her father to destroy her sympathy with him. He was to be part of her life always.

She had the resilience to continue writing the novel she had begun after Rupert's death. In *Non-Combatants and Others* the heroine's father is dead, her strong mother is absent for the first two-thirds of the story, and the man she loves rejects her. But although Alix Sandomir falters physically and emotionally, she continues to paint and in the end finds some grounds for hope and purpose. Rose Macaulay's novels are not stories of victory but of gallant survival.

The major plot of *Non-Combatants* is not Basil Doye's abandonment of Alix Sandomir (which occurs two-thirds of the way through the story); the major action is Alix's quest for her own peace, a slow recovery shared by the novel's author.

Feeling is the heart of Alix's identity and experience, but in the end ideas dominate the novel. In the final section, the larger-than-life figure of Alix's mother, Daphne, a strong, independent woman with a cause, arrives from abroad, rescues Alix, and becomes the central character. She is 'gracious, competent, vivid, dominating, alive'. And Alix welcomes her, admires her, and is 'glad her mother had a sense of humour, and didn't rant or sentimentalize'.[35] Daphne Sandomir is in complete contrast to Grace Macaulay. Except for her activism, Sandomir is a model that Rose herself was coming to resemble. Bereft of her father, she now created her own ideal mother; she was healing herself.

In creating Alix's mother Rose Macaulay has put her heritage of intelligence to work. She has realized George Macaulay's best qualities and her own in a woman with traditional male and female virtues. Daphne, an agnostic, is a crusader for a plan for world peace. Her viewpoint is both mature and far-sighted. She ignores sexual stereotypes: 'She didn't draw distinctions, beyond the necessary ones, between men and women; she took women as human beings, not as life-producing organisms; she took men as human beings, not as destroying machines.'[36]

But Rose Macaulay always has a double vision; she consistently both honours and mocks untiring do-gooders. Even Daphne's idealistic hope for world peace is attacked through her affectionate son's sceptical opposition. Yet Daphne Sandomir remains the hero; she is a warrior among the non-combatants, fighting against war itself. Daphne's forward-looking secular crusade and her courageous example, together with the hope which the Church gives, offer Alix a positive view of the future. She also has an emotional support. Her companion in the last scene is the brother who has survived the war. Their shared humour, affection, and memories comfort them both.

By the autumn of 1915 Macaulay had finished her VAD stint. She had fulfilled her six months' obligation under considerable stress. In the next few months she finished the novel.

Not surprisingly, *Non-Combatants and Others* was not a conspicuous success with home-front readers. Alix Sandomir's emotions were out of tune with the general public's feelings; the *Englishwoman*'s reviewer said Alix Sandomir's misery blotted out 'all that is splendid or pitiful in life or death, belittling those who fight'.[37] And the novel's ruling ideas about world peace were ahead of their time. The review criticized pacifist Daphne Sandomir as one of those 'who act from a nervous desire to be doing something different from the common task ... without any clear idea of the result of their activities'. In real life, the reviewer argues somewhat smugly, the conscientious home-front volunteers enjoy exhilaration and the comfort of 'a good conscience'. Today the book seems wise despite Alix's confusions. But in 1916 it was not popular. It was the last book Rose was to publish with Hodder & Stoughton.

In February 1916, six months before the book appeared, Rose had turned away from the literary world and found a temporary anodyne for her grief. She took up war work more congenial to her nature and more lifting to her heart than nursing – work on the land. It also provided a daily escape from home where she lived with the self-dramatizing, grieving, restless Grace.

The former VAD joined Margaret Stewart-Roberts, the daughter of the Macaulay's neighbour, who was working with a group of young women on nearby Station Farm where Rose had often tramped with her fierce mongrel chow, Tom. She began work in a particularly bitter winter, herding sheep and, without agricultural machinery, helping to prepare the half-frozen fields for spring planting.

These toughening, labouring days do not appear in any of her novels, but Rose Macaulay wrote five short poems about them. Their sharp sensory images are more memorable than the mystical language of her more ambitious poetry. The section 'On the Land: 1916' in *Three Days* (1919) includes 'Driving Sheep', 'Burning Twitch', 'Hoeing the Wheat', 'Spreading Manure', and 'Lunch Hour'. Rose does not attempt pastoral romance. She evokes the mist and misery of early morning; she hates the cold. We hear the sheep's 'lilting bleat, their sharp, scuttling feet. ... horn feet and quavering cries/ In the young cold hour,' see the smouldering and darkening of the twitch bonfire, feel the sting of blinding smoke, the stabbing of a north-east wind, and the numbing dampness of the soaked clay underfoot.[38] The camaraderie of the women's lunch hour is a brief jolly respite:

> Withdrawn for a little space from the confusion
> Of pulled potatoes littered on broken earth,
> We lay in the shadowed ditch, a peaceful circle
> Of food, drink, smoke, and mirth.[39]

Hard as it was, for Rose this vigorous male life was bearable, even sometimes enjoyable; she compared the ordeal of the cold with that felt by the soldiers in Flanders.

The exhausting work must have helped numb her grief for her father. She had found ways to endure emotional pain. But in the future how would her father's death affect her as a thinker and writer? To what degree, in those ten years during which she had chafed as a daughter-at-home writing novels, was George Macaulay a direct influence, a consultant, an editor, or a critic of her work? Did she depend on his judgement? What indeed was his opinion of his daughter's fiction and poetry? No letters between them exist; no public word of gratitude from her for any direct involvement of her father in her writing can be found.

George Macaulay was her teacher, a critic of literature, an editor, and a writer himself. He could not have been contemptuous of fiction, for he nourished his children's imagination on nineteenth-century novels. Because he made it possible for her work to be read by his old Eton schoolmate, John Murray, a helpful act which led to her first publication, it is likely that he read her first and second novels, *Abbots Verney* and possibly *The Furnace,* as they were written. It may have been he who had advised her that the editor's word was law and that she must accede to Murray's suggestion that she end her first novel with a hint of wedding bells if she wished to have it published.

But both the violent *Valley Captives,* which recreated the unhappiness of her Aberystwyth life, and the idiosyncratic *Secret River,* which she wrote in the seclusion of the Macaulay boat-house, read like declarations of independence from her father's tutelage as well as evasions of her publisher's appeal for happy endings.

Finding her own form and style as a writer at home away from other writers had intensified rather than weakened Rose Macaulay's independence. George Macaulay's affection and companionship, as she acknowledged, had given her the sort of 'mental vitamin' she needed, but to depend on inspiriting conversation for creation is not the same as to be 'a disciple' or 'an acolyte' of her male companions – George, or

Rupert, or her editors. Although she had no high opinion of her fiction, she made sure it bore the unmistakable stamp of her own mind.

Rose Macaulay, as Olive Willis had said, even when a young, diffident, stammering, and inconsistent Somerville student, was 'confident about her own opinion'. She defined herself as a novelist of ideas, and, although she liked to keep several conflicting points of view under consideration, she had no doubt about the right way to examine them – by logical analysis, with humane magnanimity, and with the long, historical view which produces comedy, not tragedy or popular love stories. Reason was her father's ruling mode of thought; she had made it her own, mingled it with compassion, and practised it independently. Analysing her first successful novels we see, not the influence of a living master or editor but her emulation of the work of writers she admired; she paid homage to Forster, to the early Huxley, and to Anatole France – to the irony, pity, and control of their authorial voices.

Her last editor, Mark Bonham Carter, says she liked, even *needed,* to talk about minor decisions in her novels as she wrote them – and preferably with a man. And she had enjoyed those hours when she was for Rupert 'a companion to discuss things with'; she had liked talking with her father, 'the happiest of companions'. She wrote most fluently with the inspiration of a male Muse. Yet her writing itself was a solitary enterprise. She consulted Mark Bonham Carter about such choices as gender-blind names for her female characters. But when a manuscript was completed and delivered to the publisher, Bonham Carter says, 'There was not much you could do with it. It was an original. In spite of criticism, she didn't change her manuscripts.'[40] In the end, Miss Macaulay made independent choices and stood by them.

In one scene of *They Were Defeated* (1932) the 15-year-old would-be poet Julian Conybeare, who is the pupil of Robert Herrick, is questioned by Sir John Suckling. He wishes to charm her and he asks to see her verses.

> 'Mr. Herrick's seen 'em,' she added. 'He tells me how to mend 'em.'
> 'And do you mend 'em as he says?'
> 'Not always.'
> 'I thought not. No one mends his own verse to order; 'tis not in human nature.'[41]

John Murray had supported and encouraged her, but although his advice was the fruit of knowledge, experience, and goodwill, it was sometimes incompatible with her idiosyncratic bent. She stopped modifying or evading his suggestions and left his fold, unwilling or unable to change. Defending her independence, she said goodbye to his patronage apologetically. 'I don't think my novels will ever sell very well.'[42]

She continued to look quizzically at the world of ideas and people –
now using one angle of vision, now another, but always with the same
level gaze and the same humane values. 'Nobody ever zig-zagged more,'
said Alan Pryce-Jones, 'either driving a car or walking through life; yet
the essential part of her was perfectly still.'[43] More and more she concealed
her deep emotions in that 'essential part of her'. Introducing the reprint
of selections of her poetry in 1927, Humbert Wolfe wrote, 'The dark
lantern is a true image to apply to her work, because those who like it
best have always been aware of something held back, some quality in
reserve. They believe she will someday bring that quality into play, and
they believe that it will prove to have in it as much of tears as laughter.'[44]

Rose Macaulay holds something back in *Non-Combatants and Others*.
Her second voice, filled with pain, is represented by Alix, yet this young
girl displays humour and self-mockery and her saddest tones are in the
end muffled by the slightly satirical first voice of the narrator. The
audience for that first voice was in London. And London continued to
call. When later in 1916 a registry of university women was compiled by
the government and a recruitment questionnaire was posted to her, Miss
Macaulay saw the opportunity for a return to the city. Could she support
herself there? We do not know Rose's income at this time, but she did
not have to assume the financial responsibility for her mother's expenses.
Grace had money of her own and had inherited £10,000, George's entire
estate. Money aside, what was Rose's responsibility for the widowed
mother, who had always had the complete emotional support of her
husband?

Grace Macaulay must have known that her daughter's departure from
Great Shelford was inevitable. Within months of her husband's death,
Grace decided to sell Southernwood and move to Hedgerley, nearer to
London, to remain close to Margaret and to the city where Rose was
bound to settle. We can guess that Miss Macaulay was struggling with
the desire to break away once more. And we know from a witness that
she was struggling with the problems of living with her mother. In a
letter to Constance Babington Smith, Father Hamilton Johnson tells of
witnessing that distress in August 1916 (a year after her father's death).

Between the summer of 1914 and November 1916 Rose had made
regular appointments for confession at St Edward's House in London.
During that time her usual confessor Father Lucius Cary was away;
Father Johnson took his place. He recalls Rose attending a Retreat for
Women and asking to talk to him after her confession. Of this quiet
conversation he writes:

> We sat upright on chairs facing each other, both of us stiff and shy – much
> more stiff and shy than in the addresses in the little chapel, talking, I think,
> of nothing save only of how a young lady living with her family might most

suitably conduct herself. .... Oh, yes, and I remember looking out from the little parlour where I was put, into the little dull, square garden, and seeing Miss Macaulay pacing up and down very gravely and slowly, I think, on the grass, for a long while, in steadily drizzling rain, tall and grave and thoughtful, wearing some sort of dark tweed suit – no overcoat or rain-coat. This she did for a long time.[45]

A period of intense conflict was about to begin. Grace had purchased a house in Hedgerley, near Beaconsfield, within commuting distance of London; mother and daughter were to take possession in October. Meanwhile, Rose had applied for a post as a temporary civil servant; she was to become a wartime bureaucrat. And she was also to write *Potterism,* a best-selling novel, and to fall excitingly and painfully in love with a married man. That man was Gerald O'Donovan.

9

The Debate

GERALD O'DONOVAN HAD, wrote his wife Beryl, 'exceptionally thick, heavy eyebrows, shadowing his keen blue eyes.'[1] In one sharp glance he could signal the presence of what Rose Macaulay described as his 'sardonic wit'.[2] H. G. Wells once found the exact simile for that arresting image: 'Look at O'Donovan, his eye like a rifle barrel through a bush.'[3] But his piercing intelligence was not the whole self; in her unpublished memoirs Beryl O'Donovan described her husband as a man 'who could not be other than stimulating and interesting, and whose unconscious charm nobody ever resisted'.[4] And his oldest daughter Brigid testified, 'He was an extremely affectionate man.'[5]

To Rose Macaulay's astonishment and against her reason, within months of their meeting at the Ministry of War in 1918 she was overwhelmed by her responses to his searching mind, his power of sympathy, and his sardonic wit. In *What Not*, her novel written that year, the spirited and independent heroine Kitty Grammont speculates helplessly, 'What was it, this extraordinary driving pressure of emotion, this quite disproportionate desire for companionship with, for contact with, one person out of all the world of people and things, which made, while it lasted, all other desires, all other emotions, pale and faint beside it?'[6]

But before she became entangled in feelings which were so at odds with her principles and her good sense, Miss Macaulay spent the year 1917 as a junior administrative clerk in the Exemptions Bureau of the Ministry of War in London. In her twelve-month tour of duty in this maze of hidebound officialdom, she created a departmental reputation for bold *ad hoc* solutions. It was perhaps her unbureaucratic common sense that first attracted Gerald O'Donovan to her when, in February 1918, he became Head of the Italian Section of the Department for Propaganda in Enemy Countries in the new Ministry of Information.

The Ministry was founded on a new concept of warfare: the dissemination of persuasive rhetoric and misinformation. The Department for Propaganda attracted such literary and journalistic celebrities as H. G. Wells, Arnold Bennett, and Wickham Steed. In 1918 its Italian Section was distributing messages to Austrian citizens through England's Mediterranean ally. Gerald and Rose were both chosen to serve in it because they were writers; Rose's knowledge of Italy and Italians made her particularly valuable. (Her tendency to inject a caustic and personal note into the turgid official correspondence of the Bureau of Exemptions may also have contributed to this shift of assignment.) The question of how Gerald O'Donovan and Rose Macaulay would revise their lives to accommodate the intense friendship that grew out of this close association would face them both for the next three years.

In January 1917 Rose Macaulay had joined many other well-educated and well-connected young women to work in the grey buildings of the wartime civil service. The routine was tedious; the days were long; oddly, the war could be kept distant. Rose worked ten hours a day at Crewe House and spent three more hours commuting to and from Hedgerley near Beaconsfield, her weekday journey between present and past. Contrasting Old Beaconsfield with new wartime London she described the former as 'an enchanted city; as it was in the seventeenth and eighteenth centuries ... an ancient country town, full of brick walls and old houses, and courtyards and coaching inns, and dignity and romance and great elms'.[7] Part of the island magic of place for her was the quiet and beauty of the surrounding beech forest where at weekends she enjoyed long, brisk walks.

But her life at Hedgerley with her mother was not enchanting. Rose's friends believed that she was devoted to Grace, and when she took a few carefully chosen intimates home with her for a visit she allowed her mother to be the garrulous, anecdotal hostess. Yet Jean reported that in private the exhausted Rose – often irritated by Grace's emotionalism and the repetitive parade of her prejudices – interrupted, contradicted, and patronized her mother. The hypersensitive Grace, who craved emotional support, became miserably conscious of Rose's impatience with her. With characteristic exaggeration she asked Jean, 'Why does Rose hate me so?'[8] Rose may have believed she was paying a debt to her father by keeping up a vestige of the old home life, but her sacrifice was misguided, made at the expense of both of the survivors.

Yet Rose was not socially isolated in Hedgerley; she kept in touch with her London literary friends, many of whom were also in government work. She had reluctantly given up her London flat when she was tied to Great Shelford, first by her VAD duty and then by her land-girl work, but now she often spent weekends at Naomi's country cottage in Sussex and after a time rented a room in Naomi's flat for occasional overnight stays during the week.

By 1918, the London Miss Macaulay had acquired a worldly air. Her deep griefs were hidden; her manner was urbane. She was described as 'rather argumentative', but her conversational challenges, though brisk, were impersonal and entertaining. The main character of *What Not*, which she wrote during the last war year as a satire of the imagined regimented peacetime life to come, suggests her new ideal identity.

Her heroine Kitty Grammont is a synthesis of the lively, nonchalant Edwardian Rosamond Ilbert of Macaulay's first novel and of Macaulay's image of what the future career woman would be – accomplished at her professional duties but a little cynical about male ambition, and at all times independent, playful, amused, and amusing. This sophisticated young civil servant reads the *New Statesman* and the *Tatler* with equal interest as she takes the Tube to her middle-level job in the Ministry of Brains. Her creator says she is 'a learned worldling ... something of the elegant rake, something of the gamin, something of the adventuress, something of the scholar ... [and with] a travelled manner, and an excellent brain, adequately, as people go, equipped for the business of living.'[9] Although she is a 'gamin' and not a 'gamine', the post-war Kitty has an unmistakably female name and an unmistakably female charm. Her defining modernity – in contrast to the occasional unconventionality of the turn-of-the-century Rosamond Ilbert – is her complete freedom to live as an intelligent, insouciant bachelor, wearing 'cap and bells' in a changing, insecure world.

Yet Kitty differs from Rose herself; she is long-lashed and lovely, smartly dressed and stylishly made up. Here Macaulay breaks new ground; it is difficult to know whether this character, a blend of fashion and wit, was Rose's fantasy *alter ego*, a rare bow to popular novelistic convention, a sign of self-confidence, or all three. Perhaps Macaulay, now socially successful and outwardly assured, was by this time less at odds with feminine beauty. She had, as a friend said, developed her own style. Some years later Compton Mackenzie praised her appearance in a battered jockey cap, which made her look, he said, 'like a faded print of William Archer running the Derby in 1878,' and on another occasion he admired her *tailleur* as that of 'a Light Blue Hungarian Hussar'.[10]

The descriptions of Kitty as a fashion-plate are always interwoven with those of her intelligence and her insouciance; indeed, her cool powers of decision almost protect her from falling in love. Her character clearly has the author's sympathy; the vivid, gallant Miss Grammont comes to life in *What Not*. And the Miss Macaulay whom Gerald O'Donovan met in February 1918 was quite as independent and incisive as Kitty. Gerald said he was attracted to Rose because she had a 'mind like a man's'.

But who was Gerald O'Donovan, the man whose companionship the self-possessed Miss Macaulay came to desire with 'an extraordinary driving power of emotion'? In February 1918 he was 46 years old;

Rose was 36. The two were thrown together in their work. Rose had opportunities to observe the discrepancy between his background and his look and manner. Although born in Western Ireland, the son of a Supervisor of Public Works who built municipal piers along the Atlantic coast, Gerald had an upper-class British accent and the manners of an English gentleman. He was 5 feet 8 inches tall; his dark reddish hair had not greyed (although it formed the fringe around a balding head); he had kept the figure and the energy of his youth. His voice was melodious and his conversational allusions reflected his experience as a novelist and a publisher's reader. As a member of his staff, Rose would before long have learned that he was married and had a daughter and a son and perhaps she might have heard through office gossip that his wife was expecting a third child. In fact, she may have met Mrs O'Donovan. Although Gerald's family was living in Cromer, his wife Beryl, fluent in Italian, was for a brief time an employee of the Ministry, acting as her husband's translator on an official trip to Rome.

And in the course of her duties Miss Macaulay could assess Mr O'Donovan in his role of fellow civil servant. She discovered that he was an able administrator and an excellent speaker. He had a quick and critical mind and a forceful presence; Brigid O'Donovan said he had a photographic memory. Like Rose, he was skilled in repartee. What most surely won her notice and then her sympathy as she came to know him was his passion for social justice and his record of failure as an impatient battler for near-hopeless causes.

In 1918 she witnessed one manifestation of his quixotic behaviour: the Ministry recalled him from a diplomatic mission to Italy because, although only a minor representative of the British government with a well-defined brief for action, he had exceeded his authority. He attempted to participate in the premature planning of the post-war partition of the Austro-Hungarian Empire by calling for the independence of the oppressed southern Yugoslavs. Harold Nicolson had written tactfully: 'The energy and enthusiasm which made him so valuable a propagandist rendered him somewhat dangerous as a diplomat.'[11] Like Rose, Gerald was independent, impatient with authority. The impulsive Gerald and the impulsive Rose came to understand each other quickly, and as new friends and potential lovers do, gradually unfolded their life stories to each other. But Gerald's oral autobiography may have come forth slowly and disjointedly – his past was buried in secrecy. Even his children did not know the events of his early life until they were adults.

He might have offered Rose some of his story, disguised, by lending her his first novel of Irish life, *Father Ralph* (Heinemann, 1913). At the turn of the century he had been Jeremiah O'Donovan, a young Roman Catholic priest of national prominence – a man of spiritual, economic, political, cultural, and social influence in Irish life. But thwarted in his local reform projects by his bishop, reprimanded and suspended for neglecting his parish duties in favour of activism in nationwide liberal causes, he had in 1904 given up his leadership in the Irish revival movement. Disheartened, he had left his post as administrator of St Brendan's Cathedral in Loughrea, and, like Father Ralph, had eventually left the priesthood, an apostasy then almost unheard of in Ireland.

In 1901 D. P. Moran, editor of *The Irish Leader*, wrote that Jeremiah O'Donovan 'is admitted on all hands to be one of the most vigorous and gifted of the Irishmen of these times.' *The Irish Catholic* called him 'a patriot priest', and in February 1903 Edward Martyn described him as 'a leader of opinion in Ireland'.[12] But in 1942 there was no notice of his death in any Irish newspaper.

However, in 1985, across the space of over eighty years, he was still remembered as a young priest in Loughrea by Mrs Mary Conlon: 'A very handsome, good-lookin' man. You'd love to look at him, a fine, lively, lively lookin' man. Everyone loved him. Lovely man. He was loved and liked in this town and why wouldn't they for what he done in this town?'[13] Only recently has the scholarly research of Irish historian John P. Ryan rediscovered, documented, and honoured Gerald O'Donovan's eminent and significant, though brief, role in his country's history.[14]

His mother had dedicated him to the priesthood from his birth in 1871. Gerald's children never met this grandmother or any member of their father's side of the family, but Brigid deduced from his warm nature that her father must have had a secure, happy, even pampered, boyhood.

After an indifferent education in the parochial schools of Galway, Cork, and Sligo, Jeremiah O'Donovan entered Maynooth in September 1889 to prepare to be a parish priest. His scholastic record in its narrow theological curriculum included recognition as one of the runners-up for several prizes, but was on the whole undistinguished; the most interesting entry in his seminary history is the reproof issued to him for ordering 'books of a somewhat unbecoming kind'. Father Thomas O'Dea, later to be his bishop and political adversary, commanded him to return these to the publisher. O'Donovan was an ambitious autodidact; from *Father Ralph* we can infer that he had ordered books by modernist theologians who challenged the church's rigid views of the past and called for a course of social action that anticipated the agenda of the much later Second Vatican Council. Hearing the new idealistic voices, Father Jerry and a dozen other young clerics in Ireland attempted a spiritual, nationalistic Irish revival. They crusaded for the Church's involvement in social problems and the laity's participation in Church affairs.

As a priest with a vision, Jeremiah O'Donovan was a creative force in the small village of Loughrea near Galway between 1897 and 1904. Even if reduced to a mere list, his activities are exciting and impressive – a sum of imaginative and practical projects designed to help his parishioners become better educated, healthier, more prosperous, more culturally and spiritually alive, and, above all, more proudly Irish.

A brief night scene in *Father Ralph* shows the young priest standing in the muddy, narrow street watching men entering a pub – a dirty hole, yet a brighter refuge of an evening than their own wretched homes. Absentee landlordism and the fall of agricultural prices had contributed to the village's decay. The local farmers were discontented, resentful of the shopkeepers' high profits and of the Church's lack of interest in improving their miserable circumstances; the higher clergy saw its task as encouraging dutiful piety and eliciting large gifts from the parishioners. The tenant farmers dared not speak out; the Church had the power to cut off their livelihoods. This fictional village of Bunnahone was like Father Jerry's own parish, Loughrea, a rural corner of the moribund Ireland from which James Joyce fled in 1904.

Apathy was Loughrea's predominating mood; emigration offered the only hope for escape from this death-in-life. Yeats's nearby Ballylee Tower made him a neighbour, and, on one occasion, calling on O'Donovan, he noticed a hole in the glass fanlight over the Presbytery's front door. Father O'Donovan explained that it had been made by a brick thrown by a drunken old woman with a dislike for the bishop. Yeats observed, 'That is the first sign of secular activity I have seen in this town.'[15]

Standing in cold rain, the fictional Father Ralph imagines an alternative to the pub where much of the community's meagre income is nightly spent on drink. He dreams of forming a men's club in the village. The real-life Father Jerry O'Donovan did found such an organization – the St Brendan's Total Abstinence Society; its original membership of 200 grew to 300. Classes were begun in crafts and drawing, and also in Gaelic, history, and music, subjects not taught in the parochial schools. The men formed a brass band. Lectures, concerts, plays were organized. Father O'Donovan arranged for the Abbey Theatre to stage Yeats's *The Pot of Broth* in Loughrea in 1904, the company's only performance outside Dublin. And he not only collected a lending library but also organized a national contest for the best list of 100 books for any village library to acquire. By 1904 there were fifty such libraries in Ireland.

O'Donovan tried to reform the dreaded workhouse, to improve the town's lighting and housing and sanitary arrangements. Nor did he neglect the women's special interests. He began a national speaking campaign against the inadequate education of young girls, believing they were being trained to enact what he called a 'false gentility' which cramped their minds and left them with no practical knowledge or skills.

Father Jerry's most lasting contribution to the town's culture gave St Brendan's Cathedral the title of 'The Pride of Loughrea'. Together with the sympathetic Bishop John Healy and the landlord patriot and playwright Edward Martyn, he initiated and commissioned a treasury of native Irish art in the cathedral's interior. Lest this expense be one more burden on the bent backs of the farmers, O'Donovan made two speaking trips to America to raise funds for the project; the first, in 1902, was successful, bringing £1,500 to the cathedral treasury. On his second tour the following year the climate had changed; he found that Irish-Americans were more eager to give money to the IRA than to nourish the culture of the starved Ireland from which they had emigrated.

The realization of O'Donovan's harmonious vision for St Brendan's is still a wonder. The stone and wood carvings and the stained-glass windows bloom with the Irish imagery of the life of St Brendan; they were created with Irish materials by Irish craftsmen. (The English stained-glass artist, A.E. Childs, whose teacher had been a student of William Morris, was given a post in the municipal school so that he could train and work with local craftsmen.) Large church banners, depicting Irish saints, were designed by Jack Yeats and Sarah Purser and executed in silk and wool by Yeats's sisters, Lilly and Lolly. These three-by-five-foot embroidered hangings are still used by the sodality; they are strikingly beautiful, at once simple and rich.[16]

Father Jerry also engaged himself in the new national movements which addressed Ireland's widespread poverty, although they were not approved by Church policies. By setting up co-operative creameries, Sir Horace Plunkett's Irish Agricultural Organizational Society directly addressed the problem of the dairy farmer's loss of profit to the town middlemen. The clergy was not friendly towards this economic reform because the profiteers gave liberally to the Church. In addition to supporting the IAO movement, O'Donovan, believing that a way to improve the economy and to de-Anglicize Ireland was to develop electrical power and industry, threw himself into that cause as well. His approaches were all positive and pacific; he did not instigate violent anti-English political activity or anti-Protestant sentiment. His dream was a combination of social reformism and the Christian concern with the individual, the creation of an institution which would combine the benefits of Violet Markham's settlement with Sister Margaret's All Saints' House.

He was an animating voice in the Gaelic League, which encouraged both the teaching of Irish in the schools and the revival of Celtic literature. O'Donovan believed the old legends should be read in English as well as in Irish, and to learn more of the Celtic Literary Revival he spent hours with Lady Gregory, Yeats, George Russell (A.E.), and with George Moore, who became a lifelong friend. He was captivated by the literary world. (Moore said O'Donovan was his model for the priest in *The Lake*.) He published articles and short stories and was invited to speak on prestigious platforms across Ireland, fearlessly confronting his superiors, charging them with indifference and, indirectly, with ignorance of their own people and their own culture. 'Is Ireland Doomed?' was one of his subjects. His answer was, 'No, not if it could be inspired and led by Irish priests who were men of action as well as men of faith.'[17] Obviously, he was provocative, neither politic nor tactful to his superiors. And he ignored a cardinal rule of the clerical vocation – obedience to authority.

But his rebel causes seemed to prosper. He was invited to give addresses at Maynooth on three important occasions. Rumour reported that Father O'Donovan's peers put forth his name as a candidate for the bishopric when Bishop Healy was transferred to the diocese of Tuam. If so, the Vatican rejected the nomination. Placed over Jeremiah O'Donovan's head was his orthodox former disciplinarian from Maynooth, Father Thomas O'Dea. His judgement was predictable. O'Donovan's national career and possibly his local influence were to be cut short.

Bishop O'Dea's privately addressed charges against Father O'Donovan can be surmised and were uncontestable: he had delegated his routine parish duties to the Carmelite brothers; he had spent time out of the diocese, speaking, arranging publication, and meeting with reformers throughout Ireland – some of whom were Protestants. His friendship with Lady Gregory and her friends whom she entertained at Coole Park was a mark against him; they had nothing to do with Church life. His local reforms had built up organizations which were not controlled by the clergy. He was seen by his bishop to be a proud and negligent young priest. Naïvely, impatiently, egotistically, he had believed that he could persuade many to share his utopian dream of Ireland's rebirth and that both the people and the Church would heal factional divisions to achieve a united national glory.

But the end of his crusade had come. On 28 September 1904, he said to Horace Plunkett with sadness that he could not go on with his work because 'my bishop has no knowledge of life whatsoever'. Thomas O'Dea had suspended Father Jeremiah O'Donovan from his clerical duties. The 33-year-old priest felt he could not follow the narrow path his superiors had laid out for his future. Father Jerry's departure by train from Loughrea on 8 October 1904 was a scene crowded with young and old weeping and asking for his blessing. As the young priest hero of *Father Ralph* prepares to leave Bunnahone, he thinks of those who love him, 'He suffered, but they suffered, too, and the thought of their suffering was his heaviest blow.' Jeremiah O'Donovan never returned to Loughrea.[18]

The last pages of his novel are hopeful, however. Father Ralph 'took up his clerical collar and looked at it curiously. He smiled as he thought of how he had dreaded laying it aside. And now there was only a sense of escape from bondage, of freedom ... "I have found myself at last." '[19] But six unhappy years of wandering, loneliness, depression, and struggle with disillusion lay ahead for the real-life Father Jeremiah. And for another eight years, from 1910 to 1918, officially removed from the Church Registry of clergy, he worked to create a new self – to become the quiet, courtly Anglo-Irish Mr Gerald O'Donovan, the literary gentleman and civil servant who so strongly attracted Rose Macaulay.

The self-transformation was a painful task; the simultaneous loss of prestige, authority, identity, and purpose was a bitter dose. By May 1905, Gerald was bankrupt and discouraged. The clergy had sent emissaries urging him to return, but he could not bring himself to do so. Friends – Yeats, Moore, Plunkett, Byrne, Sarah Purser – gave and lent him money or tried to find him literary work in London. He went to America on a humiliatingly unsuccessful money-raising venture for the Co-operative Movement. He wrote book reviews. Still active in the Rural Library Association, he visited Ireland several times, but he was estranged from his family; a 'spoiled priest' was a figure of deep shame in Ireland. He rarely spoke of those years in a barren wilderness, but all his life he was subject to periods of depression.

However, there proved to be a wonderfully suitable place in secular life for his talents and goals. He was in April 1910 appointed as the subwarden of Toynbee Hall, the first settlement house, founded by the Reverend Samuel Barnett in 1880. It was a large residential hall and night school in the East End, a community dedicated to social reform. The social reintegration of men of all classes through communal living and mutual study of the complex problems of the time was its chief aim. Gerald O'Donovan was so excellently suited for the work of its administration and its inspirational educational mission that many of his friends believed that in social work he had found his true vocation. But his private life took a surprising turn.

In the summer of 1910, in his thirty-ninth year, O'Donovan went to a house-party at Marble Hill in County Donegal, the estate of Hugh Law, MP. Upon the arrival of a fellow guest, the 24-year-old Beryl Verschoyle, Gerald stepped forward and handed her down from the 'outside car' in which she had arrived. In her memoirs Beryl records that she was wearing 'an enormous cartwheel hat' and was dressed all in black, in mourning for the death of King Edward. She also observed that her courteous welcomer, with whom she made a mild joke, was 'charming'.[20]

'Five days later', she continues, 'Gerald proposed in so determined and authoritative manner I could only say "yes," but did not agree, much to his astonishment, to being married at once.... When our engagement was announced I could see it came as a shock. Gerald was considerably older, and exceedingly brilliant intellectually. Nobody thought me at all up to his standard, which was true, and I was humbly aware of it. He loved me for what I was, gay, young and enthusiastic.' Revealing little of her own emotional response, she writes that she tried to be worthy of 'the entire devotion' he gave her, and makes it clear that he found her youthful high spirits a welcome tonic for the gloom which had surrounded him for so long.

Their marriage followed in the autumn, and during the waiting period Gerald wrote Beryl letters almost daily, declaring that her love would provide a centre and purpose for his alienated life. He confided his past to her, explaining that they would have to be exiles from Ireland. Catholic friends who had stood by him up to this point were shocked at his marriage plans; some rejected him angrily. And the hasty union, unwisely hurried along by Gerald's emotional starvation, was in more than one way a mismatch.

Florence Emily Beryl Verschoyle was the younger daughter of an Army colonel from an Anglo-Irish Protestant family and an English mother. Throughout his years of active service, Mrs Verschoyle accompanied her husband to his assigned posts in India and South Africa, and the parents saw their children only once every four years. The two young daughters were shipped back and forth according to the seasons, from one grandmother in Rome to the other grandmother in Ballinamallard, Ireland.

In both Rome and Ballinamallard, the circumstances were comfortable, even prosperous, the adult social life around the children an exciting pageant, the servants kind. But although Beryl described her education as 'ample' (tutors and governesses and a year at a private school in Brussels until she was 15), the conventional and superficial teaching provided her was not designed to create intellectual curiosity. She enjoyed music and the theatre, and was accomplished at languages. But her husband's first novel and *The Wind in the Willows* are the only books mentioned by name in her memoirs although she said she admired H. G. Wells as a writer.

She had suffered, too, from the absence of parental love. Her seldom-seen mother died when Beryl was in her teens; her father remarried, arranged an allowance for his daughters, and told them they must manage on their own. As a result of this emotional neglect, Brigid O'Donovan says, 'My mother found it hard to be as genuinely affectionate as my father.'[21] Some who knew her in later life described her as self-absorbed. Beryl's sexual instruction to her older daughter in her adolescence was a brief and frigid description of resigned wifely passivity.

The greatest feeling shown in Beryl O'Donovan's memoirs, written after Gerald's death, is in her sensuous account of her lifelong love affair with the warmth and colour of life in Rome. She records less about human affections than about sensory pleasures – sunsets, dresses, parties, balls, and an especially rapturous response to food. She pictures herself in the memoirs as a tall, slim-waisted young girl waltzing in Rome, but, not surprisingly, over the years her waist greatly increased, and as she was over two inches taller than Gerald, they never made what people call 'a handsome couple'.

Neither Gerald nor Beryl had paused to fathom the gulf between them. Symbolically, Beryl confesses that while Gerald wrote her long 'delightful letters' each day they were parted, she could not at first read his minute handwriting. She carried his first letter about all day and 'at intervals tried to piece it out'. (Rose Macaulay described that writing precisely in a 1942 story which mourned the loss of her love letters from Gerald: 'close small writing, the o's and the a's open at the top'.)[22]

Beryl remembers Gerald and A. E. discussing subjects which were 'very abstruse and founded on knowledge I did not possess'. She pictures herself during the thrice weekly visits of George Moore to their Chelsea home in London in 1917, curled up on the sofa 'out of the way' as a non-participant in their late-night debates. Gerald believed in women's education; he sent his two daughters to Oxford and Cambridge. But there is no evidence that Beryl made any attempt to take advantage of his natural talent as a teacher or to share his intellectual life. She describes dinner parties in the Twenties at which Shaw, Wells, Arnold Bennett, and Maynard Keynes held forth, and although she enjoyed the company of Wells, who became a family friend, she felt left out: 'Literary subjects and the function and practice of art, as well as various literary reputations and output were analysed and discussed, and I sat very quietly and wished very intensely I had better brains!'

There were other incompatibilities. Beryl was always admiring of Gerald's mental accomplishments but complained that he would not go calling with her to see her friends or allow her to accept 'delightful invitations' for the two of them, preferring to work on his novels or to mind the children and to let her go unaccompanied. He was a sociable man, yet he was quite capable of going upstairs and remaining absent from the festivities when she gave a formal dinner for those whose company she enjoyed. (Rose Macaulay uses such an incident in *The World My Wilderness* but reverses the sexes of the pair.) The O'Donovans were plainly bored by each other's friends.

Gerald and Beryl were not quarrelsome; Rebecca West described Gerald as 'a man of gentle manners'. They were not dramatically unhappy, but neither, as those who observed them comment, was their mid-life together warm and joyful. 'It was a misalliance,' said their daughter Brigid O'Donovan, 'but one which both parties were prepared to make the best of.'[23] Beryl always looked up to Gerald. Gerald, thirteen years older, was paternal, even patronizing; he called Beryl 'my dear child' and took over the management of her allowance of £500 a year. (He probably knew of her private means when he proposed, for at that time he was not in a position to support a wife.) Brigid said he disbursed his wife's allowance wisely and unselfishly for the good of all the family, but that her mother did not like his assuming this power. Unlike Rose, Beryl was in sympathy with the suffragettes, but she did not rebel. For the first year of marriage she behaved, as she had done in her grand-parents' homes, like a good child, respectful of her elders.

The two near strangers were married at the Whitehall Registry on 15 October 1910. Gerald took his bride straight to her new home, which she had not yet seen – the Lodge at Toynbee Hall. Two rough shocks awaited her: the cold unattractiveness of her living quarters and the weight of her new responsibilities. The University Settlement was in a dingy part of London. She describes it: 'In the neighbourhood a short distance away flourished a dust destructor and a brewery, and when the streets were wet after rain the windows had to be shut to keep out the sickening smell, and the slime that covered the pavements seemed to seep through my shoes and make my toes curl.... The rooms [of the neo-Gothic Lodge] were large, dark and dirty. It was a curious and violent contrast to the life I had always lived.... To my great dismay I was asked to "take on" the housekeeping. Never in my whole life had I ordered a meal or interviewed a maid. In my grandmother's flat we were not allowed in the kitchen.' She was put in charge of a housekeeper and a cook who quarrelled constantly; she had to arrange three meals a day for twenty-five to thirty men. The warden was unmarried; there was no other woman of her class to help or advise her.

In the evening Gerald often superintended night classes or was in charge of concerts, debates, or lectures; Beryl reports attending only the concerts. She remained distanced, on the fringe of the real and exciting working life of the Hall to which Gerald was so committed. She recalled, 'Many social abuses were being studied and brought to notice by the group of brilliant men living in the settlement house at the time. I was too inexperienced to share in any of the work, but I could sympathize whole-heartedly with all that was being done.' By custom at meals she was always seated between her husband and the warden; she had no opportunity for instructive conversation with those crusading 'brilliant men'.

Next year, in 1911, when Beryl was pregnant, she refused to go on living in the settlement as head housekeeper and tour guide. Gerald had come to understand her justifiable dissatisfaction; she had remained an outsider in a close community. Yet the parting from Toynbee Hall was a painful sacrifice for him, for he had once more achieved a position of visionary leadership and might very shortly have been appointed warden. But Beryl, though she had been co-operative and had coped with unan-ticipated difficulties, felt exploited. She was certainly not happy there. Gerald was right to recognize her needs; it was unfortunate for both that they did not harmonize with his. This was the first but not the last contretemps to face them.

As Gerald's position required his residence, resignation was obligatory. They moved to Edwardes Square where he began his first novel and Beryl prepared to bear her first child. With the help of a French maid she began, ineptly, she confesses, to learn to keep house.

From 1911 to 1917 Gerald wrote three novels about Ireland, did freelance publishing work, and held two positions in succession. In both of these posts he rashly repeated his pattern of attempting to make radical reforms without authorization, and from both he departed in moral indignation and in unhappy circumstances. In their life story Beryl makes no report of these disappointments. Such self-destructive, self-righteous acts were characteristic of him; they were to bind him sympathetically to Rose Macaulay, always a champion of courageous failure. Gerald's social conscience may have reminded her of her father; surely the age difference between them did so.

Father Ralph, published by Macmillan in 1913, was controversially and widely reviewed; it soon went into four editions. The story of a young reformer's gradual disillusionment with Church politics sold well in England in spite of its Irish subject. The reviews in Ireland were hostile, but the book was an under-the-counter success. However, representatives of the Church in New York informed Macmillan that the publisher's profitable Catholic business would be lost if the firm brought out *Father Ralph* in the United States. The novel was pirated there and had a good press and sales, but, of course, O'Donovan received no American royalties.

Despite that particular disappointment, 1913 was the best period of the O'Donovan marriage. Beryl writes, 'I was delighted with the daily pile of reviews and the flow of invitations which gush for every successful author. The new book and our first child [Brigid] brought us great happiness. I myself felt secure and wanted, no longer an "amusing" visitor, but the very centre of our dearly loved home'.

After the birth of their son Dermod in 1913, the O'Donovans moved to large, charming old Northrepps Cottage, near Cromer on the Norfolk coast, within sight of the sea and within calling distance of interesting and talented neighbours. Gerald was working on his second novel, *Waiting*, also critical of Irish conditions and Church politics.

But a year later the war broke out, beginning for the O'Donovans a series of separations. Except for the winter of 1917, which she and the children spent in London, Beryl was to stay at Northrepps until after the Armistice, doing some Red Cross nursing and struggling with wartime shortages, the fear of Zeppelin raids, and the care of her three small children – Brigid, Dermod, and Mary – whom she describes as beautiful, wild, and unmanageable. Gerald wrote to her almost every day he was away, but their lives ran separate courses for much of this time. She was increasingly resourceful about the family's practical difficulties. Her account of these years is understandably homebound, showing little empathy with Gerald's experiences. Both suffered from her lack of perceptiveness. Her memoir does not imply that their marriage created common interests or a deep mutual understanding.

On 24 May 1915, Gerald volunteered and was commissioned as a First Lieutenant in the Royal Army Service Corps and sent to Hull. Given the task of feeding and billeting troops, he discovered widespread graft and exploitation in the civilian financial transactions with the Army. Indignant at the greed and waste, he reduced the government payments to the townsfolk for housing, and, as he could have anticipated, found himself out of favour not only with the public but also with his superiors. O'Donovan's novel *How They Did It* (1920) is a bitter story of wartime corruption and favouritism. (Rose's bureaucratic novel *What Not* (1918) more good-humouredly attacked other perennial flaws of officialdom – institutional stupidity and government invasion of privacy.)

In October 1915, Gerald was invalided out of the Army and after over a year of piece-work editorial jobs began acting as the London representative for William Collins, the Scottish publisher. Their head-quarters were in Glasgow, where they had for years been leading pub-lishers of textbooks. But the firm was increasing the publication of fiction and Gerald represented their cosmopolitan outpost. Not surprisingly Gerald discovered, however, that the one-man London office he was expanding was eventually to be headed by someone from the Scottish headquarters rather than by himself. Once more his ambitions had been unrealistic. And again working against his own interests in what he believed was the cause of justice, Brigid O'Donovan reported, he sided with Collins's London authors in a royalty negotiation. As a result of this advocacy and his disappointed hopes, he left the job in 1917 after less than a year.

Nevertheless, he had the firm's respect, and continued as their first reader until 1919. Their records show that he was involved in the pub-lication of Henry James's unfinished fragments, *The Ivory Tower*, *The Sense of the Past*, and *Within the Rim*, in addition to works by minor novelists. Gerald O'Donovan eventually not only persuaded Rose Macaulay to become a Collins author but was also put in charge of seeing her books through the press. She was to publish her fiction with Collins for a quarter of a century.

His next post was with the Ministry of Munitions from which, one year later, in February 1918 he was promoted to the Ministry for Propa-ganda where his close friendship with Rose Macaulay began. It is naïve to read the relationship between Kitty Grammont and her Ministry chief Nicholas Chester in *What Not* as a literal transcription of their friendship. But there are four similarities to Rose's own character and situation in the love story embedded in her novel; Kitty (like Rose) prizes her freedom and that of others; the Minister and Kitty fall in love; though neither is married, under the rules of the novel's particular world each knows that their marriage to each other would be both illegal and immoral. Most significantly, the novel creates scenes in which a man and woman spark each other's laughter and sharpen each other's wits.

The scene of the satire is post-war England. The ideas that control it are taken from the last pages of *Non-Combatants and Others* and the conception of a worthy end implemented by absurd means creates a comic plot. In the last chapter of *Non-Combatants* Daphne Sandomir had exclaimed, 'Oh, for more *brains* in this poor old muddle of a world! Educate the children's brains, give them right understanding, and then let evil do its worst among them, they'll have a sure base to fight it from.'[24] To raise the national level of intelligence, the post-war government in *What Not* launches not only compulsory adult education but also an arbitrary and impractical national programme of eugenics enforced by a Ministry of Brains. The bureaucracy assesses the intelligence of every citizen, prescribes the proper class of mate for each, and fines the parents of children from unsuitable unions.

In *Non-Combatants* Nicholas Sandomir had predicted that despotic systems would arise as a consequence of the war. 'War is the tyrant's opportunity. The Government's beginning to learn what it can do.' Daphne's dream of intellectual excellence and Nicholas's pessimistic prophecy of government control are both made official policies in the Ministry of Brains. Once more Rose Macaulay produces a problem novel of deadlocked concepts.

What Not's hero, one-dimensional Nicholas Chester, is the idealistic, ruthless Minister of Brains; he is like Gerald in his pursuit of a vision. But he faces increasing public objections to government intrusion into the most private areas of life. Kitty, believing in Brains, assists him. But, also believing in Individualism and understanding the intransigent independence of 'the great stupid pathetic aggrieved public' as well as the randomness of heredity, she is sceptical about the possibility of the plan's success.

The Brains Regulations affect both Kitty and Nicholas: Kitty has been classified 'A' and must marry a 'B' to lift the race's level. The genius Chester has been classified 'A (deficient)'; because he has two retarded sisters he may not marry anyone. Inevitably, the two colleagues fall in love. Their guilt is defined by the law and by Chester's duty to his Ministry, their emotions are similar to those of would-be adulterous lovers. (Rose dedicated the novel 'To Civil Servants I Have Known', a rather bold gesture since obviously the ascription included Gerald O'Donovan.)

In 1918 Rose and Gerald enjoyed each other's company in compatible groups outside office hours. Rose was probably included in working parties as Kitty was in the novel. Gerald, as a literary friend of Rose, was included in such ritual social events as the weekly luncheons given by

Naomi Royde-Smith and Reeve Brooke (a Toynbee Hall alumnus, a civil servant, and a cousin of Rupert); the guests lunched in Brooke's sunny rooms on Mitre Court, around the corner from Naomi's office. Brooke regulary entertained a cross-section of his literary and social reforming friends, including Rose's old hero, Walter de la Mare. Mary Agnes Hamilton, the Fabian MP-to-be, was a regular guest. She writes, 'Reeve had a rare gift for drawing people together and getting them to talk interestingly about interesting things.'[25] On such pleasant occasions the friendship between Rose and Gerald prospered. Beryl was in Norfolk; the two colleagues were often invited together to London gatherings. Their intelligences were so in tune that during one period they did *The Times* crossword puzzle over the phone together daily.

If *What Not* cannot be read as a transcription of Rose's own experience, it does contain some accounts of similar social encounters between Kitty Grammont and Nicky Chester. The novel quickly plunges the reluctant Kitty into love with her equally smitten chief. His own moral resistance to an illicit relationship might be seen symbolically in his cutting a poisoned thorn out of his hand and nearly biting off his tongue in an accident just before he tells Kitty he loves her. They love chastely; they try to part. Their stern effort fails, says the narrator: 'The fact remained that when two people who love each other work in the same building, however remote their spheres, they disturb each other, are conscious of each other's nearness.'[26]

When Chester pleads for a secret childless marriage, Kitty, refusing, makes a long speech summing up Rose's own view of the *pis aller*, making the best of the second-best:

> But there *are* other things. There are jokes, and shops, and music, and plays and pictures, and nice clothes, and Russian politics and absurd people, and Greek poetry, and the world's failures caged together on one island, and things to eat and drink, and our careers, and primroses in woods, and the censor.... Good gracious, it's all like an idiotic, glorified revue. We mustn't let the one thing, just because it matters most, matter alone. It's so commonplace. Our hearts aren't broken, and won't break. We're out to have a good time, and we'll let love and marriage go to the – anywhere they like, if we can't have them.... By the way, if it's any comfort to you (and it is to me) I shouldn't make at all a good wife; I'm much nicer as a friend. I want too much out of life. I'm grasping and selfish. You'd find me tiring.[27]

The reader suspects that this is meant to be rationalization by the infatuated Kitty. But it reflects Rose's characteristic effort to resist tragedy, to remain *toujours gai*, and to taste life's delights; she subtitles the book 'A Comedy', although it ends in a fiasco, not in a comic reconciliation. Kitty Grammont, like Rose, braves life 'in its more formidable aspects' by nailing 'a flag of motley to the foundering ship and keep[ing] it flying to the last'.[28]

Rose and Gerald's regular companionship was publicly acknowledged. The chief evidence for Gerald's committed affection for Rose is that he was content to be constantly coupled with her by London friends and colleagues and that after a time he made visits to Hedgerley with Rose to meet her family. Though she knew Gerald was married, Grace Macaulay was charmed by him and said to Jean that she thought it was 'wonderful' that he obviously cared so much for Rose. Grace believed in romantic platonic friendships; Rose did not sentimentalize, but this was a just description of their situation.

The Macaulay sisters were an exception to Beryl's axiom that no one could resist Gerald O'Donovan. Jean Macaulay disliked him, saying 'he was not a man to be trusted'. Both she and Margaret tried to persuade Rose to give up the company of a married man; Jean believed that sexual sins 'poison the whole of life'.[29] Rose was adamant, even against the pleas of the sisters with whom she had so close a bond. The three finally agreed not to discuss the subject.

Fictionally Rose Macaulay pictures Nicholas Chester as a passionate wooer and Kitty Grammont as an adventurous risk-taker. And in this quality Kitty is like Rose Macaulay. Lance Sieveking of the BBC remembers walking down Regent Street with her one evening in the Twenties and coming across a hansom cab sitting driverless in a side street:

> 'Come on,' she exclaimed. 'You get up in the driver's box and I'll get inside.'
> She obviously meant it and began to climb in. I hesitated, and I could see that I had gone down in her estimation. The expression of gaiety and zest faded from her face. Looking back, I wish I *had* driven her madly about London and, later, appeared beside her at Bow Street. It would have been well worth the fine.[30]

Equally careless of the cost, Kitty, after realizing with a shock her own susceptibility to Nicholas's attraction, thinks, 'And, after all, why should one turn one's back on life, in whatever curious guise it should offer itself?'[31] In the novel this only means that she should let herself love him. The narrator repeatedly attempts to play down the love affair against the background of Ministry politics and the country-wide protest against its decrees. Macaulay insisted to her publisher that her book was not a love story, but chiefly a satire against bureaucracy.

But the tender and fierce debates between Kitty and Nicky about their future are credible emotional interludes to the satire. Kitty yields. They marry; they go to Italy for a fortnight and are recognized by a fellow worker as they dive ecstatically into the waters of Rose's pastoral paradise, the Mediterranean near Varazze. Through the press's persistent pursuit their treason is published; the Ministry falls; Chester is nearly torn apart by an angry mob. The novel ends with the disgraced couple's rueful laughter.

'Individual desire given way to, as usual, ruining principle and ideals by its soft pressure,' says the tolerant narrator.[32] In context this is more a fatalistic description of fallible human nature than a stern moral condemnation. *What Not* offers the bemused sense of a muddled world: the author-narrator is for a more intelligent citizenry but against any legal coercion that would create it; the writer's fictional voice celebrates the joy of romantic love but laments its inevitable destructive selfishness.

But Rose's double concentration on *What Not* and on her friendship with Gerald was broken by the news which came on 12 October 1918, less than a month before the Armistice: Will Macaulay had been seriously wounded, and would be condemned to live with a permanently disabled right arm and a collapsed left lung. The Macaulays were once more bound together in grief. That *What Not*, to be published by Constable, was being held up by the censors because of its irreverent views on the civil service could not have seemed overridingly important to Rose at this time.

The story of Rose and Gerald is a private story, experienced on another level from that of Rose Macaulay's public success and busy social life of the Twenties and Thirties. The pervading light tone of *What Not*'s love story can be understood only in terms of Rose's already quoted statement to her audience: 'Readers do not know how even the most improbable novelist may have tried to be truthful. He no doubt knows how life – some life that is – is actually lived, but his lips are sealed: he cannot tell.'

Any account of the secret life Rose Macaulay 'actually lived' must be in part speculation based on shards of evidence: contradictory opinions of outside witnesses; unexpected flashes of revelation in Rose's acts and writings; reported spontaneous confessional remarks; several critical letters; significant omissions in Beryl's memoirs; repeated plot situations in the novels; and the occasional serendipity of biographical hindsight that suggests the relationship among all three members of the triangle. Much of the underlying pattern of events and feelings emerges; the whole truth about any human relationship cannot be known.

'I would be private,' Rose Macaulay said to the press. Even before meeting Gerald she was passionately opposed to any publicity about her personal life, although she wrote essays about her memories. She refused to give so much as her address to *Who's Who*, and begged even admiring critics not to write articles about her. Yet to invade that privacy at this distance is not merely to practise the fascinated voyeurism of literary biography. We can fully respond to the resonance of Rose Macaulay's best work by being attuned to the minor notes of her second, private voice of love and conscience and the third transcending voice of the imagination which create the counterpoint of her best novels.

On 4 November 1918, Beryl came down to London at Gerald's invitation to celebrate with him the delirium of the signing of the Armistice. For the next two years Rose and Gerald were intermittently separated, at one time by a painful decision to end their relationship, apparently made by Rose; at another by Gerald's financial circumstances which made it impossible for his family to live in London.

Just after the war, the fortunes of both Rose and Gerald were in confusion. The Propaganda Section had been dissolved. Rose had been moved to the Ministry of Information in the winter of 1918–19 and was acting as a reader of fiction for Constable; Gerald's post had been discontinued.

The O'Donovan family was in financial straits. To economize they moved to Burton Bradstock in Dorset, to a primitive, small, leaky cottage with an outdoor privy; their discomfort was mitigated by the charm of the village. Gerald, working on a new novel, went up to London occasionally.

All Rose's physical and emotional reserves were called upon at this time. She was worn thinner by concern over Will's operations and suffering; her mother's resulting distress; the strain of the months of long working hours and commuting; and her debilitation from a case of the virulent influenza of that year. The pain of conscience about her love for Gerald and the uncertainty of its future exacerbated every misery. Everything we know points to the chastity of their relationship at that time; Rose was still going to confession.

Her career was not stable; *What Not* finally came out in March 1919, but was only mildly successful. (It is ironic that when she at last almost inadvertently wrote a love story, 'which I seldom mean to do,' it did not find a public.)[33] She began writing poetry again, with that plangent note that had always dominated her verse – in contrast to the ebullience and laughter of most of her fiction. *The Two Blind Countries* of 1914 and the newly published *Three Days* of 1919 both reflect a vague melancholy, conveyed in a similar sibilance of voices, 'whispering, hesitating . . . muted, cautious . . . threatening us with terrors at once ghostly and earthly,' as one reviewer wrote.[34] Most of the poems are the embodiment of anguish, disquiet, griefs, and fears suppressed and never exorcised.

The collection, however, is not all a grey lyrical monotony. Some of the war poems have clear images, and one curious, vivid piece closes the volume. 'To Thomas: An Easter Address' is a poem of seventy-three tetrameter couplets spoken to Rose's dog Thomas as they walk in the beech wood at Beaconsfield. There are hints of 'distant guns and shells and sorrows' still threatening the forest's peace, but the month is not the month in which Easter Sunday fell in wartime 1918, but the April of Easter 1919. The late war's griefs still haunted her.

1. Emilie Rose Macaulay, aged 3

2. George Campbell Macaulay in his
early forties

3. Grace Mary Conybeare at 18

4. The Macaulay family at Clent on holiday from Varazze, 1892
Standing: William H. Macaulay, George C. Macaulay
Sitting: Grace Macaulay, Mary F. Macaulay, Kenneth A. Macaulay, Aulay, Margaret
On the ground: Rose, Will, Jean

5. Margaret Campbell Macaulay

6. Jean Babington Macaulay

8. William John Conybeare Macaulay

9. Aulay Ferguson Macaulay

The Five, with Rose Macaulay, centre

10. Olive Willis at 30, at the time of starting Downe House in Kent

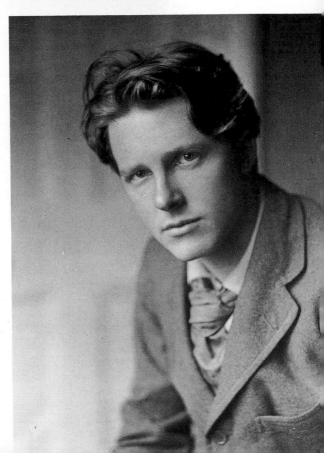

11. Rupert Brooke, London 1913

12. Rose Macaulay, 1924

13. Landgirls, Great Shelford, 1916.
Rose is drinking from the bottle

14. Storm Jameson in the late 1920s

17. Rose beside Will's Essex, California, 1929

18. Rose on Metacombe Island, Florida, 1929

19. Reginald Heber
    Macaulay
    (Uncle Regi) in
    late life

20. Will, Eleanor, Margaret, Jean,
Rose at Lees, Petersfield, 1926

21. Leonard and Virginia Woolf at Cassis, 1928

22. Ruth and Victor Gollancz at Brimpton during the Second World War

23. Harold Nicolson and Vita Sackville-West at Sissinghurst, 1932

24. Rose Macaulay
    speaking at a Freedom
    of the Press rally,
    London, 13 August
    1942

25. Stephen Spender, Paris, 194

26. Rosamond Lehmann

27. E. M. Forster

28. Ivy Compton-Burnett, 1950

29. Rose Macaulay in her London flat, 1958

30. Gilbert Murray with Emily Penrose at Somerville, 1920

31. Father Johnson at the Monastery, near Boston

32. Rose Macaulay in the garden of Peggy Guggenheim's villa, Venice, May 1957

33. Rose Macaulay going down the gangway from the SS *Hermes* to board a boat taking her to the island of Lemnos, September 1958

The poem is the expression of a longing to escape her self, to take on the nature of Tom, who was in life a wildly active, fierce half-breed chow, notorious for fighting and for biting even Rose, who defended him against all criticism, even when he chewed up part of a manuscript. (Uncle Edward fulminated in his diary about 'Rose's beastly chow'.)

The speaker of the poem, envying the dog's ignorance and freedom, stands with him 'on the bounds of fairy land', longing to enter, to forget that 'she is human/An earnest, grown-up, working woman/Writing books and reading news/Thinking thoughts and holding views,/Meeting friends and talking sense'. She watches him become 'a tawny flash/A leap, a scuffle, a yelping dash.' But she fears that to feel such joy (and perhaps such aggression) will make her mad, and fears as well that if she releases her feelings and then returns to the world where she must 'feign sense': 'men will guess the secret ill/I bear in my heart, all hid and still,/And know that, hide it as I will/I really am an imbecile'. This line collapses into doggerel, bathos, and a self-pity uncommon to Rose Macaulay. Uncle Edward recorded in his diary, 15 May 1919, 'Rose broken down'.

For many others in England, after the first exhilaration of the Armistice, the year 1919 was one of purposelessness and giddiness. Macaulay describes this mood in *Potterism*: 'It was a queer, inconclusive, lazy, muddled, reckless, unsatisfactory, rather ludicrous time. It seemed as if the world was suffering from vertigo.'[35]

But she drew once more on some of the fundamental experiences in which she had found unfailing strength and joy in childhood: the company of her brother and sisters, the beauty of the natural world, and the escape of story-telling. In the latter part of the summer Rose, Margaret, and Will, temporarily out of hospital, went to stay at Uncle Regi's Argyllshire shooting lodge – a happy island. She describes this long, low, grey former farmhouse, its beautiful garden and surrounding lakes, streams, and moors in *The World My Wilderness* (1950). Soon after this inspiriting change of scene and company Rose began working on the new novel which was to make her a celebrity.

She still saw Gerald when he came to London, sometimes at Naomi's and sometimes at Hedgerley. He persuaded her to put her business affairs into the hands of the literary agent, Curtis Brown; he now also persuaded her to become an author on the Collins list. He encouraged her to continue writing in the dry, satirical, sometimes flippant vein which so successfully captured the ironic 'first voice' of her public self. Their professional companionship bore fruit; Rose said it stimulated her invention. They laughed at the same jokes. But the secrecy of their personal relationship meant the continued suppression of emotion in her work.

The emotion was intense. Increasingly it was clear to both that there was an urgent private question to be settled between them. It does not seem to have been one of marriage, although in both of Rose's novels with similar situations she shows the man in the story eager to abandon his responsibilities in order to marry. Brigid O'Donovan did not know, but said that she did not believe Gerald ever proposed divorce and marriage. Brigid said, 'He was fond of my mother'; Beryl clung to him and to the respectable status of wife in spite of any suspicion she had of his double life. The O'Donovans had tacitly worked out the mutually tolerant habits of their lives. Gerald was a good and loving father and cared greatly for his children. He had experienced one dreadful uprooting of his allegiances. He was impulsive, but would he, at 50, with severely limited personal resources, have faced another abandonment of vows and the desert of ostracism?

More to the point, however enchanted she was with Gerald's company, Rose had always been and was at the time opposed to marriage for herself. Her parents' marriage and Gerald's were examples for her of the hampering bonds of wedlock. Fictionally, she has the dashing Kitty Grammont say, 'For after all, what is marriage? A tying down, a shutting of gates, the curbing of adventure which seeks to claim all four corners of the earth for its heritage.'[36] More than once she said the same thing in her own voice.

Since the beginning of the war Rose Macaulay had been faced squarely with her identity as a woman. Love intensified this recognition, however much she wanted to remain, like Kitty, like a man. Man's sexual urges, she kept insisting, are more powerful than woman's and they are designed to create a trap for both parties. Nine years later she wrote in her newspaper article, 'People Who Should Not Marry': 'Some men and women might well prefer to live alone, meeting their beloved only when it suits them, thus retaining both that measure of freedom (small though any human freedom is) enjoyed by the solitary, and the delicate bloom on the fruit of love which is said to be brushed off by continual contact.' And 'Love does not spoil separateness, but households do.'[37] She wanted to control her time, her life, her choice of friends, her moments of companionship and love. And she did not want to destroy Gerald's home.

In late life she revealed her inner struggle of love, conscience, and independence during that time. To Father Johnson in 1951 she wrote, 'Oh, why was there so much evil in what was in so many ways so good? Why did it have to be like that, all snarled up and tangled in wrong, when if we had been free it would have been the almost perfect thing?'[38] The word 'free' does not necessarily imply freedom to marry – only the absence of the guilty betrayal of Beryl.

But in her last years Rose Macaulay did break stride once in her fiction to compare happy marriage with happy adultery: her character Laurie in *The Towers of Trebizond* says of her love affair, 'I supposed that the every-day life that married people live together after a time blunts romance, but we did not think we should mind that, if we had all the other things, even the tedious things to do together ... and marriage would still be our fortress and our peace, just as love was now when we could be together but could be a sadness and a torment when we were apart.'[39]

In 1920 Rose and Gerald had to decide whether to be lovers or to part. Rose had deep scruples of conscience. Beryl must have sensed Gerald's unrest; whether or not she divined the reason, she had reasons of her own to make a bold decision. In March 1920, after a miserable winter of 'fog, rain, snow, and colds' and 'deep dullness' in Dorset, she announced that they were all going to Rome to live near her relatives – more comfortably, more economically, and in a warmer climate. She pictures Gerald's astonishment, but asserts confidently, 'He wanted to leave as much as I did, and we said good-bye to our kind landlady and set off.'

The year ahead was critical for this triangle. It was a turning point in Rose's career, the year of Rose's first popular success and of the final stages of the debate between the emotionally needy Gerald and Rose, who wanted both love and freedom. It was the year in which they moved toward a lifetime commitment to be both together and apart, in disregard of their moral convictions. Many years later, looking back, Rose Macaulay wrote, 'Human passions against eternal laws – that is the everlasting conflict.'[40]

10

Secrecy and Success

THE ROSE MACAULAY of the spring of 1919, when Gerald moved to Dorset, and the Rose Macaulay of the autumn of 1920 contrast sharply. At Easter 1919 she had stood on the road looking into the beautiful Burnham Beeches – reminding herself in graceless verse that the 'world's a place/ Where I must run a strenuous race/ And make my mark, and use my wit,/ And earn my bread and do my bit'. And, wavering between the hard road and the 'magical' wood, she had seen herself 'held in doubt/ One foot in and the other out' and confessed that 'loth to trust myself in either/ I am a denizen of neither'.[1]

By late 1920, when Gerald was making occasional visits from Rome, Rose had been transformed into an outwardly confident, joyful woman by success, love, and her own resilience. She was receiving congratulations for the popularity of *Potterism*, which was to run through four impressions in England and to sell 20,000 copies in the United States. And she was described at 39, in spite of the marks of her illness of 1919, as radiant. In that autumn of 1920 she was beginning a period of great fertility as a writer. The final stage of the change from lonely, despairing paralysis to an active life of work, love, and enjoyment can be partially deduced from the masked arguments of Gerald's and Rose's novels of the Twenties and from the record of their outer lives.

We know of Miss Macaulay's renewed state of vitality and magnetism in 1920 because her minor celebrity drew unwanted publicity. A newspaper interviewer gushed somewhat: 'She is tall, very slight in build, with a tendency to tie herself into knots, and yet graceful with the strong grace of the born walker.... Her energy is amazing ... her face, worn, and yet retaining the inexpressible candour of a child about the large, wide-open, heavily lidded eyes, blue as the eyes of a child are rarely blue, suggests this ageless energy.... every action is with her quicker than with most of us.'[2] Storm Jameson, reminiscing about one of the Thursday salons

Naomi and Rose held every week for fifty to sixty guests, describes her more precisely: 'She was enchanting to watch, a narrow head covered with small curls, like a Greek head in a museum, with that way she had of speaking in arpeggios, and the lively hands, the small arched nose and pale, deep-set eyes.'[3] And in the same passage she comments on the number and distinction of the guests who sought out Rose. 'One Thursday evening, I watched her with Arnold Bennett. He hung over her, mouth slightly open, like a great fish mesmerised by the flickering tongue of a water snake.'[4]

In early 1920 Rose Macaulay began to live in a world kept exciting by public and private tensions, which is (up to the limits of tolerance) the best of all possible worlds for a writer. She wrote eight novels in the next ten years – all but one of them both penetrating and witty – and much literary journalism and criticism. Her life was to accelerate, to fill with new opportunities and new friends, to be happily interrupted by travel, and to require a hectic, brilliant, even reckless balancing act of her talents, time, and affections. Rose Macaulay always relished risk and action.

At the same time, beneath the surface ebullience for which her company was prized, there ran a dark undercurrent of fatalism. She did not lose her interest in religion, but she lost her faith. Writing to Rosamond Lehmann in 1957 about her last novel, *The Towers of Trebizond*, her only novel wholly in the first person, she said, 'It's a book I have had in mind to write for a long time ... the heart of the matter being my own story.'[5] If the heart of the book – the effect of the love affair on Laurie's spiritual life – is Rose Macaulay's story, one passage presents some facts that only she could tell us:

> I was a religious child, when I had time to give it thought; at fourteen or so I became an agnostic, and felt guilty about being confirmed, though I did not like to say so. I was an agnostic through school and university, then, at twenty-three, took up with the Church again; but the Church met its Waterloo a few years later when I took up with adultery; (curious how we always seem to see Waterloo from the French angle and count it a defeat) and this adultery lasted on and on, and I am still in it now, steaming down the Black Sea to Trebizond, and I saw no prospect of its ending except with death – the death of one of three people, and perhaps it would be my own.[6]

The debate between Rose and Gerald about the direction of their future together seems to have been concluded in late 1921 or early 1922 when their platonic romantic friendship became a secret commitment to each other for life.

The last stage of their controversy began when Gerald's departure for Italy forced their separation. When the five O'Donovans arrived in Rome in March 1920, they were taken in only briefly by Beryl's grandmother, then settled by relatives in a primitive but charming villa on a family farm in Tuscany. In August, when Beryl began to worry about the prevalent malaria, they returned to Rome to live in an attractive flat which Beryl fortunately located in the densely overcrowded city. She was near her family, and she later remembered the time between the autumn of 1920 and the autumn of 1921 as a very happy one for her, a less happy one for her children, and a time of concentrated writing for Gerald. (Brigid said Gerald had a brief breakdown at one time and went to Ostia for a rest in the company of his sister-in-law, Glay.) The spring was lit up by the excitement of a visit from H.G.Wells. (Rebecca West was with him, but significantly Beryl makes no mention of his extra-marital companion.)

Some incidents of this period which Beryl describes suggest that Gerald may have been absent more than once on trips to London, possibly supervising the publication of the two novels he brought out that year or consulting his editor about *Vocations*, his anti-clerical Irish novel about the recruitment of nuns from well-to-do families, to be published in 1921. This was a period in which Rose and Gerald could have met and talked and laughed at Naomi's or at Hedgerley; the separation, their brief times together, and perhaps the letters from Gerald seem to have intensified their love. They were in constant touch, for Rose was acting as Gerald's literary agent. In the autumn of 1921 Gerald insisted that he must be in the English publishing world again. And the children did not want to stay in Italy.

When the family moved back to London, Gerald and Rose began to see each other again regularly. The O'Donovans gave a party to which Dorothy and Reeve Brooke and other friends of Rose were invited, but this could not have been a very successful occasion. Beryl does not mention it, and there seems to have been no sequel. In fact, although in her memoir she mentions many writers who were friends of the family, nowhere does Beryl O'Donovan record the name of Rose Macaulay. To her reader it eventually becomes clear that the autobiography, which in late life Beryl made several efforts to get published, was designed in part to present its writer attractively, in part to present her marriage as a success, and in part as a denial of any sadness in her adult years. She does not mention the death of her daughter Mary at 23 or the death of Gerald, and she attempts to prove by omission that Rose Macaulay did not exist as a character in the story of Gerald and Beryl O'Donovan.

But during the O'Donovans' year in Dorset, Beryl knew, at least, that Gerald was part of Rose's professional and creative life. He had provided encouragement for *Potterism* which had been published shortly after the O'Donovans had left for Italy. Rose, writing and living a busy social life all that year and seeing Gerald from time to time, had captured in what she called that 'Tragi-farcical Tract' the outer tensions of her London world – the frantic activity and the chilling commercial pushiness of society in the first years after the war. But she had added a subplot which spoke of the inner tensions – a struggle between love and right reason.

In its picture of public life her 'newspaper novel', as it was called, showed the forces of disinterested integrity fighting hopelessly against the prevailing opportunism in England. 'Potterism' is a state of intellectual immorality – 'sentimentality and cant and cheap short-cuts and mediocrity' – a state nourished by greed and vanity. Potterism is indestructible – a kind of original sin of the mind.

The novel pits the forces of good – scientific objectivity (Katherine Varick), generous disinterestedness (the young Anglican curate, the Hon. Laurence Juke), and the passion for truth (Arthur Gideon) – against the greedy and the ruthless. Both sides have a voice in telling the story, but the voices of truth are muffled and finally overcome by that prince of mediocrity, the press baron Potter; his clever, greedy twin children; and his sentimental, shallow, complacent wife, the popular novelist, Leila Yorke.

The novel's theme is the debasement of language and thought by the popular press. All characters except the failed heroes are shown to be subtly corrupted by contemporary life. In a 1920 letter to an unidentified recipient, Rose, spiritually modest but a little cynical, confesses to being herself – like almost everyone else of her era – part Potterite. She says she 'minds' her own weaknesses, 'but resignedly and without remorse'.[7] The prolific mystery writer Edgar Wallace was the best-selling author of the day; several reviewers accused Rose Macaulay of Potterism in forcing a quite improbable and irrelevant semi-murder mystery (as she called it) into her morality play. But Rose said she put the murder in because her brother Will begged her to write a book in which her characters stopped talking.

The hero of the crusade for truth in *Potterism* is Arthur Gideon, 'one of those rare people who can really throw their whole selves into a cause – lose themselves for it and not care'. Like Gerald he is a prophet and the martyr to an ideal, the third altruistic man in her novels to be attacked by a mindless mob. (He is half Jewish, one of the numerous signs in her work and in her correspondence that Rose Macaulay was one of the few well-known writers of the Twenties and Thirties who were not anti-Semitic.) But his secondary role is as a man in love. And in his dialogue with himself we hear Rose's second voice, her conscience battling her love for Gerald. Gideon falls in love with Jane Potter Hobart, a married woman. Although, in a personal letter, Rose writes that she herself is not a noble Gideon, his inner dialogue is consistent with some of her convictions about relations between men and women, and consistent with her own sternly willed rationality about the control of her own love for a married man. The book is dedicated to 'the unsentimental precisians of thought'.

First Gideon says firmly:

> I claim the right to be intimate with Jane – well, if you like, even a little in love with Jane – and yet to keep my head and not play the fool. Why should men and women lose their attraction for each other because they marry and promise loyalty to some one person? They can keep that compact and yet not shut themselves away from other men and other women. They must have friends. Life can't be an eternal duet.[8]

But moments later he counters this urbane rationalization of his passion for Jane:

> We couldn't go on. It was too second-rate. It was anti-social, stupid, uncivilised, all I most hated, to let emotion play the devil with one's reasoned principles and theories. I wasn't going to. It would be sentimental, as in a school girl's favourite novel.... I hate the whole tribe of sentimental men and women who, impelled by the unimaginative fool nature, exalt sexual love above its proper place in the scheme of things.[9]

Sometime during this period Rose did try to break off with Gerald. We can read this reasoned argument as part of her struggle, and we can imagine the prick of her Anglican conscience.

Virginia Woolf, reading *Potterism* in August 1920, not having met Rose, wrote in her diary, 'Potterism – by R. Macaulay – a don's book, hard-headed, masculine, atmosphere of lecture room, not interesting to me'.[10] (She was hearing only Rose's first voice.) And in October to Hope Mirlees, she added another judgement: 'Poor dear Rose, judging from her works, is a Eunuch – that's what I dislike most about Potterism. She has no parts. And surely she must be the daughter of a don?'[11]

But Rose Macaulay was not the invulnerable cold-blooded intellectual. And Gerald O'Donovan, too, could argue about the state of their relationship through a novel's voice. His winning rebuttal, in his novel *The Holy Tree*, was published near the time when Rose seemed to signal her capitulation to sexual love: she stopped going to confession and communion at St Edward's House. Sometime in late 1921 or early 1922 there seems to have been a crisis like that in a critical chapter in *What Not* – 'The Breaking Point'.

Of Gerald's persuasiveness Rose wrote to Rosamond Lehmann three weeks after his death in 1942:

> To me his real work, the one I love, is 'The Holy Tree,' he wrote it in 1922, for me. In it he puts his whole philosophy of love, through the medium of Irish peasants – all the things he would say to me about love and life, all he

felt about me, all we both knew. He wrote at the beginning of my copy the lines from Yeats about the holy tree. It was burnt up with my other books, but he gave it to me again and inscribed it, so at least I have that, and can hear his voice talking to me through it.[12]

'Beloved, gaze in thine own heart,' the first lines of the poem command, 'The holy tree is growing there.' Yeats's 'The Two Trees', from his 1893 volume, *The Rose*, calls up two Blakean visions of the holy tree: the first is benign and beautiful; the second is malign and ugly. The trembling flowers of the first tree represent sexual desire and divine energy; the broken boughs and blackened leaves of the second represent selfhood, morality, and abstract thought. Gerald urged Rose to see the power and the glory of the first vision.

His novel uses the image potently. *The Holy Tree* is centred in the consciousness of an unworldly, unlearned, emotional Irish peasant girl, Ann Logan, who, to aid her family, marries a dull man and too late falls catastrophically in love with a passionate political reformer. Brian Hogan's eloquent response to her feelings overwhelms and transfigures her. For a brief time he makes her feel that their love is not a trouble but a divine gift which will branch out in its beauty, like the holy tree at its loveliest, to shower blessings on all the others in their lives.

Family and priest rage at her, but Ann is moved to choose the vision of joy. In the end, however, troubled by fear of harming Brian, she decides that they must part. Moments later, her husband and Brian are called out to sea to make a lifeboat rescue. Ann believes her husband to be drowned, but the drowned man proves to be Brian. She is left empty-hearted, but, believing her lover's central doctrine, she resolves to teach her child how to love.

The Holy Tree is all quivering feeling, exalting romantic love; it opposes Arthur Gideon's assertion that 'the love of an idea, a principle, a cause, a discovery, a piece of knowledge or beauty, perhaps a country is more valuable and beautiful than the love of lovers'. For Brian Hogan, life and love were synonymous. He had said to Ann, 'Like two dead suns a man and a woman were, wandering about aimless until they found each other.'[13]

The triumph of *The Holy Tree* is its power to place the reader in the mind and heart of a young girl swept away by love. Gerald O'Donovan's success in this imaginative creation is a sign of his own intense and open emotional nature – of the woman in him. Gerald's novel of feminine sensibility argues with Rose's masculine novel of sense. 'Most of the wrong of the world came from thwarted love,' says Brian, pleading with Ann.[14]

Gerald's philosophy of love implied that if he and Rose made a place in their lives for caring for each other, they would be more caring for all others, including his family. Rose's letter to Rosamond Lehmann says that this novel contained 'all we both knew' about life and love. Despite her admiration for logical rigour, she did not until many years later judge the argument of *The Holy Tree* to be self-deceiving.

The subsequent behaviour of Gerald and Rose suggests that they came to an agreement in the light of Gerald's 'philosophy' – believing they could make their love benign and fruitful for themselves and others by being together yet living apart. They met in Rose's literary world where Gerald, as a novelist, had a place; Rose became an ancillary and benevolent figure in O'Donovan family life; the two arranged their private time as lovers with great discretion.

In almost every way this agreement seemed to work for Rose; she was not a back-street wife waiting for the telephone to ring, but a very busy author, a friend to many, and a public figure. As a writer of topical novels, she had to be in the swim. She belonged to the University Women's Club and to the new Bohemian and Socialist 1917 Club where she may have first met her future friends from Bloomsbury. She was free – alone, or with company as she pleased. She went to the theatre; she went to crossword-puzzle parties with the circle formed by Dorothy and Reeve Brooke and Sylvia and Robert Lynd. She lectured amusingly at the London School of Economics on 'What People Want'. She immured herself and wrote.

Her time with Gerald was precious and without question creatively enlivening for her, but she did not depend on him to fill her appointment diary or to take responsibility for her happiness. Although Rose Macaulay was not a declared feminist, she seems to have solved some difficult problems faced by independent women. Her life was a compromise. She had no children, but she hugely enjoyed Gerald's. She paid a daily price for compromising with her principles; on the surface she had always to be nonchalant – in both the dictionary and the root French meaning of the word. But from day to day this arrangement was a workable answer to her wish for 'love and no ties'. She was as free as a man, but beloved as a woman. She was seen by all as a life-enhancer.

Before this time she had loved two men. She had respected and admired George Macaulay and intellectually had thrived on his companionship, but he had hampered her freedom. She had enjoyed going about with Rupert, 'someone to talk things over with', but he had not loved her or been interested in her writing. With both men she had enjoyed mutual laughter. Gerald's love offered her the best of both relationships. Knowing his secret story, she honoured him. Like her father, he felt himself a failure, and failure had always attracted her warmest sympathy. They walked mind-in-mind; he aided her career and assented to her liberty. They shared a scorn for those in the seats of power. They were alike in their chief interests – literature, language, and ethical questions –

but they were unalike in their habits and temperament: he never learned to cycle or drive or play sports, although he was a keen swimmer. He was apt to lose his temper; she was argumentative but not combative. She was less outwardly passionate than he. These differences were unimportant, for they found the same things amusing. As Father Johnson said of her, 'She was never *not* a humorist.'[15]

Rose still had some of the 'fastidiousness' about sex that characterized her adolescent fears; she disliked D. H. Lawrence's novels and rejected detailed physical descriptions of sex in fiction on aesthetic grounds. She continued to argue against Freud's thesis that sex was the chief controlling human impulse, believing the latter to be vanity.

Confronting the sexual aspect of their love, Kitty Grammont of *What Not* observes to Nicky Chester that while she can tolerate a chaste friendship, he cannot. In a rare Macaulayan generalization about women and men, Kitty concludes that they differ on the subject of the most satisfying means of enjoying love:

> And the difference is that for me a half-way house would always be better than nothing while for you it would be worse. Men seem to value being married [having a sexual relationship] more than women do – and friendship, going about together, having each other to talk and play with and all, seems to matter to them so little. Love seems to take different forms with men and women, and to want different ways of expression.[16]

Yet Virginia Woolf was mistaken about her. Rose Macaulay was not 'a Eunuch'. It is improbable that her argument to Father Johnson against sexual abstinence in marriage (as a method of birth control for parents of a large family) did not reflect her own sexual experience: 'To ask them not to live together normally would be asking a frustration (anyhow to the man; women do feel differently about it, I think) which might starve and poison their relations together. That act of love eases intercourse, heals quarrels, fulfils affection; I don't think it should be given up except for some very weighty reason. . . . I can never quite see how birth control is wrong.'[17] By this time she may have understood some of her father's depression and sexual frustration in Varazze when the family grew too large for its means.

One protection for Rose's secret life was her unromantic androgynous image; most who knew Rose saw her as the confirmed spinster who mixed on equal terms with men. This was how Brigid O'Donovan always saw her. She could never believe Rose had been her father's lover, although she said she believed her mother was capable of turning a blind eye had this been true. But Brigid was, for much of the time when Rose and Gerald were seeing each other, away at school. When Rose's private life was revealed after her death, Evelyn Waugh said, with characteristic malice, that he wondered whether Rose's adultery was a hallucination.[18] But Alan Pryce-Jones, who knew her better, said that 'her response to life was far more warm-blooded than might have been supposed by those who knew her only as a delicate spinster'.[19] In any case, her friends could not imagine her as a one of a pair; her independent spirit defied capture.

Again and again in her novels Macaulay describes falling in love as an inevitable calamity. Her character Denham Dobie of *Crewe Train* (1926), the beautiful young woman who likes to live and play like a 12-year-old boy, lets out this *cri de coeur*: 'One was trapped by love, by that blind storming of the senses, by that infinite tenderness, that unreasoned, unreasoning friendship that was love. That was the trap ... that was the snare ... love.'[20] And she goes on, 'Love broke one in the end, locked the fetters on one's limbs.... Love was the great taming emotion, perhaps the only taming emotion. It defeated all other desires in the end. You might struggle and rebel but in the end love got you.'[21] Rose did indeed find love for Gerald irresistible, but if she was less free, she was never truly trapped or tamed.

The world saw Rose's thorniness, her defences against being possessed; Gerald saw her potential for flowering friendship and tenderness. But Cesar Saerchinger, a *New York Evening Post* reporter, interviewing Miss Macaulay in 1929, intuitively saw the whole Rose:

> I have called Rose Macaulay a spinster. The language is unjust, inadequate. She is unmarried but who could venture to say why? Love could not have been absent from so complete a personality. She has true feminine charm; one would even call her 'sweet,' if that did not suggest something maudlin. She has nothing that is mannish. On the other hand, there probably are few men who could withstand the acid test of her satirical judgement. To most men she would be someone rather difficult to live up to.[22]

The life of Rose and Gerald began. For a time Mr O'Donovan was Rose's companion at professional and social events in London. But some of her close friends, among them Dorothy and Reeve Brooke and H. B. Usher of the *Westminster Gazette* and his wife Grace, did not greatly care for him.[23] Perhaps there was a snobbish prejudice against his nationality; some believed he was cynically using Rose's new success and prosperity as aids to his own ambitions. They saw him as an *arriviste*.

Rose did indeed try to help him as she helped many others. She was always generous with gifts, and it is more than probable that she paved the way for the publication of his last two novels with her American publisher, Boni and Liveright, and that she arranged for him to write reviews and to read manuscripts for an American publisher. This employer's identity was kept a secret, even from his children, lest, Brigid O'Donovan said, it 'get out' and the Catholic powers that blocked *Father Ralph*'s publication in the United States should block him again.

Other friends said simply that a relationship with a married man was 'not good enough for her'. But there are often hidden, selfish reasons for such hostility to the outsider. Rose was lovable and entertaining; friends with such a treasure are often jealous of it. These underlying antipathies erected barriers. Gerald attended Naomi Royde-Smith's Thursday evenings, but Royde-Smith was in the end the power that pushed him out of the more intimate parties of this bookish, cliquish social world for good.

By 1921 Rose had come to spend several nights a week away from Hedgerley in a room she rented from Naomi at 44 Prince's Gardens, Naomi's large Kensington home. Naomi took herself seriously as a woman of letters, a literary hostess and patron, and a *femme fatale*. Reactions to her were mixed. Dorothy Brooke, who knew her well, said, 'She was very amusing and attractive, but I didn't like her.' Back in the Rupert Brooke days, Naomi had chosen Rose as a protégée for her drawing power as 'the golden talker', but perhaps also because, unlike herself, Rose did not pretend to beauty. Naomi did, and thought Rose no social threat.

At their salons, however, which were wonderfully successful, Rose was often the centre of attention. More than one guest observed that Naomi did not savour the competition. We are fortunate to be able to see these weekly affairs from three angles of vision, as in a modernist novel: Mary Agnes Hamilton praised them as creative occasions; Storm Jameson said they were attended chiefly by the unadventurous older generation of writers; Virginia Woolf thought them crowded gatherings of mediocrities.

Hamilton described the weekly parties as a generously planned opportunity for literary cubs to meet the leading lions. Elizabeth Bowen was enchanted to find herself in the same room as Edith Sitwell, Walter de la Mare, Aldous Huxley. And benefits ensued for the neophytes. Rose helped Bowen get her first story printed and later recommended her first book for publication. Of Royde-Smith, Hamilton wrote:

Every Thursday evening she was at home, charmingly attired and most attractive to look upon (her dangling crystal earrings gave the note), receiving guests in a long succession of various abodes, to each of which she gave the distinct accent of her own highly individual taste. ... There was excellent coffee; there were chocolates and cigarettes – hard liquor had not yet come into vogue with the intelligentsia; there was conversation. It was enough, more than enough. Over a long series of years, everybody in the literary world, the not yet arrived as well as the established, was to be met with, there, at one time or another.[24]

Storm Jameson says that she found Naomi 'a little formidable with her air of a younger more affable Queen Victoria'. But Rose Macaulay was a contrast. Jameson writes that on her first visit to the salon Rose had been kind to her, and that she felt no fear of her, 'nor of her salty tongue'. (It was Rose Macaulay with whom the young novelist was to remain in touch for twenty years. Rose agreed with Storm that she would rather write than cook, and rather travel than write.) But in 1921, after many Thursday evenings, Jameson judged Naomi's milieu to be 'an urbane backwater', frequented by the rear rather than the avant-garde; she stopped attending. 'The great figures who sometimes glided through were none of them rebels – Arnold Bennett but not D.H. Lawrence, Eddie Marsh, not T. S. Eliot.'[25]

The Woolfs came – probably only once – and even a brief excerpt from Virginia Woolf's diary account (5 June 1921) shows her keen distaste for the atmosphere:

> We went to Miss Royde-Smith's party on Thursday to discuss Ireland. Never did I see a less attractive woman than Naomi. Her face might have been cut out of cardboard by blunt scissors.... She is slightly furred, too; dressed à la 1860.... There she sat in complete command. Here she had her world round her. It was a queer mixture of the intelligent and the respectable.... I detest the mixture of ideas and South Kensington.[26]

Leonard Woolf was to write of his wife, 'Her most obvious fault, as a person and as a writer, was a kind of intellectual snobbery – and she admitted it herself.'[27] Royde-Smith's salon was not the salon of Lady Ottoline Morrell.

Virginia's description of the detested company includes a comment on Rose's general popularity: 'Rose Macaulay chipped in with her witticism all in character, at which the clergyman, Duncan Jones, said, "Oh, Rose!" and everyone laughed loud as if Rose had done the thing they expected.'[28] This description of Rose's role as jester is not meant to be admiring, but the other guests' unanimous amusement explains Naomi's jealousy, a reaction observed by more than one guest.

In 1922 Rose moved into her own flat at St Andrews Mansions near Baker Street. In the mid-Twenties Naomi vented her resentment of Rose's independence in a campaign of leaked confidences about Rose and Gerald which made it embarrassing for them to go about together. The two women's relationship was never to be the same again, although later their differences were patched up, and they still saw each other through the years in the company of mutual friends.

A chief character in Macaulay's *Crewe Train* (1926), which satirizes the vanities of the London literary world, is a wildly imaginative and destructive gossip who bears an identifiable resemblance to Naomi; she irrevocably damages a marriage and a friendship. Perhaps in retaliation, in 1931 Royde-Smith published her historical study *The Double Heart:*

A Study of Julie de Lespinasse. Mlle de Lespinasse, an eighteenth-century Parisian bluestocking, turned her back on her generous patron Mme du Deffand, opened her own rival salon, and wooed away some of the most brilliant members of du Deffand's circle. In an interview Royde-Smith said she drew the subject of her book from memories of her post-war joint salon with Rose Macaulay. Macaulay's frequent fictional pictures of wounded egos in the world of letters are not exaggerated.

The salon displayed Macaulay's party self. In her private life Rose created still another identity. In the O'Donovan family she was from now on an honorary courtesy maiden aunt, a fortnightly guest at Sunday lunch, and in later years a delightful godmother to Gerald's first grand-daughter. Brigid O'Donovan described Rose's position in their lives as 'one of the many people who were very fond of my father, fond of us children, and not so fond of my mother'.[29] One of this company was another novelist whom Rose introduced – the attractive Canadian, Marjorie Grant Cook, who had been a VAD with Rose. Marjorie also enjoyed a lifetime welcome in this domestic scene. Muriel Thomas, Dermod O'Donovan's first wife, describes her: 'She had great style, a wry wit and a good kind heart ... a most attractive and amusing person.'[30] Gerald always drew and held good conversationalists as guests and friends.

In being what Brigid described as 'a faithful family friend', Rose was applying Gerald's philosophy, which included loving all those in the lover's life. According to its principle, she could be with Gerald in his home and enjoy his son and two daughters. She took great pleasure in the children and they in her, although she was more interested in Dermod than in Brigid. But the picture of her sitting down to tea with her lover's wife is not as sympathetic as that of her taking Dermod, Brigid, and Mary to the pantomime. In her last years, looking back on her affair, Rose felt keen remorse about her relationship with Mrs O'Donovan. After Gerald's funeral Rose dropped Beryl completely, although she kept in close touch with the O'Donovan children and grandchildren.

In *The Towers of Trebizond*, written thirty-five years later, Rose looks back at her years of secret love. She has the first-person narrator Laurie confess:

I had come between Vere and his wife for ten years; he had given me his love, mental and physical, and I had taken it; to that extent I was a thief. His wife knew it, but we had never spoken of it; indeed, I barely knew her. We had none of us wanted divorce, because of the children; I liked it better as it was, love and no ties. I suppose I had ruined the wife's life, because she had adored him. Vere always said that he was fonder of her because of me; men are given to saying this. But really she had bored him; if she had not bored him, he would not have fallen in love with me. If I had refused to be his lover he would, no doubt, sooner or later, have found someone else. But I did not refuse, or only for a short time at the beginning, and so we had ten years of it, and each year was better than the one before, love and joy drowning remorse, till in the end it scarcely struggled for life.[31]

Although she described *The Towers of Trebizond* to Rosamond Lehmann as her 'own story', it is a work of fiction. And we can, in this passage, confidently identify at least one artistic variation from the facts – 'I barely knew her'. Perhaps this is true in the deepest sense, but the real situation may have been slightly changed in the novel to make the confessing 'thief' seem less brazen and less culpable. We can, of course, wonder whether there are other departures here. The heroine is younger; the love affair lasts ten rather than twenty-four years. But these last confessional passages of the book move the reader with the ring of truth.

Rose and Gerald are seen to better advantage as escaping lovers, joining each other to travel in Europe as a couple for a week or two, after having departed from England separately and in the company of others. Rose would sometimes embark with Dorothy and Reeve Brooke, Gerald with Maurice Bireley, his former co-subwarden at Tonybee Hall. It would have been like her to enjoy the adventurous trappings of conspiracy and the private world created by travelling incognito *à deux*. Gerald's alleged purpose was to study church architecture, in which he was still interested. Beryl was ill with a thyroid disorder at one time, but could not have been for twenty years too disabled to travel. When the children were young, Beryl and Gerald took them to Normandy or Norfolk during school holidays. But later, Beryl writes of taking sketching trips alone to Ireland where Gerald would not go. She took up volunteer work with council schools and destitute children and helped him in the Second World War in his work with Czech refugees.

When Rose and Gerald went together secretly, they seemed to believe they were injuring no one. In her short story, 'Miss Anstruther's Letters' (1942), Rose's main character recalls her lover's letters, which recorded memories of paradisal journeys together in Italy, Southern France, and Spain:

> He would run over a list of places they had seen together, in the secret stolen travels of twenty years. The balcony where they had dined at the Foix inn, leaning over the green river, eating trout just caught in it. The little wild strawberries at Andorra la Vieja, the mountain pass that ran down to it from Ax, the winding road down into Seo d'Urgel and Spain.[32]

Detail follows detail in a long, ecstatic catalogue: 'the little harbour at Collioure, with its painted boats, morning coffee out of red cups at Villefranche ... truffles in the place at Perigeux ... Lisieux with its crazy-floored inn, huge four poster, and preposterous little saint.'[33] The lover counts over twenty towns and villages they had visited, as though they were gold pieces. And the passage ends, 'Baedekker starred places because we ought to see them, he wrote, and I star them because we saw them together, and those stars light them up forever.'[34] Such passionate hyperbole is the language of *The Holy Tree*.

Postcards and letters Rose sent from these towns still exist, and when Rose's library was burned in the Second World War, she listed the guidebooks which described those remembered trysting places and lamented their loss. In *The Towers of Trebizond* she tells of the 'doped oblivion' in which such happy lovers live: 'We each understood what the other said, and we laughed at one another's jokes, and love was our fortress and our peace, and being together shut out everything else and closed down conscience and the moral sense.'[35]

Rose and Gerald had a permanent island of escape as well – Rose's flat, where they could enjoy each other's company and the laughter and talk that nourished her. (She made clear to her friends and the public – verbally and in published essays – that she did not welcome unannounced visitors.) She liked to talk to Gerald about alternative plans for the ideas, plots, and characters of her books. He was her perfect audience, the lover who was a creative listener. His most important influence, both as her publisher's representative and her dearest friend, was to encourage her to go on writing in the light, ironic style which was bringing her a wide audience.

He was her supporter and adviser, but not her teacher. Rose Macaulay's novels were nothing like those of Gerald O'Donovan. In fact, of his six books she praised only *Father Ralph* and *The Holy Tree*. Although still in the depths of grief after his death, she wrote to Rosamond Lehmann: 'Writing was not his medium, really. His novels were too documentary, and, as he knew, he lacked style. I don't know who wrote this in the Lit Supplement, "a bright style, and full of incident". That is all wrong. They weren't.'[36]

By 1922 Gerald was finished as a novelist. He had used up the raw material of his Irish crusade and his battles with British bureaucracy. Neither the Irish nor the English were interested in attacks on the Irish Catholic Church, and the war was over. No longer at ease with Rose's closest friends and with her sisters, he built up his own literary set and joined Rose's social life only occasionally. Brigid O'Donovan says he spent long hours lying on the sofa, reading a detective story a day, studying the *Cambridge History of Literature*, and amusing himself with the Irish anecdotes of Somerville and Ross. It was he who was excluded from Rose's professional and public social world, not she from his.

But her love affair was not the only reason for Rose Macaulay's burst of creativity and for her success during the Twenties. In her disorderly flat she and Gerald were happy together, but there, as in Varazze, she also enjoyed the necessary solitude for reading and imagining. There day-dreaming could temporarily blot out the world outside. Her rooms were cluttered with manuscripts, pictures, unopened letters, scraps of paper, trays, and teacups, and walled with more than 1,500 books – the couch spilled over with them, the tables held towering piles. Her library comprised chiefly old tomes from the sixteenth, seventeenth, and eighteenth centuries which she read and reread with absorbed delight, from Hakluyt to Addison. Novels, she said, were dispensable – except for Jane Austen and E.M. Forster and perhaps the great Russians. 'I do not put novels in my necessary shelves, with poetry, biography, letters, voyages, history, dictionaries, and essays.'[37] She judged almost all fiction ephemeral and borrowed contemporary novels from the library. (But she did keep her childhood adventure stories on her top shelves.) Her most cherished books were the twelve volumes of the *Oxford English Dictionary* inherited from her father. As the daughter of a don and a lover of words, she added her own marginal annotations to those pencilled in by George Macaulay.

These crowded shelves, and those of the British Museum and the London Library, and party-going, lengthy telephone conversations, newspaper reading, and travel – all provided raw material for her writing. Her greatest interests were in ideas, language, exotic places, and the tragicomic oddness of human behaviour throughout history. It is no surprise that her novels were in large part stylish essays, peopled by amusing talkers with differing views.

Rose was a bookish writer. Although she acknowledges, in a 1957 review entitled 'Sources of Fiction', that all novelists make use of their experience (sometimes 'to purge it out of the system', sometimes to enhance it), she cautions the critic Morton Zabel against depending wholly on a study of writers' lives to understand their works. She advises him not 'to underrate the two factors of creative imagination and the assimilation of literary sources'.[38] Her reading played a major part in her writing.

The contents of her 'necessary shelves' help us understand the form of her fiction: her love of biography attests to her interest in character and temperament; her love of homilies and essays is reflected in the commentary on behaviour and ideas in which she embeds the action of her novels; her pleasure in plays is compatible with her heavy use of dialogue to display a spectrum of opinions; her passion for accounts of voyages is seen in the various quests of her fiction and in her successful travel books; her absorption in history explains her tone – that of the distanced spectator who observes human folly with amusement and compassion, *sub specie aeternitatis*. And her childhood books and the records of exploration always nourished her love of escape.

Most important, her first love – poetry – is at one with her fascination with style. In her essay, 'Writing', in *Personal Pleasures*, she says that for her the charm of writing lies 'in arranging words in patterns, as if they were bricks, or flowers, or lumps of paint'.[39] Her description of this pleasure rises into a long lyrical tribute to words. Her panegyric begins,

> And so we come to words, those precious gems of queer shapes and colours, sharp angles and soft contours, shades of meaning laid one over the other down history, so that for those far back one must delve among the lost and lovely litter that strews the centuries. Such delving has rewards as rich, as stirring to the word-haunted fancy, as the delving into the deeps of human emotion has to the novelist of psychology, or the weaving of intricate plot and counterplot to the story-teller, or the laying down of subtle clues to the detective problemist.[40]

To read this essay is to experience vicariously her swimming in language and diving for the treasures of rare phrases, a pleasure she enjoyed alone, as she had done as a child. She collected her spoils in her small loose-leaf notebooks. But, she laments, 'No one desires ... such loose jetsam. I must write novels.'[41]

In 'the loose jetsam' of her jottings for her last and unfinished book, 'Venice Besieged', we can see her way of building up a novel: lists of images ('wreckage swept to Venice – boat full of lunatics'); a quotation from Jung and a description of Bosch's pictures of Hell from an art book; a catalogue of the ghosts who haunt Venice, from Marco Polo to Henry James; a cynical couplet from Clough's 'The Latest Decalogue' – 'Do not adultery commit, Advantage rarely comes of it'; and a proposed piece of dialogue on escapism: 'Going to bed [making love] is cosy and comforting, you can forget everything else, it wraps you round in forgetting like music and drink, and religion can, too. Religion, music, love, drink – they could wrap you round in dreams, you can hide in them, till everything seems a dream.'[42] Such bits and pieces for the novel-to-be are inserted between the gems of her collection. She wrote her musings while travelling on buses and trains, in libraries, and in the retreat of her flat.

In addition to Gerald's support and the pleasures of her solitary exploratory reading of old books, there was a third profound influence on Macaulay's novels of the Twenties – contemporary history. The first sentence of her critical monograph, *The Writings of E.M. Forster*, sets it out: 'Writers, like other people, are rooted in time and place, embedded in, growing and flowering out of, these conditioning soils, so that you will only with some pains sort their elements, disentangle the individual from the background, and never (I think) quite.'[43] Immersion in the past and dreaming in the present could only temporarily isolate Rose Macaulay from her workaday times.

Her values were of the pre-war world; they were rooted in and flowered out of the nineteenth-century libertarianism and liberalism she had embraced in adolescence. But in the Twenties, as with many of her contemporaries, her ruling conviction was the disquieting belief that applying those values to post-war politics and ethics was increasingly difficult. Dilemmas could be described but not solved. If religious faith could not give answers, the repetitions of history might offer solace and comedy.

Rose Macaulay, like all those in the West, had been shaken since 1914 by the quakes of an unstable world. Intellectually, however, she was quite aware that the nineteenth century, too, had been a time of social change and ideological turmoil. And as a historian she was inclined to say of human experience: '*Plus ça change, plus c'est la même chose.*' But there were significant differences between her own personal pre- and post-war worlds. As a child in Italy she had lived in two insular, stable cultures – the free world of play and the static world of her isolated parents' manners, beliefs, and reading. Her later childhood, adolescence, and young womanhood were spent chiefly in the community of the university – a culture encouraging rational controversy but with its own ancient and fixed laws and customs. Her earliest pre-war novels, although they foreshadowed the ethical conflicts of her adulthood, were written in the midst of that calmer, more insulated life.

But England in the Twenties was not calm. It was a great country undergoing accelerating social change; many forces were at work – experimentation, iconoclasm, social mobility, commercialization, sensationalism, economic upheavals, internationalism, institutional evolution, and scientific and technological discovery. Rose Macaulay saw and reacted to most, but not all, of these changes.

She observed with amusement the fads and trends, the doubt, drift, fecklessness, and changing institutions of the time. She was a fascinated witness, as well as a part of its galvanic energy. She recorded the surface changes, but continued to call attention to the ways in which human folly gave those changes a deeper meaning and linked them to the past. She saw the comedy in life because she saw the littleness of the egotistical actors; she felt, and concealed with humour, the pathos of their futility.

Macaulay was concerned with both contemporary and eternal questions, but her view was necessarily circumscribed. She was a keen observer of a limited section of English society: most of her characters were from the educated upper middle class; those from the lower middle class were seen from the outside, with interest and a certain human sympathy, but without any possibility of empathy. Unlike her sisters, she did not know or seek to know the working class or the poor, and the aristocracy that she knew was intellectual, not hereditary. Quite wisely and modestly, like Jane Austen, she worked to recreate the social world of her experience, although as a political observer she addressed the affairs of all Europe.

However, if Rose Macaulay kept her eye on the surface of things, she did not look at the surface in a superficial way. The intelligence of her observations almost always saves her contemporary comedies from triviality. The new fictional forms created by diving below that surface to imitate consciousness were impossible for her; she was obliged to conceal her strongest feelings, a reticence that was, in any case, natural. She wanted to withdraw her earliest books because they exposed her emotions. In truth, she saw herself less as a novelist than as an amused commentator; she presented her ideas candidly and revealed her inner self – as a writer cannot help but do – only by indirection, by a general confession in the name of all humanity.

Her strengths and weaknesses as a social historian are displayed in an essay she was commissioned to write for the American monthly *Current History* in 1926. Its subject was the change in London since the beginning of the war. The editor introduced her as the author of *Told by an Idiot*, her novel of three English generations.

Virginia Woolf bridled at the news of Macaulay's assignment: 'It is this sort of thing I so distrust in her. Why should she take the field so unnecessarily?'[44] But Macaulay was a university-educated historian with the credentials for such a task. Woolf, herself the daughter of a don, later attempted, with great difficulty, to write a historically documented chronicle of family life like *Told by an Idiot*. She began by calling *The Years* 'an essay-novel', an accurate generic term for much of Macaulay's fiction. After a struggle, Woolf eventually changed its form to encompass what she did best – the imitation of the inner life. Woolf found writing *The Years* according to her initial plan to be a task undertaken against the grain, just as incompatible with her imagination as Rose would have found an attempt to plunge into the confluence of many streams of consciousness as Woolf had done in *To the Lighthouse*.

Macaulay's historical article, 'The New London Since 1914', is not as irreverent in tone as her fiction, but it is sprightly enough to be read for delight as well as for instruction. First she lists the phenomena of change in London's appearance; then through images she brings them to the mind's eye: electric illumination ('ruby wine poured and repoured from bottles eternally full ... a gay spasmodic vision' in bright lights above Piccadilly); commercial vandalism ('Nash's Regent Street, one of the graces of London for over a century, in 1925 stood in ruins'); population growth ('the main street was jammed with jostling crowds like the Thames with boats at Henley').[45]

Her technique is to light on a small, telling detail from which a thesis may be inferred: 'The top hat became, both during and after the war, increasingly rare in public life.' The select, brilliant world of formal, extravagant high society, in which entertainment was private, had been dimmed by the expense of keeping up country houses and diminished by the large, levelling world of public spectacle and popular recreation – the film, the night-club, the revue, the dance-hall, wireless entertainment, and the motoring holiday. She speaks of this change – and of arts and fashions, the young, the press, middle-class morality, divorce, women, politics and religion. She writes effectively and succinctly, always ironically sceptical of the generalization or the easy deduction.

She asserts that the young, those not directly affected by the war, were much as the young had always been and that their elders, as elders had always done, deplored their conduct. She briskly exposes the fallacy of broad statements about 'the modern girl':

> People wrote to the papers about her and said that 'she' (as they called her) was fast, dissipated and selfish, or alternatively, loyal, generous and straight, apparently never thinking it at all strange that all girls of the moment should be of the same disposition whether good or bad, as if their minds and characters depended, like their clothes, on the fashions of the year, as if, as well as saying, 'Girls are slim this year,' you could say, 'Girls are selfish this Spring, or honest.'[46]

She writes that immorality had not so much increased as that hypocrisy had lessened: 'What had once been practised in discreet secrecy was now flaunted.' But she does admit, 'There was more freedom of intercourse between the sexes, in all senses.' On the whole she concludes, as a historian with a sense of centuries of human life, that London had changed more than Londoners.

Although Macaulay discusses all that seems to her most significant, she omits changes that might seem equally important to other observers: as a writer, she naturally speaks of the new in literature, but says nothing of the revolutions in the visual arts and in music. More significant omissions – she has nothing to say about the industrial pollution and mechanization of life that so outraged Lawrence, or the economic displacement caused by new technology, or any of the major scientific or economic changes that affect everyday life. She does not, for example, mention the material changes which improved life for the lower middle class; her view is almost always from her upper-middle-class standpoint. She writes, 'Servants had become poor in quality and quantity,' but does not add that this was because many working-class women had been emancipated by new kinds of employment from ill-paid drudgery in a tyrannical domestic system. Twenty years later, in her brief social history, *Life Among the English* (1942), she sees the Twenties as a party: 'The twenties were, as decades go, a good decade; gay, decorative, extravagant, cultured.' But she does not add that the party she describes was for the privileged few.[47]

However, her novels bring so much of upper-middle-class daily experience to life and present so many of its dilemmas that we cannot reasonably fault her for presenting a limited view. And if she did not provide answers to the hard questions of the time, she provided examples of those who found ways to live, like Kitty Grammont, with *élan*, courage, intelligence, and humour in the midst of modern confusion.

In part, her Twenties' novels were popular because her nostalgia for dying liberalism and her derision of the stupidity of political leaders, the sensationalism of the lowbrow press, and the destructiveness of commercialism reflected the views of many. And her books were certainly popular in both England and America because of their wry humour, their moments of flippancy and even cynicism, their amusing surprises, their puncturing of pomposity, their lack of self-righteousness, and their sense of style. (Their 'modern' tone and content were not popular with some of the older generation – Uncle Edward, Uncle Willy, and Uncle Kenneth. Uncle Edward found *Dangerous Ages* and *Orphan Island* 'nasty'. We do not have comments from Uncle Regi but Rose herself remained a favourite with him.)

As Macaulay acknowledged, all dialogues between ideas lack a strong narrative structure. 'Heaven, never, I think, destined me for a story-teller, and stories are the form of literary activity which give me the least pleasure. I am one of the world's least efficient novelists; I cannot invent good stories, or care what becomes of the people of whom I write.'[48]

It is surprising that her childhood passion for strong plots of adventure did not make more of a mark on her creative imagination, although their inevitable victories were admittedly at odds with the uncertain times. Yet vivid details of secret passages and lost mermaids and desert island life suddenly surface in her fiction as fantasy. Today these digressions would be called 'magical realism' – although the ancient literature she loved is crowded with such sudden symbolic visions.

However, she did find two ways to give unity to her most successful novels. As always, the omniscient author's voice is heard throughout. And she used conventional fictional formulas to satisfy the reader's expectations.

But more important, the topical subjects and ironic tone of Rose Macaulay's fiction suited the taste of the times. *Potterism* had aimed at the right target at the right moment. During the war the reading public had increased. There had been a great hunger for news and yet a scarcity of it because of censorship. What facts were available were exaggerated, mixed with propaganda, printed in giant headlines, and hawked in the streets. The public was ever more avid for sensation and information, yet ever more sceptical of the press's reliability and ever more suspicious of its power and wealth. The educated reader judged journalism to be a vulgarizing force.

And Macaulay went on to choose other subjects which were appropriate for the opinions and interests of the Twenties. Although she did not want to be a woman's writer, she liked to write for *Time and Tide*, she told its politically conservative editor Lady Rhondda, because its feminist position was moderate, never militant. There is no question, however, that her next novel, *Dangerous Ages* (1921), commanded attention because it presented central problems in women's lives. Rose Macaulay's story of four generations of women went into four impressions in four months and won the prestigious *Femina-Vie Heureuse* Prize. (It had been established in 1904 by the reviews *Femina* and *Vie Heureuse* 'to encourage literature and strengthen the bonds between women of letters' and was awarded annually for a novel.)

The germ of Macaulay's idea derived from a Danish novel, *The Dangerous Age* by Karen Michaelis, translated into German, French, and English, and widely read in 1912. It is the fictional journal and correspondence of a menopausal woman neurotically destroyed at 43 by the horror of growing old.

Doubtful of the novel's premise that a woman losing sexual attraction will become a little mad, and both curious and sceptical about psychiatric treatment, Rose disguised herself as an older woman and visited a psychiatrist. Her childhood attempts at playing Sherlock Holmes, however, were too amateurish to qualify her as a professional spy. The doctor saw through her ruse at once, and angrily sent her away. But she did not need his counsel to form her opinion. The epigraph of *Dangerous Ages* both expands and qualifies Michaelis's assumptions about the effects of ageing: 'We may say that all ages are dangerous to all people, in this dangerous life we live.'[49]

The characters of each generation of *Dangerous Ages* have different problems – as much related to their temperaments as to their times and their ages. The grandmother at 84 is serenely resigned to old age; the neurotic mother, Mrs Hilary (earlier discussed as drawn from Grace Macaulay), is wretched and aimless because her children have grown up; two of her daughters in mid-life – Nan, a writer, and Neville, the mother of two, who wants to return to medical school – must make compromises with their desires and ambitions; only young Gerda at 20 confidently reaches out and takes what she wants.

The final chapter's title is 'The Key', and the novel's last word is from the unmarried Pamela Hilary, a social worker, 'going about her work, keen, debonair, detached, ironic, cool and quiet, responsive to life and yet a thought disdainful of it, lightly holding and easily renouncing, the world's lover not yet its servant, her foot at times carelessly on its neck to prove her power over it.'[50] Pamela says, 'Age has very little to do with anything that matters. The difference between one age and another is, as a rule, enormously exaggerated.'[51] Although this indifference is recommended, the novel won its readership, as the reviews make clear, not because of its detachment, but because of the sympathy which lies beneath its cool tone. The narrator implies what she says explicitly in *Told by an Idiot*: 'The heart alone knows its own turbulence.'[52]

Her next novel was a shallow *jeu d'esprit*, a parody of a detective novel. *Mystery at Geneva* (1922) is based on a trick: the male detective hero proves to be a woman, an intended deception of the reader in which the author takes delight. The novel is also a repetitive satire on the hostile ethnocentricity of a large cast of League of Nations delegates who are national stereotypes. Rose had attended a League meeting both as an official observer and as a journalist and was supportive of it, but she could not resist this easy mockery of passionate, blinkered jingoism.

Her imp of the perverse was at work; the joke got out of hand. Seeing it as a possible canard against the League, she firmly denied her satirical intent in a prefatory note. She says specifically that the novel is not 'a skit on actual conditions at Geneva, of which indeed I know little.'[53] But she could be marvellously disingenuous. A friend says that upon being stopped by a policeman as she was deliberately driving in the wrong direction down a one-way street, she pretended to be a timid, confused old lady. The officer gallantly gave her directions.

The novel is ephemeral and self-indulgent. But the frivolous gambit of *Mystery at Geneva* was succeeded by two of her best novels: *Told by an Idiot* (1923) and *Orphan Island* (1924). The first is a sparkling *tour de force* – a family chronicle covering the years 1879 to 1923, peopled with members of the delightful Garden family, some of whom enact aspects of the author's personality. Fads, religious beliefs, books, politics, customs, professions, fashions, art, ideas of the Victorian, *fin de siècle*, Edwardian, and Georgian periods flash by the reader in short dramatized essays, illuminated by the vivacity of the characters and the epigrammatic comments of the narrator.

The six Garden children are both eternal types and identifiable individuals; Rose's selection of the trivial details of their milieux and their experience creates a solid social history. What might have been fragmentary is a colourful whole. Rome Garden, 'the elegant diner-out', so much like Rose in her public role, unifies the pattern at the close: 'The brief pageant, the tiny, squalid story of human life upon this earth, has been lit, among the squalor and the greed, by amazing flashes of intelligence, of valour, of beauty, of sacrifice, of love. A silly story if you will, but a somewhat remarkable one.'[54]

This sprightly commentator is a delight, but in Rome's meditation on her love for a married man, we hear Rose's second voice, musing on her private trouble: 'Harder and harder, and cooler and more cynical she would grow, as she walked the world alone, leaving love behind. Was that the choice? Did one either do the decent difficult thing, and wither to bitterness in doing it, or take the easy road, the road of joy and fulfillment, and be thereby enriched and fulfilled?'[55] We never know

Rome's answer, for her lover is killed as he proposes to her on a bench in Bloomsbury Square.

Rose's choice of enrichment and fulfilment as against 'the decent difficult thing' had been a hard one. Her next novel, *Orphan Island* of 1924, understandably begins a series of escape novels. This one is related to both *The Swiss Family Robinson* and *The Admirable Crichton*, and also, as Alan Pryce-Jones says, to Mallock's *New Republic* and Butler's *News from Nowhere*. At the same time, it is, like her two previous novels, a satire that mingles present and past.

Rose recalled that her earliest childhood stories, written in Varazze and Oxford, almost always began: '"Man the lifeboats," shouted the captain, "because we have struck a reef and are sinking fast."'[56] She seizes upon this rousing opening scene for *Orphan Island*. But at this point reality stops and fantasy begins. In 1854 a shipwreck brings to a Pacific island the seeds of a whole society: Miss Charlotte Smith, the daughter of an English Evangelical country clergyman; the Irish Catholic atheist Dr O'Malley; the Scottish Presbyterian nurse Jean; and forty orphans, all on their way to an orphanage in San Francisco. Their small world becomes a microcosm of Victorian Britain, wonderfully and comically distorted.

Seventy years after the shipwreck Mr Thinkwell, a Cambridge lecturer in sociology, and his two children set out to find and rescue the castaways. The search begins with a map bequeathed by a Thinkwell ancestor who pre-empted the only lifeboat, abandoned the orphans, and escaped.

The Thinkwells discover that in the decades since the orphans first came to shore, this small Anglocentric colony has developed an unjust class system, rigid social customs, a wrangling Parliament, religious differences – indeed, all the comforts of home – under the stern matriarchal rule of the humourless Miss Smith, a woman sufficiently like Queen Victoria to earn protests from humourless readers. It was as though injustice and intolerance were the original sins of all governments.

The jokes come thick and fast. Through Miss Smith's guile, the rescuers are in the end robbed of their means of returning to England. The Thinkwell party will attempt to reform this world, but eventually become assimilated into it. And the happy island-lover Rosamond Thinkwell can spend the rest of her life eating breadfruit and combing the perfect beaches. Macaulay has succeeded in combining almost all of her pet themes and characters in a social parable and a child's adventure story. Alan Pryce-Jones writes, 'Perhaps the chief reason for reading *Orphan Island* is that it gives so many clues to the character of its creator.' And he adds, 'If only you had known her!'[57]

All seven of the Twenties' novels are works with much in common, and much of the quintessential Rose Macaulay is in them. But there was a break in their continuity. No Rose Macaulay novel appeared in 1925, a year that was marked by the pain of loss.

Grace Conybeare Macaulay had a serious heart attack on 2 April 1924 and was not strong during the following year. In late April 1925 Rose was in Europe with Gerald; the only address she left the family was a European poste restante. On 2 May, Uncle Edward writes, 'Alarm about Grace'. Margaret and Jean had already begun to try to reach Rose, but she did not call for her post. By the time she finally received the news of her mother's critical condition and rushed back to Hedgerley, Grace was unconscious and remained so. She died on 5 May in her sixty-ninth year.

Rose was pierced with guilt. Jean said 'I believe Rose was rather conscience-stricken about Mother's death.... she and mother didn't understand each other very well, in spite of mother's devoted love for her'. Rose's pain was deep and long-lasting. Twenty years later, when Forster's mother died in her eighties, Rose Macaulay wrote a letter of condolence and confession:

> One thing, one touch of bitterness that her going can't have for you is what one so often feels – to wish that one had been different and nicer oneself, which does so enbarb the pain of loss.... My own mother (whom I loved) died in her 60's and I could envy you; only that she would have been too much of an invalid for one to want her to live so long. But oh dear – what a wrench of one's whole life and being it is when people one loves die – all one has shared and had together now halved or gone.[58]

The Macaulay family home was empty. At 44 Rose Macaulay was left with the freedom she had longed for – and with remorse.

I I

New Friends

Miss Macaulay concealed her private sorrow and painful conscience and began to lead an even more crowded life. By her midforties her self-created London image was well known. In 1972, looking back at Rose in her heyday, Storm Jameson wrote, 'Anatole France might have cast her for one of his rebellious angels, detached, searching, amused. She looked like one, too, with her short, curled hair, quick movements and sexless elegance.'[1] Elegance is preferable to chic; she was not modish but timeless.

She had made her mark. Now she was active in at least six demanding roles. In the years before the Second World War she was a public figure in literature and in debates on international politics; a favourite among diverse groups of literary friends; a constant supporter of and correspondent with Margaret, Jean, and Will; a prolific novelist; a hardworking critic, reviewer, and journalist; and a 'beloved companion' to Gerald O'Donovan.

Even a selective list of her encounters, engagements, and tasks is dizzying: she attended (and eavesdropped at) the Royal Garden party; was the welcomed, entertaining guest of hosts as unalike as Dean Inge and Ivy Compton-Burnett; was honoured at a luncheon party for the descendants of famous writers; and appeared at cocktail parties 'more spirited on orange juice than others on champagne', as another partygoer observed.[2] Between 1926 and 1941 she published seven novels, a monograph on language, a critical study and a biography, an anthology, and a volume of essays. She wrote ephemeral newspaper articles on subjects such as 'Why I Dislike Cats, Clothes, and Visits' and 'Have We Done with Hell Fire?'; she wrote a play about Milton for the BBC (waging a principled battle royal with its producer over cuts in the script right up to the moment of its transmission); she wrote an unpublished, unproduced farce, 'Bunkum', and regular columns in *Time and Tide* and in the

Spectator. She took a jolting and adventurous trip in an old Essex down the American West Coast with Margaret and Will. She gave speeches for the Peace Pledge Union. And she continued to travel secretly with Gerald and tramped ecstatically around southern France with him one hot July. 'We never knew her tired,' wrote John Betjeman.[3]

Like all those who choose to live alone and to enjoy the company of differing groups and incompatible friends, she had to be sensitive to the unique character of each relationship. Rose was known, as Josephine Sackville-West said, for 'the way she had of meeting people on their own ground, without ever becoming less than herself'.[4]

That is not to say she was always the same. To strangers who presumed intimacy or made foolish or pompous remarks, she could be chilling. (E.M.Forster thought her 'a bit arrogant' in the Twenties, but as time passed he grew increasingly fond of her.) To her close friends she was faithfully committed. To those in need she was generous. (Jean said her beneficiaries often let her down.) As a political advocate she was her usual divided and sceptical self; to those with whom she debated, she was a keen but sometimes maddeningly elusive opponent. To her siblings she was once more the Varazze hobbledehoy Rosie. Jean said that after Rose's death she had burned many of her sister's 'indiscreet' letters – 'the really dangerous ones' (a regrettable loss). To dour Jean the 'danger' of their survival lay in their spontaneous humour and their jokes about the historical failures of the Church; she thought that in her correspondence to her younger sister Rose had probably shown 'a more frivolous side to her nature than to other people'.[5] In the life of her faithful allegiance to Gerald she was a rare, private person whom we can only imagine.

To be so many-sided and yet to maintain integrity takes emotional and intellectual self-knowledge as well as a mingling of candour and reticence. She was never hypocritical, but she was occasionally duplicitous, being both talkative and secretive. Like all who live a double life, she assumed that most others around her also had hidden lives. One verse of the poem she wrote as an epigraph for *Staying with Relations* (1930) is an image of human elusiveness:

> Shifting as mist, men's secret selves
>   Slip like water and drift like waves,
> Flow shadow-wise, and peer like elves
>   Mocking and strange, from the deep caves.[6]

But because she had chosen to conceal her private emotional life, she was all the more scrupulous about the honesty of the intellectual self she chose to display – the enemy of humbug, the tough self-critic. When she was once more urged to write a love story, this time by her American publisher Horace Liveright – on the grounds that she was 'a great writer' and that all great writers must deal with the greatest subject in the world – she responded, 'I have no ambition to be a great writer. My touch is for trivial topicalities.'[7] She had a passionate admiration for the first-rate major writer, and rightly she did not rank herself in that class. Yet she was a first-rate minor writer; her art required a rare ironic intelligence. High comedy is not without high seriousness.

Despite her success in the position she defined for herself, and despite all the pleasure she gave and took in her active life, as an educated woman she began to feel a certain élitist embarrassment about her general popularity. Her agents Curtis Brown brought well-paid journalistic assignments her way. She refused those which she thought silly, such as articles focusing on 'Woman' as a class, but she depended on writing for her livelihood. Her growing ambition, however, was to write chiefly about matters in which she was interested as a woman of letters, even if this interfered with such an obligation as her ten-year contract with Collins for an annual profitable novel.

The popular novelist Daisy Simpson, Macaulay's creation in the novel *Keeping Up Appearances* (1928), complains, 'Why would they not let her write about inhuman things, about books, about religions, about places, about the world at large, about things of which intelligent persons had heard.'[8] But Daisy also timidly defends her novels. They are not, like Macaulay's, based on ideas, but two of their attributes fit Macaulay's self-deprecating sense of her own work: 'When Daisy turned the pages of her advance copies it seemed to her that they were, these pages, no worse than those that occurred in most novels. But then, of course, this was not to say much. They were not ill-written ... and here and there, Daisy thought, there was humour.... she was surely not on the lowest level?'[9]

At the height of this period of popularity and prosperity, Rose Macaulay changed her direction as a writer; she limited the number of journalistic assignments she was accepting and satisfied her longing to write of what most interested her, although doing so reduced her income considerably. The publication of two characteristically light-hearted and successful novels, in 1926 and 1928, and her formulaic third one in 1930 was followed by a happy five years of scholarly research and creativity which resulted in one of her finest fictions, *They Were Defeated* (1932). This historical novel was flanked and complemented by *Some Religious Elements in English Literature* (1931) and a brief controversial critical biography, *Milton* (1934). In creating both her anthology *The Minor Pleasures of Life* and her essays *Personal Pleasures* for Victor Gollancz in 1934 and 1935, and in publishing *The Writings of E. M. Forster* (1938), she continued to satisfy her desire to write about things 'about which intelligent people have heard'. Her journalism rose to the level of critical and social commentary. Mark Bonham Carter says she was always far more concerned about what London critics said of her writing than about sales figures.

A strong case can be made that this shift in 1930 towards a more intellectual level of creativity was influenced by her self-conscious entrance in 1921 into the hypercritical atmosphere of Bloomsbury. But it can also be argued that the best of her topical satires up to this point do not lack intellectual distinction. None of her novels could adequately be described by Leonard Woolf's definition of a best-seller: 'Most contemporary best-sellers are written by second-class writers whose psychological brew contains a touch of naïvety, a touch of sentimentality, the story-telling gift, and a mysterious sympathy with the daydreams of ordinary people.'[10] Rather, hers were what Q.D. Leavis described as the upper-middlebrow bestsellers to be found 'on the shelves of dons, the superior kind of schoolmaster (the other sort has sets of Kipling, Ian Hay, P. G. Wodehouse, and Masefield's poems), and in the average well-to-do home.'[11]

Less anxiously than the popular novelist Daisy Simpson of *Keeping Up Appearances*, Rose Macaulay nevertheless fretted about the opinion of highbrows. Identifying them was a literary-critical parlour game of the day and the name of Virginia Woolf led all the rest. (It was a journalistic tag neither Woolf nor Macaulay approved of.) But in a 1941 posthumous tribute to Virginia Woolf in the *Spectator*, Macaulay defines the term in relation to her subject – one who was 'cultured, scholarly, fastidious and fine in mind'.[12] Such a phrase also fitted Rose Macaulay's own background, intellect, education, and temperament. And inevitably the world of Bloomsbury attracted her.

Although Macaulay knew nothing about painting or music and was not a francophile, was interested in religion and not interested in the structural aesthetics of the novel, she still had much in common with this group of individualists: her anti-authoritarianism, liberalism, and libertarianism, her hatred of cruelty, her respect for reason. The word 'civilization' meant to Macaulay what it meant to Bloomsbury. And her part in the civilized world, Rose said during an evening's conversation at the Woolfs', was 'to stick up for common sense'. Virginia responded by defining Rose's role as 'being Cambridge'.[13] In that aspect of her identity she is like the straightforward Forster or the ruthlessly honest Leonard Woolf. (Yet this university identity was another division from Virginia Woolf. In *A Room of One's Own* Virginia Woolf was to make much of the injustice of the privations of women at Oxbridge. But Rose Macaulay, born a year before Woolf and from the same background, had a good university education – proving that for a woman of her generation to enjoy such an opportunity was not impossible.)

Yet despite her overall intellectual sympathies with Bloomsbury, Miss Macaulay's behaviour as a guest there was a notable exception to her usual style of meeting people comfortably on their own ground. If Macaulay was formidable to others, Woolf was formidable to Macaulay. She was so ill at ease in her first meetings with Woolf that Virginia described her as 'humble'. ('You could not be yourself, quite yourself, with anyone who mattered to you,' thinks Rose's character Daisy Simpson.)[14]

Virginia Woolf writes an ambivalent account of one of the first meetings that began the complex twenty-year friendship which was to become so important to Macaulay. On 18 February 1921 Rose made her first appearance as the Woolfs' dinner guest:

> Rose Macaulay dined here last week – something like a lean sheep-dog in appearance – harum-scarum-humble – too much of a professional, yet just on the intellectual side of the border. Might be religious though; mystical perhaps. Not at all dominating or impressive; I daresay she observes more than one thinks for. Clear, pale, mystical eyes. A kind of faded beauty; oh badly dressed. I don't suppose we shall ever meet for she lives with Royde-Smith, & somehow won't come to grips with us.[15]

'Come to grips with us' suggests that, despite Virginia's suspicion that Rose Macaulay was tainted with commercialism, the Hogarth Press may from the first have considered wooing her as a writer. The supposition that they would not meet proved wrong; after Rose moved away from Naomi she did indeed go more than once to Tavistock Square.

Woolf's diary entries describing their first meeting and an evening of party conversation in 1926 show Macaulay, in the presence of Bloomsberries, uncharacteristically self-conscious and uncharacteristically talking about herself. Rose did introduce self-centered topics which offended Virginia – her literary social life and negative reviews of her books. Virginia, annoyed by Rose's 'chittery-chattery' conversation during this 1926 visit, says perceptively, 'But this was partly nerves, I think; and she felt us alien & observant doubtless.'[16] Leonard Woolf's description of T. S. Eliot's first visits to the Woolfs' home in Richmond draws the same scene – the uneasy outsider among the intellectual aristocrats, compulsively behaving in just such a manner as to cause the company's laughter after his departure. (Virginia writes to Roger Fry, mocking Eliot: 'Poor Tom . . . is behaving more like an old maid who has been kissed by the butler than ever'.)[17] Leonard quotes Eliot as saying after a visit to Lady Ottoline Morrell's Garsington: 'And I behaved like a priggish pompous little ass.'[18]

A friendship developed – on Rose's side totally admiring, but a touch defensive. There were affinities. As Virginia Woolf knew, she and Macaulay were both descended from the same intellectual aristocracy. 'After all she had no humbug about her; is exactly on a par as conventions go.'[19] And to Vita, 'What I say about writers is that they are the salt of the earth.... With both of these people, Rose and George [Moore] one can tell the truth – a great advantage.'[20] Virginia, too, wrote Leonard, 'had a streak of the common-sense, down-to-earth, granitic quality of mind and soul characteristic in many generations of her father's family.'[21] But, in the end, candour did not prove to be the bond which underlay their slowly developing friendship.

Rose Macaulay (sometimes with Elizabeth Bowen) continues to appear as a dinner or weekend guest in Woolf's diaries and letters from the time of their first meeting until Virginia's death in 1941. The Woolfs were not likely to invite bores out of kindness. (They did not entertain Leonard's mother and sisters.) And the Hogarth Press was to commission three non-fiction books by Rose Macaulay. Leonard Woolf was a stern, impartial critic – he courageously rejected one of Vita Sackville-West's novels. And although Virginia Woolf wrote, 'No creative writer can swallow another contemporary,' she maintained some interest in Rose Macaulay's fiction over the years.[22] In a July 1940 diary entry she notes that she is reading Rose's Spanish Civil War novel, *And No Man's Wit* (1938).

But for snobbish reasons and sometimes for comic effect, Woolf's letters and diaries contain far more disobliging remarks than sympathetic comments about Rose Macaulay. She often wrote of her as 'Old Rose', although Rose was only a year older than she. Most who knew Rose characterized her as ageless.

In Woolf's published correspondence and diaries Rose is most frequently described with a dash of teasing mischief. To young Quentin Bell his aunt writes that Rose looks like 'a mummified cat'.[23] (Animal images for humans are a Woolf trademark, of course. She had been 'Goat' as a child; she called Leonard 'Mongoose'.) But she also calls Rose 'a spindle-shanked withered virgin'.[24] Yet, in one of her characteristic balancing reversals, she writes: 'Rose showed up rather well in argument.... In some lights she has the beautiful eyes of all us distinguished women writers; the refinement; the clearness of cut; the patience & humbleness. It is her voice and manner that make me edgy.'[25]

Virginia held some contempt for Macaulay's mixing with what she called 'the literary riff-raff' of South Kensington and for her practice of writing reviews and newspaper articles. Rose Macaulay lived by her pen at that time, achieving a female independence she should, on principle, have admired. But, of course, Leonard was an editor and both Woolfs wrote reviews. Leonard's careful charting of Virginia's earnings from 1919 to 1924 shows that although her work steadily gained a wider reading public, the higher percentage of her income in that early period of her writing was from literary journalism, not from those first novels which have since become classics.

Both Woolfs, however, had a low opinion of the journalists who spent time in Soho restaurants and pubs, eating, drinking, and talking what

Virginia Woolf called 'dingy literary shop'. The Woolfs called this scene 'the underworld', and they believed that Rose Macaulay sometimes lunched in Grub Street. Virginia Woolf identified her fellow guests at a formal dinner party which Rose gave in a restaurant as – '10 second rate writers in second rate dress clothes, Lynds, Goulds, O'Donovan; no, I won't in any spasm of hypocritical vanity include Wolves.'[26]

We can wonder whether Woolf may have used her descriptions of Rose to ameliorate the honest, unflattering views she sometimes had of herself. ('I am not so nice as I was, but I am nicer than Rose Macaulay.')[27] She criticized Rose's dress; she was always self-conscious about her own choices of clothing. She repeatedly damned Macaulay for sensitivity about reviews, although she herself suffered from the same skinless vulnerability. Virginia wrote her novels in a state of deep concentration, yet of Rose she said, 'How she grinds.'[28] Woolf withdrew from a sexual life with Leonard, but she said Rose 'was devoid of private parts'. Woolf called Macaulay 'spiteful'. But she added, 'I think I shall be like that and I thought her awful.'[29] In 1934 she called Rose 'a ravaged sensitive old hack', but added, '– as I should be no doubt, save for L.'[30] (Perhaps at that moment she was remembering both Leonard's emotional support and the freedom she so prized as co-owner of the Hogarth Press: 'I am the only woman in England free to write what I like'.)[31]

However, there are other explanations for Woolf's caricaturing than this apparent tendency to accuse Macaulay of exaggerated manifestations of what Woolf saw as her own flaws. Although today it seems absurd to discuss the two as writers on a par, Leonard Woolf makes clear their relative place in the public eye at the time they met: 'In publishing a book by Virginia Woolf in 1923, you were publishing a book which the vast majority of people, including booksellers and the literary "establishment", condemned as unintelligible or absurd.'[32] Rose Macaulay was certainly among the admiring minority and said so privately and publicly, but she herself was the darling of those booksellers who were baffled by *Jacob's Room. Dangerous Ages* eventually went into seven impressions. During the early years of their friendship Macaulay's talent was recognized; Woolf's genius was not.

Understandably, after an evening spent in Rose's company, Virginia Woolf scoffed at the public attention paid to 'our leading lady novelists'. She disapproved of such activities as Rose's attending the second Assembly of the League of Nations as a reporter for the *Daily Chronicle* and responding to invitations to speak at public meetings. Yet she candidly admits: 'I am not quite one of them. I see my own position a great deal lowered and diminished & this is part of the value of seeing new people.'[33]

What was probably more vexing to Woolf was Rose's great admiration for E.M. Forster, which she had early put in print. When the Hogarth

Press published Rose Macaulay's *The Writings of E. M. Forster* in 1938, Woolf wrote in her diary [March 1938] 'Re Morgan: he likes, I think, and very naturally, the praise which now comes from the young. And do I grudge it that *he* should be the best living novelist? He handed me a cutting, about Rose's book, in which he is thus saluted. And so, jealous as I am, rather mean always about contemporaries, I got my dejection, to run into the dirty drop.'[34]

What might have been most irksome to Woolf, however, was that Leonard Woolf, Vita Sackville-West, Harold Nicolson, and Morgan Forster were all fond of Rose. Vita had known her since the days when they worked together in the Ministry of War. The friendship lasted long after Virginia's suicide. Rose spent Christmas at Sissinghurst in 1950 and, uncharacteristically, her hosts were sorry to see their house-guest depart. Harold Nicolson wrote of Rose after her death, 'In comparison with her, other witty people appeared conceited, snobbish, or harsh.'[35] Such unalloyed admiration could not have pleased Virginia. Elizabeth Bowen said of Woolf, 'And, of course she was a jealous person, I think.... I think that was a side of her that one had to watch. Sometimes her judgements were queered, I think. I was reminded sometimes of "The Lord thy God is a jealous God; thou shalt have none other God but me." '[36] In one entry about Rose, Woolf accuses, then confesses candidly: 'She is jealous of me; anxious to compare us; but I may imagine it & it shows my own jealousy no doubt, as suspicions always do. One couldn't know them if one hadn't got them.'[37]

But despite Virginia's *ad feminam* attacks, in 1926 the Woolfs published a 45-page monograph in the second series of the Hogarth Essays. It was *Catchwords and Claptrap* by Rose Macaulay. And it began disarmingly, 'These discursive and random comments are the indulgence of a private taste, which finds in language as used one of the most amusing subjects for meditation and speculation.'[38] Miss Macaulay is sweetly reasonable, but she is in deadly earnest. She goes on to attack the imprecise use of words and continues more vigorously to cite and castigate the cant, false rhetoric, 'haloed' phrases, and 'facile and inaccurate symbolism' which corrupt and cloud thought, consequently corrupting politics and the press. Her constant use of the Oxford English Dictionary ensured that her own language was inevitably precise.

Although, like Virginia Woolf, Rose loved poetry, her essay's subject is not the emotional power of connotative language, but the importance of using language according to its exact denotative meaning. (Her essay echoes G. E. Moore's 'What exactly do you mean?') She writes, 'Most of the better writers of verse and prose, in all countries, seek more or less after precision, and have gained in truth what they have perhaps lost in loveliness.'[39] By Woolf's standards, this essay was another 'donnish' piece of writing and once more placed Macaulay on the male side of the intellectual spectrum. (Woolf was not in perfect sympathy with the cool precision of Cambridge.)

Rationality, then, was not the basis of the friendship which grew between Rose Macaulay and Virginia Woolf. They shared a common trait in their love of imaginative escape and irreverent humour. Although of far lower wattage than Virginia Woolf's power of fantasy, Rose Macaulay's imagination could suddenly cast a wild light on the quotidian world; that light was essential to her satire. Although in her scholarship she was rigorous, in conversation she could, writes Raymond Mortimer, 'force merry moans from her friends by the extravagance of her assertions'.[40] This was not a side of her mind that she at first wished to display to the male company of Bloomsbury.

The talent for fantasy and imaginative exaggeration and the interest in gender identity may have been the most important links between Macaulay and Woolf. Rose Macaulay's few surviving letters to Virginia Woolf suggest that a writers' friendship – with considerable warmth on Rose's side – could exist side by side with Virginia's flare-ups of irritation at 'Old Rose'. In 1928 Macaulay wrote enthusiastically to its author about *Orlando*, which she had just reviewed; its imaginative leaping and soaring and its theme of androgyny entranced her. She began her admiring letter, 'Dear Mrs Woolf'. But in 1940 she was writing more fondly ('Dear Virginia') about a proposed imaginary biography of her own which she began working on the following year:

> How I wish I could see you! It's one of the sad things about the war, seeing people has become so much more difficult, at the same time more important. I like it so. . . . I'm glad you're getting on with Coleridge. I would like to talk about him sometime, as I have long had in mind a novel about a girl who would be his descendant (great great grandchild, the fruit of mild and rural sin) and would take after him – I suppose she would be a very odd girl, wouldn't she – opium, metaphysics, flow of talk, cadging on friends, even poetry, but it needn't be as good as his.[41]

Rose's reasons for her buried thesis that a woman poet would probably not equal a male poet might have provoked a lively discussion; Rose was eager to discuss her playful plan with the author of *Orlando*. And her last letter to Monks House was an effort to fix a date in response to an invitation for a weekend visit. Rose closed 'With love', a phrase she did not use lightly; she knew that Virginia wanted always to be loved. In 1954, looking back, she wrote in a letter, 'She had so much fun, and humour, and a kind of genial friendliness, though also much malicious comment (discreetly *not* published).'[42] The absence of their full correspondence is a lamentable black hole. (Did Woolf ever read *They Were Defeated*, a work she may have influenced?) The tone of Rose's letter of condolence to Leonard after Virginia's suicide is one of horror: 'She is the one person who *should* not have died, who could not be spared. No one like her ever was nor could be.'[43]

Rose Macaulay's affection for Virginia Woolf was nourished by an understanding of her own function as a scapegoat in Virginia's life. In her elegiac tribute, 'Virginia Woolf' in the *Spectator*, she writes, 'For it amused her to embellish, fantasticate and ironise her friends, as she embellished, fantasticated and ironised all she wrote of.'[44] And in her more developed *Encounter* eulogy, Rose Macaulay, 'the golden talker', needed an extended metaphor to do full justice to the dazzlement of 'the flashing, many-faceted stream' of Virginia Woolf's conversation as she mocked her visitors by assuming the pose of the recluse, eager to hear 'their fine stories of the world.'

> To tell her anything was like launching a ship on the shifting waters of a river, which flashed back a hundred reflections, enlarging, beautifying, animating, rippling about the keel, filling the sails, bobbing the craft up and down on dancing waves, enlarging the small trip into some fantastic Odyssean voyage among islands of exotic flowers and amusing beasts and men.[45]

Turning one of the themes of *Potterism* into *Catchwords and Claptrap*, an essay to be published with the Bloomsbury imprimatur – a Vanessa Bell cover – must have given Rose Macaulay pleasure in 1926. Bloomsbury friends, however hypercritical – of themselves as well as of others – offered more heady stimulation than Naomi Royde-Smith's 'urbane backwater'. This commission for the Hogarth Press was not the sole cause for the new direction Rose Macaulay was to take in 1930, but the monograph's publication coincided with an inward turning point for her and was prophetic of the new phase of her writing which was to begin four years later.

Both Rose Macaulay's 1926 novel, *Crewe Train*, and the one to follow it, *Keeping Up Appearances* (1928), although quite different from each other, satirized the egocentricity of the 'professional' literary world in which Macaulay moved. These two novels foreshadowed the independent mood of the five years (1931–4) during which she would abandon her successful topical satires.

Each of the two novels shows longing for escape – but escape of different kinds. *Crewe Train*'s boy-woman, Denham Dobie, seeks escape from being a female, from her husband's talkative, book-mad, jealous London set, and from domestic responsibilities. *Keeping Up Appearances* expresses its heroine's longing to escape the dishonest concealment of a double life: a self-supporting writer, embarrassed at writing for the vulgar public, aspires to live, love, and write among the more attractive, graceful, cultured upper classes. Both novels end in defeat for the would-be escapee.

In *Crewe Train* the unsociable, gauche Denham Dobie finds that an irresistible mutual sexual attraction leads to marriage with an editor-author. Her entrapment by social custom hints at pathos but generates comedy; Denham is the Barbarian come to Town. Marriage and London life fetter her. She is expected to supervise maids instead of sorting out jigsaw puzzles or studying maps of the South Seas. She must attend a dull literary party at which her dinner partner is put off by her animated account of her dog's mange. Her naïve queries expose the vanity of authors and show the egocentricity of the literary world to be boring and ridiculous; she is baffled by the nonsense of writing about writing. Her annoyance at a pregnancy that promises unasked-for misery and trouble leads to her miscarriage through self-neglect. This casual selfishness is perfectly consistent with her small boy personality, but it shocked some reviewers.

Denham's retreat to a contented Robinson Crusoe life in a rude cabin by the sea includes an episode about a secret underwater passage and cave which Rose happily borrows from her old childhood favourite, R.M. Ballantyne's *The Coral Island*. The temporary separation of the married pair is complicated by Denham's Aunt Evelyn, who bears an identifiable physical resemblance to Naomi Royde-Smith. She is a fashionable, meddling arch-gossip. But in spite of Denham's happy temporary escape, she is finally captured and condemned to suburbia.

Few reviewers or critics have been able to resist quoting the memorable doom-filled last lines of the book. Denham, once again pregnant, is settling down in her new home after a reconciliation with her husband. Her mother-in-law explains the daily schedule of the model lady of the house:

> 'You see,' said Mrs Chapel.... 'There needn't be *any* empty moments in one's day if it's properly schemed out. Think of that! Not one empty, idle, useless minute.'
> Denham thought of it...[46]

Hedonistic, non-intellectual Denham is the opposite of ascetic, intellectural Arthur Gideon of *Potterism*, yet they are like each other and like Rose – they resist the pressures of society. Denham is another part of Rose, her solitary, tomboy self, minus her love of books and people; one reviewer called this runaway heroine a 'mental' case. But *Crewe Train* is not a psychological study of social retardation; it is Macaulay's sustained comic protest against the narrowness of literary life and the domestic incarceration of women. It is part subversive feminist fantasy and part escapist nostalgia for a boyish childhood.

Keeping Up Appearances (1928), also concerned with escapism, is far more complicated, although it is compound rather than complex. Two half-sisters, Daphne and Daisy – one chic, self-possessed, gifted with a mind that 'grabs and holds', and the other, five years older, unconfident, evasive, and obliged to support herself by writing popular trash – prove, one-third of the way through the novel, to be one person. The two selves continually exchange places. Daisy has a fully detailed life, both outward and inward; Daphne is revealed to be her social pose. 'A casual beckon from a stranger, and here again was Daphne, debonair, youthful, beloved. And with her came Daisy, her shadow, weaving with lies the garments in which she appeared.'[47]

When Daisy, hiding behind Daphne, is at last exposed, she loses the upper-class fiancé she adores. He feels contempt for her when he discovers her true identity, not because she writes novels and has a carefully concealed jolly, lower-middle-class mother who drinks, but because she has failed tests of courage and has lied to him. In remorse she calls herself 'a liar, a snob, and a cad'. In the last chapter Daisy sails to America on a lecture tour, reverting to deception and to her pseudonymous identity as the popular novelist, 'Marjorie Wynne'.

This use of the double is not subtle. The reader is mildly annoyed when the author's trick is baldly announced on page 127: 'Daphne and Daisy were actually one and the same young woman, Daphne being Daisy's presentment, or fantasy (as the psychologists call it), of herself as she hoped that she appeared to others.'[48]

Macaulay's alter egos here are not from Conrad or Dostoevsky but from farce. Both Daphne and Daisy are visible and whip in and out of doors to exchange places. The reader finally suspends disbelief because Macaulay's device makes possible the comic treatment of a number of serious themes: the coexistence of a confident social self and a vulnerable private self; omnipresent human vanity; the vulgarity of the intrusive press; an exposure of the lies women believe they must tell to be sexually attractive; the failure of family loyalty because of snobbery; and some derision of Freud as a modern-day Casaubon with the Key to All Psychologies. (Several scenes in *Keeping Up Appearances* are identical to dreams analysed in *The Interpretation of Dreams*. This seems to be a private joke for the author.) Rose's analyst was not Freud, but the sage of Ecclesiastes.

Keeping Up Appearances suggests that Rose Macaulay longed for confession at the time she was writing it. And in 1927 she did speak of her life with Gerald to her cousin Jean Smith, who was about to enter a religious order as a postulant. Rose, believing her secret would be forever immured within the convent, confided in Jean Smith and asked for her prayers. After six months, discovering that meditative seclusion was not her vocation, the novice Jean returned to secular life, but she never spoke of the secret love affair until it was revealed after Rose's death.[49]

Somewhat discontented with her work as a novelist, perhaps wanting escape from her pangs of conscience about Gerald and about her mother, Rose either instigated or quickly agreed to a holiday plan to return to Varazze life by taking a trip to America with her brother and sister. (She had refused offers to go on an American lecture tour.) In 1929 she and Margaret, whose order of deaconesses had closed its doors in 1925, sailed to New York, crossed the Northern United States by train, and met Will in Portland. (Jean had not joined their trip to Scotland after the war, and she was not able to join them on this exploration. She made several Continental trips with Rose in later years, but disappointingly was always too tied to her duties as a nurse and too committed to her house-mate Nancy Willetts to holiday with the remnant of the Five.) The three Macaulays drove down the Pacific Coast together in a chronically ailing automobile and re-crossed the continent through the South-west and the South to Florida.

Rose's letters describing the two-month trip are effervescent. The travellers' route was a great rectangle; they followed the two borders and two coasts by car and train and avoided big cities. As a result, Constance Babington Smith notes, they skirted the political and economic woes of the Depression in America's big cities and acquired a selective view of the United States. The mood of the expedition was carefree. Margaret still wore her deaconess's habit and Rose her city cloche hat, but the travelling conditions were informal and the journey adventurous, a revival of the spirit of the Five.

Rose explored the religious beliefs of the Americans she met – among them a Fundamentalist black Pullman porter and a loquacious evangelist who had been saved from such wickedness as dancing and movie-going by the warning voice of the Lord. She was fascinated by such exotica as American slang, cactus plants, a swim (or paddle) in brilliant, shallow Florida waters, and two brief glimpses of Mexico. To the three's chagrin, the anti-clerical Mexican government would not let Margaret cross the border, refusing to believe she was not a member of a Catholic order. Their plan to go to Guatemala was thwarted.

But the brother and two sisters had hugely enjoyed each other's company and the holiday had been for Rose a wonderful flight. Significantly, during those two months of everyday adventure and realized fantasy, Rose wrote much poetry. In 1949, at 68, she said in a BBC interview that poetry for her was 'a bridge between the business and the dream'.

The exuberant explorer returned reluctantly. Miss Macaulay was welcomed back to London by a group of friends at a celebratory luncheon in a Soho restaurant. And she began again to fill her appointment book, ignoring a cardiologist's warning of the previous May that she had a third-rate heart. 'Really I can do all I want with my heart as it is, so I shan't bother about it,' she had written to Jean.[50] She continued to speak of her heart metaphorically rather than physiologically. Looking back on her frustrated attempt to see Guatemala, she wrote 'My heart still pants after it.'[51]

As a result of that longing, she wrote a novel illustrating that the creative imagination can redeem lost opportunity as well as capture and transform experience. Macaulay set *Staying With Relations* (1930) in her new dream country – Guatemala. But she once more made the central character a novelist and again used the theme of the social pose and the private self that dominated *Keeping Up Appearances*. This time, however, the doubling provides merely a repetitive device, not a plot which examines deception and guilt. The result is an entertaining, forgettable summer fiction, a falling off from her best work of the Twenties, yet it has survived and has recently been republished in America.

Staying With Relations begins: 'Catherine Grey, a young female, and, like so many young females, a novelist, went to America one autumn and lectured to its inhabitants on the Creation of Character in Fiction.'[52] Both the rhythm of the sentence and its promise of further irony recall Jane Austen, and when the reader discovers that Catherine arrives at a rococo jungle ruin made into a modern mansion, peopled by diverse types and permeated by mystery, and that her quick perceptions of human character consistently prove to be wrong, Macaulay's allusion to *Northanger Abbey* is obvious. She means the reader to get the joke; after all, Austen's self-deceived heroine was also named Catherine.

The reversal of Catherine's expectations occurs with predictable regularity. But occasionally there is a little twist. One of Catherine's perceptions is a commonly held generalization about the sexes:

> Feminine creatures too often appear and feel unseated, alien, and a little lost, as if they knew no way of coming to terms with a world too strong, too swift, and overpowering for them. Catherine had seen that lost look in the eyes of many little girls, while their brothers seemed to be immediately at home in the odd world into which they had strayed, recognizing it as something which their papas and grandpapas had made and bequeathed to them.... Baffled and afraid; that, thought Catherine, was what women were when they stopped to think. Men, on the other hand, seemed competent, assured, at home, full of energy and physical and mental robustness.[53]

Is this Rose Macaulay's view – that woman is the perpetual insecure outsider? No. The authorial voice immediately undercuts the statement: 'So Catherine meditated, succumbing to the facile temptation to classify mankind according to sex, to age, to type, to anything but temperament, which so readily besets the writer.'[54] So much, says Macaulay, for gender labels: it is temperament that most dependably identifies the individual. And the temperaments of some men and women, she implies, make them exceptions to any generalization about the sexes. Yet the metaphor of the brother as the natural inheritor of the world of power is effective enough to stick in the mind. She has it both ways.

The novel ends in a comic wild chase in a collapsing, steaming car, lurching up the rough roads of southern California. Catherine and her family are in pursuit of a smiling villain, a Christian Scientist con man who can see no evil and feels no guilt.

Rose's creative imagination made good use of her trip, and the Guatemalan disappointment is turned into a compensatory literary success, for the set piece of the novel, presaging her success as a travel writer, is a nightmarish jungle landscape in which a hysterical young woman is lost. Vivid imagery crowds the pages – piebald butterflies, a little yellow-jawed snake, sinister clutching vines, a ruined grey stone temple, fluting birdsong, the darkness and turmoil of a tropical storm. If readers remember this ephemeral book at all, they will remember the surreal chapter, 'Wandering Lost'.

Macaulay herself must have known that this novel would not rank among her best, although it did have a good share of what she herself enjoyed in a light novel – 'wit and style and good nonsense'. Much of her creative energy at this time seems to have been directed toward the building of important new friendships, among them her relationships with Ivy Compton-Burnett and Victor Gollancz; each would develop into almost three decades of conversation, brought about by Macaulay's inclusion in two quite different milieux. (Gerald was not a part of either circle. Their time together was now only rarely spent at London literary affairs; they saw each other either with his family or tête-à-tête.)

Rose Macaulay met Ivy Compton-Burnett on 25 July 1929, just after the publication of Ivy's enthusiastically reviewed first successful novel, *Brothers and Sisters*. Rose invited Ivy to a party she was giving for a large number of guests in the basement of a Soho restaurant. The meeting of minds was immediate; Rose dined at Ivy's flat the following night. Each could snub strangers briskly, yet, to close friends, each was generous, loyal, and tender; for both women, a true friendship was for life.

Different as Macaulay and Compton-Burnett might seem at first, there were many affinities. Rose and Ivy were not unusual, of course, in being single women over 40; in 1929, forty per cent of all women over the age of 30 in Britain had never been married. And they were not unusual for their generation and class in having been born into large bookish families or in having lost a beloved brother. But there were less common areas of likeness: both women had a university education, and their mutual dark views of what Rose called 'the continualness' of marriage and 'that formidable affair, family life' were particularly pronounced. Also common to their fiction are sensitive portraits of brothers and sisters 'banded together in defensive alliance ... a sort of underground movement', as Rose described the fraternal clannishness in Ivy's novels.[55]

Rose Macaulay and Ivy Compton-Burnett could each be described as *sui generis*. Each gradually became fixed in appearance, manner, and speech, and in her own socially useful kind of eccentricity. (Ivy dressed austerely, like a governess.) They relished each other's conversation. Their similar powers of observation and irony ensured that no nuance of their dialogues would be lost. Each had a gleam of mischief in her eye, masked by what Hilary Spurling calls 'a deceptive spinsterish primness'.[56]

It is rare for two such conversational *enfants terribles* to share a drawing-room so happily, but their methods of discourse and disruption were different. Although Ivy's novels are made up almost entirely of dialogue, she did not habitually indulge in repartee; rather, as Francis King remembers, 'if she felt at her ease with people whom she knew well, she could talk about a fascinating range of topics. (I particularly remember what she said about the Victorian novelists whom she so much admired. But as a rule Ivy was laconic and Rose loquacious.)'[57] But Ivy could sabotage an uninteresting conversation by discussing the price of groceries or by asking intrusive questions with the licensed impertinence of the celebrated hostess. And if really in strong disagreement with the speaker, she could shout her antagonist down. Rose used a different ploy; she asked of any pretentious, canting speaker, 'Do you really mean that?' Sometimes the two friends put on a dazzling set-piece argument on religion for the benefit of others, but there was no rancour in it.

In defining the lifelong intimacy of the two, Elizabeth Sprigge, a Compton-Burnett biographer who was a good friend of her subject, says, 'Ivy was the recipient of Rose's private confidences.'[58] It must have been comforting to Rose to talk about Gerald to a friend who could say with cynical compassion, as Ivy did, 'People have a way of not coming out well in a temptation. They generally behave quite as ill as they can, don't they? Well, not any worse than I should expect them to behave. I mean, people have to consider themselves before anyone else, don't they, and one wonders what would happen to them if they didn't.'[59] Ivy, more pessimistic than Rose, thought humans were more likely to be wicked than good; she did not believe people were well armed to fight successfully for virtue – conscience was likely to be the still, small voice that speaks when the wrong-doer fears exposure. She was unshockable; Rose was sometimes surprised by human behaviour. Ivy judged her own life as morally impeccable; Rose was deeply aware of her own peccability. Yet they were alike in their capacity to forgive.

Hilary Spurling writes, 'Ivy loved Rose's vitality, audacity, gaiety – what Rosamond Lehmann called "her wit and crackle" – her fearlessness, and, above all, her integrity.'[60] And she adds, 'Rose was by all accounts incapable of doing a mean thing or saying a dull one.'[61] She became a familiar at the regular luncheon, tea, sherry, and dinner parties given by Ivy and her life companion, Margaret Jourdain, who was a successful published critic, connoisseur, and authority on English furniture and interiors. The company opened a new social world for Rose. Ivy's regular guests were, like the young novelist Francis King, from the literary milieu, but many of Margaret Jourdain's guests at these affairs were homosexual young men of the world of art and interior design, new and fascinating personalities to the untiringly curious Rose. (Ivy described herself and Margaret as 'neutrals' and did not enjoy married couples, while Rose had a gift for making friends with both husband and wife.)

Rose quickly became a favourite of the favourites regularly visiting this art-conscious household. One of them, Herman Schrijvfer, echoed the aesthetic admiration of some of the other guests: 'I adored her. I loved her appearance, her delicious speaking voice, her little curls which covered her rather skeleton-like head, her elegance of movement.'[62]

Figures peripheral to Bloomsbury sometimes appeared at Linden Gardens – Vita Sackville-West, David Garnett, Raymond Mortimer – but Ivy's only contact with the inner circle of Bloomsbury had been the Hogarth Press's quick rejection of her third novel, *Brothers and Sisters*. (The first two had been published by a vanity press.) To the apprentice publisher's reader, Richard Kennedy, who submitted a report offering the opinion that it was 'a work of genius', Leonard had answered coldly, 'She can't even write.'[63]

But when Compton-Burnett's blood-freezing domestic drama became an overnight *succès d'estime* (enthusiastically praised by both Raymond Mortimer and Arnold Bennett), Virginia Woolf tried to charm its author into submitting her next book to the Hogarth Press. She underestimated Compton-Burnett's cool guile. Ivy resisted, took Rose's advice, and turned her affairs over to the agent Curtis Brown. She signed with Heinemann for three novels, and eight years later, at Rose's suggestion, became an author of the Gollancz publishing house.

Rose was an admirer of Ivy, but not a completely uncritical admirer of her novels. 'I find her entertaining and sometimes brilliant,' she wrote to Father Johnson in 1955, 'but her novels are certainly odd, and often awkwardly written.'[64] Yet she said to Ivy, perhaps thinking of the top-icality of her own work and the timeless absence of background in Ivy's, 'My novels won't live. Yours may, Ivy.'[65] Her review of *A House and its Head* avoids any negative criticism of her friend by precisely describing the whole body of Ivy Compton-Burnett's work: its 'macabre psychological world', 'the gradual and terrifying unveiling of character', and 'the light, deft touches ... the elegant precision and formality of her wit' which build up the reader's growing sense of 'the enormity' of her plots. She closes her assessment with an analysis of the novel's effect upon the reader: 'It is the intercourse of character, the spinning by passion of plot, the enchanting *étincellement* of wit, that engrosses our fascinated attention throughout.'[66]

The social meeting-place for friends and friends of friends – Compton-Burnett, Macaulay, and Gollancz – on several occasions was the Friday Hampstead Circle, whose gatherings Rose regularly attended. The clique was first presided over by Dorothy and Reeve Brooke, later by Sylvia and Robert Lynd, all old friends. Robert, skilled in 'bland irony', as Rose said, wrote a popular column as 'Y.Y.' for the *New Statesman and Nation* and was literary editor of the London *News Chronicle*. Victor Gollancz described Sylvia as 'handsome, immensely energetic, ambitious, and a trifle ruthless and domineering'.[67] She relentlessly drew everyone into games, charades, recitations, and sing-songs – her recipe for keeping a party bubbling. Impromptu theatricals gave Rose a chance to shine; as a deadpan character actress she was hilarious. And Ivy, upon becoming an overnight celebrity, was also sometimes invited to the Hampstead gatherings. Gollancz reported that such lions as Max Beerbohm and James Joyce were regularly produced as surprises. (Joyce's presence at such a London soirée is difficult to imagine, but he would certainly have won all the word games.)

Victor and Ruth Gollancz were not to be outdone by the Lynds as creative hosts. When Rose wrote to thank the Gollanczes for the many lavish festive occasions they arranged at Brimley, their Berkshire home, she said that before they had begun giving parties, 'life was much less like a circus!'[68] But the guest-list of the Brimley circuses differed slightly from that of the Hampstead parties. Gollancz invited members of the Hampstead Friday group, but chose them selectively on the basis of their political awareness. He was at this time shifting from liberalism to Socialism; and because, he said, Rose was 'on the side of the angels politically', he used his characteristic hectoring tactics to try to convert her. But she stood her ground. She was all for Socialism – 'later'. Her consistent role in the body politic at this time was that of the gadfly.

Rose describes Gollancz as 'a very generous-minded, courageous man, so egotistical that he shocks some people, so unreticent in what he prints about himself that he embarrasses others; and so entertaining as company that he makes any gathering a roaring success. A unique character; I am very fond of him.'[69] Victor Gollancz returned the compliment; he entitles a section in his *Reminiscences of Affection* (1968) 'Rose Macaulay: and Others'. He is recalling the many weekends in the 1930s which Rose spent at Brimley, along with the Lynds, the David Lows, and Humbert Wolfe. But he finds it hard to break off his anecdotes of Rose's idiosyncratic tastes and behaviour to go on with the book: 'There were many things about Rose that I must pass over with a word, for this, I am sure to many people's disappointment, is not a book about her, but a book, I was going to say – about me.'[70]

But he does describe her connoisseurship of such oddities as an exotic and ridiculous musical bird-in-a-box; her love of artificial ruins and imaginary beasts; her generous secret charities; her habits as a driver – habits so perilous for passengers that, unless positively disabled, most people preferred to walk rather than to ride with her. Compton Mackenzie, being given a lift by Rose, was terrified at the sight of angry pedestrians and fist-shaking drivers in their path. He insisted on alighting: 'She stopped on the wrong side of the road as I hastily got out. I see now Rose Macaulay sweeping on southward in a series of ample zig-zags.'[71]

In her car she was a nonchalant Toad of Toad Hall: 'All is bliss;' she writes, 'we hum songs of triumph, as all charioteers have'.[72] Talking constantly at the wheel, 'she simply didn't pay attention,' says Mark Bonham Carter. One friend says Rose sped through red lights when no other cars were near; another says her attitude toward traffic was 'sporting', and that she consistently ignored speed limits. But Rose's own sense of her motoring style was rather like Laurie's description of Aunt Dot at the wheel in *The Towers of Trebizond*: 'Aunt Dot was a clever, impetuous driver, taking the sharpest bends with the greatest intrepidity. A brilliant and unorthodox improviser, she usually managed to work her way out of the jams she not infrequently got us into.'[73] This cavalier technique reflected Rose's love of danger, but its irresponsibility threatened the security of others. Jean said Rose's driving frightened her. Rose Macaulay's debonair driving was like the gay risk-taking of her clandestine trips with Gerald.

And she also showed a kind of social ruthlessness – mixed with her indefatigable kindness. Although Gollancz speaks as Rose's admiring friend, he finds one fault in her. Ironically, but not surprisingly, she could practise the same kind of intellectual intolerance that as an outsider she saw so clearly in action when visiting Bloomsbury. Gollancz writes:

> She was a snob: in relation not, God forbid, to the working class, but to tedious and uninteresting members of the middle one, particularly to the wives of famous men and the husbands of famous women. 'Poor so-and-so,' she would say, 'It's a pity one can't see him more often, but, really, his wife!' The chances were that there was nothing wrong with the lady, apart from her conversational inferiority to her husband; and the certainty was that Rose would have sacrificed a great deal to do her a service.[74]

She had suffered the inferior conversational styles of two wives of good talkers – Grace Macaulay and Beryl O'Donovan.

Compton-Burnett and the Gollanczes were her near contemporaries, but she did not confine herself socially to her own age group. Writing of Rose Macaulay in the Thirties and Forties, Alan Pryce-Jones says: 'One of the most striking things about her life was her agelessness. Most writers are imprisoned within their own generation. They neither can, nor wish to, establish easy contacts with readers much younger than themselves. She, on the other hand, shared many of the preoccupations of her juniors. Veronica Wedgwood, John Betjeman, Rosamond Lehmann, Stephen Spender; these are only four writers who might have accepted her as a contemporary, so closely identified were their interests with hers. Even the newest writers on the scene found she knew all about them.'[75]

Pleasant parties were not the only occasions for Rose's making new friends. She began her long epistolary and collaborative relationship with Daniel George Bunting by accusing him at their first meeting of borrowing one of her ideas. His gracious response sparked her shamed apology and from that day they became friends and collaborators. She made a friend of Veronica Wedgwood when they were both doing research daily in the British Library and invited her to lunch across Great Russell Street at the YWCA canteen. Her important friendship with Gilbert Murray began during the war when he sent her copies of his translations of Greek drama to help restock her bombed-out library. They began to correspond and to see each other regularly.

These new relationships were not merely cordial acquaintanceships. John Betjeman said, 'She was not exactly social, so much as a maker of friends.'[76] Her candour cut across insincerity and gush, simultaneously shocking and attracting. Veronica Wedgwood says Rose Macaulay was the obligatory guest for a successful dinner party. In 1951 Stephen Spender records such a party in his diary; the guests were T.S. Eliot, William Plomer, Veronica Wedgwood, and Rose Macaulay. Rose was then 70. They talked of childhood and Rose amused them with her Italian memories.

Friends wanted her presence at important moments. She was both sympathetic and unsentimental. She comforted Rosamond Lehmann when her beautiful young daughter died of poliomyelitis. And although Rose was nineteen years older, she and Rosamond corresponded with each other in 1950 about the griefs of their love affairs. Lehmann once described a grandmother whom she knew only through the letters she left behind, saying that she loved her for 'her genius for friendship and her sense of the ridiculous'. She found the same gifts in the living Rose Macaulay. And Rose took great pleasure in Rosamond Lehmann's statuesque beauty, which Mark Bonham Carter said made her seem like 'the Queen of Nineveh'.

These four names do not exhaust the list of those of the younger generation who prized her company. Alan Pryce-Jones adds hyperbolically: 'There was in the last decade of her life, no intelligent house in London where she might not appear, be the household rich or poor, hip or square.'[77] There were many friends, young and old, to grieve with her and to rejoice with her in the eventful decades ahead.

12

New Directions

THE DEATH OF Uncle Edward Conybeare in 1931 marked the end of the Cambridge past for all the Macaulay children, although they still had a meeting place. Margaret, after leaving Bethnal Green, had bought a house in the village of Liss, near Petersfield in Hampshire. Rose and Jean both visited regularly, Rose sometimes taking her bicycle on the train to Godalming and cycling the last twenty miles. But without Uncle Edward, the family patriarch and critic, there was no 'old family home'. Still, whatever backward looks Rose cast toward the unforgotten old days, she did not break stride.

For 1931 also began her happy period of literary and historical research. She brought out no novel that year. Instead, the Woolfs published her monograph *Some Religious Elements in English Literature,* No. 14 in the Hogarth Press Lecture Series. (By this time Rose understood Virginia Woolf, and, in spite of Virginia's epistolary gibes to others, their friendship had developed. Recalling her fondly, Rose wrote to Father Johnson, 'Virginia Woolf – yes, I was devoted to her, and am a great admirer.')[1]

Rose Macaulay's short Hogarth Press book was an attempt, as she says in a prefatory note, to 'dip into its enormous subject'. In doing so, she perfectly achieves the tone of a lively lecturer, as Forster had done in *Aspects of the Novel* (1927). Her empirical mind, like his, reluctantly and cautiously sets up a working theory: 'that most religious literature was the outcome of some kind of clash or conflict, and bore stamped on it the nature of this conflict, and the fusion, victory, or defeat which had been its outcome.'[2] Such conflict was the pattern of her own experience.

Clashing forces conveniently provide the titles to the five sections of the book – from 'English and Latin', to 'Reason and Passion' – but sceptical of abstractions, Macaulay avoids grand claims for her hypothesis: 'I do not know that there is very much in it after all.'[3] *Some*

Religious Elements in English Literature begins with the earliest anonymous Anglo-Saxon poetry, which, she says, reflects 'a depressed, though always courageous, and never discouraged fatalism', a view of life at odds with Christianizing influences.[4] She ends the book with a mere catalogue of poets from Tennyson to Alice Meynell, arguing that the nineteenth century is a period when literature and religion as subjects become 'too voluminous' to include in her study. The book trails off.

Throughout its first sections, however, Macaulay explores the influence on English literature of cycles and patterns of theological argument, of invasions and religious wars, and of domestic sectarian clashes. But she never forgets the ultimate creative independence of the major artist; she writes, 'Not that Dr Donne himself could ever have been called typical of anything,' and 'Milton, almost alone in his time, shows no sign of the dualistic conflict between religious and profane.'[5]

The reviewers praised her for encompassing such a mass of material without dulling the reader's taste for the literature itself. Most critics preferred the earlier sections to the later ones, but, unsurprisingly, given her Oxford studies, her own preference was for the seventeenth-century chapter, 'Anglican and Puritan'. Her next novel emerged from this chapter.

She finished *Some Religious Elements* in March 1931 and left with the congenial Dorothy and Reeve Brooke for a two-month tour of Sicily. She continued her trip without them to travel in Italy, probably with Gerald. But even before she left England, the idea for *They Were Defeated* had begun to germinate.

Her original plan, as she wrote to Jean, was to write a life of Robert Herrick, who was both one of her favourite poets and a distantly related forebear. (George's paternal grandmother had been a Herrick.) Herrick's contradictions attracted Macaulay: in *Some Religious Elements* she says that Herrick must be 'nearly the only seventeenth century clergyman who continued to write love-poems and light odes after his ordination, and lightened the cares of his incumbency by maying-songs and lampoons upon the more irritating members of his flock.'[6] Here, in this tension between Herrick's religious and secular lives, is an example of her theory of conflict as a source of literary inspiration. Her own work is another.

Rose's original idea grew and changed: she had intended a biography; it turned into a historical novel. Macaulay says she began it by 'brooding on Cambridge life as it was about 1640. ... It was a lovely century in Cambridge; or anyhow those immediately pre-civil war years were. So much poetry, so much flowering of Anglicanism in the midst of Puritanism, so much idealism on both sides.'[7] Her imagination began to live in that time and place.

She even assumed with enthusiasm the daunting linguistic task of an accurate imitation of the colloquial speech of 1640. The *New Statesman* praised her for her success – for 'her characteristic audacity': 'She has gone to the labour of adopting, in all speeches (and much of the book is dialogue) the very words and rhythms of the period. ... This device is seen to have a formal beauty of its own, to make a full and gracious pattern most suited to the world Miss Macaulay is making live again.'[8]

Some linguists found anachronisms and some critics found the antique language jarring. After the book's publication Rose was vexed that she had used the word 'scientist' before it had come into the language. Roger Thompson, historian of the seventeenth century, in a letter to the author, said that for him the novel suffered from 'epithetitis' and the 'verily, verilies'.[9] He agreed with E. L. Brown, the *New York Times* reviewer, who said that the outmoded language gave the book an air of 'tushery', but Brown ended by saying that the disadvantage was slight and that he had enjoyed the book so much that he wished it had been longer. For most critics 'the savoury language' of the period was convincing and added liveliness and immediacy.[10]

The problem of historical accuracy is another matter. In a letter replying to a query, C. V. Wedgwood wrote, 'As far as anachronisms are concerned, I don't think Rose aimed at a precisely accurate-in-every-detail historical novel. I think she was quite prepared to take a chance if it suited her theme. She was not after all writing a history book.'[11] But Rose Macaulay was a scholar and, if there are anachronisms, they are not glaring and do not flaw the novel. (It is typical of Rose Macaulay's careful research and her way of making imaginative fictional use of her findings that she discovered the androgynous name for her leading female character in Robert Herrick's life; Julian was the Christian name of the poet's mother.) As a work of historical recreation, *They Were Defeated* succeeds in bringing to life a moment of crisis in both public and private lives as the two cultures of Anglicanism and Puritanism struggle for dominance.

Writing it brought together her own life and education, her deepest feelings about being a woman writer, and her passion for delving in the past. Veronica Wedgwood describes discovering Rose hidden among the library shelves: 'A great place for chance meetings with Rose was the London Library ... burying herself under the avalanche of her own notes and knowledge from so many sources. Turning a dark corner among the bookstacks, one would come suddenly upon Rose squatting – an awkward position for one so tall, but squat she certainly did – in a narrow cleft between the shelves with an enormous tome upon her knees.' She goes on to describe Rose's swiftly mounting the precipitous ladders from floor to floor of the library, which members were warned to use only at their own risk. 'Perhaps the idea of risk appealed to the streak of romantic daring in Rose's nature, or perhaps she just wanted to get the books by the quickest possible route,' Wedgwood continues. 'Whatever the reason, she was for ever up and down those ladders like a chamois, until the library suppressed them.' Dame Veronica surmised that the library worried about her safety.[12]

Later Macaulay said that *They Were Defeated* was her favourite among her novels. But writing it was not easy. Both supportive and depressive influences acted upon her as she worked. Her supports were her love of her subject and her delight in a new home. The negative influence was the absence of Gerald's catalytic encouragement.

The book's plan never ceased to fascinate and stimulate her, and she writes that she especially liked writing 'the part about Cambridge, which was very real to me, so were – and are – all the people in it.' She says that she built the imaginary characters around people she knew: 'Dr Conybeare [Julian's loving, neglectful father] . . . was the son of an Eliza-bethan schoolmaster who was my ancestor; we have the line of descent. . . . I invented Dr Conybeare in a sense, but I made him as like as I could to my cousin Fred [Conybeare] of Oxford, atheism, appearance, and all.'[13] The historical Cambridge and London characters like John Cleveland and Sir John Suckling had been alive in her imagination since Oxford days.

As well as the perfect subject, she had found the perfect island on which to write about it. She and her books were settled into a new and charmingly located flat up three steep flights of stairs in Luxborough House, Marylebone. She wrote to Jean, 'I sometimes feel no-one has a right to be so happy as I am in the flat, looking out on trees on both sides, and so uninterrupted and comfortable with my library all around me and my pen and typewriter to hand.'[14]

But the privacy of this leafy eyrie did not wholly compensate for the fact that only Margaret and Jean seemed interested in the work of imagination for which she was doing such painstaking research. Her friends the Brookes told her they preferred her comic vein. Gerald, her most important critic, believed that the authentic historical novel could never be successful, either aesthetically or commercially. As her friend, her literary adviser, and the representative of Collins, he argued for what he believed were her best interests and suggested that her project was ill-advised. The lack of his encouragement was disheartening, but her subject drew her on. If proof of her artistic independence is needed, it can be found in her determined isolation as she wrote *They Were Defeated*. Her solitude was fruitful. In an unusual working pattern for her, she began to conceive the novel by creating full-blooded, credible characters for whom she cared and involving them in a dramatic action in which her imagination and sympathies were engaged.

They Were Defeated is an elegy – for two human beings and for a culture. The eight months of 1640 during which the novel's action takes place encompass the suspense and sorrows of three defeats: as London poet, country parson, and 'the sturdy sylvan god', Robert Herrick embodies the learning, tolerance, grace, humour, and hedonism of the late Renaissance spirit. He is driven out of his parish by the victory of the Puritans. However, although in the opening pages he appears to be the novel's centre, his story does not dominate the book. The focus is on the pitiable destruction of Julian Conybeare, Herrick's beautiful, intelligent 15-year-old pupil, a would-be poet. She is killed trying to reconcile her Cavalier brother and the Puritan John Cleveland, her callous seducer. Saddest of all the losses, in Rose Macaulay's eyes, the flowering humanist culture of Cambridge is stripped of its bloom by the chill of Puritan austerity.

The novel is too rich for summary. Macaulay uses many of her recurrent themes and situations: a closely bonded father and daughter; two brother and sister pairs; mingled paternal love and neglect; the horrors of ignorance and cruelty· religious intolerance; the blindness of romantic love; the scorn of most men for female intellectual ambitions. Yet this novel rises above and beyond her earlier work because it synthesizes rather than mingles her central insights and creates human beings rather than mouthpieces for ideas.

Macaulay brings the historical Robert Herrick to life as an engaging, worldly parson whose courtly and pastoral lyrics are going out of fashion. His pupil, the fictional Julian Conybeare, attracts the real-life brilliant poet and don, John Cleveland, by her delicate beauty. He agrees to her father's request that he tutor her while she is on a visit to Cambridge. But Cleveland is interested in her body and not her mind:

> A strange lovely enticing maid she was, but shy and remote, like a visitor from another star; and with her pretty head stuffed with maggots derived from her father about learning and books. Mr Cleveland kept a firm hand on this nonsense, teasing it out of her with raillery and kisses. ... he would tell her sometimes that she knew nothing of such matters, and should not talk of them.[15]

After a few lessons, which Julian drinks in with delight, he seduces her and then refuses to read her poetry and her thesis on Pythagoras. He is bored by her stubborn passion for learning and casts her off. (Cleveland's indifference to Julian's verse and his rejection of a woman in the role of poet reflect Rupert Brooke's attitude, not Gerald O'Donovan's.)

This is the first Rose Macaulay novel after the war which fulfils Humbert Wolfe's prophecy that sometime in the future her work would reveal her capacity for tears. And it is the first in which the humiliations and difficulties of the exceptional woman in love are presented without levity. 'For there *is* sadness in love. Always, always. For no two can feel alike in all things, and that hurts 'em. ... They must denounce being themselves and lay down their wills, and deny their whole lives, just for love,' says Julian.[16] Rose's customary narrative role as *l'allegra* was in this book complemented by her alter ego *la penserosa*; the mood is often sombre. (The story of Julian Conybeare may have been inspired by Virginia Woolf's imaginary tale in *A Room of One's Own* (1929) in which Woolf tells of the fate of Judith, sister of Shakespeare, who goes to London to realize her talents for acting and writing and ends as a suicide.) Julian Conybeare's poignant reply to John Cleveland's question, 'What does a lovely maid do with rhyming, pray?' is the heart of Rose Macaulay's individual feminism: 'It makes no differ being a maid. ... men or women, if we crave to write verse, we must write it, and write it the best we can.'[17]

What freed Rose Macaulay's cool, sceptical mind to write a novel of such self-revealing human interest? Writing without the repartee and laughter she enjoyed with Gerald, she did not work with the surface only, as writing good intellectual comedy requires. This novel demanded and called forth new creative talents and the deeper emotional resources of a mature woman.

Yet writing *They Were Defeated* also offered freedom from her own identity. To imagine a world locked in the past was to escape from the twentieth century; to reinvent a language was to write poetry; to bring to life historical characters like Cleveland and Herrick was to enter their emotional lives as well as to understand their politics. And dramatizing the widespread practice of witch-hunting demanded, as C. V. Wedgwood reminds us, that she look at the habitual cruelty as well as the graces of the age she loved. One of the conscious or unconscious creative forces behind her writing at this time could have been the pleasure of compensating for her Aegrotat failure by returning confidently in this novel to the very questions of judgement which her abandoned Oxford examination had posed.

The critics' praise for *They Were Defeated* delighted her, even though it was not unanimous. On 21 February 1932 Winifred Holtby reported to Vera Brittain that because of the splendid reviews, Rose Macaulay looked happier than she had ever seen her. Ralph Strauss of *The Sunday Times* wrote: 'I place Miss Rose Macaulay among the three most interesting and distinctive women novelists in England today.'[18] And L. A. G. Strong of the *Spectator* made the judgement: 'Her great achievement ... is not so much that she has lightly blended with her romantic story a great deal of learning as that she has succeeded in presenting historical characters without any distortion and has yet made them integral and proportionate parts of the whole ... this is perhaps the rarest achievement of the historical writer.'[19]

Part of her happiness about the book's success was Gerald's recantation. We have proof of his reversal of judgement in a letter he wrote in 1935 to Joseph Hone, who was working on a biography of Yeats: 'The historical novel is an almost impossible form of art, and I know of one only in which at least some of the major difficulties are faced and surmounted – a novel of the eve of the Civil War, "They Were Defeated" by Rose Macaulay.'[20]

They Were Defeated was reprinted four times and was reissued by Collins in 1960 and later by the Oxford University Press (1981). But Gerald was right about the undertaking being a financial risk. *They Were Defeated* had lower sales for Collins than the ironical comedies the public had come to expect. And in the United States, where it was entitled *The Shadow Flies* in order to avoid the use of the word 'defeat' during the Depression, the book nevertheless suffered; it did not earn its advance. The mass American reading public knew and cared little about the English Civil War.

After imaginatively wandering in seventeenth-century England, Rose did not immediately return to the present. Her next task, commissioned by Duckworths, was to write a short biography of Milton for its Great Lives series. Macaulay's *Milton* is no cut-and-paste précis from secondary sources. With a thoroughness reminiscent of George Macaulay, Rose, in order to write a 35,000-word book, undertook to read all of Milton's Latin and English polemical and political prose and correspondence as well as all of his poetry. She read the voluminous pertinent scholarship and criticism too. As a result, what might have been an unnoticed auxiliary school text became an original biographical analysis, and, to many Milton scholars, a red flag.

Rose Macaulay's *Milton* does not challenge the poet's genius; she celebrates his poetry appropriately in mannered (sometimes over-mannered) prose. But she finds him seriously flawed as a man, and some Miltonists were appalled at her irreverence. James Douglas, she wrote to her friend Daniel George, called her 'a shrew, a vixen, a harpy, and a blasphemer'.[21] Basil De Selincourt said, 'It is almost as if something hypnotic or maenad were mingled with her ruthlessness, so persistent is it.'[22] But the *Times Literary Supplement* found the book 'a readable account of Milton, the man, both well informed and eloquently written'.[23]

Without mentioning either name, Macaulay effectively replied to De Selincourt's attack and his charge that she had 'written in the Strachey style'. She wrote to the *Spectator*, in which a friendly review by Bonamy Dobrée had appeared, responding to Dobrée's surprise that she had omitted the criticism of Denis Saurat from her bibliography. She replied that she judged his work as 'largely unsound', because it was 'tainted with a readiness to jump to conclusions which mark the psycho-analyst let loose upon literature'. (This was her description of Strachey's writings in private.) In contrast to both Strachey and Saurat, she described her own analysis as 'perhaps pedantically over-cautious'.[24] She is just and compassionate towards all parties in discussing Milton's treatment of his wives and daughters. Of his first wife, Mary Powell, she writes:

> Mary's side of the story and account of the honeymoon is sadly lacking. Milton is his own eloquent counsel. She has none. He, in passionate language of often haunting beauty, has engaged our sympathies for all time with ideals of marriage many of them so modern that, even three hundred and fifty years after, they are still unrealized. It is perhaps not fair. There seems in this tragic piece, no villain, only two victims.[25]

Macaulay's Milton is a man isolated from other human beings by his huge and humourless ego. Believing that all writers are vain, she thinks him the vainest of all. She also believes his genius and vanity set him apart in a lonely universe: he was 'an arrogant self-dedicated solitary, a superb and monstrous alien'.[26] Her critical conclusion is: 'His tremendous imagination penetrates chaos and spheres, but never the human soul, creates for us a universe, a glorious garden or the very desolation of human despair, but not the subtler play of mind and heart.'[27]

Of the critics who accused her of emotional prejudice, Rose wrote to Elizabeth Bowen, 'To a passionate Miltonist like me, it is disconcerting to be accused of hatred.'[28] And in other private letters she suggests that the scholars who scold her for charging Milton with lying have perhaps not read all his correspondence and political prose.

In the summer of 1934, in the midst of her absorption in this academic task, Rose's remorse about her mother was aroused and quickened by a mildly comic incident. A former Great Shelford nextdoor neighbour, Mrs Ernest Stewart Roberts, widow of the Master of Gonville and Caius College, Cambridge, had written an innocuous little memoir to be called 'Recollections of Oxford and Cambridge'. She wrote to Rose describing it, asking her to write an introduction. She knew that the name 'Rose Macaulay' on the title page would catch the public's eye.

At first Rose categorically stated that she never wrote introductions except to her own books. But Mrs Roberts sent her the manuscript and Rose discovered, with horror, that the author had described in some detail the private life of the Macaulays, with special emphasis on Grace and Rose. Rose Macaulay regularly went to great lengths to block the appearance of any articles about herself, no matter how friendly and factual. Mrs Roberts's picture of Grace Macaulay as an invalid in 1912 and 1913 particularly distressed her, although its truth is verified by Uncle Edward's diary, which records that in 1913 the doctor ordered Grace to take a twelve-month rest cure, allowing only one visitor a day. Rose hated complaint and talk of illness; she did not want such weakness associated with her mother, particularly in print. She explained to Mrs Roberts that being mentioned in books made her 'shy and embarrassed

... a stupid kink I have'.[29] She particularly objected to the passages about her mother. She offered to write an introduction if the material about her family was omitted.

Her correspondence with Mrs Roberts is agitated and uncharacteristically repetitive. After consulting with Margaret, she writes: 'We both do feel that mother, who was so active and interested in seeing her friends, taking classes, gardening, etc. comes out rather as an invalid in a chair, going out only in good weather!' And she writes again: 'I felt you had, without meaning to, given the impression she was completely on the shelf & able to do nothing, in the Shelford days. ... I suppose what I – we all – feel about our mother, was that she was the most *alive* person I have ever known.'[30]

The 'aliveness' was Rose's chief memory of her mother in Varazze; in her remorse for having treated her unkindly in her last years, she wanted that ideal picture of vitality preserved undimmed. But the Mrs Hilary in *Dangerous Ages,* a picture drawn from Grace Macaulay at her worst, is a self-pitying woman who feigns activity and enthusiasm but who uses her ailments to manipulate her family. Perhaps Rose did not want any published evidence to give credence to the cruel picture in the novel.

Mrs Roberts could only accede. The published *Recollections* has more about Rose's rogue dog Tom than about the Macaulays. Rose's preface to the book is somewhat tongue-in-cheek, praising Mrs Roberts's charm and wishing her well, but making it clear between the lines that the charm rests on complacency and that the recollections are memories of a tame, incurious, conventional life.

This genteel but tough negotiation (in which Rose was careful to see the galley proofs before she wrote the preface) took place in the midst of her pressured but pleasant task of selecting and editing the literary excerpts of the anthology *The Minor Pleasures of Life* (1934) for Gollancz.

Analysis of a writer's humour produces dismal prose. But one way to hear what Victor Gollancz describes as Rose's 'dry mocking laugh' at the oddness of human nature is to read the table of contents of *The Minor Pleasures*. Beyond the predictable Macaulay choice of topics – 'Abroad', 'Bathing', 'Conversation', 'Solitude', and 'The Single Life' – there are others, represented by both prose and poetry, such as 'Being Flattered', 'Eccentricity', 'Malice', 'Smells', 'Showing Off', 'Sloth', 'Taking Umbrage', 'Xenophilism', and 'Xenophobia'. The anthologist apologizes for the preponderance of selections from the seventeenth century, but no reader could complain of a lack of variety or wit in the collection.

Her next volume, *Personal Pleasures* (1935) – also published by Victor Gollancz, who was enchanted by Rose's idiosyncrasies – was a natural and an even more humorous sequel. She dedicates it to her brother and sisters. Of this series of very short alphabetically arranged essays (the 'loose jetsam' she most enjoyed writing), some of the titles are the same as in *Minor Pleasures* ('Bathing' and 'Taking Umbrage', for example), but there are a good number which are more unusual.

The essays can be enjoyed as pieces of a jigsaw puzzle entitled 'A Self-Portrait'. Of parties she says: 'Anything may happen. A man has just come in who stands charmingly on his head at parties.... That is what people should do at parties... it gives parties of pleasure the right note.'[31] Of the pleasure of throwing out the 1937 equivalent of junk mail, she writes in 'Getting Rid': 'Life is one long struggle to disinter oneself, to keep one's head above the accumulations, the ever-deepening layers ... which attempt to cover one over, steadily, almost irresistibly, like falling snow.'[32]

And gregarious as she was, one of Rose Macaulay's most ecstatic essays is 'Departure of Visitors'. After the house-guest leaves, Rose rejoices: 'The easy chair spreads warm arms of welcome; the sofa stretches guest-free; the books gleam, brown and golden, buff and blue and maroon from their shelves; they may strew the floor, the chairs, the couch, once more, lying ready to the hand.'[33] (This was a clever ploy. After this published hymn to solitude, few would invite themselves to spend a weekend with Rose. She told Jean that when she had a spare bedroom she 'suffered terribly'. In fact, house-guests kept Gerald away.) Other pleasures are more active: her account of flying in a two-seater plane piloted by her future publisher Hamish Hamilton is a variation on the theme of 'enormous bliss', her phrase and Milton's.

But by this time Collins was beginning to demand another novel. And her friends the Brookes, to whom she dedicated it, wanted her to write a novel of 'unredeemed levity'. And so Rose Macaulay set about writing *Going Abroad* (1934) – the kind of fiction her readership expected from her. The characters are an English party vacationing in the Basque country, which she had recently visited with Gerald. Its plot involves the kidnapping of the entire group of tourists and some non-violent extortion in the name of poetic justice.

One of the novel's satiric targets is fraud in the cosmetic and face-lifting industry. But its major source of amusement is the naïvety of the Oxford Group, the youthful evangelical sect which at this time was urging its prospective converts to make public confession and restitution for all their sins, after which all parties – sinners and their victims – would experience a Change of Heart.

To develop material for the novel, Macaulay disingenuously attended a number of the Oxford Group's meetings. Its members were delighted and made much of this celebrity as a potential convert. But the resulting novel, while acknowledging their engaging sincerity, sees the Groupers as rather like puppies who drag one's knickers into the drawing-room while the vicar is calling. In the author's eyes and in those of the older generation in *Going Abroad,* public confession is bad form – vulgar, exhibitionist, and likely to expose truths embarrassing to all concerned – in short, un-English. The subject of confession always attracted Rose Macaulay's attention, but the Group's methods offended her sense of reticence and made her wonder whether the changed sinners might not be encouraged to sin more in order to continue enjoying the spotlight.

In 1950 Rose said she really should not have lampooned those earnest efforts for good. (On the other hand, Compton Mackenzie wrote that he wished Cambridge had supplied her pen with more gall.)[34] But though 'kind (within reason)' as Rose described herself, she always struck in her own fashion, and then – remorseful – apologized. (After a dinner party at Rosamond Lehmann's home in 1954, she wrote to her hostess the next day, mildly conscience-stricken about her behaviour toward a 'superbly irrational and eloquent' guest she had 'bullied' in a 'theological disputation': 'He is so likeable & teasable – I hope he didn't mind our teasings.')[35]

Her good-natured laughter at naïvety in *Going Abroad* is mixed with another more biting attack. She exposes as charlatanism the 'art and science of cosmetology', just beginning to be a thriving business among women in England's leisured classes. Two of its practitioners, M. and Mme Josef, have ruined the appearance, emptied the purse, and destroyed the marriage of a Mrs Dixon. The Josefs have also exiled their two daughters because their plain appearance might be bad for business. They are the villains; they are unmercifully excoriated.

Perhaps Rose had paid an investigative visit or two to beauty salons, but although she had the same early-ageing, delicate complexion as Mrs Dixon, it is not likely that she had been cheated by false promises of miraculous rejuvenation. She is morally indignant at the Josefs' greed, insensitivity, and fraud. But she deplores the gullibility and vanity of their clients as well. She has more kindly fun with her heroine, the beautiful and infatuated Hero Buckley, an illegitimate descendant of Lord Byron.

Going Abroad produces easy laughs and bounces along to a satisfactory enough close, but there is a flicker of cheerful nihilism at the abrupt conclusion. The absolutely correct Sir Arthur Denzil suggests that the holiday's events have been like 'a rather absurd comic film'. A bit later his brother-in-law, the missionary bishop, thinks, 'No, it would never do to let oneself think that life in this world was anything of that nature. No; dear me, that would never do at all.'[36] Summarily rejecting this trivialization of existence, the bishop settles back into untroubled peace and the story ends. But the sense of life as an absurd comedy remains. One reviewer charged Rose Macaulay with caring nothing about people. As Constance Babington Smith says, this would have been an unthinkable criticism of *They Were Defeated*.

Going Abroad was a best-seller; it was republished in 1951, and Rose herself seems to have enjoyed it, and gave copies to friends. But from the happier time of writing about what most interested her, she had slipped back into producing the well-paid formula. Her interests lay elsewhere. She wrote one more, much weaker, such novel – *I Would Be Private* (1937), a story about a young policeman who fathers quintuplets and, to escape the publicity which swamps his family's life, sails off with his wife and their embarrassing brood to a desert island. Some of the novel's excursions into foibles of interest to Rose have charm, but it was not a success. Perhaps its irreverent attitude toward parenthood and the burden of babies hit a discordant note with the public. But besides being a one-joke novel, it has another flaw; it presents its lower-middle-class bangers-and-mash family with unwitting condescension. The young Scottish policeman McBrown is a model of common sense and virtue, but the rest of the family is a set of caricatures. It is meant to be 'an absurd comic film', or as Daisy Simpson of *Keeping Up Appearances* had said of her own novel, 'a foolish, clattering stream, running frothily beside the real stream of life.'[37] The novel's most memorable feature is the epigraph, a pastiche, which Rose herself wrote and which she attributed to a fictitious source:

Press me not, throng me not, by your leave I would be private. Jupiter Ammon, is a man then not free? What a pox, may he not choose his road, is he to be bethronged, beset, commanded, as he were a beast in a drover's herd, or a zany in a fairman's show? Stand back, you knaves, you buzzing flap-dragons, give me leave to be private, by Cock's death I'll walk free, or I'll not walk at all.

Roger Rampole's Cheaping[38]

There is another element of *I Would Be Private* which is equally personal: in a spirit of reprisal, Rose began the story with a fatal automobile accident, caused by an MP, Sir Walter Brentwood. Crossing against the lights, he hits a car and kills its driver, a young schoolmistress. In spite of the testimony of the constable and other witnesses that he was at fault, the coroner's verdict is 'accidental death', with a rider acquitting the distinguished Member. Discredited, the truthful PC Ronald McBrown resigns from the force 'in a mood of white-hot Highland rage'.

In this incident Rose Macaulay is reliving her own emotional response to a successful libel suit brought against her and the *Spectator*. In December 1935, Lord de Clifford had been charged with the manslaughter of a fellow-motorist and with driving on the wrong side of the road on the Kingston bypass; the car he struck, according to witnesses, was in perfect control. Tried by the House of Lords, at considerable expense to the taxpayers, he was acquitted. Scandalized, Rose Macaulay had written a column in the *Spectator* (17 January 1936) attacking the inequity of the traffic laws: 'The laws by which motoring offences are tried certainly seem to be in a state of chaos only matched by the traffic chaos itself.'[39] In the course of this scolding, she had by implication scolded Lord de Clifford himself. The *Spectator* published an apology, but their humble words did not block the suit or the judgment of £600. Virginia Woolf wrote to Elizabeth Bowen of her sympathy with Rose in this 'monstrous affair'. In a sadly ironic fashion, it all came back to haunt Rose Macaulay three and a half years later in a traffic accident of her own.

I Would Be Private is a prank, a rather mechanically assembled comic story, and its frivolity was ill-timed. The best-sellers of 1937 were being published by the Left Book Club of Victor Gollancz. This slack fiction left Collins with a damaging loss of £465; her publisher had a right to be indignant. W. A. ('Billy') Collins saw its hasty production as a breach of faith. In a letter to her agent, he chided Rose indirectly as though he were a schoolmaster writing to the parent of a truant child. ('Billy' in a temper was known to rebuke Collins authors by dropping a huge account book on the floor in front of them with a tremendous bang.) He referred to Rose's signing of a contract in 1929, 'a time when Miss Macaulay was writing novels regularly at two-yearly intervals and when her sales were steady in the neighbourhood of fifteen thousand [books]. ... there have, however, been longer and longer intervals between each of Miss Macaulay's novels, as she has been spending much of her time in doing other work, and ... she [has] kept finding it difficult to think out plots for her novels.'[40] He goes on to say that there had been a fifty per cent drop in their sales, 'a very considerable drop'.

Just at the time of this professional and financial crisis there was another loss in the Macaulay family. It brought Rose grief but freed her from financial worries and left her able to write as she pleased without reduction of income. Reginald Heber Macaulay, her last surviving uncle, died on 15 December 1937 at the age of 78. In death he was once more her godfather and liberator. Among the bequests from his large estate he left £10,000 each to four of his nephews (Will Macaulay and three sons of his sister Alice Smith), but to only one of his nieces – Emilie Rose Macaulay. This timely inheritance did not alter Rose's frugal style of living; she did not even buy a new car. But it increased her powers of generosity and her choices of occupation. As a *rentier,* she could afford to write literary, political, and historical commentary in leading journals rather than features in newspapers or reviews of detective stories and thrillers. (In the Twenties she had asked to review the latter because Grace enjoyed them.) She was also free to escape the world's woes by researching odd antiquarian subjects which fascinated her. Best of all, she could enjoy what she called 'dear abroad', 'the Englishman's picnic', whenever she pleased.

The inheritance was an important support at this time, but financial difficulties or no, Rose Macaulay had already begun to refocus her interests. Even before Uncle Regi's death she had probably accepted the Hogarth Press commission to write a critical study of E.M. Forster's work, for it was published the following year. And as we know she had found other ways to write about things 'in which intelligent people are interested'.

Observing the Macaulay books from other presses may not have been the only cause for William Collins's ire about Miss Macaulay's inattention to novel-writing. His indignation had probably been spurred by assessing the demands on her time made by the increasing volume and intellectual scope of her 'other work': her regular column, 'Marginal Comments', in the *Spectator*, frequent articles in the *New Statesman*, and her intermittent assumption of the 'Notes in the Margin' column of *Time and Tide*, as well as her frequent appearances in BBC debates and broadcasts. She was in the public eye and her famous challenges and ripostes earned her a following. Forster called one of the debates in which she had come to his defence as a moralist 'a glorious dust-up'.

Rose Macaulay's reviews are carefully composed essays; they reflect high standards and are discriminating, but also tactful, and whenever possible, generous. She says that a writer wants 'a moderate, a reasonable, a delicate flattery, spiced with criticism'; when she can in conscience do so, she provides this.[41] When analysing scholarship or critical editing, she sometimes avoids carping by first telling us what the pedantic or 'captious critic' might say – and then offering deserved praise. And her praise often proved to be important to rising young writers whom she encouraged and to whom she gave practical help. Although she did not have a high opinion of her own novels, she was deeply discomfited by unfavourable or dismissive reviews. She wrote to the hypersensitive Hugh Walpole saying that because her interests lay elsewhere she wrote novels only to make money and did not care what people said about them: 'Heaven knows I shouldn't mind what anyone said of them – except in reviews, of course, which I suppose we all mind a little.'[42] Mark Bonham Carter says she was anxious her books should not fall into the hands of reviewers to whom she might have been particularly formidable in conversation. She thought opinions about novels a matter of taste and she wrote a signed review of her own *Dangerous Ages* for *Time and Tide* which closed, 'Some may like it, others had better not try'.[43]

In her own reviewing she aimed at the humorous balance which takes into account that reviewing is a world of competition and that the vanity of the creator is 'the most profound, the most sensitive vanity in the world'. One of her favourite sources of amusement was Isaac D'Israeli's *Quarrels of Authors*. In *Crewe Train* there is a scene in which a young publisher-reviewer-author reacts with wounded rage to the assessment of his first book. In the *Times Literary Supplement* under 'New Books and

Reprints' his novel rates several patronizing lines: '. . . a certain pleasant talent', 'would not suffer from considerable pruning'.[44] He decides that the review was written by a man whose book he had turned down. He plots revenge. And in *Keeping Up Appearances* a supposedly disinterested young biologist is given the task of reviewing a book on the lamelibranch, the small mollusc on which he was planning to publish a treatise. He had been forestalled. 'He did not feel disposed to make much of this book; it was possible to find in it a few faults, disagreements with himself, even mistakes, and to make it seem of small importance, in a short notice obviously written to be set up in minion, or even nonpareil type. He saw no reason to puff the book.'[45]

The London world of reviewing was incestuous and political; all writers had need to feel wary. The reviewer had power. One author could receive publicity, £8, and some valuable goodwill by praising a fellow writer; another could achieve a reputation for critical acuity and damage the purse and vanity of a rival by unkind cuts. In her 1939 essay 'Reviewing', Virginia Woolf, disapproving of a craft that could have a negative effect on the author's sales and on the author's sensibility, discusses the possibility of doing away with reviewing altogether in favour of professional paid consultations between critics and authors. She prefers the critic's considered judgements to the reviewer's necessarily hasty, impressionistic opinions – what Rose Macaulay called 'the *ad hoc* quality reviews must contain.' But in an afterword, Leonard Woolf, as a practical publisher, defended reviewing as a necessary, although flawed device to serve the needs of the new and larger reading public.

Equally sensitive to the faults of the system, Rose Macaulay nevertheless continued to write reviews, but she began to raise them to the level of criticism by accepting only books which interested her – chiefly history, biography, travel, and novels of ideas. She developed some criteria for these genres, although she presented them as opinions, not dogma. She did not believe in the establishment of eternal laws determining literary value because human emotions are too much involved with taste. In 1945 she wrote 'An Alphabet of Literary Prejudices', a list of literary antipathies nursed by literary persons from Anthony à Wood to Zoroaster, from the hatred of Quakers to a dislike of women; she entertainingly shows that literary preferences are idiosyncratic and are affected by religion and politics. She includes her own antipathies, which largely have to do with the misuse of language. Her aesthetic analysis of the works of Evelyn Waugh may have been influenced by her Anglicanism; she is convinced that he had made an error of aesthetic judgement in forsaking the hilarious ironical detachment of his early satires to become an emotional and reactionary Roman Catholic apologist. Unfortunately, she says, his dry style had liquefied. Biased or not, she was not alone in this opinion.

As always her analysis of the work of others tells much about her own standards: Rose Macaulay believes that a good biographer should display faults as well as virtues and 'should lift the lid from the subject and let it reveal itself ... through a number of carefully selected sources'.[46] She abhors the use of psychological terms. And she insists that biographies be enlivened by the inclusion of small amusing details and anecdotes of eccentricity. She praises John Aubrey for his *Brief Lives* because of 'his racy turn of phrase, his mixture of scholarliness and gossip, his lively and sympathetic characterizations, his gay, rueful, colloquial style'.[47] In contrast, a good travel writer, she says, concentrates not on people but on the romance and beauty of the landscape, although 'with learning and zest [he] keeps his head and does not gush'.[48] In her opinion the author of a novel of ideas should not be his own protagonist, 'using imaginary discussions as a platform from which to train his own guns, bringing down his birds right and left'.[49]

The Writings of E.M. Forster (1938) was her major critical work, a study to which Forster obviously gave assistance by lending unpublished manuscripts – a youthful novel and an early version of *A Room with a View* – but not *Maurice*. Rose Macaulay was his unswerving admirer, but Morgan Forster, as he wrote to Leonard Woolf, thought her study 'tamely conceived and badly written ... not a good book', although he acknowledged that it was 'considerate, tactful, gratifying, and, in a sense, intelligent'.[50] Outsiders were more positive. Elizabeth Bowen wrote, 'This is an outstanding piece of critical work. To begin with, Miss Macaulay has succeeded in writing for those familiar with Mr Forster's writings and for those who do not know them at all. ... The structure of her book – which might be a difficult problem – is excellent; here is an intellectual portrait, with its background, and a comprehensive study of all of Mr Forster's work, with a simultaneous running analysis.'[51] M. L. Elting of the *Forum* called it 'an alert and graceful critical estimate that combines a rare sensitivity with robust common sense'.[52]

Lionel Trilling, however, who was himself to write the major study, *E.M. Forster* (1943), was predictably less enthusiastic. He patronizingly called *The Writings of E.M. Forster* 'a labour of love'. And he found its style 'coquettish' (a female adjective), concealing Forster's 'toughness' (a male noun).[53] In his own study of Forster he writes, 'Both Rose Macaulay and Virginia Woolf, who write of Forster with admiration, perceive the delicacy but not the cogency of his mind.'[54] Even though these judgements are set forth as disinterested criticism, the bias of gender seems to be at work. Rose usually escaped a critical whipping for being a woman, because, unlike Virginia Woolf, she had chosen to write in a traditional genre. She did not pose any threat to the canonization of the Great Tradition.

When Trilling's own book appeared, Rose Macaulay's review of it was generous, but she found that as an American, writing out of a different culture and society, he was occasionally obtuse about the nuances of idiom and wit in Forster's work which were characteristically English. Rose was right about the beam in each reviewer's eye.

Forster's disappointment might at first seem surprising. The ethical and political values of both subject and critic were in harmony; both were descendants of nineteenth-century liberalism; both were engaged in separating the sham from the genuine; both valued human relationships. She praises him highly for achieving 'uncommon beauty and charm; the fusion of humour, perception, social comedy, witty realism, and soaring moral idealism [which] weaves a rare, captivating, almost hypnotic spell'.[55]

They were alike enough to become increasingly good friends and they were to see each other often through the years. Forster sought out her company more and more. When, in late life, he was relatively immobile, he asked Rose to drive him from London to Abinger and back to visit the scenes of his youth. After hearing her arguing on the BBC, he wrote her that the sound of her voice in 'the mêlée' made him 'so happy'. But there were differences in their work and their conceptions of the novel which account for his dismay at her assessment of his writing. And in part his dissatisfaction is related to Forster's image of himself.

In a personal interview, P.N. Furbank said that Forster was disappointed that in *The Writings of E.M. Forster* Rose Macaulay did not focus on the aspects of fiction which most interested him. Far from using his own critical methods to analyse his fiction, she begins her chapter on *Aspects of the Novel* by saying that to her it is 'his least interesting book', although it was 'his highest feat', for he had made a success of 'a tedious subject'. This irked him. Unlike Bloomsbury artists and critics, Rose Macaulay was not interested in aesthetic theory, however diffidently and engagingly posed. She only reluctantly acknowledges that 'novelists must, one supposes, be interested in the art of the novel'.[56]

In discussing his much praised *Aspects,* she challenges Forster on almost every point. She says, 'It is an uneven book, full of excitements and opening doors, and sudden flaggings and peterings out, and thin bits, as if some of the affair suddenly became too tangled for investigation and must be left at that.'[57] Her passion for debate is in opposition to him on a subject in which he took the keenest interest. The only critical assessment of his work which greatly pleased Forster was Peter Burra's 'Introduction' to *A Passage to India*, which used Forster's own critical terms for the analysis. Burra gave unalloyed praise.

She is, however, much engaged by Forster's ideas and analyses 'the ideas surrounding him', and 'the way in which they are connected', as she assesses the credibility of his characters.[58] She treats the plots descriptively. Looking at Forster's own more elegant style, it is not hard to see why he judged her book badly written. It is heavily adjectival, and Macaulay used more of the arcane words of which she was so fond than was appropriate for the task. And the book ends with a mixed metaphor.

Forster may have been most irritated by her tone. She writes to him as a fellow craftsman, most often praising but occasionally questioning the effectiveness of his authorial decisions. Forster had a reputation for personal modesty, but he did not underestimate his fiction. He may have thought the less honoured Rose Macaulay was presumptuous in writing from the standpoint of a peer. Her last chapter is entitled 'Some Conclusions', but Forster writes to Leonard Woolf, 'No conclusion is reached'. The book's last sentences are speculative rather than definitive:

> Never has such a stabilizing imagination as his been needed to focus and interpret the human scene. Presently it may be too late for this particular interpreter; neither that murderous chaos to which we so confidently look, nor that as yet dubious rearrangement of society which he has called (vision or nightmare? he does not know, but thinks both) 'the new dawn,' will throw down suitable reflections for his mirror, they would both crack it. The future will be someone else's pigeon. The present might still be his, if he would attempt it.[59]

In 1938 Rose Macaulay was beginning to be involved in the turmoil of the present and to feel the threats of the future – the struggles of European politics and the portentous events leading to war. Although E. M. Forster did not like her prophecy, it proved to be sound. He did not write another novel after *A Passage to India*.

Even this brief summary of some of Rose Macaulay's writing in the last half of the Thirties testifies to a busy professional life, but her anthologizing and critical writing during these five years did not absorb all her time and energy. Certainly some of her journal columns discussed literary and linguistic subjects – the difficulties of modern poetry, the invective of literary quarrels, the fascination of semantic and etymological analysis. But the greater part of her strength in the late Thirties was spent in considering 'the murderous chaos (vision or nightmare?)' which lay ahead. Hitler had come to power; the Spanish Civil War had polarized London intellectuals. Forster's humane Edwardian tolerance seemed to her a frail defence against what lay ahead. She was much engaged in two activities demanded by the times – political writing and political activity.

13

Politics and Escape

Dᴇsᴄʀɪʙɪɴɢ ᴀ ᴠɪsɪᴛ to Rose Macaulay's flat, Alan Pryce-Jones writes:

> The darting presence which ran from kitchen to bedroom, turning off gas, finding a lithograph, brushing away towers of literature to make a second place on the sofa: all this is resumed in the discursive nature of her books. Certainly she turned from one thing to another. Practical at one moment, she could be cantankerously vague at the next. An idea trotted into her head. It must be brought out at once, set in its place, displayed to the company. She must rush off to the London Library in order to check out the true facts about bread-fruit or land crabs. She must copy a reference to one of the seventeenth-century poets she loved, or of the divines she loved still better.[1]

But though in the midst of this disorder Rose was prone to lose gloves and mislay manuscripts, she created order in the end: those land crabs and bread-fruit appear in *Orphan Island*; references to seventeenth-century poets appear in *They Were Defeated*; old lithographs illustrate *Pleasure of Ruins*. 'All her findings had to be given a place, and a place pre-determined by strict professional discipline,' Pryce-Jones concludes.[2]

Her *Spectator* and *Time and Tide* columns of the Thirties are indeed learned and discursive, but their wanderings are lucidly connected, and they conclude gracefully, exactly at the pre-determined end of the single column allotted them. It is characteristic of Rose Macaulay's darting mind that few of these columns can be filed by category: she writes a literary essay, 'Autumn Meditation', but is actually playing a linguistic game, seeing how many obsolete words she can use to describe the season; she brings together politics and literature (the State and the Arts); she connects a contemporary political figure with one from the past (Sir Oswald Mosley and Guy Fawkes).

In the late Thirties she wrote of the contemporary scene in the light of her literary and historical knowledge. And she was playing a lively part in that drama. As a critic of literature and politics she attended both meetings of PEN and sittings of Parliament. Although she had always regarded politics as an absurd show, in the years just before the war she became more than an amused spectator. She declined the offer of a CBE, fearing that accepting honours would oblige her to support the Establishment, and in a high proportion of those *Spectator* 'Marginal Comments' columns of 1935 and 1936 she challenged the decisions of leaders. 'I don't want a Leader,' was her stated principle. 'I like to think I am capable of leading myself.'[3] She protested against domestic and international policies which offended her sense of justice: laws which limited personal freedom; the support of the terrorist Blackshirts by rich backers in high places; England's passive collusion in Mussolini's annexation of Abyssinia. And like many other British writers in those years, she became more and more troubled by the imminence of war.

But although much of the time she was acting responsibly as a critical citizen, she knew how to escape from the anxiety and indignation roused by thoughts of war and violence and the troubling search for solutions. In 1935 she had traded her near-obsolescent car for a year-old Morris and was sometimes tempted, she said, to drive about in it all day. In odd moments she happily collected notes for a book on real and imaginary beasts as characters in literature. This new avocation brought back her childhood; in Varazze, over thirty years before, when George Macaulay was translating Herodotus, he had told his children tales of gryphons, tritons, dog-faced men, and other strange creatures. So, although she went to Peace Pledge Union rallies at Hyde Park Corner in the numbing cold, she sometimes entered too a warmer world, inhabited by lovesick turtledoves and life-saving dolphins, rare white tigers and camelopards, and even rarer unicorns, mermaids, and chimeras. She noted questions for research: 'And what about the sea-horse's love-life in literature? I must find out.'[4]

At the end of her public activity in the peace movement and her private pursuit of enchanting oddity in myth and legend, she was to write *And No Man's Wit*, a novel set in Spain just after the Civil War; it would encompass both the viewpoints of a political world and the mysteries of a magical one. All her findings would be given a place.

She had always listened carefully to the many opposing voices of her times. So, moving from describing the Twenties to summing up the Thirties in her *Life Among the English* (1942), she assessed the changing tone and volume of that chorus:

> The next decade was more serious, less cultured, less aesthetic, more political. The slump blew like a cold draught at its birth, war stormed like a forest fire at its close; between these two catastrophes Communists and Fascists battled

and preached, and eyes turned apprehensively across the North Sea towards the alarming menace which had leaped up like a strident jack-in-the-box from a beer cellar to more than a throne. Bets were laid on the date of war. Ivory towers and those who frequented them were under a cloud. People who had never sat on committees for the defence of liberty, democracy, or culture, sat on them now; and culture, losing caste, came to mean anti-Fascism. During these stormy years the Spanish *pronunciamiento* split the British public; the fashionable continental tour was to government or rebel Spain, according to the tourist's political colour.[5]

Though never before a joiner, Rose Macaulay, too, now sat on committees. She was a member of the National Council for Civil Liberties headed by E.M. Forster, who distrusted slogans and organizations but who distrusted those in power even more. Among her fellow Council members were H.G. Wells and J.B. Priestley, Professor Julian Huxley and Clement Attlee. She was also aware of the more radical goals and commitments of those younger writers who were, as the historian C. L. Mowat says, 'inclining towards a world view, social consciousness, and a platonic affection for the proletariat'.[6] Rose Macaulay never visualized the Proletariat very clearly, although she did take a keen interest in her char's summation of 'my 'ubby's' views on Labour politics. She read the *Daily Worker* and was amused and irked by the predictability of its harangues. All forms of bigotry offended her. She admittedly had a weak grasp of the economic forces which had brought about the social instability of the Depression years, but she believed in a fairer economic distribution. However, she did not in the Thirties suffer from the typical middle-class writer's Marxist *crise de conscience* about the lives of the working class. Her work appeared in John Lehmann's *New Writing* rather than in the *Left Review*, and she tentatively considered Socialism as a distant national goal rather than hotly pursuing Communism as a near one. But at the same time she shared many of the ethical concerns of the younger generation about injustice and the use of force. And so she was often in the company of the young partisans such as Stephen Spender and his friends.

As a writer she pondered the aesthetic and moral questions raised by Spender's statement at the 1936 Book Exhibition: 'I am not concerned with writing a particular kind of poetry, but with writing about something I believe to be very important. The poet has to make a synthesis out of the moral life of our time, and this life is lived at this moment on a political plane.'[7] She quoted this credo of her friend with sympathy in 'Marginal Comments', yet she wondered a little wistfully if there would ever again be for writers 'a time to fiddle and a time to dance'.[8] Yearning for fantasy, she was nevertheless engaged in *Realpolitik*; her own musings and queries about specific moral problems in political life appeared regularly, not only in the *Spectator*, which C.L. Mowat calls 'independently conservative', but also in *Time and Tide*, which he calls 'so independently liberal that at times it became die-hard conservative'. And Rose herself was so independent that she sometimes wrote for the *New Statesman*, which Mowat describes as 'independently socialist, exasperating, and bitchy'.[9]

Her chosen role was to disturb the complacent and to oppose the demagogue. Never unreservedly committed to a party platform, she was still a Liberal sympathizer. But when the Liberals became too weak to mount a candidate in her borough in 1935, she voted according to her own eccentric principles. She wrote to Jean, 'My reason for voting for the Labour candidate in Marylebone is to increase the opposition to the Conservative candidate who is a safe winner.... It is very bad for any member to have a safe seat.'[10] In the midst of the savage anti-Semitic wave generated by the rhetoric and thuggery of Sir Oswald Mosley's followers, she wrote a *Spectator* column on 26 April 1935, boldly questioning his assumption that there was a monolithic structure of 'Jewish interests' in England.

As well as taking an anti-Fascist stand, Rose Macaulay returned to the pacifist evangelism of her character Daphne Sandomir in her 1916 novel, *Non-Combatants and Others*. In a lecture to a village meeting, Daphne says, ' "In this dim, dubious future, let us see that we build up one positive thing which shall not fail us." And by that, of course,' the narrator adds, 'she meant Peace'. Peace would be achieved by rational means: 'Understanding, clear thinking, it nearly all turns on that, everything does.'[11] In the Thirties Rose Macaulay worked for peace alongside other writers, including Aldous Huxley, Vera Brittain, Virginia Woolf, and Storm Jameson who, like her, believed that no condition could be worse than a world at war and that rational means to achieve peace should be continually explored. The strength of a similar pro-peace position had first come to widespread public attention after the Oxford Union debate on 9 February 1933 when the young men of the future officer class voted 275 to 153 that 'this House will no longer fight for King and Country'. Many polls taken by working-class groups expressed the same resolve but earned less publicity. A countrywide League of Nations Union questionnaire answered by eleven and a half million people in 1933 showed firm support in all classes, constituencies, and countries for the strengthening of the League, for mutual disarmament, and for the implementation of international economic sanctions. This Peace Ballot was 'not for peace at any price', say Margot Heinemann and Noreen Branson in *Britain in the Thirties*, 'but for a mutual stand against aggression.'[12] But the government was almost more wary of cooperation with other nations that it was of the threat of Germany.

Rose Macaulay's views were at one with the poll's stand on the necessity of peace-making, and, until Germany's march into Poland, at one with the general public's approval of conciliatory negotiation. With patronizing historical hindsight Malcolm Muggeridge wrote of her in 1964, 'Dear Rose, so earnest, so clever, so wrong!'[13] But Mowat observes, 'In retrospect everyone was against appeasement; at the time not so many.'[14]

Rose Macaulay was not a political prophet but an intelligent observer who was making judgements based on the lessons of the First World War. Like other contemporaries she was sensitive to the inequities of the Treaty of Versailles, which she defined as 'another battleground'. As a private citizen she only gradually came to perceive and deplore the rationale of the secretive, fatally blinkered, internationally isolated, personal diplomacy which was being carried on by the Chamberlain government. She did not seem to grasp the fact that Hitler was being increasingly supported by the German people. And she was among the many – including those in government – who failed to understand at first that Hitler's militaristic strategy did not include keeping agreements and that his vision of *Lebensraum* had no boundaries.

As a humanist working for a rationally achieved peace, Rose Macaulay learned some painful political lessons about the Fascists when the Blackshirts began to mount raids in the East End on the persons and property of Jews and trade union members (automatically termed 'Reds'). Because their 'Leader', Sir Oswald Mosley, was a wealthy Englishman who had been for thirteen years a Member of Parliament, the Blackshirts were generously funded by men in high places, as *Britain in the Thirties* points out. But those who thought to use Mosley did not comprehend the extent of his brutality. Mosley believed in force as well as in oratory; a huge Blackshirt rally held at Olympia on 7 June 1934 resulted in serious injuries for protesting questioners of the speaker inside the hall and a bloodletting clash between police and the gathering of a few protesting Communists and many trade union representatives outside. The press, by mutual agreement, did not publish the details of this fracas.

Rose Macaulay's suggestions about how the British public might silence Mosley's ranting are both temperamentally characteristic and politically naïve. In a column of 13 March 1936 she suggests that her readers take tickets for a Blackshirts rally announced for 26 March just as they would 'take seats for the Marx Brothers' and laugh at the prancing pomposity of 'The Leader' and the 'impassioned frenzy' aroused by his glorification of the 'white forces of civilization' and his 'storms of vulgar and vicious Judeophobia'.[15] She believed that Sir Oswald Mosley and his British Union of Fascists could be laughed off the stage of politics by the sensible and fair-minded English public. The Blackshirts should, she suggests, be kept like chimpanzees in the Zoo. She soon discovered that her advice was not only quixotic but also dangerous.

She attended the rally. And on 27 March she publicly withdrew her hope that the power of intelligent mockery could silence sadistic fanaticism. The scene was not comic. She commented that 'crowds have the half-ludicrous, half-sinister suggestibility of the pack, who may be sent by the huntsman's word after any quarry. One felt, woe to any Jew who should that night cross the path of that applauding mob.'[16] And after witnessing the 'violent ejections' of some protesting members of the audience, she concluded that this was not 'entertainment', but 'a meeting in a mental home'. On 4 October of the same year her column deplored a brick-heaving conflict at Tower Hill between the Blackshirts and angry working men from Leeds. Throughout these disruptions the police seemed to have been instructed to bring their batons down on the heads of Mosley's enemies; a double standard on freedom of speech was being applied.

Rose's moral indignation at what she judged to be the government's tolerance of bullying at home and abroad increased. In mid-May 1936, visiting Italy, she observed in her column: 'The speed with which the London Sunday Press accepted the announcement made late on Saturday night in Rome of the annexation of someone else's empire, the deposition of its Emperor, and the assumption for all time of his title by the King of Italy, beat all records of obliging complaisance.'[17] Sympathetic to Italy, she was loath to condemn its citizens, blaming the annexation of Abyssinia entirely on Mussolini. In a letter to Jean she flippantly volunteered to bring honour to the family name by assassinating him. But while criticizing in print the British government's methods of conciliation and their snubbing of Haile Selassie on his visit to London, she nevertheless was thankful for peace – even 'Peace with Ignominy', as she candidly termed it. And she privately admitted that if Italy could occupy Abyssinia without bloodshed, she would approve of their transforming it into a more fruitful land. Her views were never uncomplicated, but she was consistent in deploring violence.

In the first two weeks of June 1936, with her customary insatiable curiosity, she arranged both to attend Haile Selassie's press conference and to have a private interview with the Reverend Dick Sheppard, former vicar of St Martin-in-the-Fields, then Canon of St Paul's. Some called him 'the radio peace crank'. But Sheppard's Peace Pledge Union, founded in 1934, had attracted many supporters, including public figures such as Bertrand Russell and Siegfried Sassoon. Sceptically prepared to find Sheppard charming and shallow, she was instead moved by his belief in the ultimate power of an organized and determined 'goodness' – mass non-violent resistance. She became a sponsor of the Union, which entailed speaking engagements, letters to the press, and recruitment. Victor Gollancz, gaining many adherents through his Left Book Club to his belief in preparing for an international military defence against Fascism, was critical of her conversion to non-violence. As a Jew, he knew what was happening in Germany. And when in 1937 Rose published a pamphlet, 'An Open Letter to a Non-Pacifist', and sent it to him, marked 'Victor, please read', he refused to do so. Despite their disagreement, however, he and Rose remained good friends.

Rose Macaulay's arguments in the eight pages of the pamphlet set forth concerns which were to dominate her thought for the rest of her life: Is there hope that civilization will win out over the barbarism that has periodically overrun it throughout history? Can we reasonably believe that, by what E.M. Forster called 'a slow crab-like motion', humanity can progress morally? These were the very questions pondered by her ancestors who had fought against slavery. The dream of the Enlightenment and the social Darwinism of the nineteenth century were mingled in her tentative hopes. But what she saw was disheartening: 'The gamble of armed contest has not brought us very near to anything that I care to call freedom, or to anything that any of us would care to call civilisation or decent Christian living.'[18]

She knew nothing of Auschwitz, and as a former civil servant in the 1918 British Department for Propaganda in Enemy Countries, she disbelieved all atrocity stories. And so she points to some limited improvement: 'the abolition of slavery, torture, of the burning of heretics and witches, of public floggings, brandings, pillories.'[19] She challenges the non-pacifist:

> You truly point out that war is only a symptom of the whole horrid business of human behaviour, and cannot be isolated, and that we shall not, even if we abolish war, abolish hate and greed. So might it have been argued about slave emancipation, that slavery was but one aspect of human disgustingness, and that to abolish it would not end the barbarity that causes it. But did the abolitionists therefore waste their breath? And do we waste ours now in protesting against war?[20]

And yet, as always, in the spirit of fairness, she undercuts her own argument. She acknowledges early on that 'if someone were to attack and try to rob or injure me, or if I saw him attacking some weaker person, I should endeavour by all means (though probably unsuccessfully) to knock him down'.[21]

In October 1937 the Peace Pledge Union suffered a fatal blow. The Reverend Dick Sheppard died of a heart attack, shortly after he had impressively defeated Winston Churchill and several other candidates for the rectorship of the University of Glasgow on a peace platform. Rose Macaulay had campaigned for him; her name had been so effective a drawing card that a larking group of undergraduates opposing Sheppard had attempted to kidnap her upon her arrival in Glasgow to speak. Fortunately, she was at once rescued by a pro-Sheppard student faction.

Without Dick Sheppard's leadership the Peace Pledge Union lost momentum, and when the Germans goose-stepped into Austria on 12 March 1938, Rose Macaulay resigned from it. By 1940 she had firmly decided that although non-violent resistance might work between individuals, it was ineffective in modern war.

After the bombless 'twilight war' came to a close and France fell in June 1940, the first aerial conflicts of the Battle of Britain began. In September Rose wrote to Jean, 'We must embattle everyone's *mind*'.[22] Non-violent resistance was futile against terrifying aerial bombardment. But until the last moment she fought for peace, frequently doubted the possibility of achieving it, and periodically regained her emotional balance by escaping the ever-worsening news reports. One way to chart her oscillations between hope, scepticism, and escapism in the late Thirties is to read the earlier of the surviving 155 postcards and letters she wrote to Daniel George Bunting between 24 June 1936 and 6 June 1956.

In addition to recording some of the events of those years, the correspondence gives the history of a friendship and shows Rose Macaulay's conscious methods of choosing the people in her life. 'As a matter of fact,' she wrote to Jean ten years earlier when her books first became popular, 'I select my friends with great care, and only have those who please me a great deal.'[23] She prized and cultivated such selected friendships; she also determined and controlled their level of intimacy. She gave generously, but she protected her privacy.

As a well-known woman she was sometimes sought after by strangers. In 1926 she had written to Jean, 'What do you do with mawkish female admirers who vent their passion by leaving you expensive flowers and begging to have meals with you?'[24] One such persistent young lady, lilies-of-the-valley in hand, had arrived at her door. Rose at once set about disengaging herself without hurting the worshipper's feelings by demonstrating to her that she had many friends and no time for tête-à-tête luncheons with fans. When the young woman insisted on a lunch engagement, Rose arranged in advance for several of her friends to join them when they arrived at the restaurant. The pushy young woman did not push herself again. 'Writing books is a terrible magnet for such as her,' Rose told Jean. 'They are so boring as a rule. I suppose no one who wasn't would force their way into people's lives like that.'[25]

'Daniel George' (his pen name and the name by which Rose addressed him) was also an ardent admirer, but an appreciated and accepted one, although they first met in a chilly atmosphere. When he was introduced to her, she expressed her annoyance at his copying her format of alphabetized selections (*The Minor Pleasures of Life*) in his anthology of human miseries, *A Peck of Troubles*. Afterwards he wrote a polite note of apology, offering to acknowledge his indebtedness publicly in his next book. She apologized in turn for being 'peevish', although she did admit 'that at the time I was so little magnanimous as to feel rather aggrieved at losing my special invented method.'[26] Apologies accepted on both sides, they became friendly and remained so. He did not bore her. Mark Bonham Carter describes him as 'clever, astringent, and discriminating'.

She asked him to assume a project which, with her Forster book in progress, she was too busy to undertake and ended in generously assisting him in the task. The International Peace Campaign had suggested that she compile an anthology of anti-war poetry and prose written throughout twenty-four centuries. At her invitation Bunting agreed to take over the project. Rose Macaulay culled his proposed selections, wrote an introduction for the book, and persuaded Collins to publish it, all the while insisting that 'Daniel George' take full credit. He responded by becoming an indefatigable and resourceful volunteer researcher for her proposed 'Animal Book' and a long-standing friend.

At the time of that first meeting in 1936 Rose was 55; Daniel George Bunting was ten years younger. 'The son of a naval man', as his *Times* obituary puts it, he was born on the Isle of Portland and grew up in Southsea. He left school at about 16, and in 1914 joined the Queen's Westminster Rifles as a private. He served in France, was awarded the Military Medal for an act of conspicuous bravery, and was commissioned in 1918. After the war he rose to become the general manager of an engineering firm in London and a successful automotive inventor. But his true identity was 'autodidact'. He was, as *The Times* carefully phrases it, 'an almost omnivorous reader', and a collector of inexpensive second-hand books. In his late middle-age he entered the literary world, where he had always longed to be, as a reader for Jonathan Cape. He began to give book talks for the BBC as well, and he was known in publishing circles for the 'practical and often laborious help, encouragement, and advice' he gave to innumerable writers.[27] He was on a lower rung of the literary ladder, but like Rose Macaulay he was fascinated by obscure and recondite reading; his antiquarian literary tastes harmonized perfectly with her love of 'rummaging' in odd old books. They shared and analysed their discoveries with enthusiasm. Yet she kept their quite genuine friendship on a little island of its own.

Rose Macaulay's letters to 'Dear Mr George' are cordial but not intimate. Her tone is by turns matter-of-fact, jocular, scholarly, conspiratorial, grateful, delighted, and complimentary, but she maintains a certain distance. He does not seem to have been introduced to her family or to her close friends, and she does not address him as 'Dear Daniel' until the fourth year of their correspondence. She worries a bit about taking advantage of his constant research on her behalf. He made her gifts of flowers from his country garden and gave her books – mostly uncommon ones, although they were not technically 'rare'. In 1952, after knowing and corresponding with her for sixteen years, he sent her an antique Valentine which she described as a 'delicate concoction ... a lovely piece of Victorian elegance'. In a warm thank-you letter, she indicates exactly the tone of their long and mutually loyal relationship, for she adds to her praise of the Valentine's charm, 'And the nice word on it – "affection" – which I like'.[28]

The high point of their relationship seems to have been Rose's visit to his seaside home in 1949, where, during a cold June weekend, she took 'sea dips' in the Atlantic and upon emerging was cosseted with hot-water bottles and plied with whisky and lemon by his wife Margaret. Thanking her hostess she wrote, 'My sea bathing has quite set me up'.[29] She was 68 at the time. This example of Rose's enduring passion for bathing recalls Harold Nicolson's story:

> I remember that once when she was staying with us in the country during those ice-days that mark an English Easter, she manifested a desire to swim. We told her that, apart from the English Channel which was sixteen miles away and cold in April, all we could offer her was our pond. It was a muddy pond, not very deep, and thick with weeds and water snakes. We told her of these disadvantages. 'Oh, I never mind things like that,' she answered, and within ten minutes there she was swimming happily in the viscous pool. She made us all feel middle-aged.[30]

But the greatest biographical value of the Macaulay–George correspondence is not anecdotal. Because the two treasure-hunters compared their appointment books to arrange regular editorial consultations at lunches near the London Library or tea near the British Museum, the letters record a bit about her social life, more about her political work, and much about her doubts as to its effectiveness. And her letters also give details of the real and imaginary journeys she made to escape the pessimism aroused by reading and thinking about war.

These letters are not confidential; her personal news to Daniel George usually lacks detail. She speaks frequently of going for a day or a weekend to Surrey, but she never mentions that she is visiting the O'Donovan family, which was by this time living in Albury. From 1938 on, Gerald O'Donovan threw himself into the assistance of Czech refugees; he was particularly successful in placing young Czech students in good English schools. Rose would have heard a great deal from him about the plight of Hitler's victims, but she does not mention this subject to George. She often makes extended visits to Margaret in Liss, but although she talks about its weather and the landscape, she tells nothing about her sister until 1941. (Jean does not enter the correspondence for some time; she was in South Africa as a missionary-nurse from 1936 until 1939 when her health broke down.) Rose writes of 'a brother's visit' in February 1938, and says 'we are never indoors', suggesting Will's love of action, but she reveals no more about him, not even his name. She mentions borrowing a book from Leonard Woolf or discussing the peace anthology with Max Plowman when such meetings are relevant to their task, but she does not send along news about eminent friends as she does in letters to Jean. Her letters to her collaborator centre on the research they are sharing and their mutual anxieties about the political climate.

The discursiveness, the humour, and the conversational style are unfailingly spontaneous and give the letters range and life: 'The worst of looking through these writers is that one gets so beguiled and seduced by the way, and runs a-whoring after the ladies fine as fi'pence and the man with bright rose-noble hair – so much nicer!'[31] But her chief focus is on an exchange of facts, ideas, and opinions with her correspondent, not on personal display, emotional autobiography, or virtuoso stylistic performance. She perfectly controls the tone of the conversation and the relationship. Rose Macaulay's letters never seem to be written with one eye cocked on the mirror or on posterity; she focuses on the person to whom she writes. It was another form of what a friend called her 'playing the telephone'; it was as though for a moment she stopped her busy darting and brushed away towers of literature to make a second place on the sofa.

During the first months the two considered selections for the anthology, which was finally entitled *All in a Maze*. George did the searching; Rose read, commented on, checked translations and variants, and edited page after page of excerpts. Her impressive erudition is lightly worn. Finding eloquent laments about war throughout recorded human history proved too easy; Collins at last insisted they cut the book to 450 pages.

Rose continued to believe in the anthology's interest and value, yet in the midst of editing it she suddenly bewailed the futility of crying out against violence: 'It's like trying to shout above the storm, or stem Niagara with bare hands, or like frail human voices among a jungle of wild beasts.'[32] In another letter she predicts that man's folly will probably crush him in the end. And in her introduction to the book she quotes Euripides, 'Fools rush on war, and mankind are fools.'[33] Of the well-attended Writers' Anti-Fascist Meeting on 4 June 1938 which she had helped Hugh Walpole and Philip Guedalla to organize, she wrote Bunting, 'Yes, I think the Meeting was a success.' And then, 'I'm glad we had it, though heaven knows what good we think it will do.'[34]

Her happiest letters come from her trip to Provence and Italy in September 1938 when she speeds off, she says, 'to sunshine and idleness'. In the short story which recounts the heroine's travels with her lover, 'Miss Anstruther's Letters', Rose names one of the towns she visited on this trip; it is possible that Gerald was with her. If he was, her euphoric mood is perfectly explained. In *The Towers of Trebizond* ('my own story') Laurie says of spending a fortnight with her lover: 'In ten years I had not got used to all that brilliance and delightfulness, nor to the fact of our love. When we were together, peace flowed about us like music, and fun sprang up between us like a shining fountain.'³⁵ But magic holiday or no, she had to keep in touch with George, for he was struggling with the proofs of *All in a Maze*. And so he hears from her along the way: 'I am in bliss in Provence. I had a glorious mountain run from Grenoble and Aix is exquisite.'³⁶

She was in Varazze when Hitler met Chamberlain at Munich and gained the concession that the German army could march into the Sudetenland without English opposition. Her mood was that of an irresponsible truant: 'I am lotus-eating (or rather fig and peach-eating) in this Eden, in a blue warm sea or on sweet-smelling hills. Everyone is charming. I read the oddest news in the local press. But I eat another fig and forget it.' And on 15 September, 'Our P.M. seems to have saved the world! ... If war is so easily averted as all this, it does seem a pity no P.M. ever thought of it before. I gather from my *Corriere* that Londoners have quite lost their heads, and stand all day and night in Whitehall and Downing Street as if there were a motor-crash to watch. The *Corriere* rather admires this. I'm glad I am out of the hysteria. In Varazze we are very placid and gay, and I don't think we know what a Crisis it all is, or quite who these Sudetichi and Cechi are.'³⁷

But such a hedonistic flight was only occasionally possible. She had another way to replenish her resources from day to day so that she could face her moral responsibilities as a citizen in difficult times. Back in Luxborough House, she continued collecting esoteric legends and pseudo-science about animals in literature, creating a counter-world which she planned to turn into a book. George began sending her his finds – tales and fables about asps, pelicans, pismires, and crocodiles found in Aristotle and Pliny – even a delightful picture of a romantic snail, captioned 'tossed here and there by divers tides of thought and desire'.

All in a Maze was at last finished and was published in November 1938, but it was still-born. Neither Macaulay nor George could find any evidence that Collins ever advertised it. The firm may have considered it an embarrassment, for it was ill-timed. England was awaiting and fearing war, and the anthology's material about such contemporary peacemakers as the Prime Minister, which the compilers had hastily added at the last, gave the book the air of propaganda. It displeased even those who admired its literary charm. Neville Chamberlain's appeasement was failing.

In March 1939, still hoping for peace, Rose enrolled in the Voluntary Ambulance Corps and began training. Many Londoners, certain of disasters ahead, were resettling in rural areas. Rose could have gone to Margaret's home, but she was determined not to be removed from her flat. Being an ambulance driver would ensure that she remained there, and more importantly, would offer the opportunity to serve side by side with men under dangerous conditions, as she had wanted to do in the First World War.

At the same time she began working on a new book, and in April she was studying Spanish history, preparing to write a novel on its Civil War. Discussions of its events and ideas had dominated conversations in London literary and political circles since July 1936. Several of Rose's friends had joined the International Brigade. She had attended fund-raising rallies for the 4,000 Basque children who had been brought to England under private auspices. She had warmly supported Gerald's son, Dermod, who had gone to Spain with a Quaker mission to deliver tins of milk for children. She was very fond of him and they were good friends. Although she had visited the Basque country in more peaceful times, he doubtless furnished her with some important details for her novel. *And No Man's Wit* was to bear what was for her an unusually demonstrative dedication, 'To Dermod O'Donovan, with my love'.

If the nature of war in modern life was ever to be comprehended, contemporary Spain was surely the historical landscape to be studied. The Spanish Civil War had been marked, especially in its early stages, by ruthless cruelties. It was a struggle of factions within factions, religious as well as political, and an international as well as a national conflict. Its causes had recruited fighting men from all classes in England. The names of famous English writers who went to Spain – W.H. Auden, Stephen Spender, John Cornford, George Orwell, Julian Bell – are fixed in historical memory, but eighty per cent of the men in the English Battalion of the volunteer International Brigade were working-class. Italians, Germans, English, and Americans as well as Spaniards had killed and been killed. Spanish priests were photographed giving the Fascist salute; churches were burned and bishops were murdered by the Republicans. The products of modern technology had been tested as engines of total devastation. Spain had been a cauldron of human suffering.

It was a painful subject, and Rose began the planning and writing of *And No Man's Wit* under painful conditions. A deeply disturbing event at the time she was beginning to write the novel weighed on her throughout its creation. In June 1939 Gerald, who had never learned to drive, asked his daughter Brigid to drive him through the Lake District for a holiday. She had done so in two earlier summers but was not particularly enthusiastic about a third trip. So, with the full knowledge of members of the family, their old friend Rose was asked to be Gerald's chauffeur and companion. There seems to have been no question of Beryl's participation; apparently she had no wish to go. Bookings at separate hotels were discreetly made. 'Mother and I helped pack Rose's car and waved them good-bye,' Brigid recalled.[38] The journey was to be disastrous.

On the trip's fourteenth day, 26 June, Gerald and Rose in 'Elk' (licence number ELC 299) headed for Hadrian's Wall. Rose was driving up a road near Hartside so steep that an approaching car could not be seen until it breasted the hill. On the rise she swerved to the middle of the road and hit an oncoming car. 'My friend', Rose was to testify in court three weeks later, 'called my attention to a signpost and I had looked to the side for a moment.'[39] The other driver was not injured, but Gerald O'Donovan was concussed. Rose, in shock, climbed out of the wreckage repeating, 'It was all my fault,' and fainted. The memory of her public criticism of Lord de Clifford's driving on the wrong side of the road may have passed through her mind. After the accident, Gerald, at 68, was in a grave condition and, as Constance Babington Smith tells us, Rose said to Jean, 'If he dies, you won't be seeing me for some time.'[40]

She was charged with careless driving, and her offence was recorded on her driver's licence. But because the *Penrith Observer* identified her as Emily Macaulay (the name on her licence and the one under which she had frequently received parking tickets), the London newspapers did not pick up and publish the story.

However secret her disgrace, guilt haunted her. Gerald was unconscious for some time; six months later he suffered a stroke. She felt the weight of all his suffering. In the climactic automobile crash of *The Towers of Trebizond*, the heroine Laurie is responsible for her lover's death. 'I had plenty of time to think about it; no doubt my whole life,' Laurie says. 'It seemed impossible to think about anything else.'[41] In like torment Rose Macaulay suffered because of Gerald's injury and his subsequent debilitation. But she had to go on living and working; she had to report for ambulance training in London and she had contracted to write the Spanish Civil War novel.

In writing *And No Man's Wit* she protected her feelings: its action is intellectual rather than emotional. Except in the creation of one lovely, pitiable escaping character and the relation of one poignant event, the narrator speaks in her ironic first voice. The novel considers the question of whether the cruelty inherent in unbending beliefs can ever be transformed into civilized tolerance. Surveying the pain and waste of war, Rose Macaulay asks whether John Donne accurately pictures the modern world in the lines from his 'Elegy' which she chose for the book's epigraph:

> The Sun is lost, and the earth, and no man's wit
> Can well direct him where to look for it.
> And freely men confesse that this world's spent....
> 'Tis all in pieces, all coherence gone;
> All just supply, and all Relation.

In *And No Man's Wit* Rose Macaulay's professional discipline found a place for her seemingly disparate findings, her feelings, and her experiences: her detailed review of Spanish history and politics, her anti-war activism, her intermittent despair about humanity's inhumanity, her admiration for strong women, her love of bathing, her delight in travel, her engrossing study of strange, imaginary creatures, her belief in the loyalty of friendship, and her private guilt.

The frame of *And No Man's Wit* is a quest through Spain for the missing Englishman Guy Marlowe, late of the International Brigade. Within this frame Rose Macaulay examines the ideas and ideals that cause strife between human beings who are neither saintly, nor devilish, neither heroic nor villainous. There is no fanatic revolutionary Communist Republican and no fanatic reactionary Fascist Nationalist among its chief characters, although all but one of them are aligned with some system of belief by which they live and judge others.

Rose summarized her novel superficially for Collins when she finished it: 'If I wanted to describe the book shortly, I think I should call it the adventures of a well-meaning English family in contact with the new and old Spain. There are other threads running through it, but this is really what it is about. I have tried to hold the balance between Left and Right – perhaps not quite successfully.'[42]

Gerald O'Donovan had written a novel of conflicting beliefs about the Troubles in Ireland. Perhaps the two lovers discussed the problems of such a plot as he convalesced from the accident. In his even-handed *Conquest* (1920), Irish and Anglo-Irish argue passionately for their causes throughout the book. But *And No Man's Wit* is less emotional than *Conquest*, and it cannot really be described as a dialectical novel, for it contains only a few scenes of genuine intellectual debate. The characters assert unshakeable points, ask each other disagreeable questions in a falsely agreeable manner, or quarrel and bicker like children over their differing loyalties. The narrator's comments and long passages of exposition provide enough action and historical background to show how their temperaments, experiences, and cultures have formed their convictions and tastes. Almost all are educated and intelligent, neither barbarians of the Right nor barbarians of the Left. If these people cannot live together, what hope is there?

The English Dr Kate Marlowe, 'a mother, a doctor, a liberal, and a humane, active, fussy woman'; her son Hugh, a Cambridge graduate with a job in a London publishing house; her 19-year-old romance-struck daughter Betsey; and her son Guy's beautiful and mysterious fiancée Ellen Green are all driven into Spain by their working-class chauffeur from Kidderminster, Ernie Kent, in search of the missing Guy Marlowe. He was last glimpsed by Ernie, his fellow soldier, during the fighting, just before he vanished into the darkness of a Pyrenean pass.

By affectionately mocking Dr Marlowe, Rose Macaulay subjects her own beliefs and behaviour to ironic scrutiny. The tireless committeewoman Mrs Folyot of *Keeping Up Appearances* is Dr Marlowe's precursor, and in Aunt Dot of *The Towers of Trebizond* she will appear again, galvanized by eccentricity and forceful feminism. Kate Marlowe is an admirable, independent woman, a conscientious defender of human rights, dispatching telegrams of protest to heads of state by night and day in the present-day spirit of Amnesty International. The narrator also says she sometimes leaps to unfair conclusions.

In a lengthy essay called 'Moral Indignation', published in 1938, Rose defines that emotion as characteristically English, and she details a long line of eloquent ethical scolds through English history.[43] She always makes fun of reformers' pretensions to god-like rectitude, but she does not in the end disapprove of them. As she wrote to Jean about the English: 'We get called busybodies: as indeed we are, and always have been. We annoyed Europe dreadfully in the 17th century by sending deputations abroad to investigate continental cruelties and we are still at it. I *think* it's a good thing, on the whole, though it makes us unpopular.'[44] The ever-inquiring high-mindedness of Dr Marlowe's civilized concerns is rarely allowed to tire the reader, however, for she must sometimes throttle her criticisms of the barbarism of Spain in the interest of finding her son, Guy.

For finding him is dependent on the help of a young Spanish marquis, Ramon del Monte, who had been Guy's friend at Oxford. At first the search party is hospitably entertained at his run-down manor, although their liberal and irreligious beliefs are anathema to him and to all the del Monte household stands for, however much its members disagree among themselves. In this country-weekend setting, the hopelessly incompatible divisions between the Left and Right are displayed with what Anthony West calls 'an odd sparkling pessimism'.[45]

All save one of the characters in the novel live by different sets of beliefs: Dr Marlowe by the principles of humanistic liberalism; her son Hugh by Cambridge Marxism; Betsey by faith in the romantic scenarios of trashy popular novels and films; and Ernie by working-class egalitarianism. The pale, delicately lovely Ellen Green exists in some other world. Her odd ways slowly divulge a mysterious alien identity, eerily incongruous in this political novel. In the end, she attempts to find a way to escape from its deadlocked strife.

On the Right, Ramon del Monte, the charming, handsome hidalgo of whom Rose said she became rather fond, is Dr Marlowe's ideological antagonist; he lives by the myth of feudalism. His obligations are to his ancestral estate, not to the nation; to his proud manhood, not to the Church. Consequently, he disapproves of education for peasants and women. The two agree that men are the more intelligent sex, but Ramon says women should be left in charming ignorance. Dr Marlowe maintains that women's intellectual deficiency makes it all the more important to educate them. When she argues against his convictions, he urbanely replies, 'If my views are so strange to you, it is Spain that is strange and that you don't know.'[46] And he reminds her that his country has always made political changes by assassination, coup, or revolution rather than by the ballot box – a device which the Spanish ruling class judges to be a corrupter of the common people. A flashback to the bloody murder of a Marquis del Monte by his king brings to life the cruelty and hate which lie at the heart of Spanish history.

Yet Ramon does provide a challenge to Dr Marlowe's occasional dogmatism. He graciously demonstrates that the duty of a feudal lord is defined by *noblesse oblige*; he offers to accompany the party on its journey and to provide access to the prison camps which they plan to visit in search of Guy.

The other del Monte family members are less accommodating and easier to dislike; each represents a conservative myth of Old Spain. Only two characters in the novel have found a way to live with completely genial tolerance and *joie de vivre* – without either political cause or religious shrine: Ramon's worldly, cynical, good-humoured grandmother, the old Marquesa, and his friend, Armand Arachon, a wealthy and conservative young Frenchman, who gaily follows a code of *laissez-faire*. If Rose Macaulay has created some unattractive representatives of the Right, she is even-handed in making the most rational, happy, and moderate characters Right-wing also.

In the midst of these confrontations of ideas sits Ellen Green – 'a nymph, a lost Persephone ... a pale, green-eyed nereid listening silent to strange far tunes'.[47] She seems to have no ideas at all, only antipathies (to Christian symbols and cats and the hot arid inland plains of Spain) and affinities (with dolphins and song and the sea). The world of the other characters is rhetoric; her world is poetry. Ellen responds to Ramon's wooing, but shows no human affections. She comes alive only when she enters the sea for the first time in her life and discovers that it is her natural element. She swims and dives with superhuman agility. She at once knows herself to be 'part of the ancestral ocean, whose salt tide flows through our veins, beats forever in our blood.'[48]

Ellen Green's story is told in Rose Macaulay's third voice, that inner voice which she said reminds us all of our queer amphibious life of dream. Three-quarters of the way through the novel the nereid swims out to sea, away from the summoning voices of the search party, on and on, in the loveliest passages of the book, seeking to rejoin the mermaids from whom she now knows she is descended. Though Ellen has not been told of her antecedents, we are given the story of her mermaid ancestor, who had, in 1675, married a parson in Cornwall. Ellen's beautiful, unearthly forebear had pined on land, and had run down to the sea in the full light of the moon one night and was never seen again. But in the contemporary

Spain of *And No Man's Wit* Ellen, swimming out to sea in the starlight, cannot return to her origins; she is 'lost utterly, forsaken of earth and sea, of humankind and all other, quite doomed.'[49] Fishermen next morning discover a fair, drowned, naked girl in their nets.

Reviewers found Ellen enchanting but so strange an anomaly in the modern-day political wrangle of the novel that the novelist and reviewer Kate O'Brien suggested she should have had a book of her own. Unlike the other characters, Ellen's connection with the ideological myths of *And No Man's Wit* is not spelled out. The meaning of Ellen Green's life and death must be grasped by intuition and symbol. This lost mermaid does not *live* by a myth but represents one: she is a creature of the imagination, a power which can in times of peace transcend the earthly. But in 1939 she cannot survive either on the arid Spanish field of battle or in her own supernatural universe. She cannot really breathe under water indefinitely and the shadow of a shark threatens her. Even in the sea there is the inescapable law of violence: one must eat to live.

And No Man's Wit was an effort to achieve the goal Stephen Spender had described – to synthesize the moral life of contemporary politics. But Rose had longed for 'a time to fiddle and a time to dance', a time to create art, which gives, not political instruction, but delight. Her novel sadly implies that the myth of art is not strong enough to provide escape from the violent contemporary world.

But in addition to this generalized emotion – the failed hope for liberating joy – Rose Macaulay realized her private feelings in Ellen Green's death. Its pathos is personal as well as symbolic. One of Rose Macaulay's selves, she implies, was a lost mermaid, for, speaking of her love of bathing, she wrote to Father Johnson in 1951, 'I am vaguely icthyous and mer.... I dare say some Conybeare rector in Devonshire once married a mermaid, tho' it doesn't seem to have gotten into the family records.'[50] Ellen Green is not boyish, or androgynous, or female – she is feminine – described as an exquisite Botticelli angel. Rose's mermaid self could not swim away from the coming war or wash away the guilt of Gerald's injuries, and her most feminine self could not survive in the masculine landscape of war and politics. Delight for its own sake must die in a world of violence.

Once Ellen is drowned, the book loses momentum. 'I am dead sick of my novel,' Rose wrote to Daniel George.[51] Guy, a wanted fugitive, disguised as a gypsy, has been found by Ernie and Ramon, but he swears them to silence. He cannot take the risk of being exposed by his mother's rescue attempt. Dr Marlowe drops out of the story, and at the close there is no strong female figure like Daphne Sandomir of *Non-Combatants and Others* to prophesy a better tomorrow. The travelogue of damaged Spanish towns becomes less interesting, and the examples of Nazi domination and Spanish cruelty are repetitive. In reading her galleys, Rose herself decided the book was too long.

The last scene is in a bar at St Jean-de-Luz, two months after Dr Marlowe's search had begun and immediately after the Russo-German pact had been signed on 22 August 1939. The war lies just ahead. Guy has escaped across the Pyrenees and by chance finds Armand and Ramon in this chic French resort. Ramon and Guy are reconciled, and over their drinks the three old Oxford friends imagine a better world of small powerless principalities in which the individual is respected. Here world warmongers can do limited harm. Wars are inevitable, the three conclude, but in such a system of petty princedoms conflicts would be local, not international or global. The only positive value that would remain is the central article of Forster's creed – faith in personal relationships. The book's last paragraphs are melancholy, even bitter:

> Cruelty was the devil, and most people were, in one way or another, cruel. Tyranny, suppression, persecution, torture, slavery, war, neglect – all were cruel. The world was acid and sour with hate, fat with greed, yellow with the triumph of the strong and the rich.
>
> The answer would appear to be a lemon. Still here they sat and talked, three friends together in the Bar Basque, with perhaps some nuisance coming tomorrow.[52]

Robert Littell of the *Yale Review* wrote of *And No Man's Wit*: 'For all the lightness of tone, it never seems callous. It is like seeing the figure of Wit himself walking behind the black plumes and mourners and shooting off his fireworks as the procession goes – a procession which is somehow not incongruous with Miss Macaulay's direction.'[53]

She finished *And No Man's Wit* in late January 1940. The funeral procession had begun. By then England had been at war with Germany for almost five months. In June the book was published, and in July Rose Macaulay wrote a charming historical daydream for the BBC, entitled, 'I Wish I Had Been Born in 1850'. But there was no escape.

14

War and Grief

D URING THE LAST war [wrote David Wright in 1972], one of the famous sights of London, a peripatetic phenomenon usually seen chained to the railings of the London Library, was a lady's bicycle: angular, battered, with a wickerwork basket strapped to the handlebars and, boldly inscribed on the frame in white paint, the name ROSE MACAULAY.

When Wright was introduced to its owner in the late 1950s he remembered that famous sight and 'recognized at once in the erect figure of the slender, delicately formidable but not unkindly elderly lady ... the unmistakable personality that had emanated from that bicycle – a *mélange* of toughness, independence, enterprise, courage, and good humour.'[1]

Reporting on the Blitz in the London weekly journals of 1940, that 59-year-old cyclist, who was not only driving an ambulance by night but was also pedalling about between the craters and rubble of London streets by day, protested strongly and repeatedly against the cheery smugness of the national boast heard over the BBC, 'We can take it.' She disliked braggadocio; she admired honesty. One of her wartime *Time and Tide* columns was censored because she had reported a demolition worker saying, in the midst of fire, smoke, explosion, and ruin, 'How long can people stick it? Where will it all end?'

Rose Macaulay herself neither boasted of her wartime courage nor voiced such despairing cries. Bruised by witnessing suffering and death, both in the sick-room and in London's ravaged streets, she soldiered on through three major wartime losses and through post-war bouts of illness and depression. She put to work her proven methods of survival to weather eight years of inner pain and struggle. Her jaunty jockey cap, admired by Compton Mackenzie, perished in the Blitz. She purchased a duplicate.

She nourished old friendships. And she was always in touch with Gerald; perhaps, like the lovers in *The Towers of Trebizond,* they posted diaries to each other. Other opportunities for sharing mutual support included regular visits to Jean in Romford; London dining with the Woolfs until their Mecklenburgh Square home was destroyed; visiting Ivy Compton-Burnett in Thatcham where Ivy and Margaret Jourdain were sheltering from the bombs; lunching with Veronica Wedgwood with whom she shared many interests; and seeing a good deal of Harold Nicolson as she pursued her political activities. She continued to meet and correspond with Daniel George. And she also turned former acquaintances into significant friends. Chief among them was Professor Gilbert Murray; 116 letters to him survive from their long correspondence.

After the war she took up travel writing and historical research until her creative powers could revive. When Jean retired, Rose advised her sister to write because 'nothing makes one happier or more interested.'[2] As a writer, she kept her spirit alive by continuing to explore fundamental questions both of history and of private lives: the nature and powers of Good and Evil; the struggle between barbarism and civilization; the problems of rebuilding after destruction; the possibility of mankind's slow and wavering moral progress. Her underlying grief for the victims of the post-war Waste Land was to infuse her dark and compassionate novel of 1950, *The World My Wilderness.*

For Rose Macaulay the war's strains began with the imminent jeopardy of London. Using her motorist's alias of Emily Macaulay (a disguise soon penetrated by her fellow workers), she had been an emergency ambulance driver for the London Auxiliary Service even before war was declared. During the early period Londoners were obediently sandbagging, digging trenches, blacking out windows, and carrying gas masks everywhere. In the sky overhead the Oxbridge graduates who six years earlier had vowed not to fight for King and Country were preparing to fight and win the aerial Battle of Britain. Still hoping for peace, Rose spent three weeks training for her volunteer post – practising car maintenance, map-reading, and participating in stretcher drills. On 30 August 1939 she wrote to Daniel George in gratitude for a new Animal Book item: 'Thank you for the mortified elephant – he must have felt just as I did this afternoon when I couldn't put a stretcher together after taking it apart. Only I didn't cry and weep.'[3] She had signed up for a 10 p.m. to 3 a.m. shift so that she could go home to try to rest in the early hours and to write during the day. During this period, she helped to evacuate hospitals in the East End dock area by transferring recovering patients to their homes.

In June 1940 the reviews of *And No Man's Wit* were, with few exceptions, favourable. Anthony West's charge in the *New Statesman* that the novel's humour was heartless and its view of Spain shallow was refuted in the next issue by a letter from the loyal Daniel George, who pointed out West's inaccuracies and what he saw as his misreadings. The novel sold well. Rose modestly attributed this success to the fact that few books were being published. She, too, now put fiction on the shelf. She did not begin a new novel again for eight years.

Before long she stored her car at Liss, took to her bicycle by day and drove an ambulance by night, living and working from the late summer of 1940 until the late winter of 1941 through the noisy danger of the worst bombing raids on London. Virginia Woolf wrote to Ethyl Smythe that she 'very much' admired Rose's ambulance service; she noted in her diary that one of Rose's letters describing her duties 'almost broke my day'.[4]

Even in the midst of war's dangers, suffering, sleeplessness, and emotional exhaustion, Rose Macaulay recorded her experiences in the Battle of Britain in her BBC broadcasts and in her columns. On 5 October 1940 her column in *Time and Tide* began:

> Where an hour back two houses stood in this small street, there is a jumbled mountain of fallen masonry, rubble, the shattered debris of two crashed homes; beneath it lie jammed those who lived there; some of them call out, crying for rescue. Others are dumb. Through the pits and craters in the rubbled mass the smell of gas seeps. Water floods the splintered street; a main has burst; dust liquefies into slimy mud. The demolition squad stumble in darkness about the ruins, sawing, hacking, drilling, heaving; stretcher bearers and ambulance drivers stand and watch. Jerry zooms and drones about the sky, still pitching them down with long whistling whooshes and thundering crashes, while the guns bark like great dogs at his heels. The moonless sky, lanced with long, sliding crossing shafts, is a-flare with golden oranges that pitch and burst and are lost among the stars. Deep within its home a baby whimpers, and its mother faintly moans, 'My baby. Oh, my poor baby. Oh, my baby. Get us out.' The rescue squad call back. 'All right, my dear. We'll be with you in just ten minutes now.' They say it at intervals for ten hours.[5]

Although she once wrote, 'I have always avoided tortures when possible,' Rose was one of those workers who nightly had to stand helpless, witnesses to prolonged suffering.[6] No other task of her difficult ambulance service made such painful demands on her. 'One wonders all the time how many people are at the moment alive under some ruin, and how much they are suffering in body and mind,' she wrote to Jean.[7]

Her active duties were satisfying and suited to her talents. 'Emily' Macaulay's driving skills were now life-saving rather than life-threatening. The streets were totally dark except for the lightning flashes of combat; most landmarks and street signs had disappeared. 'Cars crashed all night into street refugees, pedestrians, and each other,' she writes.[8] Hoses, rubble, and the rushing streams from broken water mains blocked the thoroughfares; the ambulances were themselves targets. Drivers had to take chances, had to improvise routes, had to get the victims to hospital. Her innovative boldness was in demand. She liked this chance-taking for a good cause, the mateyness of the rescuing teams, their disregard for a driver's dress or peacetime occupation or gender. Citing discrimination in other branches where women served, she writes, 'Only, I think, in the ambulance services, are the sexes on the same footing and doing exactly the same work.'[9] In contrast to her volunteer work in the First World War, she had the satisfaction of dangerous duty beside male and female comrades stationed on the front lines.

In fact, there were no rear lines in London. Her flat was constantly at risk. On 11 September she interrupts a letter to Jean to mention the 'deafening and continuous pounding'. And then she reassures her: 'The house rocks – but I read today houses can rock a lot without harm.' She sealed her ears with wax balls or slept under the staircase. Twice before the end of October 1940 bombs fell near Luxborough House. She was not at home on either occasion, but 'any time things may crack ... and one lives from day to day,' she wrote to Daniel George.[10] And on 25 October she wrote: 'I returned from a walk this afternoon to find that for the second time a bomb had fallen in the Public Institution garden under our windows and had blown out all the cardboard with which the windows had been replaced last Friday, smashed some more china, brought down some more ceiling, and generally played the hooligan in my flat. It is annoying, but, of course we're lucky.'[11] She had come home from her ambulance duty the week before to find the bed where she should have been sleeping strewn with glass.

At that time she was still driving for the ambulance service at night, feeling somewhat disappointed by the collapse of her assignment to go overseas with the Quakers to transport refugees, learning touch-typing, and still collecting tales of basilisks, centaurs, and unicorns from Daniel George by post. She seemed almost invincible.

But in January 1941 her worst griefs of the war began. She entered upon another painful tour of duty, one which also required her to be a helpless witness of suffering. Margaret, at 61, was diagnosed as having cancer, and Rose spent more and more time with her in Liss. At last she had to leave London and stay there, unable to concentrate, read, or write in the company of 'a bright little nurse' whose chatter filled her ears while the anxiety about Margaret filled her mind. In contrast to London, Liss was physically safe, but the friendly ambulance service shelter and her bomb-rocked flat were more emotionally secure than Margaret's sick-room. After an operation in late January, Margaret sank gradually, too weak and in too much pain even to be read to. Anguished by her sister's suffering and steady decline, Rose – doubtless knowing that her request must and would be denied – desperately asked the doctor to practise euthanasia. Margaret died on 1 March.

Jean, home from South Africa, was now living and working in Romford as the District Nurse, so the melancholy task of disposing of Margaret's possessions and selling the house fell to Rose. She spent two months 'choked in house cares', as she wrote 'Dear Mr. George'. Such a work of sorting and dispersal releases years of memories; Margaret was her favourite sister. If she had saved Rose's letters, Rose destroyed them, just as she must have destroyed her letters to her parents when she dismantled Grace's home. But no surviving correspondence is necessary to understand that Margaret's death was the bitter loss of part of Rose Macaulay's life. The two sisters had been very close in the six years when, after Jean's departure, they had lived in alliance at home in Great Shelford. Now no Macaulay survived to share Rose's memory of that time.

On 13 May she left at last to return to London. But on 10 May, the worst bombing raid of the Blitz had hit the British Museum, the House of Commons, Westminster Hall – and Luxborough House. When Rose arrived in Marylebone, unprepared for personal disaster, she found her entire building a smoking, blackened ruin.

The next night, on the train to Romford to stay with Jean, she wrote to Daniel George on an odd scrap of paper:

> I now have nothing. I came up from Liss last night to find Lux House no more – bombed and burnt out of existence, and nothing saved. I am bookless, homeless, sans everything but my eyes to weep with. All my (and your) notes on animals gone – I shall never write that book now. I don't expect you kept any notes of what you copied for me. I've lost my Pliny, Topsell, Sylvester, everything. Isn't that desolating!
>
> I shall take a room somewhere, till I can look around. But the old address will find me, as bombed addresses go to the P.O. to be called for. Let us meet, and I will try not to be too dismal. The string bag will nicely hold all I now possess.[12]

Although this is a gallant message, for the moment she could not be as stoically independent as usual. She started to sign her note 'Much love', but she crossed this out, and closed as usual with 'Yours'. She wrote immediately to all who might worry about her whereabouts and her state – Storm Jameson and Victor Gollancz quote quite similar letters from her. To Jameson she wrote, 'my lost books leave a gaping wound in my heart and mind'.[13] As always, she kept in touch with her many friends. But refusing to accept the offers of refuge which came by return, she rented a bed-sitting room in nearby Manchester Street. She would not even take sanctuary with Jean. Next to the sorrow of Margaret's death, her consuming grief was the loss of her books and, as we know from her short story, 'Miss Anstruther's Letters', the loss of her letters from Gerald. Day after day she searched the bomb site. In a letter to Storm Jameson she writes: 'I have been climbing about my ruins (staircase gone, but I climb precariously up charred and frail laths, up to where No. 7 was)'.[14] And she found only her kitchen dresser containing her month's ration of marmalade, some tea, and – strewn everywhere in the foundations – the singed and sodden pages of her books.

She began life again. Arrangements for the sale of Margaret's house to some cousins collapsed; one of the cousins committed suicide. The house had to be offered for sale again. She had to retrieve for her own new flat some of the furniture from Liss which she had disposed of. 'It would have been less trouble to have been bombed myself,' she wrote to George.[15]

By the middle of June she had moved into 20 Hinde House, off Manchester Square near Wigmore Street, and had begun her dogged book hunt – investing in Everyman and World Classics, searching second-hand bookshops for Purchas, Hakluyt, Burton, and the hard-to-find D'Israeli's *Calamities of Authors* and *Quarrels of Authors*. 'The less I brood over my lost darlings', she wrote, 'the better for my sanity.'[16] She advertised for out-of-print rarities, and even wrote a detailed *Spectator* essay, 'Losing One's Books', which was sincere in its lamentation but perhaps a little disingenuous in its specific detailing of titles. In it she mourned her inability to afford replacement of her thirteen red morocco-bound volumes of the *Oxford English Dictionary*. Victor and Ruth Gollancz filled this particular hole in her life. She thanked them for their gift in what is perhaps the most ecstatic letter of her surviving correspondence: 'My darling Dictionary again, in the same vestage [*sic*] and habit as I have always known. ... I think it is the most generous act of friendship I ever knew. ... I begin to feel I can live again. My O.D. was my Bible, my staff, my entertainer, my help in work and my recreation in leisure. Nothing else serves.'[17] Other friends sent her miscellaneous old volumes, copies of her own books, and copies of theirs. She welcomed each one. Professor Gilbert Murray, whom she had known casually since 1919, at once sent her copies of his translations of Greek plays. Thus began their sixteen-year correspondence, enlivened by teas, lunches, his visits to her London flat, and her weekend visits to his home, Yatscombe, at Boar's Hill.

For all the generosity of friends and strangers and for all her tireless searching, there were still irreplaceable losses which continued to grieve her. Eight years later, in July 1949, still bereaved, she gave a talk on the BBC – 'Books Destroyed and Indispensable': 'When the first stunned shock begins to pass, one knows that something must be done about lost books. One makes lists. A list of the books one had; that is the saddest list, and perhaps one should not make it. .... There are many books that one cannot live without, and yet one has to live without them, for too many are unprocurable again.' She goes through the catalogue of her treasures and rejoices over those she has been able to replace, but she closes the broadcast, 'I am still haunted and troubled by ghosts, and I can still smell those acrid drifts of smouldering ashes that once were live books'.[18]

This was another loss of the past: the core of her burned library had belonged to her father.

But even after catastrophe, she went on working. She was researching and writing a book for a Collins series, *Britain in Pictures,* designed to hearten an England at war. Her *Life Among the English* (1942) is an amusing social history which begins with the dissimilar images of life in a mud-and-wattle hut and in a Roman villa in the third century AD and ends in a London bomb-shelter where high and low unite. It economically covers such aspects of British life as domestic decoration, banquets, fashion, drama, marriage ceremonies, and education – all in the course of forty-seven illustrated pages. 'What a scamper,' she wrote Daniel George.[19] She kept working away at it, but by 3 December 1941 she was in King's College Hospital, Brixton, with a gastric ulcer. When released, she went on to Romford, where Jean plied her with milk, which she disliked. She complained of being 'milk-soaked'. By Christmas she was back writing and was trading epistolary book reviews with Daniel George. But for the time being she was too weakened to go on with ambulance work; she suffered some ominous heart palpitations. And so she resigned from the ambulance service. She had worked through the four heaviest months of the bombing. The worst of the Blitz was over, England was fighting in North Africa, and the flying bombs aimed at London were yet to come.

By the New Year she had recovered enough to participate gaily as godmother at the christening of Mary Anne O'Donovan ('Boo'), the first child of Muriel and Dermod. (Dr Mary Anne O'Donovan today has a daughter named 'Emily Rose'.) Rose wrote for the occasion a twelve-verse toast, which closed with a summary of her own creed at 61:

TO BOO FROM HER GODMOTHER, 1942

Well, here are a few
Godmother's precepts to see you through:
Think for yourself, and don't mind who
Thinks something else, as they'll surely do;
If they can think something, you can, too.

Know life's a joke, and so are you,
And few, how few,
Things are worth much of a hullabaloo.
If you can't get one thing, another will do.
(But I hope you'll get the lot, my dear little Boo.)

Use your wits, and don't lie and coo
(After the age when it's seemly so to do),
Think, and ask, and wish you knew,
About all there is, why, when, where, who.
It'll take your life, and a bit more, too,
So you'd better get busy enquiring, Boo.

Keep alive and kicking, and set your shoe
In every land. Look at every view,
Strolling blandly through
Barrier, frontier, and taboo.

Make enough friends to drop a few
With no tears shed, and never rue
Spilt milk, smashed pitchers, but find some new
Jug in which to mix a brave new brew.
And toast life deeply as you can do.

Be a clever, brave, *ça-ne-fait-rien* Boo,
A laughing, quaffing, don't-give-a-damn Boo.
And I hope you'll do
Far finer things than I promised in the pew.

Adieu, my Boo,
And here's to you,
Drinking at the gate of 1942.[20]

This represents not optimism but a tough-minded courage. In the penultimate year of her life, she was to say in a BBC interview, 'I think happiness is important.' And she added, 'Happiness is a matter of temperament.'[21] She was not, she herself said, naturally phlegmatic, confident, or armed against adversity, but she exercised a will to achieve and to share what Dermod's wife Muriel, who for over twenty years knew her well, described as 'a gallant high-hearted happiness'.[22] And so, with her characteristic *brio* and her belief in making the best of the nearly inevitable second-best in life, she faced the new year. All notes lost, she was beginning again where her ten years of research for the Animal Book had left off. 'The Animal Book was my heart's blood,' she wrote to Storm Jameson.[23]

But this bravado could not shield her from the most crushing sorrow of her life, which lay just ahead. Shortly after the christening, Gerald O'Donovan's doctor told him he had rectal cancer. Gerald asked him many questions, consulted medical texts, and announced to his family that he had six months to live. His prediction proved accurate.

From January to June 1942, Rose was in the anguished position of being unable to visit Gerald often because of petrol rationing and of having little time alone with him when she did. He was not without comforters, for although Beryl, like Rose, had no talent or taste for nursing, his old friend Marjorie Grant Cook helped care for him, and the Revd Philip Grey, the vicar of Albury, called on him daily and became a friend. (After Gerald's death the vicar said that over the months he learned to admire Gerald's forthright outlook, his sympathy, and his freedom from all pettiness.) Rose brought friends from London to visit him; one of them was Victor Gollancz. Although the two men had not met since 1919, when Gerald accepted a book of Gollancz's for Collins, Victor represented the world of which Gerald had so much wanted to be a part. But Rose herself could not regularly be at Gerald's side.[24]

Storm Jameson describes a revealing moment with her old friend at this time: 'In my eyes she had not altered a hair since the evening twenty years before when, timid and dazzled, I saw her for the first time. [But] listening to her rapid talk, watching the movements of her small head and abrupt flickering smile, I thought that in some persons age makes a sudden leap; overnight the flesh shrinks from the bones and hidden lines rise to the surface. But age did not account for a trace of sadness, or lassitude, given away by her voice, for all its liveliness. ... Despite her letters I did not believe that the change in her had much to do with the loss of her books and manuscripts. Something sharper was biting her.' And she continues:

> One day, when she was leaving, she stood for several minutes, still talking, on the stairs down to the lift. I looked at her, profiled on the wall, narrow shoulders, delicate arched nose.
> 'You're very tired,' I said.
> She moved down a step, paused and looked back at me.
> 'Margaret, you don't know what it's like to watch the person you love dying.'
> She spoke calmly, and I felt her anguish pricking the ends of my fingers.[25]

Rose had watched Margaret Macaulay die and had spent the last weeks at her side. But watching Gerald leave her, she was blocked from intimate conversation with him. She sought for a way to send him a message of love and a plea for forgiveness for her attempt to part from him twenty years before. In mid-May she wrote the short story, 'Miss Anstruther's Letters', which, because it was written for a collection called *London Calling,* to be published in America, she believed no English reader would see. As she wrote to Daniel George at the time, the story was a 'mainly veracious' account of the Luxborough House bombing one year before. But she departs from the facts in two ways: she places Miss Anstruther on the scene on the night of the disaster (Rose had witnessed so many victims experiencing catastrophe that she could picture the circumstances all too clearly), and she had the courage to place the time of the story after the death of Miss Anstruther's lover, the event which both Rose and Gerald knew was soon to come. In this story, written for him, she could and did picture for him how deep her grief at his loss was to be.

In the story Miss Anstruther rushes from her burning flat, carrying a few hastily snatched belongings, and leaves behind to the consuming flames her dearest possession – her lover's letters. Afterwards, she searches the blackened site for them, recreating over and over in her mind what had been a diary of their happiest moments together. But she finds only a burned scrap: '... leave it at that. I know now that you don't care twopence; if you did you would ...' The story ends: 'She had failed in caring once, twenty years ago, and failed again now, and the twenty years between were a drift of grey ashes that once were fire, and she was a drifting ghost, too. She had to leave it at that.' Rose had tried unsuccessfully to part with Gerald twenty years before. 'Miss Anstruther's Letters' is her most moving piece of writing.[26]

Brigid O'Donovan said that her father did not suffer constant intense pain but slowly starved and failed after an operation, from which the incision never healed. For six months Rose came as frequently as she could; on each visit he was visibly nearer death. During the last month of his life, July 1942, she put aside all other responsibilities, arranged somehow for transportation in spite of petrol rationing, and visited him two or three times a week.

On 20 August 1942, she wrote to Rosamond Lehmann:

He died on July 26th. I had spent the day before with him, and he knew me and talked to me, and had been asking for me, but was only partly there. Then, late in the evening, he became unconscious and died next morning. I wasn't there then, but didn't want to be. I feel empty and dead, and without purpose. I'd like to get right away – to Portugal if I could – but must wait till I feel better; I expect Portuguese food wouldn't be the right thing for a gastric ulcer! (I *hope,* however, that won't develop again.) I think an entire change of scene would help me begin life again. For himself, of course, I am thankful he didn't linger on in pain. Isn't it odd, with all this dying, so inevitable, we haven't yet learned to accept it. We are unadaptable about that. It still comes as a shock. It's all this loving we do. Worthwhile, but it doesn't fit us for losing each other.

He was the dearest companion, you know. And had such a fine, brilliant mind. His grasp of things was so masterly – he would have been such a good statesman.[27]

She acknowledges – then brushes aside – his limitations as a novelist, and speaks of her love for *The Holy Tree*. And once more she praises him as a human being: 'You would have liked him, and he would have delighted in you.'

In *The Towers of Trebizond,* written thirteen years later, the narrator Laurie says of her lover's death:

And now the joy was killed, and there seemed no reason why my life too should not run down and stop now that its mainspring was broken. When a companionship like ours suddenly ends, it is to lose a limb or the faculty of sight; one is quite simply cut off from life and scattered adrift, lacking the coherence and integration of love. Life, I supposed, would proceed; I should see my friends, go abroad, go on with my work, such as it was, but the sentient, enjoying principle which had kept it all ticking, was destroyed.[28]

Rose's letter to the sympathetic Rosamond is intimately confiding; nevertheless, it attempts in the end to hide the extremity of her grief. She closes, 'Well, it's over, if things are ever over. The trick is not to feel one's springs are broken or worn down. Perhaps it's partly health. I'd *like* to go to Portugal, and see sun and miss spies and refugees and Portuguese.'[29]

With less intimate friends than Rosamond, however, she described herself as resolutely determined to recover. To Daniel George she wrote casually in mid-September, 'I am trying to get to Portugal for a change of scene and to relieve the brooding mind. ... I had a very close friend die at the end of July, and have not been good company since, but must get over this.'[30] She was not defeated, but seven years later she expressed the enduring pain of solitary mourning in her description of a widow's state in *The World My Wilderness*: 'Her want of Maurice grew no less; it hungered in her night and day, engulfing her senses and her reason in an aching void. She tried to fill the void, stupefy the ache, with reading, translating, painting, gambling, chess, games with Roland; but still it deepened about her, as if she were in a cave alone.'[31] Rose did not paint, gamble, or have a young child to play games with. But she tried to fill the void with absorbing research, travel, and political action.

And so she wore a mask and threw herself into wartime public life. However, there had never been a clear role for her maverick style in party politics. She had little interest in the strategies of gaining and holding power or the manoeuvres of committees; her interest was in the ethical conflict she experienced in her own life and especially in her life with

Gerald. How can a society or an individual human being simultaneously manifest love and enjoy freedom? In 1950 she wrote to Gilbert Murray about this moral question in terms of public policy rather than of a private dilemma; the problem was raised for her by the concept of the Welfare State in the light of her libertarianism:

> The Liberal problem always seems to me this. How far does one combine resistance to over-control with social justice, i.e. tolerable living for people in general? We are too selfish to be trusted, if left free, to give away enough to make people comfortable enough to give them a chance. Yet if all this is ordered for us, as to some extent it has to be, it so soon leads to tyranny. It is a very difficult problem. If only human beings had more pity, unselfishness, and justice and didn't need coercion to treat each other decently. But it is such a jungle of wild beasts on the whole.[32]

She believed 'no one is good enough to rule others or wise enough to rule himself.'[33] To Victor Gollancz she wrote in 1942, 'I have been asked to join the Council of the Liberal party! But am I a Liberal? I think not. Nor Labour. What am I? I think no party. All are so tiresome. Why is there no proper, Socialist, non-Communist, no-Transport House party? Any way, I hate party politics.'[34] In 1946 she was to sit on the Council of the International Liberal Party, but it was so internally divided that she was never asked to cleave to a party line. Her political energy was thrown largely into the work aimed at a lasting post-war peace, work which began in the League of Nations even before August 1945 when the hostilities came to an end in Japan. And she combined this evangelistic activity with research into exotic or obscure subjects and with the solo journeys which produced *They Went to Portugal* (1946) and *Fabled Shore: from the Pyrenees to Portugal* (1949).

Rose Macaulay's correspondence with Gilbert Murray during these years reveals her sad vision of the post-war morals of the West. That vision lies behind *The World My Wilderness* and the novel's bleakness implies the emotional needs which were only partially satisfied by her travel and travel writing. The letters also record a friendship which ended only with Gilbert Murray's death. They are complemented by those to Daniel George and Jean Macaulay, and by the story of a new and lasting friendship made in Portugal with the helpful young English scholar David Ley. But the letters to Murray yield the greatest number of clues to Rose's life in the late Forties.

Gilbert Murray, Regius Professor of Greek at Oxford, and Chairman of the Executive of the League of Nations Union, was a man so distinguished both in the world of letters and in the world of affairs that Rose Macaulay could not fail to admire him. He had become in the public eye a Victorian Monument. She wrote him, 'How proud I am to know you and to be allowed to correspond with you.'[35] But her reverence did not subdue the vivacity that Professor Murray prized. He said she rejuvenated him. As Alan Pryce-Jones writes, 'Her friends devoured her, for she managed to renew them in their own eyes.'[36] On one occasion Professor Murray wrote, 'Dash my buttons, Ma'am, this must not go on. I have not seen you for months – unless you count a casual meeting at the Liberal International. Will you please lunch with me at the Athenaeum Annex next Thursday?'[37] During one period when he was too ill to come to London for his regular schedule of meetings, he joked that he would gladly pay her rail fare, as he did for his grandchildren, if she would visit him regularly at Yatscombe.

Professor Murray was fifteen years older than Rose Macaulay, a handsome, graceful, charming man with a delightful sense of humour, in his early years described as 'a young Apollo'. Judging from their correspondence, Murray must have made Rose Macaulay feel like one of his brightest, admiring women students. Toward them he had always expressed a romantic affection, tempered by an unpossessive detachment. He called such relationships 'emotional friendships' and could never regard his pleasure in teaching and knowing young women as a threat to his marriage. However, his authorized biographer, Francis West, says that Gilbert Murray's wife, the rather joyless Lady Mary, who shared his political but not his intellectual life, was always jealous of his students and the young actresses who appeared in his plays. He was a faithful husband, but he was always susceptible to 'an attractive, lively, intelligent girl'. Although Rose was 60 when they began to correspond, her liveliness and intelligence were indeed attractive.

For many reasons aside from his personal warmth she wrote to him regularly and admiringly during the periods when she intermittently neglected many other correspondents: Murray was not only an internationally known classicist, but also a man who, although not a pacifist, had for years taken on national and international peace-making responsibilities. He played a principled role in Liberal politics. He was a scholar-poet-playwright, a cultural historian, an impressive actor-speaker, and an inspiring teacher. From his arrival at Oxford in 1904 he steadily offered active support to Somerville College; he and Lady Mary were active feminists. Above all, Professor Gilbert Murray was a link with Rose Macaulay's past. Like her father, he was a don, a classical scholar, a critic, a translator, and a moral Victorian agnostic. And although no one could take Gerald O'Donovan's place, like Gerald he offered Rose the intellectual stimulation of affectionate, bantering, analytical conversation.

The two shared many interests and activities. Both correspondents were frequent BBC performers, lecturing, reading, and participating in quiz shows; they were regular guests on the 'Brains Trust', a symposium in which controversial questions were posed to experts. Her letters trace the boundaries of their common ground and reflect her desire to entertain him. They move between serious and light topics: she amuses him with good-humoured tales about her fellow contestants' bad debating manners and their vanities, and she laughs at her own frustration at missing questions when she knows the answers to everyone else's. She attends political meetings and sittings of the House of Commons and writes him her candid judgements; Churchill, she says, 'is becoming a bully and a tyrant'. She arranges for Professor Murray to meet C.V. Wedgwood (then an editor at *Time and Tide*) over lunch. She writes to him of books and asks his opinions of them; she recommends a Michael Innes detective novel. She mentions 'a nice week-end spent at Cambridge with E. M. Forster'. She shares pleasures, enthusiasms, and her interest in ethical quandaries. Among these latter are amusing surprises: 'I have been waiting for a moment when I could go deeply into the matter of Cheating at Cards.'[38] Or she asks, 'What do you do about a friend whom you suspect of stealing reference books from the British Library?' And she answers herself, 'Nothing, of course.'[39] But in addition to the persiflage there are always matters of substance which both letter writers attack seriously. She discusses the relationship between Art and the State and concludes that the State as patron can effectively support every art but literature. Gilbert Murray's answering letters were briefer than hers; they contain less news of activity and more health complaints.

But he was always responsive and appreciative, for the 'rejuvenation' Rose Macaulay provided was important to him. Although he continued to be active in both politics and academia until his death at 91, in the years Rose knew him he was more and more often ill. His friends died; he lost three of his five children; Lady Mary's hearing, memory, and general health failed. He said he had begun to feel old, tired, and brittle. (Rose's reply is brisk. 'Surely not.') As early as 1920 what he believed to be his most important work had been devalued by the younger poets. T. S. Eliot had called him 'merely a very insignificant follower of the Pre-Raphaelite movement', and scorned Murray's rhymed translations of Greek dramas as decorative and wordy, devoid of creative power.[40]

Classical scholars rejected Murray's Apollonian interpretation of sixth-century BC Greek life as romantically idealized because his distaste for sexual and physical frankness blinded him to the Dionysian aspects of the classical world. He had bowdlerized his translations of Aristophanes; he thought *All Quiet on the Western Front* 'coarse'. He believed in the sacredness of Hellenic culture. He believed in Progress. He was an optimist. He was not of the Age.

But Rose declared herself profoundly moved by his radio talks and poetry readings and listened with pleasure and admiration to the BBC productions of his plays. She shared his belief that the chief problem of the times was the struggle between civilization and barbarism. But as always, she was independent of her mentor; she was to redefine that struggle in her own way in *The World My Wilderness*. However, because, like her, Murray was grieved by the diminution of order and beauty in the post-war world, and because, like her, he had in childhood become unusually sensitized to cruelty, and because – perhaps especially because – he was now being called old-fashioned, Rose Macaulay showed in her letters a deep fondness for Gilbert Murray.

In March 1943 she wrote to him of her forthcoming trip to Portugal, a neutral country, adding that before packing her books she was required to take them to the Portuguese embassy to be read and sealed by the censors. (She wondered what she could include to tease them.) She showed no apprehension about her proposed journey in one of the small civil planes with blacked-out windows that were making London–Lisbon flights at the time. In spite of the fact that Portugal was a non-combatant, such wartime travel was a calculated risk; a few weeks after her outward flight a similar flight bringing Leslie Howard home after his series of British Council lectures was shot down.

Her plan was to conduct research in Lisbon and Oporto about the lives of English citizens who had spent time in Portugal during the previous eight centuries. (About this time she reviewed approvingly a similarly structured book about English visitors to Jamaica by her friend John Pope-Hennessy; perhaps the two of them had discussed this device together.) She was to follow the footsteps of Crusaders, royalty, writers, clergymen, ambassadors, evangelists, plotters, tourists, merchants, seamen, officers. The earthquake of 1756, the port wine industry, piracy and diplomacy, the life of nuns, the rudeness of Byron – all fascinated her darting curiosity and her love of *mélange*. What amused her most and what was to be one thread that bound together the many disparate accounts was the bad manners of the British in foreign lands, 'so fatuously priggish, and often so stuck-up about the "dirt and superstition" they encounter abroad'.[41] Her amusement is contagious; Gilbert Murray said he laughed aloud on the train when he read her account of Southey in Lisbon.

From early March until May 1943, she laboured in Lisbon and Oporto, including her hostess for a time, Susan Lowndes Marquez, doyenne of the British literary colony. The grateful acknowledgements of assistance in *They Went to Portugal* show that she drew many to the aid of her search. But her chief support in Lisbon were the staff at the British Institute; she worked every morning in a small room there. The young lecturer C. David Ley, whom Rose described as 'very stalwart, intelligent, companionable', was of particular assistance, and on her return to London, he continued to assist her. He says that she never really learned Portuguese; she had decided to use her Italian to translate it roughly and her French to get about socially with non-English speakers. So because Portuguese literary texts were difficult for her to translate, Ley's willingness to go over them with her, together with his wide and deep knowledge of Portuguese history and culture, proved indispensable. So began a long, warm friendship which continued when he was transferred to Madrid and when he became a professor at the University of Salamanca; he always spent his August holiday in London and Rose always spent some time with him then. On several occasions she invited him to accompany her as a 'travel-chum', but he was unable to get leave. Later, when he and his bride Paz came to live in London, Ley, now Dr Ley, sometimes used to join Rose in her chill swims in the Serpentine and the Thames. Once, she wrote to Muriel Thomas, 'we got tangled up in a regatta'.[42]

On her return to England in May 1943 she wrote to Gilbert Murray: 'Portugal was lovely! I had two months there, and enjoyed it all the time. Very interesting architecture; glorious weather; charming towns; wine, fish, and lots of material for my great Work on the English in Portugal.'[43] And then, with the same cultural snobbery that her book mocked – not quite fair from one who did not know their language – she remarks, 'I like the Portuguese, though they are rather stupid. But animated and amiable.' And she adds, 'I am now trying to find out how much, if any, intercourse we had with them in the quite early centuries – before the 9th century. I must look it up.'[44] She was to spend the next two years 'looking it up', engrossed in the endless searching by which she tried to dull her still aching grief. She described her manuscript in a letter to Lady Mary, 'It is a vast and unreadable book – but I like writing it – and that, I imagine to be the best reason for writing anything.'[45]

She had returned to an England still at war. The flying bombs from Peenemünde were dropping on London. She wrote reassuringly to Murray on 26 June that she had become 'rather toughish', not minding bombing between hits. But she is careful not to boast: 'I don't mean I *like* those noxious insects that doodle over our roofs, with the awe-ful pause when the engine stops and then clump, which means someone else has got it and one can go to sleep until the next one wakes one up.' But she has a strategy for self-control. In July she writes, 'When they are just overhead, I will them to go on and not stop, and put my head under my pillow (if it's night) in case they disobey me. So far they haven't.'[46]

She continued to write her columns and appear on radio; over the years her public was to enjoy her brisk repartee regularly on a variety of programmes, including 'Critics', the 'Brains Trust', 'Book Reviews', and 'Frankly Speaking'. Her quickness made her the ideal panel member, although her fast speech was sometimes hard to take in. Some of her candid remarks may have led to the appearance of her name on the German list of writers to be exterminated after their invasion of Britain.

She was delighted to be included with E.M. Forster on this roster of proscription and called him to announce happily that they could be punished together.

She enjoyed the social and intellectual interchange her writing and speaking initiated, but sometimes for days on end she buried herself in libraries. In July 1944 she writes to Professor Murray: 'I am tied up with Portugal in the Records Office, twenty books around me for each separate book I tackle.'[47] She refuses several weekend invitations, for, she says, she fears she will lose the thread of what she is doing if she leaves her task. As she had no contract or deadline for the book, the motive for remaining totally absorbed was to hold at bay the sorrow that threatened even now to overwhelm her; 'I was very unhappy then', she wrote seven years later, 'and had to deaden it by work.'[48]

At last in the spring of 1945, the manuscript was delivered to Collins, accompanied by a modest note. But on 23 March, after two years of concentrated, consuming research and writing, she received a dis-heartening reply from her long-time publisher: 'It is very long. You have always said we would not want to publish it, and I am afraid we are not too happy about it.'[49] She replied in her most casual tone, 'Of course I am sorry, but as you know, I always thought you wouldn't want the book.... Don't bother to "explain" about it, as I can guess what you feel. I am sure it's too long, for one thing.'[50]

As Curtis Brown, her agent, was out of town, Rose acted in his name and passed the manuscript on to Daniel George at one of their lunches together. Ever her champion and knight-errant, he read it, liked it, made a few minor suggestions, and took the bulky packet to Jonathan Cape himself. They agreed to publish it if it were cut. In fact, she halved it, 'in the fond hope that Cape may publish it later on,' she wrote to Gilbert Murray. (Forty-five years later, in 1990, the second half was at last published in England by Carcanet under the title, *They Went to Portugal Too*.) But even thus radically edited, the published book ran to over 400 pages. 'You can't think what a load it takes from my mind, after the depressing Collins view,' Rose wrote to Daniel George in thanks.[51]

But if there was some satisfaction in the success it met, sad family news diminished it. On 14 November 1945, William John Conybeare Macaulay, aged 59, died in Canada of a heart attack. Her childhood memories of the Five were now shared only by Jean. The sisters became increasingly close, writing and seeing each other often. Jean became a guardian of Rose's health, although Rose ignored her recurrent gastritis and made little of her anaemia and the colds, bronchitis, and 'flu which plagued her through this period. Rose's flippancy about the Church often hurt her devout sister's feelings, but it did not keep them apart.

Strangely, there are no surviving letters from Rose that mention the war's end. Her concern about establishing a lasting peace, however, is expressed as intensely as ever; in April 1947 she reports a gloomy prophecy in the House of Commons that 'the next war will be about petrol'. Her usual busy London activities went on, hampered only by the material austerity which affected everyone. After finishing 'a huge index' for *They Went to Portugal,* she 'wangles' her way, she says, into the Press Room to attend 'the fascinating affair' of a series of League of Nations Security Council meetings, addresses an undergraduate literary society at Oxford, and writes a long article on 'The Future of the Novel' for *Daylight and New Writing* and another on Evelyn Waugh for *Horizon.* But these were short-term tasks, and it was imperative for her peace that she find a demanding major project which would engage her in travel and in self-forgetting concentration.

By May 1947 she had found a way to realize a plan she had been forming since 1943 when she had written to David Ley: 'I think when the war is over I shall try and visit Spain. It would be fun. . . . I shall get the ancient Morris that is mouldering in a garage, and fling it across the Channel.'[52] She described her coming adventure to Gilbert Murray:

> I am going abroad at the end of June for about 2 months. I am commissioned by a publishing firm [Hamish Hamilton] to write a book in a travel series they project about the less known cities of the world. I am to do the towns on the Spanish Mediterranean coast – not the already overwritten ones just inland such as Toledo, Granada, Seville; but the smaller ones, only I think to include Barcelona and Terragona and Gerona.[53]

She goes on to describe her proposed itinerary in detail and adds, 'It will be hot as anything can be; but I shall keep near the sea and continually enter it. . . . So now I am busy reading everything I can find about southern Spanish architecture, improving my Spanish and photography.' (She was practising her Spanish on her char, who was from Gibraltar.) And she adds, 'Tyres one can but pray about. Who is the god of wheeled vehicles? I should think Apollo.'[54]

Because the length both of her journey and of its account were determined by the publisher's deadline, Rose could not indulge in open-ended research. The kinds of details she was to report were dictated by her own criterion for a travel book: the traveller should be in the picture as little as possible. And so the information about her own experience slips in only obliquely to illustrate the charms of the world she was exploring. But her voice is unique and so is the image of the insouciant and upright Miss Macaulay jolting and slipping along nearly impassable roads and mountain mule tracks in her old car, its back seat piled with guide-books, a Roman atlas, and old tomes about Spain.

Because in driving she is pre-empting male privilege, she is hooted and jeered at by astonished and derisive Spaniards all along the way. 'It is not the custom here,' she is told. 'Spanish ladies live very quietly.'[55] Describing the Spanish view of a single woman travelling she writes: 'The fact of her sex and the fact of her aloneness, seem to the Spanish at once entertaining, exciting, and remarkable, as if a chimpanzee strayed unleashed about the streets.'[56] On foot, she was not only stared at and shouted at, but everywhere followed by inescapable packs of little boys, peering, hiding, running, pointing, mocking, laughing. Once she was struck by two or three tomatoes; once stones were thrown at her car. But she consults the history books and cheers herself; xenophobia and what she calls 'sex-unfairness' are characteristic of remote communities; in earlier centuries all visiting strangers to Spanish villages had been stoned. And the Costa Brava was not unrelievedly hostile country; in her dealings with individual Spaniards, she says, 'I encountered much friendliness.' And so, with British phlegm and in her own independent spirit, as she had advised her god-daughter, she looks 'at every view, strolling blandly through every barrier, frontier and taboo', a lone adventurer. 'I saw only one GB licence in two months.'

She disregards both Spanish and English customs. She keeps her dignity and her sense of humour, demonstrates her resourcefulness, and has a very good time. Where she cannot drive up a mountain path, she climbs and scrambles on foot. One evening, unable to obtain a room in the only inn for miles, she sleeps on her rubber mattress under a tree. And at every opportunity she bathes: 'On that hot July evening, I bathed in the smooth curve of the sea, that lapped about me as cool and warm as silk, while stars came out, and the great rock jutted into still water against a rose-flushed west.'[57] In *Fabled Shore* she creates a living landscape: the 'wild and disconcerting' roads climb and slide; the sea whispers and croons; the ruins have 'the awful fascination of dark towers in a dream'.

The book is more than a series of accomplished descriptions and a stylistic feast. Woven through the tapestry of word pictures is an account of the long history of the 4,000-mile shore. 'All the way down this stupendous coast I trod on the heels of Greek mariners, merchants, and colonists, and of trafficking Phoenicians, conquering Carthaginians, dominating ubiquitous Romans, destroying Goths, magnificent Moors, feudal counts, princes and abbots. History in Spain lies like a palimpsest, layer upon layer, on the cities, on the shores, on the old quays of little ports, on the farm-houses standing among their figs, vines, and olive gardens up the terraced mountains.'[58] She writes of unfinished baroque cathedrals, abandoned towns, and ruined castles. And she does not forget the history of the Civil War as she drives past bombed fishing villages and burned-out churches.

But her journey into the past is not all romance, although it was always adventure. She was driving an eleven-year-old car. 'I learnt that cars are not as firmly held together as one had hoped. One piece after another is apt to drop from them; there is a sudden intimidating clatter, and it will be either a bumper or an exhaust pipe (or more perilously, for I was once all but over the edge of a very steep mountain precipice) the steering axle, that, still attached at one end, has broken its bolts at the other and is clattering with the noise of machine guns along the road.'[59] But she is undaunted. She straps on the dragging bumper; when the axle breaks she walks to the next town for a mechanic. Once she 'became involved with a vineyard' and is stuck in a ditch. In spite of what she calls the 'inimical' male attitudes, she gives thanks for the willing help she received from young peasants and workmen in her automotive emergencies. Sometimes their concern is rather too exuberant. She relates to Jean, but does not include in *Fabled Shore,* an account of her car's bonnet's catching fire. 'The whole of Lisbon' surrounds her and stages a slapstick farce. Six shouting policemen come to her aid, her bags are flung into the street, all her documents must be produced, a corps of helmeted firemen arrive with a hose long after the small flare-up in the fuel line has been extinguished by a handful of earth. Rose alone remains calm.

She has rounded the peninsula into Portugal and spends her last night there in Sagres, from which the small inn listed in each of her three guidebooks has long since disappeared. In the last pages of the book she describes her solution with a minimum of complaint: 'I made my bed in the roofless apse of what had once been a chapel; all night the wind whispered and moaned coldly about the Sacred Cape; the long beams of the lighthouse ... speared and shafted the desolate wastes of the sea that bounds the known world.'[60] To lie down supperless in a cheerless, cold, uncomfortable place, however romantic, and to know that no one you love knows your whereabouts is to be alone indeed. So many conditions of her journey were harsh that it sometimes seems that either self-punishment or a tough testing of herself lay at the centre of her aesthetic joy.

Yet when she heads back to the known world at daybreak, she leaves the Iberian peninsula with regret. For two months Spain had been, as she said, 'a lovely dream of beauty and interest', a land of delight linked to her boyish childhood – to the bathing; to her retreats to the top of a wall, book in hand; to the daydreams which had always 'magicked' her. Spain's fabled shore had offered the beauty of landscape and the pleasure of the warm sea. And just as in those youthful daydreams of male adventure, she showed 'on all occasions, great courage and resource.'

Back in London, she read 'the learned books and the tourist books, the intelligent books and the silly books, the critical books and the gushing books' about Spain and wrote her own. Reviews were enthusiastic. C. V. Wedgwood wrote in *Time and Tide,* 'Miss Macaulay has made her own witty, erudite, observant, and poetic addition to the literature of travel in Spain. . . . She has the sense of the past perhaps more strongly developed than any other contemporary English writer. In this book it comes out in moments of an intense feeling which is near to poetry.'[61]

But months before its publication in June, Rose had taken up another task. On 7 April 1948, she wrote to Gilbert Murray, 'I have finished my Spain book and am starting a novel,' and in May, 'I am writing a novel, rather a rest after several books which needed mugging up, to sit about and spin fiction out of an uninformed mind.'[62] But the mind out of which she was spinning *The World My Wilderness* was richly informed – not by research in the library, but by pondering on the questions which had engaged her for the last ten years and by her lone journeys, the war, her mourning, her conscience, and her spiritual longings.

Her penultimate novel is a dark story. *Fabled Shore* records not only the beauty of the Costa Brava but also 'the dark turmoil of history'. The ruins left standing in Spain, after centuries of exploring, trading, building, and warring, had been outlined against the sky throughout her journey as reminders of the conflict between forgotten rival causes and between life and time. Many hours alone, travelling across a landscape to which she responded intensely, without 'the dearest of companions' to share it, created quiet spaces for memory and sorrow as well as for sensory delight. A consciousness of destruction and of irrevocable loss permeates *The World My Wilderness,* a story of post-war France and London, Rose Macaulay's first novel since Gerald O'Donovan's death.

Rose's three voices are allowed full expression in her last four books. *Fabled Shore* is a journey recounted in two of her voices: the first – that of the cerebral self, the careful scholar and observer, and sometimes the dry humorist – and the third voice – that of the poetic, prophetic dreamer in contact with other times, who writes, 'Ghosts of a hundred pasts rise up from the same grave.'[63] Elizabeth Bowen described this combination of voices in *Fabled Shore* as 'high intelligence and second sight'.[64] Both also speak in *The World My Wilderness,* but they are joined by Rose Macaulay's second voice, the plangent voice of feeling and conscience. Virginia Woolf wrote of writers' 'many and complex' selves that 'it is when they bring these selves into relation – when they simplify, when they reconcile their opposites that they bring off (generally late in life) those complete books which for that reason we call their masterpieces.'[65] In *The World My Wilderness* and *The Towers of Trebizond* Rose Macaulay allows all three of her selves to speak. Both novels take themes and characters from her past work and develop them with a new richness. But both are strikingly different from her other novels, and from each other.

After a decade without the appearance of a Rose Macaulay novel, the publication of *The World My Wilderness* was a noteworthy event in London literary life. The short novel was warmly praised by Anthony Burgess, by Frank Swinnerton, by the *Times Literary Supplement*. It was selected by the Book Society and the *Evening Standard* for wide circulation, translated and kept in print. But such commercial promotion views a book primarily as 'a good read for all brows'. And as a result some of its subtlety may have been overlooked, for few critics of the moment looked for the techniques which distinguish *The World My Wilderness* and intensify its emotional effect: the symbolism; the effective economy of a tight, intricate, interdependent poetic structure; the allusiveness; and the layered complexity of thought and emotion. Gilbert Murray, who admired it, was to write, 'I missed the point dreadfully the first time. It is rather heart-rending and frightening.'[66] And those who read this novel more than once, as Penelope Fitzgerald notes in her preface to the Virago edition, see that for all its grieving, in the end *The World My Wilderness* puts its faith in love.

Assuredly, the admirer looking for Rose Macaulay's characteristic novel of ideas is rewarded by *The World My Wilderness*. While graver than before, the narrator acutely observes and assesses all characters, even the minor ones, in terms of their moral values in 1946, a year after the war. The central figure is a 17-year-old English schoolgirl, but every connotation of that phrase is utterly misleading. Barbary, who looks 14, is 'a lost, strayed, derelict girl'. She lives in France with her handsome, careless, gifted expatriate English mother, Helen, and a younger half-brother and a step-brother. Barbary is slackly indifferent to the obligations placed upon her by authority, propriety, custom, property, traditional morality – by rules and laws of all kinds. But she is more intelligent than the anti-social barbarian Denham Dobie of *Crewe Train,* and her behaviour is more shocking; it is not playful but criminal.

During the war Barbary is a juvenile hanger-on of the rural French Resistance, the Maquis, who fade in and out of hills and bushes, harassing the Germans by theft, vandalism, obstruction, and occasional murder. Their code is pack loyalty and their behaviour is anarchic. At the end of each day Barbary returns home to Les Fraises, the charming villa at the foot of the Pyrenees near the fishing village of Collioure. There her mother lives a dilettante life, painting without seriousness, perpetrating clever scholarly frauds for her own amusement, and secretly grieving for her second husband, the genial Maurice, drowned by the Maquis. The Resistance had damned his reasoned toleration of the German occupation as traitorous collaboration. Now that the war is over, Helen drifts indolently, and Barbary, out of habit, continues her dangerous outlaw adventures. She is not so much rebellious as sullenly subversive.

But when the novel opens Helen, without emotion, is sending Barbary to London to study at the Slade and to live with her father, Sir Gulliver Deniston, a brilliant, respected, and wealthy barrister, whom Helen, bored by his proper life and proper friends, had casually deserted some years before and since divorced. Barbary adores her unloving mother; she does not want to leave. Sir Gulliver has remarried and has a baby son. His attractive new wife, Pamela, is a decent young woman who is a model representative of the mores and tastes of her upper-middle-class Roedean background. Pamela is possessive, unimaginative, and conventionally moral, understandably hostile to Helen and to Barbary. One triumph of the novel is that it makes jealous ploys of self-preservation human and sympathetic. Sir Gulliver makes some overtures to his daughter, but she is not forthcoming. She childishly resents Pamela and believes her father should reinstate Helen in his London home. Wounded, Sir Gulliver, who still loves Helen, retreats. Barbary is put at serious risk by both parents' neglect; we learn by flashback that she had been raped by a German soldier and we witness the sexual approaches of the shady characters she meets in London. The novel holds no brief for the family as a dependable bulwark of civilization and personal security; Barbary's mother's selfishness and her father's legalism cripple their power to love her.

The unhappy Barbary moves among five vividly realized landscapes. Each exists on a physical, social, moral, and spiritual level: Helen's romantic Bohemian villa; the fear-filled *maquis* forest of the Pyrenees; the classic law-abiding order of the Deniston London household; a holiday Scottish shooting-lodge with its sporting code; and Barbary's true spiritual and psychic home, the ruined City around St Paul's, where she and her other step-brother Raoul discover an outlaw world for themselves among the bombed-out shops and churches, overrun with weeds, and frequented by wild cats, deserters, petty thieves, black marketeers, spivs, and their girls.

This haunted wilderness is precisely and poetically described. Rose's descriptions were so exact in locating every bombed shop that a successful charge of libel was brought against her and her publisher for an adjective she used implying the questionable business methods of one firm, although she did not name it. Rose visited the bombed site often, sometimes with friends. Penelope Fitzgerald remembers 'the alarming experience of scrambling after her ... and keeping her spare form just in view as she shinned undaunted down a crater, or leaned, waving, through the smashed glass of some perilous window.'[67] Frank Swinnerton writes that Rose sent him sprigs of the flowering weeds from these new catacombs for botanical identification. Their names – rosebay willowherb, chickweed, vetch, fennel, bramble, bindweed, thorn-apple, and thistle – make up a long rhythmic list of the natural elements which were daily overtaking what was once a bustling, thriving human community. To the rejected Barbary these blasted cliffs and overgrown chasms seem to say, 'Here is your home, here is where you belong'.

The Deniston family knows nothing of Barbary's truant afternoons. The household makes a holiday trip to Scotland to bring her together with jolly cricketing cousins, who find her odd, and a psychiatrist uncle who threatens to probe her secrets. She steals £15 and returns to London, only to fall more deeply into trouble as a wanted shoplifter and to fall to near death running through the ruins trying to escape the police.

Suffering from concussion, she lies in a coma (like Gerald's) and Helen comes at once from France. The drama of passion and jealousy is played out by the three adults while Barbary remains in a critical state. In the end, Barbary's jeopardy awakens Helen from her emotional numbness and she rescues her daughter, as far as she can be rescued, from her lost ways, and takes her to Paris to study art in Bohemian freedom.

All the characters have been found humanly lacking in some way, but their flaws have been exacerbated and exposed by the post-war chaos. On the level of ideas, *The World My Wilderness* is concerned with the problem that haunted Gilbert Murray. But Rose Macaulay changes its terms. Though Murray was a hopeful prophet, his greatest fear in his old age was that the Vandals would come over the wall again – that the Hellenic-Christian ethical values he believed to be a 'precious approximation to truth' would be destroyed. In more than one public and private statement he reiterated the central theme of his 1947 BBC broadcast, 'A Victorian Looks Back':

> I begin to feel that we should aim not at a peaceful law-abiding world but at some form of unity of Christian or Hellenic civilisation, based, of course on the United States and Western Europe but embracing India and Ceylon and whoever else might be willing to cooperate. I get the horrors when I think of enormous numbers of Russians, Chinese, and possibly Arabs and of coloured people – a vast sea of barbarism round an island of Hellenism.[68]

In spite of his attempt at an apology ('I try to allow for prejudice'), the civilized Murray's Victorian view is racist, élitist, imperialistic, and narrowly ethnocentric. He forgets, for example, that the sophisticated culture of China long predates that of the Western world. And there are occasional traces of this racism in Rose Macaulay, too; forgetting the ancient culture that lay behind the Moors, she believed that intermarriage with them had lowered the intelligence of the Portuguese.

But Rose Macaulay does not entirely share Gilbert Murray's vision of a final Armageddon threatening a high point of civilization; her scenario of history is a drama with a series of turning points. She believes in the constant recurrence of threat, a cyclical theory like that of Murray's former son-in-law Arnold Toynbee. (In fact, five years later, on 23 December 1954 in *The Sunday Times* she chose the just published final volume of Toynbee's *A Study of History* as her most important reading of the year. She wrote to Gilbert Murray in praise of the ambitious scope of the *Study's* great historical sweep, 'For all its queerness, it did make a great impression on me, like that of an only partly understood epic poem.')[69]

The *raisonneur* in *The World My Wilderness*, Richie Deniston, the young Cambridge graduate and war veteran, observes: 'No civilisation had lasted more than a thousand years; this present one, called western culture, had had its day and was due for wreckage, due for drowning, while the next struggled inchoate in the womb of the ensuing chaos, till slowly it too would take shape and have its day.'[70] But Macaulay does not agree with Toynbee that a mystical universal and unified religion will be the ultimate result of these historical rhythms; she wrote to Father Johnson, 'He isn't always on sound ground in his deductions.'[71] In fact, she does not appear to be indebted to Toynbee's theory, for as early as the Twenties she had written of history as repetition and as a very slow moral evolution. Grand theories tend to be popularized into literary party conversation, and Toynbee's ideas, published over the years, were doubtless not new to her. But *The World My Wilderness* is not theoretical; it is a dark view of one dark time in a series of cycles, painful for those who, like Richie, mourn the passing of the beauty he knows and loves.

In the novel she transforms Murray's and Toynbee's grand metaphors of cultural confrontation and historical rise and decline into the inner drama of private spiritual conflict. She does not, like Murray, speak of a new threat from 'coloured hordes' but of the age-old threat of the evil within each human being. She does, like Toynbee, see the multiplicity of religious beliefs in the world, but she does not join him in his confidence that One Truth would be at last available to mankind. She, too, hopes for an eirenic harmony, but she believes that diversity of belief is not only inevitable but desirable. She sees the historical struggle as the eternal struggle of individual human beings with their own inner barbarism – battles constantly fought by men and women in times and societies which were sometimes more and sometimes less supportive of good against evil.

She uses a passage from Eliot's *The Waste Land* as one of her epigraphs, and ten years later she was to define the powerful emotional effect of Eliot's poem as the shock of recognition:

Here was the landscape one knew, had always known, sometimes without knowing it; here were the ruins of the soul; the shadowy dreams that lurked tenebriously in the cellars of consciousness; in the mysterious corridors and arcades of dream, the wilderness that stretches not without but within. ... The human soul is irrational and complex; the universe is desperately and crazily both. No more so than it always was; our generation has no monopoly, no increase, as has sometimes been proudly claimed, of complexity, or of waste lands. T.S. Eliot's poetry is not characteristic of our age, except insofar as it has shaped the age's poetic expression.[72]

And in this same passage about Eliot she quotes the words she uses in the most memorable scene in *The World My Wilderness*. It is a sermon on hell preached in a bombed-out nave by a mad Anglican priest who had, during the war, been trapped in the burning ruins of his own London church for two days. Barbary's only religion is a belief in that very hell which Father Roger wildly describes; her secret life in the waste land is the misery of unconfessed guilt. Absolution holds no hope for her, for she cannot undo the wrong she has done. She had known that her stepfather Maurice might be murdered; she had felt helpless and kept silent. Silent remorse separates her from the love of her mother who has suspected the truth. Barbary weeps when the tormented priest paraphrases Sir Thomas Browne: 'We are in hell now. Hell is where I am. Lucifer and all his legions are in me. Fire creeps on me from all sides; I am trapped in the prison of my sins; I cannot get out, there is no rescue possible, for I have shut myself from God in the hell of my own making.'[73] Rose Macaulay herself had begun to feel imprisoned in her own sense of guilt.

In this scene we hear the author's second voice: the emotion and conscience which caused reviewers to say that *The World My Wilderness* was the most compassionate of Rose Macaulay's novels. For its main plot is not the social drama of the family's failed relationships or the sensational lawless actions of a young girl of good family; it is Barbary's hopeless longing for forgiveness and her estrangement from her mother's love. Its climax is confession to the one she had wronged and the release of her mother's forbearance: Helen says, 'But life goes on, and you are as important to me as Roly [her little half-brother] is, and I'm not going to let you grow up without a mother. And we won't ever talk of it again. We'll talk about Maurice, but not his death.'[74] There is no promise of a rosy future for Barbary, but the renewal of her mother's love is enough.

This novel inevitably reflects Rose's own life at the time; she later assented to Father Johnson's description of *The World My Wilderness* as an unconscious prayer. But it artfully conceals all but her general compassion for the war-damaged. At first glance, the worldly Helen seems radically unlike Rose's own mother, but both Grace Macaulay and Helen were egocentric, showed favouritism towards their children, and failed to prepare them to enter formal English life in adolescence. The waif Barbary is like Rose in her dislike of London manners after the freedom of her childhood life and in being the cause of grief to her mother. In addition to Rose's guilt about Gerald and Beryl, the strife with Grace in her last years may have been part of the pain behind the creation of this novel. But all reference to her own life was concealed by the art which transforms fact but retains the truth of the experience.

Helen is the most artful creation of all. She is the *dea ex machina* of the climax. And her goddess-like quality caused some carping from the critics who could not be bounced into belief. Nevertheless, like the mermaid Ellen Green (who escapes from war) and like the strong female-male Daphne Sandomir of *Non-Combatants and Others* (who also rescues a daughter wounded by the war), Helen is created on a mythic scale. She is described in Rose's third voice – the voice of dream and archetypal imagination – as the Venus de Milo and as the Greek-Iberian lady of Elche whose statue Rose had described in *Fabled Shore*.

Helen is openly hedonistic and amoral; she enjoys sex casually and selfishly, as a necessity but not as a great emotional commitment. If morality is evolutionary, she is a moral throwback; 'I've no conscience of any kind,' she says. She gambles recklessly, her brilliant scholarship is used captiously to hoax the experts, she is for a time unloving to her child and cruel to her first husband, she is an unfaithful wife, for Barbary proves to be the daughter of a Spanish painter. In fact, Helen is a stunning Ancient, as free of guilt as a Greek goddess. Forster, too, had introduced pagan figures whom his critics found incompatible with his contemporary characters. Those who praise the novel can see Helen simultaneously as a maternal and erotic Venus and as the modern descendant of a rakish, anti-authoritarian aristocrat – a woman with a man's freedom. Helen is the complete pre-Christian libertarian. It is a fine irony that this pagan figure should bring about the catharsis of the plot by an act traditionally considered quintessentially Christian – loving forgiveness. Rose had written to humanist-agnostic Gilbert Murray in 1948 when she was beginning *The World My Wilderness*: 'I wish I knew – what about Christianity? Are we right in the face of so long a record of its poverty in international achievement, to keep invoking it as a standard, almost synonymous with civilisation?'[75]

Yet the character who seeks order and beauty throughout the novel and has its last word considers more than once that he may best find it in the Anglican Church: 23-year-old Richie Deniston, Barbary's older brother, has also suffered from the war – in fighting, emprisonment, and dangerous escape. His moral standards have deteriorated, but instead of drifting into barbarism like his sister, he chooses hedonism – enjoying 'the exquisite niceties of civilisation ... luxury, the amenities of wealth and comfort, mulled claret drunk in decorative rooms lit by tall candles.'[76] His unashamed post-war dishonesties are genteel; he does not shoplift but he cheats the customs. When he considers that Europe is now 'treading the frail plank over the abyss, rotten-ripe for destruction, turning a slanting, doomed eye on death', he also observes that

> during all this frightening evanescence and dissolution the historic churches kept their strange courses, kept their improbable, incommunicable secret, linking the dim past with the disrupted present and intimidating future, frail, tough, chain of legend, myth and mystery, stronghold of reaction and preserved values.[77]

In the last passage of the novel Richie stands in the ruins. And he quotes from *The Waste Land*: 'I think we are in rat's alley where the dead men lost their bones.' He shudders at the chaos about him – the wrecked cityscape on which the jungle of weeds presses. But he takes 'the track across the wilderness towards St Paul's.'

In the next decade, Rose Macaulay, too, was to take the track toward St Paul's, seeking a way out of her own post-war wilderness.

PART IV

Dame Rose

15

The Golden Fleece

THE WORLD MY WILDERNESS has two haunting epigraphs – a surreal image of an empty chapel from *The Waste Land* and this melancholy fragment:

> The world my wilderness, its caves my home,
> Its weedy wastes the garden where I roam,
> Its chasm'd cliffs my castle and my tomb....

The three lines are attributed to 'Anon.', but they were, in fact, written by the author herself. Yet, however appropriate to the novel and to Rose Macaulay's sense of herself in 1948, this doom-filled vision did not prove to be prophetic of her fate. At 30 she had been a wiser oracle. In the *The Valley Captives* she had unwittingly foreshadowed her depressed but undefeated state at 67: 'The very utterness of the crash and ruin, the desperation of the case, might be its hope. On ruins one can begin to build. Anyhow, looking out from ruins one clearly sees; there are no obstructing walls.'[1]

Looking out from her wreckage, Rose was clear-sighted enough to recognize that, however vividly recalled, the landscape of her happiest days existed only in memory. 'The people I loved most have died. I wish they had not. But there's nothing to be done about it.'[2] The pain of loss was worsened by her conviction of guilt and by her belief that she could not right the wrongs she had committed or receive forgiveness for them. She suffered a growing sense of her long estrangement from a God in whose existence she could not unshakeably believe but whose commandments had in childhood been deeply engraved on her consciousness. Understanding that her state of mingled belief and disbelief was illogical did not dissipate her spiritual anxiety. Her painful secret judgement of herself was unreservedly harsh; her sense of guilt was excessive; she thought the years behind her had been 'selfish and deplorable'.[3]

From this bleak vantage point she set about reviewing and rebuilding her life. In 1945 she wrote to Gilbert Murray, 'We have a conscience somewhere, and not buried very deep, but it needs waking up and instructing.'[4] Her quest for progressive enlightenment was to be the chief adventure of her last eight years.

The pain of her guilt was well-hidden – from her public, from her friends, and even from Jean. To an observer's eye she seemed composed. Between 1946 and 1950 she was intensely busy as a writer, and her letters show that she appeared often as a debonair presence on the London social, political, and literary scene: 'The BBC Critics lunch was amusing. We were an extraordinary rabble.' 'On Thursday I am dining with the Burmese ambassador to meet the Prime Minister.'[5] But during the same period she was conceiving and writing *The World My Wilderness*, a deeply felt novel about the hell of unshriven guilt.

In the autumn of 1952 she looked back and described the wretchedness of this time: 'I was in a state of darkness and tension and struggle.'[6] The struggle was marked by action. She rejected static despair and physically journeyed back to the world of her past, attempting once more to reconcile the emotional and moral counter-pulls of the Twenties when she and Gerald had first met. Four short journeys in 1948, 1949, and 1950 seem to have been planned to reignite memories of her childhood and of Gerald. But although she was nostalgic, she also forced herself to confront the conflict between those two past lives.

First, in the early stages of writing *The World My Wilderness*, at the end of July 1948, she spent a month with Dermod and Muriel O'Donovan on the Spanish Mediterranean, most of it enjoyed at a small inn on the sand about a mile from the ancient town of Denia. Rose wrote to Gilbert Murray that the three companions had 'a one-man rubber boat with a sail and a paddle', and, although they had taken a lot of books along, 'we bathe all day and play with our rubber dinghy.'[7] (Muriel says Rose was always delightful company. Muriel is, like Rose herself, quick-witted and candid.) On this holiday Rose once more enjoyed an island life; her companions were over thirty years younger; the dinghy was like the Five's canoe, the *Argo*, in which they had played at sailing in search of the Golden Fleece.

In 1952 Rose wrote that 'the indescribable beauty and joy and romance' of those childhood voyages 'returns to me still in dreams'.[8] 'One was well inside that small, dear world and can never get quite outside its influences.'[9] Varazze had a moral life as well as a playful, companionable one. The Villa Macolai had been presided over by her father; his memory stirred up in his daughter both love and guilt: 'I was always glad he didn't live to think ill of me.'[10] Through what Rose described as his 'magnificent principles', the agnostic George Macaulay had set standards of conduct.

And Grace Macaulay had inspired moral aspiration by dramatizing the fight of good against evil:

> I think it came through my mother rather like a Marathon or a Thermopylae, and we thought of striving for the incorruptible crown, though I fear our strivings were fitful. But we did glimpse the glory and the courage and the beauty of it all, and it was never made tedious for us, or drab.[11]

To this description she added the most affirmative judgement in her surviving comments about her mother: 'I think my mother was a very wonderful person, with an extraordinary magnetising gift, and she kindled a kind of fire when she spoke of religion and being good. I have never since met anyone with so much gift for it.'[12] She did not add that Grace had been just as emotionally powerful when she spoke of death and hell-fire.

Yet even as Rose Macaulay recalled both parents inspiring the love of virtue and her mother inculcating the fear of hell, she could not bring herself to regret her years of a secret life with Gerald, a life she believed had separated her from God. In 1949 she made two pilgrimages to Ireland, both times with companions to whom she could freely talk of him. In July, with Marjorie Grant Cook, Rose visited Elizabeth Bowen at Bowen's Court and then drove about Ireland. She extended the trip by visiting ruins in Wales with Jean, preparing for the 'short ruins book' she had agreed to write for Weidenfeld & Nicolson. (The book was, in the event, to become very long; ruins as symbols of destruction and survival were to be her subject for the next four years.) In September she returned to Ireland to visit more ruins with Marjorie and with Brigid O'Donovan. And before returning to London, she separated from the party, meeting Jean on the Isle of Wight to view still more crumbling walls.

But what Rose did not report in her letters was that before joining her sister, she went to Loughrea to visit St Brendan's Cathedral and the village where Father Jerry O'Donovan's hopes for the Church, for Ireland, and for his own role in leading a renewal of both had been so suddenly dashed in 1904. Altogether, in 1949 Rose spent almost a month hearing Irish speech, eating Irish food, studying Irish ways, absorbing sensory details of the life Gerald had known as a boy, a seminarian, and a young priest but to which he had never returned after his marriage. She revisited Gerald O'Donovan's youth as well as her own.

In 1950 her summer trip took her ruin-hunting once more – to an old monastery in Amalfi, a trip which prompted thoughts of Varazze and the Church. The long-standing and deep inner conflict between divine law and human love stirred up by these journeys was not apparent to the many friends who welcomed her back to London. They saw a woman approaching 70 who had created a strong identity, that of an endearing but occasionally formidable eccentric, a role of independence rightly respected in English cultural life. (Rose herself once said, 'It is the eccentrics of this world who have contributed most of its knowledge.')[13]

A character with intelligence, panache, energy, and aplomb, she enjoyed the complete social freedom from identification by gender and age to which she believed both women and men were entitled. She was astonished to learn that someone had described her hair as grey: 'I suppose one gets used to one's hair being mid-brown, and it still seems to one to be so.'[14] The thought of her brought timeless fairy-tale or supernatural images to her friends' minds: William Plomer said she carried a guardian angel in her car; Anthony Powell said she was a White Witch; Mark Bonham Carter said she was like the poised, unchanging *Vieille Dame* of the Babar books, as thin and neat as a furled umbrella.[15]

All of her friends testified to her lively presence as a memorable personality in her last decade. In spite of her intermittent debilitation from illnesses, all agreed upon her chief integrating quality – her physical and mental vitality. She still pounced on ideas; David Ley said, 'Her mind seemed to have grown sharper and sharper at the end.'[16] Patrick Kinross wrote, 'She could never be bored.'[17] She still responded rapturously to the world around her. She went on strenuous journeys to places with few amenities and little security, sometimes alone. 'I love the sea, I love swimming, I love it all; I expect you feel I should have outgrown it – but why outgrow anything one likes?' she wrote to Father Johnson at 71.[18] One Christmas she exulted, 'I am being given a pair of rubber swimming fins – they shoot you through the water at a great pace, fixed on the heels. *Won't that be nice!*'[19] And she could still be enchanted; she went to see *The Teahouse of the August Moon* with Elizabeth Bowen and said she fell in love with the hilarious, unflappable Interpreter. His temperament was like her own; in the face of disaster his repeated counsel to the play's hero was, 'Socks up, Boss'.

She could accept new social customs; her young friends, she said, called her 'Rose'. The company of her friends seems equally divided between the sexes, although she said, 'I think it so happens that I have more men friends than women; and I am sure their masculinity enhances the relationship'.[20] But she was the sought-after guest of both men and women. Her many engagements can only be reported selectively: she spent long holidays at the four-bachelor establishment of Raymond Mortimer in Dorset; she lunched with T.S. Eliot (whose humour delighted her); she dined with Natasha and Stephen Spender; and she still regularly visited Ivy Compton-Burnett. She continued her well-established pattern of helping young people; when Brigid O'Donovan had come down from Oxford in the Thirties, Rose had been instrumental in her being taken on as T.S. Eliot's secretary at Faber & Faber. Rosamond Lehmann wrote of Rose:

> She was forever in transit; physically, intellectually, spiritually; energetically not eating, not drinking, or sleeping, so it seemed; yet such was her transparency and charity of spirit that she seemed universally available to her friends. She has been called child-like; but to me she suggested youth, a girl of that pure eccentric English breed which perhaps no longer exists, sexless yet not unfeminine; naïve, yet shrewd; and although romantic, stripped of all veils of self-interest and self-involvement.[21]

V. S. Pritchett expands on this image of perpetual motion: 'As she grew old, she may have looked like a jolly skeleton but she did not fall back on the resources so often drawn upon by distinguished English maiden ladies: dottiness, vagary, awful composure or annihilating egotism. She was as lively as a needle. She remained the discreet, learned, and intrepid spinster of irreverent eye and rapid, muttering wit, always on the go, always out and about, always working.'[22] When she thought about ageing, it was to worry a bit that she might be less able to think and write. If there is a life after death, Rose speculated – and she was never very sure of this – 'Rest is *not* what we want, surely, but more scope for work and new knowledge'.[23]

And so, in the late 1940s, her friends saw her as a strong self-governing self, a self achieved by cultivating her unique powers in the spirit of Mill's 'On Liberty'. Raymond Mortimer said that 'she was conspicuous for self control – unbalanced, if at all, only in working too hard and leading too Spartan a life.'[24] But Harold Nicolson observed, 'One of the many things we shall all remember about Rose Macaulay was her combination of opposites.'[25] That private asceticism which Raymond lamented did not unbalance her; on the contrary, it was the counterweight to her buoyant love of the world. But unless her friends read *The World My Wilderness* perceptively, they did not see the long-buried God-seeking, à Kempis side of Rose Macaulay.

Her unpredictability was part of her charm; she herself believed that 'people are interesting largely because so mixed in character'.[26] Human beings are all creatures of contradictions – almost always in some part of their lives inconsistent, self-deceived, and intellectually or emotionally confused or compartmentalized. But Rose Macaulay stood out, and caught interest, because her combination of opposites often produced comic surprise. At her best she could simultaneously write both lightly and deeply about serious matters. She insisted that she was passionately in earnest in the religious and moral parts of *The Towers of Trebizond*; nevertheless, the novel begins with the unforgettable comic line, '"Take my camel, dear," said my Aunt Dot, as she climbed down from this animal on her return from High Mass.'[27] She was aware of conflicts, incongruities, and unanswered questions, and instinctively made creative use of them. Alan Pryce-Jones wrote, 'Her secret was that every aspect of this world and the next offered delightful possibilities of discovery. She disliked things to be finally settled, so she never came to the end of a subject or a friendship.'[28]

A minor event of 29 August 1950 set in motion the experiences which helped her bring her religious longing into the open; her second voice began to speak out both in her sophisticated social life and in her writing. The receipt of a quite ordinary letter, addressed care of her publisher, led to the breaching of the blank wall Rose Macaulay believed she had built between herself and God.

She returned to London from her month in Italy to find 'amid a pile of (mostly unwelcome) correspondence' a letter from America praising *They Were Defeated*, published eighteen years before. This admiring voice came from even farther back in her history. It was that of Father John Cowper Hamilton Johnson of the Society of St John the Evangelist, her interim confessor at St Edward's House in Westminster from the summer of 1914 to the autumn of 1916 when she was wrestling with the problem of 'how a young lady living with her family might most suitably conduct herself'. A few months after their most searching interview he had joined the Cowley Fathers community in Boston. In 1928 they had exchanged a few notes, in one of which he suggested she write a historical novel. In another, Rose said she would like to visit him if she came to America. She was never to see his face again, yet this revived correspondence initiated her recovery from despair.

Four and a half months after she opened this transatlantic fan letter she emerged from making her first confession in thirty years and receiving Absolution in the Anglican Church from which she had excommunicated herself. She felt at that critical moment, she said, 'winded and dazed'.[29] She interpreted the charge to 'go in peace' as a call to work toward a closer relationship with God. She began to formulate a body of beliefs by which she could live out her life as 'a good *civis* in the *Civitatis Dei*'.[30] 'Can one be good, honest, unselfish, scrupulous?'[31] She knew that the practice of religion could be dilettantish and escapist as well as inspirational.

This epistolary friendship lasted eight years, and until her death Father Johnson remained her much-loved non-resident chaplain. But, in the last years of her life, although their mutual affection never waned, and she thought him the best friend any human could have had in a crisis, she honoured but was no longer dependent on Father Johnson's paternal spiritual counsel. Without losing love, she always eventually became independent of the guidance she at first sought from her male mentors – George Macaulay, Gerald O'Donovan, and Gilbert Murray. Father

Johnson began as her reverend father-in-God, but he became as well 'My dear Hamilton, Dear Coz'. Indeed, he generously acknowledged that Rose had in their exchanges educated *him*: 'She has written me letters which have quickened and polished up my mind more than any school, college, or university ever did; besides making me laugh – for she is never *not* a humorist.'[32]

He proved to be an ideal spiritual confidant and friend for Rose Macaulay in the early Fifties, just as, during that same period, the liberal humanist Gilbert Murray was her ideal literary and political confidant and friend. Significantly, although she mentions Gilbert Murray admiringly and affectionately five times to Father Johnson in eight years of correspondence, her letters to these two older men did not try to introduce them to each other, nor did Rose discuss with Gilbert Murray her return to the Church. (She writes him an account of going with Joe Ackerley, out of somewhat mocking curiosity, to hear Billy Graham. When Gilbert Murray complains about his friends 'going churchy,' she says nothing about her own renewed Anglicanism.) Each man represented an approving voice from two quite different periods of her past – Gilbert Murray recalled her agnostic university life in Oxford (and her father), and Father Johnson recalled her active church life in Cambridge (and her mother). She wanted the blessing of both.

Although Rose Macaulay and Hamilton Johnson were unalike temperamentally, they were, in their religious and scholarly interests, intellectually compatible; both came from similar Anglican backgrounds, and, as they discovered, from the same family tree. He was four years older than she – younger in worldly experience, but at 73 far more solidly fixed in his beliefs. Because of his pastoral role and his conservatism, it was easy for her to see him as the representative of an older generation.

He was the eldest of six brothers; he was born in Bedfordshire and reared in a Norfolk parsonage, and was, like Rose, the descendant of a long line of Anglican clerics. The cost of educating so many sons was a burden to his father; going on to university was not possible. So at 17, Hamilton Johnson left Norfolk and accepted a post in Malta, working for the Eastern Telegraph Company. After five years, however, confident of his religious vocation, he returned to England, studied at home to prepare himself for matriculation, and went up to New College, Oxford, where he was drawn to the monastic life of the Cowley mission. He was trained at the Theological College at Cuddesdon and spent two years in a curacy before joining the order in 1906.

But in addition to becoming a theological scholar and an accomplished Latinist, while at the Boston Mission House and later at the Monastery in Memorial Drive, Cambridge, Massachusetts, Hamilton Johnson continued to follow his wide literary interests, including the reading of novels. He was a relative of John Cowper Powys and the two carried on a challenging correspondence. Perhaps because of his experience of life outside the cloister, both actual and vicarious, he was often sought out as a confessor and counsellor by those who might not otherwise have turned to a member of the clergy for help. (To the surprise of his community, he had in the course of his ministry been of great spiritual comfort to two tight-rope dancers from the Howard Theater in Boston.) Rose's replies to his letters show that he was not only learned, but also intuitive and tactful – obligatory qualities in a guide for a long-lapsed Anglican who found confession after thirty years a painfully humbling experience as well as an emotional relief. Rose thought him 'immeasurably wise, good, and understanding'.[33]

Until 1953 her day-to-day gratitude for his guidance and instruction was intense, for he helped her to re-enter the life of the Church. As Anglicanism was the background of her ancestry, her family life, her historical study, and above all the foundation of her lifelong ethical convictions, in returning to Anglicanism she was returning home. But ignoring the experience of Saul at Tarsus (and disapproving of Billy Graham), she said she did not believe in a lightning moment of instantly revealed and permanently bestowed salvation. She believed that she would be intermittently pulled back into a moral twilight by 'the drag and suction of the hampering, corrupting past' and would have to experience a slowly progressive illumination of conscience. Just as her sense of history was profoundly affected by Darwinism, her sense of the moral life both of the individual and of mankind was evolutionary; slow growth and change could come from increasing enlightenment. And as she was always a seeker, she said that 'Christ as Light means more to me than any other aspect.'[34] One of her favourite Latin prayers began, '*O Sapientia*', and in 1953 she wrote to Jean, 'I believe in the Light that lights every man, trained up by reason, and the Bible after all, and the Church, too, were only products of that Light, not its sources.'[35]

But her chief need at this time was not intellectual. She describes herself to Father Johnson as '*dejecta, abjecta, indigna*, and *ignoblis*', and suffering from '*timor mortis*'.[36] On the last page of *The Towers of Trebizond* (which Rose Macaulay called 'my own story'), the sad and unforgiven narrator similarly fears her own end:

> And when the years have all passed, there will gape the uncomfortable and unpredictable dark void of death, and into this I shall at last fall headlong, down and down and down, and the prospect of that fall, that uprooting, that rending apart of body and spirit, that taking off into so black an unknown, drowns me in mortal fear and in mortal grief.[37]

Although the learned Latin cools their emotional effect, Rose's words to Father Johnson do not translate into the language of reason. 'Dejected, abject, unworthy, and ignoble' are adjectives of strong negative feeling – self-hate and depression. Despite the love and admiration with which Rose Macaulay was constantly surrounded, she compared her life unfavourably to the lives of her self-sacrificing sisters. And we know she imagined her parents making a critical judgement of her middle years. Rose's warmly grateful letters to Father Johnson show that his approval and affection at this time were as vital to her redirection as was his spiritual advice.

Looking back in the autumn of 1953 to her decision to make a new beginning in 1950, she speculates: 'Perhaps, in the end, it must be a movement not of intellect but of will; perhaps sin, perhaps unhappiness, help sometimes to open the doors; perhaps sometimes mere loneliness, often, of course, personal influence.'[38] At the time that Father Johnson's letter of praise arrived all five elements were present. It was she who broached the subject of church life in her reply to him: 'I have sadly lost touch with that side of life and regret it. We do need it so badly, in this queer world and life, all going to pieces and losing.'[39]

The eleven letters she wrote between 30 August 1950 and 12 January 1951, when she made her confession to Father Wilkins at St Edward's House, do not, in their published form, include all that she wrote to Father Johnson during this time. He heavily edited the fourth letter, in which she posed a problem and asked for his advice; however, at the time the letters were published he explained that her fourth letter was not technically a confession. It is clear that by circumlocution Rose Macaulay showed Father Johnson that she felt in need of absolution. Her hypothetical example must have been transparent enough to imply her history. She sent him *The World My Wilderness*, and when he received the Latin self-description of her own penitent distress, he replied, *'nequaquam minor'* ('I am by no means surprised').

She demurred when he suggested that she approach the Bishop of Oxford as a confessor; she thought this would be an imposition on him and an embarrassment to her. But she kept her appointment with Father Wilkins. She discovered that 'confession is a desperate business. You think in the middle that you can't go through with it, but somehow you do.'[40] To her surprise and disappointment Father Wilkins said nothing to her after the formal words of absolution, but her own severe conscience was at work. She wrote to Father Johnson:

I told you once I couldn't really *regret* the past. But now I do regret it, very much. It's as if absolution and communion and prayer let us through into a place where we get a horribly clear view – a new view – so that we see all the waste, and the cost of it, and how its roots struck deep down into the earth, poisoning the springs of our own lives and other people's. ... You can't undo what's done.[41]

Yet despite her continuing remorse for having irrevocably wronged Beryl O'Donovan, there is evidence in her last years that she could never categorically renounce her love for Gerald. Despite her doubts of an after-life, her new spiritual regimen included prayers for him.

Her pilgrim's progress was to be a search for a personal vision of a forgiving God and also for a sanctuary from which to communicate with Him within the Church: 'One wants to get the right balance between Protestantism (the individual seeking after God) and Catholicism (the seeking through the Church), neglecting neither.'[42] But her Protestant questioning bent was strong; she wrote to an enquiring American critic in 1957, 'I am a little agnostic. Surely always one must be this, however much "in" the church.'[43] And in the last year of her life she wrote, 'I could never say "I believe in God" in the same sense that I believe in the sun and the moon.'[44] Her hesitation stemmed from both intellectual honesty and intellectual modesty in the face of mystery. She said she believed that it was wholesome to entertain a little scepticism about anyone's knowing the whole truth. 'How much better it is', she wrote to Jean, 'when preachers don't seem too sure.'[45]

Father Johnson apparently did not express shock at the number of central Anglican doctrines which Rose Macaulay said her brain could not take in. She rejected the Thirty-Nine Articles of the *Book of Common Prayer* out of hand as narrow and legalistic. And she said Bethlehem and the Virgin Birth had no reality for her. (Unacquisitive and busy as she was, she was a foe of the commercial Christmas bustle, thinking that people felt about it as they did about nuclear power – they did not want it but were afraid to be the first to give it up.) She could not believe 'the actual facts' of the Resurrection, and thought the Atonement as a doctrine had been much overemphasized, so she left these concepts in what she called the neutral country beyond thought. On Darwinian grounds she rejected the doctrine of the Fall. She thought that the anthropoid could always sin consciously and did so from the first, although without the full consciousness of morality that developed later.

But despite her interest in abstract questions her theological objections did not bar her search: 'One can select what one likes out of the extra-ordinary possibilities. I leave what I can't take. I sit very loose to intellectual difficulties and don't feel they matter,' she concluded.[46] What engaged her attention was moral drama; she believed that grace was meant to open humanity's eyes to the means to virtue – 'the spirit of God never lets man alone, but is forever trying to pull him upward and outward out of his primitive nature. I found it inspiring; so much more hopeful than the theory that we were better once.'[47] Her eye was on the grand battle between Good and Evil which was the central plot of her childhood stories, the very stuff of her mother's nightly homilies. And concerning differences between churches and their beliefs, she said, 'I rather like the differences. They keep up a wholesome subversiveness against unthinking conformity.'[48]

Nevertheless, although she was unorthodox and sometimes doubting, she did share in a central core of Christian belief. To Jean she wrote in 1955:

> I should call a person a Christian if he believes in God (I call it 'believe', but you can translate it into 'hope' ... I mean 'believe' enough to pray to) and in something that may be called Christ's 'divinity', i.e. that he was connected with God in some way we are not, that he survives in spirit, and can be communicated with.[49]

She felt in need of the support of the Mass and of Absolution to improve her moral life, for she did not believe that personal faith provided sufficient sustenance. This experience was intense and her purpose tough-minded; she sought 'the desire of the spirit and the will to do His commands'.[50] (Margaret, Rose, and Jean had thought the sentimental piety of the convent nuns of Varazze 'soppy'.) She believed in the tutelary aid of good preaching and the shaping discipline of regular formal prayer. She was intensely interested in the beautiful language of the liturgy, in dignified, symbolic ritual, and in church architecture – all of which gave her both spiritual and aesthetic pleasure. She began to attend early Mass daily, following a Rule of Life; once more, after so many years, at Father Johnson's suggestion, she reread Thomas à Kempis, but with 'a pleasurist's' reservations about his monastic distrust of the senses.

It was wholly characteristic of her divided nature that in addition to visiting churches of other parishes and denominations frequently, she should have belonged to *two* quite different Anglican churches and attended them regularly – sometimes on the same Sunday. They were Grosvenor Chapel and St Paul's, Knightsbridge.

The chapel on South Audley Street is an anomaly; it is not a parish church but a 'private chapel of ease', built in 1730 by Sir Richard Grosvenor on his own property as part of a housing development, to accommodate the overflowing pews of St George's, Hanover Square. His successors became the Dukes of Westminster and continued his patronage. Throughout the eighteenth century the small, beautifully austere brick structure served the aristocrats of Mayfair and the House of Lords at prayer. Rose Macaulay enjoyed its many literary and historical associations: to name but a few – Lady Wortley Montagu and John Wilkes are buried there, Prince Albert served as a godfather at its font, the Duke of Wellington worshipped regularly. In the eighteenth century, the aristocratic birth and the conservatism of the congregation were ensured by high pew rents, but in the nineteenth century the Chapel's atmosphere changed from class-consciousness to intellectual controversy about religion. By 1918 it had become liberal Anglo-Catholic and its dignified and simple High Church services were deeply appealing to Rose. She liked its combination of austerity and sensory pleasure – only one priest, no crowds, only a few singers as choir, but incense and a chastely beautiful sanctuary. She had found the quiet place for her prayer and confession and meditation; here was her still point in a whirling life.

In the Fifties John Betjeman was also a communicant there and praised the chapel's beauty and its tradition of 'poetical sermons'. Susan Lister, a lecturer in theology at King's College, London, at that time, describes Rose as a church-goer: 'Tan and thin, Sunday by Sunday, she inserted herself into the extremely uncomfortable pew on the left hand side at the back of the Chapel. The choice was characteristic. Though immensely social she was also a very private person and one who needed to look straight into the heart of the mystery.'[51] From this short back pew near the church doors one has an unimpeded view of the altar and can make an unimpeded departure; unless the Serpentine was iced over Rose headed quickly toward it for her morning swim. She wrote to Father Johnson, 'A kind of shining peace prevails in both places.'[52]

John Betjeman praised Grosvenor Chapel for another reason: 'What makes it perfect for me is that people never bother you there ... you aren't asked to join something.'[53] Rose agreed, 'I like its quiet anonymity.'[54] But despite her love of privacy, Rose did make two close friends there. She dedicated *The Towers of Trebizond* 'To Susan Lister' and she was deeply fond of Father Harry Whiteman, whose ministry as a counsellor to those in moral, intellectual, or spiritual difficulties 'spoke to her condition', as Susan Lister writes. Even though at the time of her death in 1958 Harry Whiteman was no longer the priest at Grosvenor Chapel and was unable to attend the Requiem Mass held there for her, he wrote one of the eulogies read at the Memorial Service held at her second church, St Paul's, Knightsbridge.

In contrast to the Chapel, St Paul's was a large suburban church which *did* have typical parish activities. The busy Rose participated in these very selectively, although she was always on warm terms with the vicar, both Jock Henderson and his successor, Father Donald Harris, whom she described as 'genial, unshy, and friendly'. And at St Paul's she had a sense of congregational as well as private worship; she proposed innovations: that the church have a jazz Mass one Sunday and that the Sunday Evensong be followed by a discussion of the sermon. She met fellow worshippers, and one of the happy results of her attendance there was her getting to know her young third cousin Constance Babington Smith, who was to become her biographer; they often attended services together.

Meanwhile, Rose's letters to Father Johnson flew and sailed across the Atlantic regularly and in her usual digressive and chatty style she plied him with questions and discoursed on such subjects as the adventures of her travels, the aesthetics of Church ritual, the differing sexual responses of men and women, the oddity of old heresies, the poetry of Donne, the sticky semantic and syntactic problems of translating Latin breviaries and missals, the personalities of her new clerical friends, her reservations about Graham Greene's grim *Brighton Rock*, and her assessment of Eliot's *The Confidential Clerk* – 'not v.g. I'm afraid.' And, of course, scholar that she was, in the midst of these friendly observations she plunged into analyses of liturgical texts and church history and theological questions with the same enthusiasm and attention to detail with which, in the letters she was writing to Gilbert Murray, she was attacking political and literary problems.

In the midst of serious discourse, however, she could suddenly pose a question or make comments born from her child-like curiosity and her adult wit. About manna she inquires, 'I wonder how much of that light wafer stuff one would have to eat before feeling one had had a satisfying meal?'[55] And disbelieving the harshness of Christ's recorded words, 'Depart, I never knew you,' she says, 'I wish we had a shorthand transcript – or a Boswell.'[56] Although she said she could speak to Father Johnson of things she could not speak of to others, as time passed her intellectual chatter served to screen her religious emotions. Her love of the Anglican Church grew stronger and stronger, and candid as she was with him about her memories and interests, after the first self-revealing letters she found it easier to write of her deep feelings about the Church than about her spiritual elations or her moral anxieties, although glimpses of her inner life could suddenly break through in her second voice: an exultation, 'my universe has expanded so much', or a sigh, '. . . the misuse of life, the missing of its meaning, and now too late.'[57]

On one subject she harped, however, and friends deplored the buzzing of that particular bee in her bonnet: she was offended by the Roman Catholic Church's categorical claim of possessing the only valid religious orders and sacraments. She believed that an ecumenical relationship between Christian sects which permitted intercommunion and ignored differences of belief should be encouraged. William Plomer wrote that 'after defining her own faith she firmly denied that to hold another was to be in outer darkness; all faiths were valuable as different ways of getting at the truth.'[58]

Her reading of Roman Catholic doctrine was not always fair; her responses to it were coloured by her memories of the three little English girls in Varazze who were not allowed to pray with the other children in the convent school, and perhaps by Gerald's unhappy defeat as a priest. In any case, she sometimes contended vigorously about dogma and dogmatism with fellow dinner guests – notably Graham Greene and Evelyn Waugh – and condemned the proselytizing raids she believed were being made on Anglicanism by English Roman Catholics. Both Veronica

Wedgwood and Raymond Mortimer said that the dominance of these sectarian preoccupations in the Father Johnson letters gives a narrow and lop-sided picture of a generously tolerant mind with a wide range of interests and makes Rose Macaulay sometimes seem what she never was in life – tedious. (Many of the lively comments about people then living were removed before publication, leaving letters with a much tamer tone than the unedited originals.)

Church-going brought her other new friends who were to become increasingly important – among them, the curate Gerard Irvine, whom she met at a rehearsal of a Christopher Fry play in the nave of St Thomas's, Regent Street, where Dorothy Sayers and T. S. Eliot (and later Rose herself) were church wardens. (It was this church's practice to preach the Gospel through drama.) Rose described Gerard to Jean as 'a new type to me; very social and very extreme', but he soon became 'my bright young friend' of whom 'I am very fond' .... 'It is quite fun to know him'.[59] In fact, he came to know and value her so highly that he was chosen to preach her eulogy at the second Memorial Service held for her – at St Paul's, Knightsbridge.

To move into clerical society and to mention the old-fashioned word 'sin' in her sophisticated world required some courage. She was at first so diffident about her new life that she did not even mention the change to Jean until she was a well-established church-goer; she kept her religious practice as secret as she had at one time kept her liaison with Gerald. But in fact, other than an expansion of her friendships to include members of the clergy, there were surprisingly few changes in the pattern of her social life. She kept up her very busy working schedule and cultivated old friendships. There were two exceptions: Lady Nicholson (the former Dorothy Brooke) said that she and Rose lost touch with each other when Rose became engrossed in her religious life, and Victor Gollancz wrote in 1968, at the close of a long tribute to the pleasure of her company: 'I should be less than candid if I concealed that, during her last years, something happened between us.... May it perhaps be that the more integral practice of her religion that her lover's death allowed her led to a certain lessening of her intimacy with, a certain withdrawal from, ourselves and maybe others?' Nevertheless, he ends his celebration of her rarity with, 'But how we loved her! How I love her still!'[60] Those around her agreed with his expression of affection but not with his speculation about the reasons for their estrangement. It assuredly had nothing to do with his being a Jew. Her friendships with David Ley, firm Roman Catholic; Ivy Compton-Burnett, firm agnostic; and E.M. Forster, firm anti-Christian, grew even stronger in the last years. Of Forster she wrote, 'He is one of my best friends and I see him often when he is in London.... He is a person of very strong and continuing affections.'[61]

Gradually the nature of her inner tensions was exposed; those around her began to understand or guess at her spiritual and emotional struggle. To a few she hinted that she was 'well-in' the Church again and even that her life had not been lived without a lover. Father Irvine says, 'We all knew that there had been a Gerald.'[62] And Alan Pryce-Jones reported that she would flash out such remarks as, 'It is stupid to think that just because I never cared to marry I have no experience of life.'[63]

In her last two years many observed that the occasionally farouche Rose of middle life had become a warmer, more radiant woman. Her own explanation was that for years there had been 'a God hole' in her life, and that at last it was filled. At first her progress toward belief was a wavering movement which she called 'fluctuation'. In mid-October 1953 she invited Mark Bonham Carter to attend early Mass with her at Grosvenor Chapel, but when he went to the altar rail to receive communion she did not accompany him. To his astonished question about this last minute desertion, raised afterwards as they headed for breakfast at the University Women's Club in Audley Square, she answered, 'I had doubts at that time.'[64]

In 1954 she sent Jean an account of her state of mind about Christianity:

Faith, hope, belief. I think (as I said) that hope is the first stage – hoping against all probability that what you would like to believe is true, even though almost knowing it can't be. Faith next; the affair still improbable, but worth accepting as a working hypothesis. Last, belief: really thinking the thing is true – it only (in experience) comes by fits and starts, and doesn't cover the whole ground, at best. Perhaps I shall never exactly 'believe' in God, and shall always have to stick to the faith stage. Hope, of course, goes with all the stages.[65]

She did have those moments of 'belief', and towards the end of her life she experienced them more and more often. As early as Holy Week 1951, she wrote, 'I felt, at the Easter Mass, that here was Christ risen and with us, and I didn't care how.'[66]

But although she was obeying her mother's charge to aspire to goodness, she never lost her father's sceptical honesty. She added to her definition of a Christian, 'It [faith] has nothing to do with behaviour, as non-Christians can be as good, and Christians as bad, as anyone else.'[67]

The Christmas cards she designed annually in the last six years of her life peopled the sea or the ruined landscapes she loved with both classical-mythical and Christian symbols, accompanied by verses of mixed Latin, French, and English, mingling the teaching of both her mother and her father. One greeting is crowded with memories of a seaside town and its church, a mermaid's freedom, and the old stories of pre-Christian men and gods which her father had told his children. Nor did she ever lose the respect and love for classical learning as a source of moral inspiration

Th'unchristened Creatures of the crying Sea
Make great ado to hail the Native Morn :
The Triton rides the Dolphin round the Bay,
And twice and thrice and six times winds his Horn.
The Mer-Maids singing on the drownèd Rocks
Shrill " Natus est ", and " Pray, then, Who is born,
That we twine Holly in our sea-green Locks ? "
The Sea-Horse neighs : nor know these Creatures why
The Bells all round the Bay make sweet Reply.

Christmas and New Year Greetings
from Rose Macaulay, 20 Hinde House, Hinde St., W.1

which George Macaulay had instilled in her. She thought the ancient
Church fathers had been wrong to reject great secular literature and that
some of these texts should be read in church services; 'Light, beauty,
learning, and breadth of range – they are all there for those who want
them.'[68]

And so, because she valued the cultural intellectual legacy bequeathed
to her by her father, the symbolic blessing she received from him in the
summer of 1951 was a major event of her last decade. On 5 June of that
year Cambridge University awarded Rose Macaulay an Honorary Litt.D.

Virginia Woolf had vehemently refused such recognition from the male academic establishment, but Rose did not consider the question of accepting the honour a matter of sexual politics. In fact, she did not regard the award as Virginia Woolf had – as a patronizing gesture toward an outsider or indeed as a matter touching upon the Woman Question at all. For Rose it was a pleasant family affair. For many years she had felt part of that university world; the degree ratified her relationship to it. 'I rather like to have it, as a warming little greeting from Cambridge.'[69]

When she had learned in February of the forthcoming occasion, she had written to Father Johnson with what sounds uncomfortably like false humility, 'I imagine it is more a tribute to my father and uncle, who were greatly esteemed at Cambridge, than to myself.'[70] But her self-deprecation was likely to have stemmed in part from her usual embarrassment at public recognition, and in part from her belief in her father's and uncle's intellectual superiority. But she was familiar enough with university life to know that while honorary degress might be awarded for political reasons, they were rarely awarded for sentimental ones.

George Macaulay would have had a right to be proud of her recognized accomplishments as she marched in the procession down King's Parade – velvet-capped, scarlet-robed, and endoctored – with her fellow honorees: Edith Evans, the actress; Omar Bradley, the American general; and Sir William Haley, Executive Director of the BBC. At this moment she had justified George Macaulay's confidence in her by achieving recognition in his own male world; she, too, had done the state some service. But the greater victory was receiving an honour from Cambridge which both superseded her Aegrotat and justified her youthful rebellious longing to leave home and lead a life of her own. It was both a day of closeness to her father and a day of freedom from him.

The inner satisfactions were great, but the grand public occasion did not turn her head. She described as 'great fun' her two-night stay as the guest of the Master of Trinity, her cousin G.M. Trevelyan; the ceremony in King's Chapel; the College Orator's Latin address (which alluded to her swimming); the luncheon at Pembroke College; and the student revue that evening. She said she would not use her new title except to persuade traffic policemen that as a doctor (presumably detained by attending a difficult confinement) she should not get a parking ticket. (She laughed a little at Edith Sitwell, who, possessed of three honorary doctoral degrees, bridled when not addressed as 'Doctor Sitwell'.)

Rose's next seven years were marked by the award of more honours, and, according to her criteria, the even greater fun of exotic travel. As much as possible she ignored her frequent respiratory illnesses. Invited to a party, she would reluctantly demur, 'I'm not supposed to be well.' But a few days later, she would telephone, 'May I come after all? I seem to be perfectly all right.'[71] In 1952, however, she had to succumb to a prolonged and maddeningly recurrent bout of undulant fever. (Her weight dropped to 98 pounds.) Pressed by deadlines, in February she cries out, 'I am drowning in a sea of books, papers, work, that I can't make headway against; and now this wretched disease has thrown me back by several days. Oh, for more time!'[72]

One of her projects was what was to be *Pleasure of Ruins*. It was not financial need that pressed her to go relentlessly on with it. Her income was over £1,500 a year (£3,500 by 1958) and her estate upon her death was, to the astonishment of her friends who knew her frugal ways, £84,035. Sheer fascination with the subject drove her to amass the lore of the grand, decayed monuments of the past – in Europe, Africa, Asia, and Latin America – to visit them in reality or in imagination, and more importantly, to celebrate the power of their beauty and mystery in richly ornamented and musical prose. But, because she liked being *au courant*, she was also still committing herself to deadlines by reviewing such non-fiction works as interested her.

The late summer was punctuated by sad news from Chota Naghur, India. Eleanor Grace Macaulay died from a heart attack on 2 August 1952. High praise for her Hindi translations of hymns and the Bible and tributes to her generous and self-forgetting life came to Rose and Jean through the clergy in India; the condolences shocked and shamed Rose into the realization that she had never valued or even known Eleanor. 'It makes one feel very small and trivial by comparison, and selfish,' she writes. 'It makes me cry a bit.'[73] Rose said Eleanor had always written more often, and she grieved that she had not yet written a thank-you letter for the Kashmir robe Eleanor had recently sent her – a procrastination that seemed to her to stand for years of neglect. 'Alas for chances missed, that can't return; they are bitter in retrospect.'[74]

Her always strong family feelings were intensified. No matter how busy, she never neglected seeing Jean. During the next years, when she was in London she spent almost every weekend with her, insisted on Jean's accepting a refrigerator and a hearing-aid, worried about her sister's punishing duties as a district nurse, and continually expressed her gratitude that they were close enough to see each other. She took her usual summer holidays that year – and the first one was with Jean and Nancy Willetts on the Isle of Wight, a place to which they were to return again and again. Rose became more and more attached to its tranquil Victorian gentility, in spite of having to wade half a mile through the mud to bathe at low tide.

Another event of 1952 was a three-week Italian trip with Muriel and Dermod. They drove along the Ligurian coast and spent two or three nights in Varazze. Muriel and Rose swam there in a sea which became suddenly turbulent; they were both thrown up on the beach by the waves.

Some fisherman, alarmed at their rashness, rushed to their aid, crying '*Pericoloso! Pericoloso!*' But Rose was unperturbed.

And the travellers paid a visit together to the charming old Villa Macolai. But, although Rose was very close to her, Muriel says that Rose did not speak there of her family. 'The visit to Varazze was obviously important to her, but very private.'[75]

Back in London in the autumn of 1952 Rose pushed on with her research. *Pleasure of Ruins*, begun in 1949, was not to be published until December 1953. Another year of reading, exploration, and searching out illustrations in the British Museum lay ahead. But this project generated fantastic daydreams. In the midst of it, Rose wrote, 'I am living in a ruinous world of crumbling walls, green jungle drowning temples and palaces in Mexico and Ceylon, friezes and broken columns sunk in blue seas, with crabs scuttering about among them. Such dreams of beauty are haunting, like poetry.'[76] Her introduction to the book begins, 'The approach to ruins in this highly selective book will be seen to be that of a pleasurist. It is not architectural or archaeological, or in any way expert.'[77] She says that her aim is 'to explore the various kinds of pleasure given to various people at various epochs by the spectacle of ruined buildings.' The pleasures she explores are many – melancholy, nostalgia, awe, delight, romance, sentimentality, memory, curiosity, philosophical contemplation of the folly of pride, and the very human satisfaction of being, for the moment, a survivor. This book enlarges the haunting sense of desolation of *The World My Wilderness* so that it permeates all recorded time, and yet, because it is a book about beauty, it is not gloomy. Again, as in *Fabled Shore*, we hear a mingling of Rose Macaulay's first and third voices.

But *Pleasure of Ruins* is created from facts as well as from impressions and emotions. The list of friends on whose expertise she called shows the range of inquiry behind her packed pages. The temples, monuments, castles, abbeys, minarets, and palaces of four continents are silhouetted against a panorama of sacred and profane history. On her page of acknowledgements Professor Gilbert Murray's name leads all the rest. She was chagrined when she discovered she had waited too long to tell her publishers that she wanted to dedicate the book to him.

But the task had threatened to overwhelm her. She complained to David Ley that her life was 'disordered and overcrammed'.[78] And when she handed the manuscript in to Weidenfeld and Nicolson in May 1953 she rewarded herself and flew off alone to Cyprus with a formidable itinerary in hand – Lebanon, Israel, Jordan, Greece, and the coast of Asia Minor. She hired a car in Famagusta and poked about, enchanted with the eclectic architecture; she attended a Greek Mass on Whitsunday; she was horrified by the camps of Palestinian refugees in Jerusalem; she avoided the 'mousey, nice people rather of the church-worker type' in a hostel where she stayed; and in Cyprus she made the acquaintance of 'the rather raffish young men, of the type who are apt to congregate in Mediterranean islands, and are not much approved of by the British residents.'[79] She ranged from Annam to Askalon and floated in the Dead Sea. She was 'very well and sunburnt and gay.'[80]

But on 1 July, the morning after she returned to her flat, she suffered a catastrophe. Her wireless caught fire, probably from defective wiring, and the blaze burned pictures, furniture, curtains, carpet, a few books and papers, and broke the glass front of the massive bookcase she had inherited from her father through Margaret. She reports this con-flagration to Father Johnson quite matter-of-factly: the landlord will redecorate, insurance covers much of the damage, and most things can be repaired or replaced. But she was forced to spend most of July sitting on her bedroom floor, correcting the many scrolls of galleys from *Pleasure of Ruins*, surrounded by domestic flotsam and trying not to hear the carpenters and painters at work in the next room. (She called herself 'a galley slave'.) 'I ought to be writing my last chapter, but it is very difficult in these circumstances. However, to soothe myself I think with joy of Cyprus and the Levant.'[81]

She delivered the corrected galleys in mid-August, but correcting page proofs, compiling a lengthy index (with the help of Nigel Nicolson and Raymond Mortimer), and battling with the problems of lost illustrations and a case of pleurisy all consumed the early autumn. Yet she is in a fine mood when describing her refurbished flat to Father Johnson in October – from the curtains patterned with great blue sunflowers on squares to a new carpet and deep blue couch cover. Inspired to flamboyance, she had her bedroom cupboards painted bright blue, hung scarlet velvet curtains, and, uncharacteristically undertaking a domestic project, she made a many-coloured coverlet for her bed. But despite the pleasure she took in this handsome order, she says she did not really expect 'to keep the litter under'. She thought that for her tidiness was 'an unattainable virtue'.[82]

The correspondence with Father Johnson continues at a slower rate. She often apologizes for her tardy replies. She politely disagrees with his analogy of Anglicanism as the Prodigal Son of the Roman Church; she thinks more highly of the Reformation than he. The two discuss Cardinal Newman, Joyce Cary and Sir Thomas More, and exchange books and affectionate greetings. Her daily worship continues to nourish her. *Pleasure of Ruins* appeared on 3 December and was sold out by 22 December to the accompaniment of good reviews. What meant much more to Rose, however, was Gilbert Murray's emotional tribute to her power to call up 'the stupendous Past' and its tragic transience.

Rose's next adventure was another unpleasant and dangerous one, although she once more reports it with verve to Father Johnson. Late in February 1954 she came into her flat from shopping and interrupted two men who had dumped the contents of every drawer on the floor and were sorting out her valuables.

> 'What are you doing here?,' I asked. 'Who let you in?' Upon which they knocked me down and rushed downstairs and I couldn't catch them. . . . I was furious. I wasn't hurt to speak of. They had no cosh luckily.[83]

But she regretted telling him about it, because he became, she wrote to Jean, 'very worried and anxious', and gave her a great deal of advice. 'I try not to tell him anything disturbing,' she said.[84] She quickly dropped her suggestion to him that women become servers at Communion, which she thought quite sensible. The thought of women in the sanctuary agitated him too much.

But her great adventure of 1954 was not furiously chasing thieves down the stairs: after reluctantly giving up her plan to visit Russia on the grounds that she would have to be guided about on official tours, she took a trip alone to Turkey in June. It was cruelly hot; she lagged sometimes with 'Turkey fever'; as a woman she was forbidden to bathe in the Black Sea; she stayed in a room 'not fit for a goat'; and she was righteously angry at the repressive Turkish treatment of women. But her letters to Susan Lister show that her romantic powers of enjoyment could always triumph. She was fascinated by the old city of Trebizond behind the unattractive new port Trabzon. And on Whitsunday 1954, she wrote from the deck of a steamboat:

> Here I am, sailing up the Bosphorus from Byzantium and drinking Turkish coffee in a crowd of Turkish holiday-makers, between steep wooded shores (Europe on the left, Asia on the right), old tile-roofed, balconied, wooden Turkish houses, clinging onto one t'other up to the hills, and restaurants on stakes, built out into green water, and Turks singing, eating, and drinking in turn, and now and then an immense Byzantine-Turkish castle standing in massive ruins above hamlets, hidden gardens, and (nearer Istanbul) white villas and palaces . . . A lovely trip for Whitsunday.[85]

She had escaped urban dangers briefly, but the next winter London thieves were to anger and inconvenience her once more. On 19 January 1955 her car was stolen while she was lunching with Gilbert Murray at the Athenaeum annexe, and although it was finally recovered and repaired, she had no access to it for two months, during which time, to her friends' dismay but not to their surprise, she rode her bicycle through the heavy traffic of the wintry streets. According to Alan Pryce-Jones, she commented, 'I never realized that St James's Street is a kind of alp.'[86]

The following year she was to take what was, in the eyes of many, a holiday even more exotic than her Turkish jaunt. In 1955, in late August and early September, when the O'Donovan granddaughters were 13 and

14, she broke all the rules of decorum for a woman of 74 and spent a week at a Butlin's Holiday Camp at Skegness with them. She had been happily involved in their lives since their birth. (She described the two – Mary Anne, her godchild, and Jane Caroline Rose, her younger sister – as 'intelligent, charming, lively,' and added, 'We are mutually fond of each other'.)[87] 'Aunty Rose' had taken both girls to the Fun Fair during the Festival of Britain in 1951 and had come home laden with ridiculous prizes from the coconut shies, darts, and gambling games. She had attended Mary Anne's school play, and had taken them both to children's services at St Mary Abbott's and taught them the catechism.

She spent some of her time at Butlin's working on her 'Turkey novel', but the girls were enchanted to have her companionship in the camp activities. She described the holiday to Gilbert Murray: 'It was very remarkable, and rather entertaining, quite out of this world, more like something on the moon. ... More than a week would be intolerable, and would leave one definitely backward with no initiative, everything being so organized from day to night. The children enjoyed it enormously. We slept in small chalets in rows; I had one to myself, the children next door. There were all forms of sport. ... I saw television for the first time and I trust the last. ... It was a strenuous week but amusing.' She made friends with the resident parson, swam in the sea instead of the swimming pool, and came home, she said, to chain herself to her typewriter: 'I am writing very busily and trying to get it [my novel] finished next month.'[88] It was not finished so quickly, but it was to be her last work and her most triumphant one.

The Towers of Trebizond, published in September 1956, is a *tour de force*, an unlikely combination of elements so Rose Macaulay-like that no one else could have imagined, mixed, and unified them. It is a breathless first person narration of changing moods and themes: it is a comic Middle Eastern travelogue; it is a spoof of Anglo-Russian spying, bureaucracies, and international relations in the Cold War; it is an exposé of the vanity, competitiveness, and dishonesty of writers; it is a satire on the human flaws of the Christian Church as an earthly institution; it is a hymn to the eternal heavenly Church's power to draw humans out of their willed moral blindness; it is one more Macaulayan thrust at the intrusive, opportunistic popular press; it digresses into a brief fable about an ape, which enacts humanity's moral evolution; it momentarily dissolves into a Jungian dream of the cruelties of the tyrants of history; it is a psychological and moral drama of the gradual corruption inevitably following an individual fall from grace; it comically presents the inherent painful madness of animal lust; it is a hilarious demonstration of the cultural misunderstandings of tourists; it is a feminist crusade against the repression of women. It even includes a delightful caricature of Rose Macaulay's own busy, cantankerous, peripatetic, morally committed, bold self in the person of the elderly Aunt Dot, who, accompanied by the bigoted Father Chantry-Pigg, is fighting for the liberation of women in Muslim countries by attempting to convert them to Anglicanism.

The novel is almost always wonderfully funny, told in Rose Macaulay's most delightful first voice, somewhat disguised by giddiness. But running throughout, and at last engulfing the novel emotionally, is a moving story (here her second voice is heard) of the hidden euphoria, guilt, and grief of a long adulterous love affair; *The Towers of Trebizond* is a duplicitous private confession so skilfully mingled with laughter that many readers saw only its comedy and satire. Its camel and ape and its hallucinatory vision are imaginative creations related by Rose's third, dreaming voice. In her last novel she produced a unique phenomenon, satisfying her 'passion for the fantastically impure'.

The monologue, essay, travelogue, quest, and comic-tragedy ends, like many twentieth-century novels, in a tormented impasse. Its main character is torn between earthly and heavenly love, unable to disown the former or live without the latter. The towers of Trebizond represent the Church, 'that strange bright city on the hill ... built by men seeking after gods and gods seeking after men, yet it is barred from all but those who desire it more than anything in the world.'[89] And Laurie, made wretched by her inability to give up her lover, laments:

> The towers of Trebizond, the fabled city, shimmer on a far horizon, gated and walled and held in luminous enchantment. It seems that for me, and however much I must stand outside them, this must forever be. But at the city's heart lie the pattern and the hard core, and these I can never make my own; they are too far outside my range. The pattern should be perhaps easier, the core less hard.[90]

The voice of the narrator is the thread by which Rose Macaulay holds together the improbable tangle of thoughts and events. She went to great pains to conceal the gender of that 'goofy voice', as she called it, for she believed that all of the events of *The Towers of Trebizond* would affect either an Englishwoman or an Englishman of similar education and background in the same way. Her belief in the common life of both men and women is essential to the novel's point of view. Poignantly, she gives to Laurie's lover, Vere, the status, power, and wealth she believes Gerald O'Donovan deserved, but he is a shadowy figure, real only through the passion which Laurie feels for him. The only way to test her ploy of making the narrator's gender a mystery would have been to publish the book anonymously; even then the individual stamp of her humour would have been recognizable. It is unlikely, given her known authorship, that anyone thought the tale's teller was a man.

In the midst of innumerable Shandean detours and distractions, this androgynous voice offers what seems to be a completely spontaneous, rambling, and unpremeditated account of a journey, climaxing in a painful event and a moral awakening, stopping dramatically just short of the level of faith at which Rose herself had arrived at the time of the novel's writing.

Laurie causes the death of her lover Vere by driving her car into a London intersection to defy an oncoming bus which is shooting a red light. And she is left in torment: 'I live now in two hells, for I have lost God and live also without love, or without the love I want, and I cannot get used to that either. Though people say that in the end one does. To the other, perhaps never.'[91] Laurie's anguished isolation is a far more emotionally persuasive argument for entering the Church than the climax of salvation in a nineteenth-century novel of conversion.

In 1956 Rose Macaulay wrote, for a special *Times Literary Supplement* issue on 'The Frontiers of Literature', an essay on religious writing; in it she defines the creative principle behind *The Towers of Trebizond*. She briskly rejects dull didacticism:

> It has always been too easy to suppose a religious theme enough, no need to deck it out with extraneous beauty. Hence, much religious writing has been pedestrian; in spite of its winged subject; it has sometimes trudged on flat feet. It is bound to be 'engaged'; but it often wears too obviously an engagement ring like a shackle.

Then she changes the metaphor and compares a boring religious work to a slow-moving vessel, towed behind a tug labelled Piety. She recommends a style that wings the ship:

> The sails of style may carry it out of course, through seas not charted and not planned; the voyage may turn out odd. But a voyage it is, even with no destination, and it is making literature; the odds are that it is making religion too.[92]

The Towers of Trebizond has little to do with Piety and much to do with style. Its style is its form. Its wandering voyage *is* odd and seemingly uncharted, but it 'made literature' for most readers – and 'made religion' for many.

Rose warned Father Johnson that he might think the novel frivolous and foolish in its devices. The high comedy which masked its serious themes was sometimes too successful. (Gilbert Murray said that on first reading he did not understand it.) Rose used the love-crazed camel to enact the comic misery of unsatisfied lust and the ape's lessons in playing chess and driving a car to suggest humanity's ethical evolution by trial and error. To point out these details is embarrassing; Rose Macaulay disliked heavy-handed allegory.

She feared the book would disappoint Father Johnson, because, as she told Jean, he was a man who was 'so unquestioningly devout and single-minded, and who I don't think has ever been troubled by doubts. He is so old and has been so kind to me.'[93] (He was four years older than she.) She believed he would be displeased that she had chosen to dramatize in the novel – not an uplifting conversion, but what was more deeply emotional in her own life, the tension between love and spiritual aspiration before her confession. Nevertheless, with her usual artistic and intellectual independence, she risked his disapproval.

She wrote to a friend who did not like or understand the novel, 'The central idea was ... the struggle of good & evil in the human soul, and its eternal importance, and the pull and power of the Christian Church on the divided mind, and its torment and its attraction. ... I wrote it in a kind of white-hot passion; but perhaps too many jokes as well, which confused the issue to many readers.'[94] Father Johnson understood her purpose, but was not quite satisfied. He wanted Rose Macaulay to write a letter to *The Times Literary Supplement* making it clear to her reading public that she did not, like Laurie, believe that the way to heaven was too hard.

Rose did not write the letter, but she did write to several friends saying that Laurie would have entered the church doors just as she herself had. But, in the end, although Rose recognized and confessed her own guilt, and although she had written to Father Johnson in 1952 that novelists should not show romantic love as an unstoppable force, she could not regret the love she and Gerald had shared. On 11 September 1956, she wrote to Rosamond Lehmann, referring to the just published *Towers of Trebizond*, and compared her own loss of Gerald to Rosamond's painful parting from Cecil Day Lewis:

> It's a book I have had in mind to write for a long time and writing it – like that, at a remove from myself, in an idiom not normally my own, and in a lot of circumstances that I enjoyed making up, but still the heart of the matter being my own story – writing it did sublimate and clarify life for me a little. I never, thank God, killed my lover; I don't have that to bear; I only watched him die of cancer, and couldn't often be with him during his illness. And for years after he died, I felt starved – a ghost, as Laurie did. But less hard than what happened to you; death is not a poison, only a knock-out blow.
>
> Looking back now I am getting old, I can't not be glad of the past, in spite of knowing I behaved dishonestly and selfishly for so long. Love is so odd. It can't help being everything at the time.[95]

The novel was a literary sensation. It won the prestigious James Tait Black Prize for the best novel of 1956. It was a best-seller in America, although, as in England, some reviewers did not get beyond their delight in the comedy. Rose was a social lioness. Sought after by royalty, she wrote to Jean. 'I hope I shall behave rightly.'[96] She dined on separate evenings with the Queen and the Duke of Edinburgh, attended a dinner given so that she might meet the Duchess of Kent, and another in the company of the Duke and Duchess of Gloucester. She was delighted to meet Princess Margaret at a dinner party arranged by Mark Bonham Carter, in part because the princess had read bits of *The Towers of Trebizond* aloud to her friends while voyaging to Africa on a visit. And when she went to Venice in 1957 she was entertained by a variety of hosts, from resident Peggy Guggenheim to the visiting Bishop of Tewkesbury, her old friend Jock Henderson. Rose Macaulay had always been a welcome dinner guest, but she had at 75 become a Guest of Honour and continued to be one until the last day of her life.

Regardless of the eminence of the company she was still 'a golden talker', like the women whom Helen in *The World My Wilderness* described as the most desirable friends: 'clever, curious about life, able and apt to speculate and discuss, not too solemn, funny, knowing about something, or a little about things in general, sceptical, witty, bawdy, if they like, firsthand, free.'[97]

Appropriately, Rose Macaulay's nomination by Harold Macmillan for Dame Commander of the British Empire appeared in the New Year's Honours list in January 1958; it was almost an anti-climax after the international acclaim accorded the novel. She was a little embarrassed, and wrote explaining to those whom she most respected that she had tried to commute for a CBE but had been told she did not have this choice. (Jean Macaulay had received a CBE in 1956 for her outstanding work as District Nurse; Rose did not want to outdo her.) Raymond Mortimer urged Rose to accept, on the grounds that there were too few literary dames. And so she wrote to John Hayward that her future title, Dame Rose, would be for her 'a strange translation into pantomime, or is it a muttering crone mixing a devil's brew of herbs and nettles in her country garden? I would rather it was Zenobia of Antioch – Anyhow it is something I am not at all used to and scarcely know which role of these would be most in my line.'[98]

Her new celebrity status exacerbated an old problem. As a busy writer, living alone, without a personal secretary, she had always been overwhelmed by mail. As early as 1929 she had written to Jean, 'It has taken me nearly 48 years to learn that both to answers letters and to do anything else in life without too much strain is impossible.'[99] When she began to write journal columns and appear on controversial BBC programmes, she was flooded with letters of admiring support and battered by letters of violent disagreement. She sometimes replied to the former, never to the latter, although she passed along some of the hotter attacks to Jean for her amusement. She wrote regularly to her family and to special friends, but when she was pressed by deadlines she shelved the problem of correspondence by refusing to open letters for days (or weeks) at a time. The piles of envelopes toppled. Sometimes her friends were wounded; sometimes important business matters were neglected.

But in January 1958 this problem was critical. Dame Rose, a subject for headlines, was the recipient of 'cartsfull of kind letters daily'. She was glad to receive the congratulations but dreaded answering them. 'I wish more people would type theirs,' she complained, although she knew her own handwriting could be read only by telepathic guesses. 'When they don't I often revenge myself by hand-written answers.' In a comic mood of boasting she wrote, 'I bagged 4 bishops (perhaps more, I forget), 2 ambassadors, and, of course most of my literary colleagues, and too many wires signed by names I can't identify.'[100]

If this was pride, it was followed by a fall. Rose's crippling accident of Lent 1958 has been told in an apocryphal version, which claims that after her sudden descent down his steep front steps into the street, her host cried out, 'My God, we've killed her!', and that the injured Rose had replied, 'Don't be silly. Get an ambulance.' However, the documented facts of the fall place her in a less heroic light. Responding to her request to meet Father Denis Martin, Father Patrick McLaughlin of St Thomas's Church graciously invited the two of them to lunch. He reports that it was not a successful party.

Rose provoked and prolonged a lively theological discussion, 'needling' Father Martin, who answered flippantly. The wrangle went on so long that when they rose to go, Father McLaughlin, fearing to be late for an appointment, rather hurriedly bade them farewell on the first floor, at the head of the sitting-room staircase which led to the front door. He heard the two go down, still 'bickering'. When Rose reached the front door, she turned to fire a final verbal shot. Forgetting that there was another flight of stairs to the street, she backed into space and fell to the street, where she lay unconscious with a broken right wrist and femur.[101]

But she *was* heroic during her six weeks of hospitalization – two weeks in the public fracture ward of Charing Cross Hospital, then four in University College Hospital. She mended rapidly and was a good patient, working hard for recovery because she was planning a special trip in August – an educational Hellenic Cruise with a party of her intellectual and social peers, much like the one she had taken with her father in 1913.

She refused to make heavy weather of her pain. She spent some of her convalescence planning her next book; it was to begin with a fatal automobile accident near Stonehenge, which she visited twice in June, once driving alone, rejoicing that her right wrist rather than her left had been broken, leaving her able to shift the stiff gears of her ancient car. 'Venice Besieged', her book's working title, was to follow the guilty driver's flight across Europe, trying to escape justice and conscience. The novel was to climax in a great flood in Venice, a deluge washing all sins away.

She had said to Jean in 1955 that she thought she would die in three years, and perhaps her sorrow at Gilbert Murray's death a year before had made her own death a reality. So she amused herself by picking out appropriate hymns and texts for her funeral – 'a nice occupation', she said. She was, as much as she could ever be, at peace with the past. But she was much busier preparing for the future – working on a talk on 'Image and Sacrament' to be given at Cambridge in the autumn and organizing a trip to Persepolis for 1959.

She was rewarded for her determined recovery by being well enough to go on a Hellenic voyage so varied and adventurous that she might have invented it herself. Although after six exciting weeks of travel she was to return to her gregarious London social life and her works-in-progress for two more months of life, this journey was the high point of her last days. The *Hermes* sailed from Venice on 17 August 1958. She described its itinerary in an article commissioned for *Queen* magazine, 'The New Argonauts':

> Like Marco Polo and many more, we took ship from the Venice quays for our eastward voyage. The *Hermes* lay in the dock, looking more commodious than any vessel Marco Polo had. We were some two hundred souls (for souls we become, I believe, when on shipboard). It was like some embarkation in a Poussin picture, where men run about the quays with bales and corded boxes, and eleven thousand virgins arrive on the Zaterre to sail into a sunset sky. Down the Adriatic we steamed, bound for Greece, the Golden Horn, the Pontine Sea (black and not to be trusted); we were to dip into Russia, the Crimea, Georgia, scale the frosty Caucasus, call at Trebizond, and so down the Black Sea, to the Golden Horn again, Aegean Islands, Venice. Never a dull moment.[102]

Rose was among distinguished souls – and she was not the least among them. Her modesty was such, however, that when shown to her cabin, Patrick Kinross says, she noticed a bouquet of flowers wrapped in cellophane and withdrew at once, saying, 'This must be the wrong cabin. These can't be for me.' But they were.[103]

Just as on her Hellenic voyage 45 years before, she enjoyed historical and cultural lectures about the cruise's itinerary and studied a little modern Greek. If this all recalled George Macaulay, other old memories touched her too. At one point the travellers landed on Skyros, and Rose must have stood by Rupert Brooke's grave.

To the adventures on land she addressed her full resources. Lady Diana Cooper describes Rose's athletic participation in the most rugged adventures of the trip: 'The arena and eminences of Delphi, our first stop, she scaled with no totter.... In the Temple of Aegina – reached on a donkey she chose from the herd as being the likeliest – she bestrode the highest points of the pediments.' And she tells of Rose's disappointment 'when she did not draw a place for a desperate expedition to Bakiserail: it entailed six hours of precipice-driving in a bus after dark, a brief visit at dawn to the crumbles of a Tartar city, a night in what the guide book called "a wretched kahn", and an admission by the Russians of its being "extremely primitive" – six in a bed.' At the last minute a less hardy traveller resigned his seat on the bus and Rose delightedly took his place.[104]

In her article, published on 30 September, she described her high spirits on the last day of her last voyage:

> We had been very happy on the *Hermes*. No cruise could have been better planned, managed and enjoyed. It was a perfect *mélange* of periods and places. Like Jason and his argonauts, we returned with a golden fleece woven of beauty, interest, good company, and good fun. There was no dull moment, even at sea, since we had among us scholarship, wit, beauty, and zest. . . . An enchanted voyage. Nothing but Venice could have broken the descent to ordinary life on land; but then Venice is not, of course, ordinary life, nor yet life on land; balanced on those perilous piles, she floats, man's loveliest artefact, an evanescent mirage.[105]

Two months later, not in 'evanescent Venice' but in brick-solid London, Rose Macaulay died suddenly, leaving this ordinary land-locked life. But in her best books she remains alive – that extraordinary woman – bearing the golden fleece, and talking, talking still, with scholarship, wit, and zest.

APPENDIX

This self-mocking article, one of a series of 'Auto-Obituaries' by well-known writers, was published in the *Listener* on 2 September 1936 (p. 434) when Rose Macaulay was 55. Her great sorrows lay ahead of her, but her phrase, 'active to the end', and the humour and gallantry of this account presage what was to be her triumph over them.

'FULL FATHOM FIVE'

By Rose Macaulay

Miss Rose Macaulay, who was killed in a flying accident yesterday while on her way home from her villa on the Virgin Island of Papagayo, Caribbean Sea, was one of our older writers, having recently turned 102.

Active to the end, she continued to write books of nearly every description, her last being an exhaustive monograph on the Fauna of the Lesser Antilles. Fiction, never perhaps her strongest suit (for she lacked sustained narrative power and creative imagination), she had for some time renounced, and for the last many years had confined herself to biography, essays, travel books, poetry, and little monographs on subjects in which she took an interest not shared by the majority. Her *History of Parrots* will long remain the standard work on that bird; while her long epic poem on the submarine adventures of an amphibious girl is the best poem on that topic yet written. Miss Macaulay was always much addicted to this style of poetic narrative, but unfortunately most of her efforts in this sort, admirable though they were, did not meet with the favour of any publisher, and still languish in a drawer.

She wrote from her earliest infancy, with the greatest zest, and began to publish the sprouts of her fancy at a young age. Descended on both sides from long lines of eloquent and well-informed clergymen, few of whom had denied themselves the indulgence of breaking into print, she busily wrote down from her earliest days those little thoughts that occurred to her childish fancy. Her novels and essays, if not widely read, appealed to certain thoughtful and well-regulated minds. They were written in pure and elegant English, almost devoid of that vulgarity which degraded so much of the literature of her period, and inculcated always the highest moral lessons. Those who called her a flippant writer failed to understand the deep earnestness which underlay her sometimes facetious style and the sober piety which she had inherited from her ecclesiastical forbears. She was much interested in religions; the voluminous calf-bound theological works of past centuries were among her reading, and no curious heresy or antique doctrinal squabble failed to intrigue her fancy. She was sometimes, and with too much truth, accused of having an old-fashioned mind, and indeed the nineteenth and twentieth centuries never seemed to her, in their literature or their history, so interesting as many others. No one could – anyhow no one ever did – call her a great writer, in any of the many literary spheres in which she experimented; she was called limited, finicking, lacking in vigour or robustness of imagination; she was accused of caring more for manner than matter, for words (in which she was somewhat morbidly interested) than for what they represented. The content of her writing (which may be unearthed, dusty relics of a lost age, from the unvisited shelves of libraries) and possibly also of her mind, even in its prime, was thin and somewhat negligible.

She never had any strong link with her age, or was much interested in social questions, such as the position of women, and so forth, though international affairs, disastrous as they have invariably been, never failed to entertain and shock her. She was seldom bored by the spectacle of life, though, as she complained, the older she got the more barbarous and shocking this spectacle became. Through one barbarous phase after another, through Capitalism, Toryism, World War, Fascism, Communism, and the present Anarchy, she picked her complaining way, making would-be facetious and quite ineffectual comments on the strange conditions in which all countries habitually found themselves. She was a strong pacifist and libertarian, with a passion for being let alone; like Lord Falkland and the Rajah of Bhong, she went about ingeminating, 'Peace! Peace! Beautiful Peace! I think all this bustle is wrong'. These sentiments endeared her to no recent regime. The sunset of her life was, however, luxurious and gay, for she was so fortunate as to find, on a small Caribbean island, some of that treasure which pirates, with their curious canine instincts, appear always to have buried when they acquired it and then quite forgotten where. Despite all litigation on the part of other claimants, Miss Macaulay, then sixty years of age, succeeded in retaining her find, and it secured for her a happy old age, a Caribbean villa, and a small aeroplane, which she used to pilot to and fro between Europe and her tropical home. She was, therefore, a singularly happy old lady, particularly in that her treasure trove lifted from her the necessity of earning her living, so that she was free to write the no doubt unsaleable works that poured forth from her in her latter years. Her death came as she would have chosen, in her favourite 'plane, after a pleasant visit to her island villa. She was killed outright, by her impact with the sea into which she fell, and so escaped being devoured by sharks, a fate which she always viewed with the gravest apprehension and distaste. Due (to make use of a locution she habitually deplored) to the peculiar circumstances of her decease, there will be no funeral or flowers. She would have liked both, but obviously, since she is visiting the bottom of the monstrous world, cannot have them. Let her epitaph be, there sinks an old lady of no great talent, but who managed, on the whole, to put in a pretty good time.

NOTES

Note: Periodicals from clipping services are identified by date only. Unless otherwise documented, all correspondence is from the ERM Archive of the Wren Library, Trinity College, Cambridge University. Throughout the following notes Rose Macaulay is referred to as RM. All books were published in London unless otherwise specified.

Introduction

1. Victor Gollancz, *Reminiscences of Affection* (Gollancz, 1968), p. 72. Hereafter *Reminiscences.*

2. RM, *Letters to a Sister,* ed. Constance Babington Smith (Collins, 1964), 5 May 1929, p. 49. Hereafter *Sister.*

3. Ivy Compton-Burnett as quoted by Hilary Spurling, *Ivy: The Life of Ivy Compton-Burnett* (New York: Knopf, 1977), p. 499. Hereafter *Ivy.*

4. *Ivy,* p. 378. Ivy Compton-Burnett as quoted by Kay Dick, *Ivy and Stevie: Conversations and Reflections* (Duckworth, 1971), p. 7. Hereafter *Ivy and Stevie.*

5. C.V. Wedgwood, 'Dame Rose in Calm Waters', review of *Last Letters to a Friend,* ed. Constance Babington Smith (Collins, 1962), *Daily Telegraph,* 26 October 1962. Hereafter *Last Letters.*

6. Mary Ellen Chase, 'Five Literary Portraits', *Massachusetts Review* 3, Spring 1962, p. 516.

7. Alan Pryce-Jones, 'The Pleasures of Knowing Rose Macaulay', *Encounter* 12, March 1959, pp. 25–6. Hereafter 'Knowing'.

8. Rebecca West, 'Rosamond Ravished, but Rose Rose', *Vogue* 161, January 1973, p. 113.

9. Diana Cooper, 'Knowing', p. 31.

10. John Betjeman, 'Rose Macaulay', *Observer,* 2 November 1958.

11. RM, 'Problems of a Woman's Life', *A Casual Commentary* (Methuen, 1925), p. 82. Hereafter *CC*.

12. RM, *The Towers of Trebizond* (Collins, 1959; originally published 1956), p. 253. Hereafter *Towers*.

13. RM, see 'Woman: Her Dark Future', *CC*, p. 225.

14. John Lehmann, personal interview, 5 January 1980.

15. Virginia Woolf, *To the Lighthouse* (New York: Harcourt, Brace, 1927), p. 79.

16. RM, *Keeping Up Appearances* (Collins, 1929), pp. 152–3. Hereafter *Appearances*.

17. RM, 'Problems of a Writer's Life', *CC*, pp. 50–1.

18. RM, *Letters to a Friend: 1950–1952*, ed. Constance Babington Smith (Collins, 1961), p. 31. Hereafter *Letters*.

19. Gollancz, *Reminiscences*, p. 83.

20. Typescript for BBC broadcast 'I Speak for Myself', May 1949, E.R. Macaulay Archive, Wren Library, Trinity College, Cambridge. Hereafter Wren-Macaulay Archive.

1. 'Does Ancestry Matter?'

1. Editorial introduction to RM, 'Does Ancestry Matter?', *Daily Express*, 5 June 1928. All further quotations from RM's newspaper article 'Does Ancestry Matter?' are taken from this source.

2. RM, *Appearances*, p. 25.

3. Noel Annan, 'The Intellectual Aristocracy', *Studies in Social History*, ed. John Harold Plumb (Longmans, Green, & Co., 1955), pp. 254–61. All further quotations from Noel Annan are made from this source. Hereafter *Studies*.

4. Typescript copy of obituary of Eliza Conybeare by F.A.C. [Frances A. Conybeare], published in *Guardian*, 4 February 1903, Wren-Macaulay Archive.

5. Noel Annan, *Studies*, p. 249.

6. Family records, Wren-Macaulay Archive.

7. Revd Michael David Knowles, 'Thomas Babington Macaulay', *Encyclopaedia Britannica* (Chicago: William Benton, 1967), Vol. 14, p. 496.

8. The George Campbell Macaulay letters to Francis Jenkinson are held in the Archives of the Cambridge University Library, Cambridge. All further quotations throughout from G.C. Macaulay's correspondence with Francis Jenkinson are from this source.

9. Typescript transcription of Frances Conybeare's diaries, Wren-Macaulay Archive. All further Frances Conybeare quotations are from this source.

10. Grace Conybeare's holograph diaries, 1867–9, 1871, 1873–7, 1879–80, 1883, 1886–90, and 1898, with enclosures, Wren-Macaulay Archive.
11. George Macaulay, Tripos Verses, Cambridge University Library Archives, translated by Cynthia Damon of Stanford University.
12. Copied in Grace Conybeare's hand in her diary.
13. *Ibid.*
14. Reported to Constance Babington Smith by Jean Macaulay, Constance Babington Smith, *Rose Macaulay: A Biography* (Collins, 1972), p. 22. Hereafter *RM*.
15. Revd J. W. Edward Conybeare's diaries, Wren-Macaulay Archive. All other quotations from 'Uncle Edward' will be taken from this source. (In 1901 Edward Conybeare was to resign from his church in Barrington, join the Roman Catholic Church, and live in Cambridge until his death in 1931.)

2. The Island Colony

1. Roger Fry, letter to G.L. Dickinson, 15 February 1891, *Letters of Roger Fry, Vol. I*, ed. Denys Sutton (Chatto & Windus, 1972), p. 124.
2. RM, *The Furnace* (John Murray, 1907), p. 235. Hereafter *Furnace*.
3. RM, 'Villa Macolai', *Little Innocents: Childhood Reminiscences* (Cobden-Sanderson, 1932), p. 47. Hereafter 'Macolai'.
4. *Ibid.*
5. RM, 'After the War', typescript n.d. but during Second World War, Wren-Macaulay Archive.
6. Gwen Raverat, *Period Piece* (Faber & Faber, 1952), pp. 47–8. RM reviewed *Period Piece* enthusiastically for *TLS*, 24 October 1952, calling it 'an altogether delightful book.... This, one feels, is the right way to portray one's family and oneself when young; the humour is infectious, the figures endearingly ridiculous and admirable human beings.' This literary judgement may to some extent explain the fact that RM's own memoirs are of sunny moments only, while her novels sometimes portray the anxieties and fears of children.
7. Dorothea Conybeare, 'Notes on Rose Macaulay Memories', typescript, unpublished, July 1960, Wren-Macaulay Archive.
8. RM, 'Fraternal', *Personal Pleasures* (Gollancz, 1935), p. 232. Hereafter *Pleasures*.
9. RM, 'Christmas Books: The Free Run of the Shelves', *New Statesman and Nation*, 4 December 1948, p. 487. Hereafter 'Shelves'.
10. *Ibid.*
11. RM, *Last Letters*, 15 January 1954, p. 140.
12. RM, *Orphan Island* (New York: Boni & Liveright, 1925), p. 239. Hereafter *Orphan*.

13. RM, 'Astronomy', *Pleasures,* pp. 43–6.

14. RM, *Catchwords and Claptrap*, Hogarth Essays, Second Series (Hogarth Press, 1926), p. 12. Hereafter *Catchwords.*

15. RM, 'Hot Bath', *Pleasures,* p. 256.

16. RM, 'Frankly Speaking', BBC interview, 8 July 1958.

17. RM, 'Shelves'.

18. *Ibid.*

19. RM, 'The Spice of Life: In Deep and Shallow Waters', *Listener,* 30 January 1936, p. 207. Hereafter 'Deep and Shallow'.

20. RM, 'The Age of Reason', *New Statesman and Nation,* 10 January 1948, pp. 27–8.

21. *Ibid.*

22. RM, *Furnace,* p. 201.

23. RM, 'Fraternal', *Pleasures,* pp. 229–30.

24. RM, interview, *Living Authors: A Book of Biographies,* ed. Dilly Tante (pseud.) (New York: H. W. Wilson, 1931), p. 238.

25. RM, 'Macolai', p. 48.

26. George Macaulay, Tripos Verses, Cambridge University Library Archives.

27. RM, 'Macolai', pp. 47–8.

28. Jean Macaulay as quoted by Constance Babington Smith, *Sister,* p. 15.

29. RM, *Letters,* 6 March 1952, p. 283.

30. RM, *Letters,* 12 August 1952, p. 350.

31. George Macaulay, Francis Jenkinson correspondence, 1 November 1888.

32. Grace Macaulay, diaries, 3 February 1890, Wren-Macaulay Archive.

33. Jean Macaulay as reported to Constance Babington Smith in late life.

34. 'George Campbell Macaulay', Obituary column, *Cambridge Chronicle and University Journal,* 16 July 1915.

35. RM, 'Macolai', p. 48.

36. RM, 'Church-Going', *Pleasures,* p. 124.

37. *Ibid.*

38. RM, 'Macolai', p. 49.

39. RM, *Sister,* 17 February [1935], p. 65.

40. RM, 'Solitude', *Pleasures,* p. 339.

41. RM, 'Bathing: Off the Ligurian Coast', *Pleasures,* p. 55.

42. RM, 'I Speak for Myself', typescript preparation for BBC broadcast on 10 May 1949, Macaulay-Wren Archives; *Letters,* 18 January 1951, p. 58.

43. RM, 'I Speak for Myself'.

3. Landlocked

1. RM, 'Coming to London: 13', *Coming to London,* ed. John Lehmann (Phoenix House, 1957), p. 155. Hereafter 'Coming to London'. Following paragraph from this source.

2. RM, *Letters,* 1 March 1951, p. 90.

3. *Ibid.,* p. 88.

4. Personal letter from Constance Babington Smith, 12 July 1990. She corresponded with 'several old ladies who had been contemporaries with the Macaulay girls at Clent' and the reply of one of them and the sketches which they sent her are included here.

5. RM, *Letters,* 20 February 1951, p. 82.

6. RM, 'Prize Competition', 'The Sea', *Oxford High School Magazine,* December 1898, p. 1095.

7. RM, 'I Speak for Myself'.

8. RM, review of the film, *The Constant Nymph,* newspaper clipping, hand-dated '1943'. No further documentation. Wren-Macaulay Archive.

9. RM, *Told by an Idiot* (Collins, 1923), p. 154. Hereafter *Idiot.*

10. *Ibid.,* pp. 234–5.

11. *Ibid.,* p. 220.

12. Lucy Soulsby as quoted by Constance Babington Smith, *RM,* p. 38.

13. Lucy Soulsby, *Stray Thoughts on Reading,* fifth impression (Longmans, Green, & Co., 1904), pp. 95–6.

14. *Ibid.* p. 10. Quotations in the following paragraph are from this source.

15. Lucy Soulsby as quoted by Violet Stack (ed.), *Oxford High School: Girls Public Day School Trust 1875–1960* (Berkshire: Abbey Press, 1963), p. 7.

16. 'Lucy Helen Muriel Soulsby', Obituary column, *The Times,* 24 May 1927.

17. L. H. M. Soulsby, *A Woman's Movement* (Longmans, Green, and Co., 1913), p. 30.

18. RM, *CC,* p. 82.

19. RM, 'Following the Fashion', *Pleasures,* p. 227.

20. RM, *Sister,* [13 July 1957], p. 226.

21. RM, *Letters,* 12 March 1951, p. 98.

22. Florence Ayescough née Waller as quoted in *Oxford High School,* p. 57. RM was in touch with Bertha Browne (1863–1963) in 1934 and again in 1956 and was delighted to discover that Miss Browne, even in old age, had, like herself, 'an interesting mind' and 'a great love of solitude'. RM writes to Jean, 'It is good to find that we weren't mistaken in our adolescent passion.' *Sister,* [May 1934], pp. 61–2; 29 May 1956, p. 190.

23. RM, 'Believing', *Pleasures*, p. 72.

24. *Ibid.*, 'Disbelieving', pp. 158–9.

25. RM, *Idiot*, pp. 65–6.

26. *Ibid.*, p. 194.

27. RM, *Letters*, 16 March 1951, p. 98.

28. RM, *Idiot*, p. 132.

29. RM, *Appearances*, pp. 172–3.

30. *Ibid.*, p. 174.

31. *Ibid.*, p. 176.

32. *Ibid.*, pp. 177 and 175.

33. RM, *Letters*, 15 March 1951, p. 98.

34. John Stuart Mill, *On Liberty* (New York: W. W. Norton, 1975), pp. 58–9.

35. Ernest Renan, *The Life of Jesus* (Tribuner & Co., 1864), *passim*.

36. RM, *Letters*, 24 April 1951, p. 120.

37. RM, *Idiot*, p. 208.

38. *Ibid.*

39. George Macaulay, Francis Jenkinson correspondence, 12 June [1899].

40. Florence Nightingale as quoted by Ray Strachey, *The Cause* (Port Washington, NY: Kennicott Press, 1928), p. 21.

41. The exam had been opened up to girl examinees in 1863 by the brilliant political tactics of Emily Davis. Many headmistresses supported the examination as an external ratification of their schools' credentials. Oxford High School Girls consistently placed well in it.

42. RM, 'Mr. R. H. Macaulay', *The Times*, 20 December 1937.

4. A New Island

1. Olive Willis as quoted by Anne Ridler, *Olive Willis and Downe House: An Adventure in Education* (John Murray, 1967), p. 53. Hereafter *Olive Willis*. 'College Meeting Room' was the term used at that time for the analogous Junior Common Room in the men's colleges.

2. Vera Brittain, *Testament of a Generation: The Journalism of Vera Brittain and Winifred Holtby*, ed. Paul Berry and Alan Bishop (Virago Press, 1985), p. 321. Hereafter *Generation*.

3. Vera Farnell, *A Somervillian Looks Back* (Oxford: privately printed at the University Press, 1948), p.v. Hereafter *Somervillian*.

4. Vera Brittain, *The Women at Oxford: A Fragment of History* (George G. Harrap & Co., 1960), p. 69. Hereafter *Oxford Women*.

5. *Ibid.*

6. *Ibid.*, p. 16.

7. Rebecca West, *1900* (Weidenfeld & Nicolson, 1982), p. 72.

8. RM, *CC*, p. 2.

9. Viscountess Rhondda, *This Was My World* (Macmillan, 1933), p. 107.

10. Olive Willis, as quoted in *Olive Willis*, p. 53.

11. *Ibid.*

12. RM, *Dangerous Ages* (Collins, 1921), p. 3. Hereafter *Ages*. In a personal letter to me Quentin Bell tells a story about RM in the 1930s that verifies the fact of her athletic grace: 'There were three of us on a boat, a Channel steamer moored in Newhaven Harbour, Yvonne Knapp (who knew Rose Macaulay), Dr. Elinor Singer and I. The passengers were disembarking, going down the gang plank. We were in no hurry. I think that we knew that our motor car would wait for us outside Newhaven Station, so we took it easy. We sat on a bench and had an excellent view of the endless stream of descending passengers.

'"Look at their feet," someone said. We all looked and were all struck by the fact that to descend the ribbed surface of a gang plank is to court derision. Our fellow passengers reminded us of large wading birds wearing what I think you call sneakers, gingerly and unhappily trying and failing to preserve their dignity under impossible circumstances. Just why they looked so funny I cannot say, but comic to a fantastic degree. The "Great Little Titch" who also did things with his feet at the Palladium Music Hall could reduce an audience to helpless tears of merriment. The passengers on their gangway did likewise. At first I was afraid our entertainers would realise that they were being laughed at; but clearly they did not, indeed a part of the beauty of their performance derived from the fact that it was an unconscious effort.

'It seemed to us that no one could walk down that treacherous incline without appearing ludicrous; but we were wrong. One solitary traveller made the descent with an appearance of perfect ease and grace. We were struck dumb with admiration, all save Yvonne, who exclaimed: "Good heavens, that's Rose Macaulay."'

13. Florence Rich as quoted by Vera Farnell, *Somervillian*, p. 17.

14. RM, 'Why I Dislike Cats, Clothes and Visits', *Daily Mail*, 2 November 1928, p. 19.

15. RM, *Life Among the English: Britain in Pictures* (Collins, 1942), p. [48]. Hereafter *Life English*.

16. Alan Pryce-Jones, 'Knowing', p. 25.

17. Olive Willis, as quoted in *Olive Willis*, p. 53.

18. *Ibid.*

19. Susan Leonardi, *Dangerous by Degrees* (New Brunswick: Rutgers University Press, 1989), p. 61. Hereafter *Degrees*.

20. *Ibid.*

21. RM, 'Marginal Comments', *Spectator*, 5 April 1935, p. 565.

22. Student column from the 1913 *Isis* as quoted by Susan Leonardi, *Degrees,* p. 28.

23. RM, *The Making of a Bigot* (Hodder & Stoughton, 1914), p. 137. Hereafter *Bigot.*

24. RM, 'Full Fathom Five', Auto-Obituary – VIII, *Listener,* 2 September 1936, p. 434. See Appendix.

25. Brigid O'Donovan, personal interview, 1982.

26. RM, 'Coming to London', pp. 165–6.

27. RM, 'Problems for the Citizen', *CC,* pp. 36–7.

28. RM, 'A Year I Remember – 1913', early typescript *ms.* for a BBC Third Programme broadcast, scheduled for 3 June 1950, Wren-Macaulay Archive, p. 17. Hereafter 'A Year I Remember'.

29. RM, *Bigot,* p. 153.

30. RM, *Potterism* (Collins, 1920), p. 8.

31. RM, 'A Year I Remember', p. 17.

32. RM, 'Woman: The Myth and the Reality', *Leader,* 3 February 1945.

33. RM, 'Auto-Obituary'.

34. Judith Moore, 'Rose Macaulay: A Model for Christian Feminists,' *Christian Century,* 15 November 1978, p. 1099.

35. RM, *Potterism,* p. 5.

36. Carolyn Heilbrun, *Hamlet's Mother* (New York and London: Columbia University Press, 1990), p. 3; p. 204.

37. RM, *Towers,* p. 15.

38. RM, 'Woman: Her Troubled Past', *CC,* p. 224.

39. RM, *Mystery at Geneva: An Improbable Tale of Singular Happenings* (Collins, 1922), p. 150. Hereafter *Mystery.* The concept of 'neutral' sexual personalities was a common one at this period; two friends of RM, Ivy Compton-Burnett and Margaret Jourdain, described themselves as 'neutrals'.

40. *Ibid.,* pp. 150–1.

41. RM as quoted by H. Hunter in a letter to the editor which complains of RM's review of Arnold Bennett's *Our Women: Chapters on the Sex Discord* (Cassell, 1920) in *Time and Tide,* October 1920. Reproduced in Dale Spender's *Time and Tide Wait for No Man* (Pandora Press, 1984), p. 183. RM wrote: 'Mr. Bennett has an accurate but superfluous chapter dealing with the intellectual superiority of most men to most women; superfluous (surely) because no one questions this fact, any more than man's superior physical strength or courage.... In spite of platitudes and inaccuracies it is, in the main, a sympathetic and not unfair book.' Yet, on the whole, she did not like summary judgements about the sexes. In the same review, she says about women: 'They are not Woman, or Man, not a collective herd, but a set of uncorrelated individuals, entirely

different from one another, without enough common denominator to hang a book on.'

Note that I am, in this chapter, looking at aspects of temperament, thought, and sexual identity in RM similar to those analysed by Jeanette M. Passty in *Eros and Androgyny: The Legacy of Rose Macaulay* (London and Toronto: Associated University Presses, 1988). I agree with her thesis that RM was more interested in what was common in the lives of both men and women than in what was exclusive in the experience of each. We have, however, used different evidence and different techniques in exploring this question and have come to different conclusions on some subjects, chiefly RM's relationship with her father.

42. RM, 'What I Believe', *Nation,* 16 December 1931, pp. 664–6.

43. RM, 'Onward from Noodledom', *Listener,* 18 May 1939.

44. RM, *Ages,* p. 53.

45. RM, *Mystery,* p. 70.

46. Muriel St Clare Byrne and Catherine Hope Mansfield, *Somerville College 1879–1921* (Oxford: printed by Frederick Hall at the University Press, n.d.), p. 6.

47. Vera Brittain, *Oxford Women,* p. 39.

48. Vera Farnell, *Somervillian,* p. 9.

49. Vera Brittain, *Oxford Women,* p. 57.

50. RM, *Idiot,* p. 66.

51. A. N. Wilson, 'Introduction', *Idiot* (Virago, 1983), p. xv.

52. RM, 'On Taking Sides', *Spectator,* 17 November 1933, p. 748.

53. E.M. Forster, 'The *Raison D'Etre* of Criticism in the Arts', *Two Cheers for Democracy* (Harmondsworth: Penguin, 1951), p. 129.

54. RM, 'On Taking Sides', pp. 748–9.

55. RM, *Bigot,* pp. 278–9.

56. C.V. Wedgwood, Introduction to RM's *They Were Defeated* (Collins, new edition with introduction, 1960; originally published 1932), p. 13.

5. The Valley

1. RM, *Abbots Verney* (John Murray, 1906), p. 388. Hereafter *Verney.*

2. *Ibid.,* p. 390.

3. *Ibid.,* p. 132.

4. Margaret Macaulay, *The Sentence Absolute* (James Nisbet, 1914), p. 103.

5. *Ibid.,* pp. 107–8.

6. RM, 'Some Other Problems of Life: A Preliminary Word', *CC,* p. 19.

7. *Ibid.,* pp. 17–18.

8. RM, 'Some Inquiries: Into the Sanctity of the Home', *CC*, p. 97.

9. RM, 'A Word on Family Life', *Spectator*, 20 February 1932, p. 246.

10. RM, first draft typescript for a *Spectator* column [1942? dated by internal evidence], Wren-Macaulay Archive.

11. Sir Thomas Browne as quoted by RM, *The Valley Captives* (Collins, 1911), title page. Hereafter *Captives*.

12. *Abbots Verney*, p. 39.

13. Revd. J.W. Edward Conybeare, diary, January 1902.

14. George Macaulay, letter, 31 January 1902, Francis Jenkinson correspondence, Cambridge University Library Archives.

15. RM, *Captives*, pp. 42–3.

16. Charles Lamb, as quoted by RM, *Captives*, title page.

17. RM, *The Writings of E.M. Forster* (Hogarth Press, 1938), p. 19. Hereafter *Forster*.

18. RM, 'Problems of a Woman's Life', *CC*, p. 81. She adds, 'Further, if someone has got to housekeep, there is no reason why it should be a woman rather than a man. But that is the convention.'

19. F.A.C. [Frances Conybeare], typescript copy of the obituary submitted to *Guardian* (dated 4 February 1903) from Frances Conybeare's 'Journal', Wren-Macaulay Archive.

20. RM, letter to Marjorie Venables Taylor, 17 February 1907, John Murray Archive.

21. RM, *Letters*, 1 March 1951, p. 89.

22. RM, *Ages*, p. 121.

23. *Ibid.*

24. *Ibid.*, p. 29; p. 81.

25. RM, letter to Marjorie Venables Taylor, 17 February 1907. Marjorie Venables Taylor, a fellow Somervillian with whom Rose continued to correspond, was an archaeologist.

26. RM, *Letters*, 6 March 1952, p. 283.

27. Lucy Soulsby, letter to John Murray, The Manor House, Brandesbury, n.d., John Murray Archive.

28. RM, letter quoted by Anne Ridler, *Olive Willis*, p. 54.

29. *Olive Willis*, p. 54.

30. Violet Markham, *Return Passage: The Autobiography of Violet Markham* (Oxford University Press, 1953), p. 66 ff. Subsequent quotations in the next paragraph are from this passage.

31. RM, *Mystery*, p. 96.

32. *Ibid.*, p. 245.

33. Anatole France as translated by RM, *Forster*, p. 23.

34. RM, *Idiot*, p. 314.

35. Advertisements quoting reviews of *Abbots Verney* on p. [237] of *Furnace* (1907).

36. *TLS* review of *Abbots Verney*, 14 December 1906.

37. John Murray, letter to RM, 23 July 1907, John Murray Archive.

6. Journey through Pain

1. RM, letter to Margerie Venables Taylor, 17 February 1907.
2. RM, *Verney,* p. 388.
3. Lady Robert Cecil, reader's report to John Murray, n.d., John Murray Archive.
4. RM, typescript for 'Spectator's Notebook' column, [1942?, dated by internal evidence], Wren-Macaulay Archive.
5. RM, *Verney,* p. 105.
6. George Macaulay, Francis Jenkinson correspondence, 31 January 1902.
7. RM, *The World My Wilderness* (Collins, 1950), p. 154. Hereafter *Wilderness.*
8. RM, *Furnace,* p. [v].
9. RM, letter to Margerie Venables Taylor, 17 February 1907.
10. John Murray, letter to RM, 20 June 1910, John Murray Archive.
11. RM, letter to John Murray, 27 July 1907, John Murray Archive.
12. RM, *Furnace,* p. 202.
13. A.W., reader's report, n.d., John Murray Archive.
14. RM, *Forster,* pp. 35–6.
15. Rupert Brooke, letter to Mrs Brooke [29 October 1907], *The Letters of Rupert Brooke,* chosen and edited by Geoffrey Keynes (New York: Harcourt, Brace & World, 1968), p. 113. Hereafter *Brooke Letters.*
16. RM, *Last Letters,* 25 September 1952, p. 33.
17. RM, 'Deep and Shallow'.
18. Rupert Brooke, letter to Elizabeth van Rysselburgh, '?31 May 1913', as quoted by Paul Delany, *The Neo-pagans* (New York: Free Press, 1987), p. 205. Hereafter *Neo-pagans.*
19. Paul Delany, *Neo-pagans,* p. 9; p. 45.
20. Rupert Brooke, *Brooke Letters,* letter to Geoffrey Keynes, 8 January 1907, p. 73.
21. RM, letter to Margerie Venables Taylor, n.d.
22. RM, letter to John Murray, 23 November 1907, John Murray Archive.
23. John Murray, letter to RM, n.d., John Murray Archive.
24. RM, *The Secret River* (Collins, 1909), pp. 119–20. Hereafter *River.*
25. Virginia Woolf, *The Diary of Virginia Woolf, Vol. II, 1921–1924,* ed. Anne Olivier Bell (Hogarth Press, 1978), 18 February 1921, p. 93. Hereafter *VW Diary.*
26. RM on BBC programme with P.H. Newby, L.H. Hartley, and John Lehmann, 'The Modern English Novel', 8 March 1950.

27. Lady Robert Cecil, reader's report, n.d., John Murray Archive.

28. RM, letter to Margerie Venables Taylor, 2 June 1909.

29. RM, *River,* p. 9.

30. *Ibid.,* p. 20.

31. Virginia Woolf, 'Freudian Fiction', review of *An Imperfect Mother* by J.D. Beresford, 25 March 1920, as republished in *Contemporary Writers* (Hogarth Press, 1965), p. 154.

32. RM, *River,* p. 26.

33. *Ibid.,* p. 32.

34. *Ibid.,* p. 97.

35. RM, letter to John Murray, 15 October 1908, John Murray Archive.

36. *TLS* review, 11 March 1909, p. 98.

37. 'Personal Note', *Supplement to R. E. [Royal Engineers] Journal,* August 1909, republished from the *Civil and Military Gazette of India,* p. 60, Wren-Macaulay Archive.

38. H.R. Gale (Brevet Colonel A. C. R. E., Kohat District), letter to George Macaulay, 17 June 1909, Wren-Macaulay Archive.

39. Letters of condolence to the Macaulay family, Wren-Macaulay Archive.

40. Reginald H. Macaulay, letter from India to Grace Macaulay, n.d.

41. RM, letter to Margerie Venables Taylor, 2 June 1909.

7. The Road to London

1. RM, 'Frankly Speaking', BBC interview, 8 July 1958.

2. RM, *Letters,* 15 February 1951, p. 74.

3. RM, *Letters,* 18 January 1951, p. 59.

4. RM, 'Church-Going: Anglican', *Pleasures,* p. 121.

5. *Ibid.,* p. 123.

6. RM, *Letters,* 15 December 1950, p. 40.

7. RM, 'A Church I Should Like', May 1929, typescript for article to be published in *St Paul's Review* (The London Diocesan Quarterly SPCK, London), I: 12, p. 12, Wren-Macaulay Archive.

8. RM, as reported by Eric Gillette in a letter to Constance Babington Smith, 19 July 1963, Wren-Macaulay Archive.

9. RM, 'A Church I Should Like'.

10. Lady Robert Cecil, reader's report, n.d., John Murray Archive.

11. RM, letter to John Murray, 19 January 1911, John Murray Archive.

12. RM, *Captives,* p. 154.

13. *Ibid.,* pp. 154–5.

14. RM, *Letters,* 15 October 1951, p. 207.

15. RM, *Captives,* p. 107.

16. *Ibid.,* p. 290.

17. *Ibid.,* p. 330.

18. RM, 'A Year I Remember', p. 28.

19. *Ibid.*

20. Paul Delany, *Neo-pagans,* p. 95.

21. Rupert Brooke, *Brooke Letters,* letter to Erica Cotterill [July 1910], p. 252.

22. RM, *Views and Vagabonds* (Hodder & Stoughton, 1914), pp. 191–2. Hereafter *Vagabonds.*

23. *Ibid.,* p. 195.

24. RM, *Sister,* 18 April [1926], p. 28.

25. Sister Margaret, Dss. [Margaret Macaulay], *The Deaconess* (The Faith Press, 1919), *passim.*

26. Edward Marsh, *Rupert Brooke: The Collected Poems with a Memoir by Edward Marsh* (Sidgwick & Jackson, revised edition, 1942), p. xxvi.

27. RM, 'Coming to London', p. 158.

28. 'A Year I Remember', identified as New Page Seven in typescript.

29. Rupert Brooke, *Brooke Letters,* letter to Hugh-Russell-Smith, 'September the so & so' [1907], p. 110.

30. RM, *Vagabonds,* p. 222.

31. *Ibid.,* p. 46.

32. *Ibid.,* p. 84.

33. G. Lowes Dickinson, a passage from *A Modern Symposium* as quoted by RM, *Vagabonds,* p. [v].

34. RM, *Vagabonds,* p. 57.

35. *Ibid.,* pp. 112–13.

36. *Ibid.,* p. 120.

37. *Ibid.,* pp. 137–8.

38. *Ibid.,* p. 54.

39. *Ibid.,* p. 307.

40. Lady Robert Cecil, reader's report, n.d., John Murray Archive.

41. Rebecca West, review of *'Views and Vagabonds', The Freewoman,* 21 March 1912, pp. 348–9.

42. RM, 'Frankly Speaking'. On the other hand, in two of her best novels, *They Were Defeated* and *The Towers of Trebizond,* Rose Macaulay said she began her planning with characters clearly in mind.

43. RM, *The Lee Shore* (Hodder & Stoughton, [1912]), p. 321. Hereafter *Lee Shore.*

44. RM, letter to John Murray, n.d., John Murray Archive.

45. Unsigned *Spectator* review, 26 October 1912, p. 652.

46. 'A Year I Remember'. In her broadcast, RM either inaccurately

places this cruise as part of her 'wonderful year', of 1913, or, more probably, used artistic licence in order to include it in this happy account. Grace Macaulay's date book, 'Morning Light', dates it in 1912. Jane Harrison, the eminent Oxford scholar, was also a cruise passenger; her record verifies the date 1912.

47. *Ibid.*
48. RM, *Bigot,* p. 144.
49. RM, 'The Empty Berth', page proof of the short story published in the *Cornhill Magazine,* July 1913, Wren-Macaulay Archive [p. 9].
50. *Ibid.*
51. RM, 'Coming to London', pp. 159–60.
52. RM, 'A Year I Remember', p. 28.

8. Flight and Fall

1. RM, 'Coming to London', p. 158.
2. *Ibid.*
3. *Ibid.,* p. 159.
4. Naomi Royde-Smith, review of *Potterism, Time and Tide,* 16 July 1920, p. 209.
5. RM, *Forster,* p. 107.
6. Frank Swinnerton, 'Rose Macaulay', *Kenyon Review,* November 1967, p. 594.
7. David Wright, 'Pedals and Pluck', review of Constance Babington Smith's *Rose Macaulay, Sunday Telegraph,* November 1972.
8. RM, *Bigot,* p. 47.
9. Unsigned, review of *The Making of a Bigot, The Englishwoman,* 22 May 1914, p. 117.
10. RM, *Bigot,* p. 86.
11. *Ibid.,* p. 140.
12. RM, *Non-Combatants and Others* (Methuen, 1986; originally published London: Hodder & Stoughton, 1916), p. 178. Hereafter *Non-Combatants.*
13. RM, 'A Year I Remember', p. 4A.
14. *Ibid.,* p. 19.
15. RM, *Letters,* 12 March 1951, p. 94.
16. RM, *What Not* (Constable, 1918), pp. 162–3.
17. Unsigned review of *The Making of a Bigot, The Englishwoman,* 22 May 1914, p. 118.
18. RM, 'Coming to London', pp. 164–5.
19. Rupert Brooke, *Brooke Letters,* letter to Frances Cornford, [21 October 1914], p. 625.
20. *Ibid.,* letter to G. Lowes Dickinson, 28 October [1914], p. 627.

21. RM, 'Many Sisters to Many Brothers', 'Introduction', *Scars upon My Heart: Women's Poetry and Verse of the First World War*, ed. Catherine Reilley (Virago, 1981), p. xxxv.

22. RM, 'A Year to Remember', p. 12.

23. RM, *Non-Combatants*, p. 99.

24. *Ibid.*, p. 141.

25. Mary Agnes Hamilton, *Remembering My Good Friends* (Jonathan Cape, 1944), p. 133.

26. RM, *Forster*, p. 55.

27. RM, letter to Walter de la Mare, 7 May 1915.

28. RM, *Non-Combatants*, p. 73.

29. *Ibid.*, p. 135.

30. *Ibid.*, p. 19.

31. RM, 'Picnic, July 1917', *Rose Macaulay, The Augustan Books of English Poetry*, Second Series, No. 6, ed. Humbert Wolfe (Ernest Benn, 1927), p. 11. Hereafter *Macaulay Augustan*.

32. RM, *Non-Combatants*, p. 47.

33. Vera Brittain, 'What Nursing Taught Me', *Good Housekeeping*, April 1929, reproduced in Vera Brittain and Winifred Holtby, *Generation*, pp. 317–18.

34. Constance Babington Smith, *RM*, p. 79.

35. RM, *Non-Combatants*, p. 170.

36. *Ibid.*

37. Unsigned review of *Non-Combatants, The Englishwoman*, 22 May 1916, p. 287.

38. RM, 'Driving Sheep', *Three Days* (Constable, 1919), p. 28.

39. RM, 'Lunch Hour', *Three Days*, p. 34.

40. Lord Bonham Carter, personal interview, October 1989.

41. RM, *They Were Defeated* (Collins, 1932), p. 55. Hereafter *Defeated*.

42. RM, letter from John Murray Archive as quoted by Constance Babington Smith, *RM*, p. 59.

43. Alan Pryce Jones, 'Knowing', p. 25.

44. Humbert Wolfe, 'Rose Macaulay', Introduction to *Macaulay Augustan*, p. iii.

45. Father Hamilton Johnson, letter to Constance Babington Smith, 6 August 1959, quoted in the 'Introduction' of *Letters*, pp. 17–18.

9. The Debate

1. Beryl O'Donovan, 'Locusts Food [*sic*]', unpublished memoir of 153 typewritten legal-size pages, n.d., probably written and rewritten between 1956 and 1968. Hereafter 'Locusts'. Brigid O'Donovan allowed me to read and take notes from this *ms*. She said her mother had made a number

of efforts to have it published. 'Locusts Food' and Brigid O'Donovan's memories were primary sources for the reconstruction of Gerald O'Donovan's life in this chapter.

'Locusts Food' stops abruptly in 1938 with an account of Beryl O'Donovan's visits alone to Ireland. There may have been further chapters, but this *ms.* ends three years before the death of the O'Donovan's younger daughter, Mary O'Donovan, at the age of 23. Mary swallowed an open safety pin, was hospitalized in Guildford for three weeks, and died of internal gangrene because she could not retain the antibiotics which were administered to her. Brigid O'Donovan said her father was 'grief-stricken' and deeply depressed for a long time afterwards.

2. RM, tribute to Gerald O'Donovan, Obituary column, *The Times*, 9 August 1942.

3. H. G. Wells as quoted by Beryl O'Donovan, 'Locusts Food', p. 129.

4. Beryl O'Donovan, 'Locusts Food', pp. 84–5.

5. Brigid O'Donovan, personal interviews. From 1982 until July 1988, when she died, she gave me generous assistance. She was an Oxford graduate from St Hugh's College, was awarded an MBE for her career as the Personnel Director of the British Design Centre, and was active in local politics and in community school affairs. Brigid O'Donovan was an intelligent, amusing, civic-minded, and attractive woman who, by her own personality, helped me to understand how winning her father's charm must have been. She said Gerald O'Donovan had been a very good father and had not neglected his children because of Rose Macaulay. Her image of Rose was as a good friend of the family. She thought her formidable to most men.

Rose brought Brigid O'Donovan into the literary world in 1934 by helping her get her 'first real job' as T.S. Eliot's secretary at Faber and Faber. 'From the start I fell in love with him,' writes Brigid. Unhappy, she resigned the position after two years. Her account of this period is published as 'The Love Song of T.S. Eliot's Secretary', *Confrontation*, Brooklyn: Long Island University, 1975, pp. 3–8.

6. RM, *What Not*, p. 162.

7. *Ibid.*, p. 147.

8. Jean Macaulay, in an interview with Constance Babington Smith at the time she was doing research for her biography of Rose Macaulay.

9. RM, *What Not*, p. 7.

10. Compton Mackenzie, *My Life and Times, Octave VIII, 1939–1946* (Chatto & Windus, 1969), p. 19; *Octave X, 1953–1963* (Chatto & Windus, 1971), p. 77.

11. Harold Nicolson, as quoted by John Ryan, 'Gerald O'Donovan, Priest, Novelist and Intellectual: A Forgotten Leader of the Irish Revival', unpublished thesis, p. 198. This is a significant piece of research on Irish history which, along with the generous assistance of Donal and Jennifer

O'Donovan of Kilbride Lodge, Dublin, and the staff of the National Library of Ireland, helped me to recreate the story of Gerald O'Donovan's early life.

12. D.P. Moran in the *Irish Leader,* 1901, as quoted on a programme about the life of Gerald O'Donovan by John Ryan, broadcast on St Stephen's Day, 1988, KTE Radio Centre, Donnybrook, Dublin. Hereafter 'O'Donovan Broadcast'. Edward Martyn, February 1903, as quoted on 'O'Donovan Broadcast'.

13. Mrs Mary Conlan, speaking on the 'O'Donovan Broadcast'.

14. John Ryan's thesis was presented in the National University of Ireland for the Degree of Master of Arts (Mode A) in History, University College, Galway, November 1983.

15. W. B. Yeats, as quoted on 'O'Donovan Broadcast'.

16. In January 1982 John Ryan guided me through St Brendan's Cathedral and made it possible for me to see the Dun Emer banners.

17. Jeremiah O'Donovan, 'Is Ireland Doomed?', *New Ireland Review,* Part I, Vol. XI, April 1899, pp. 67–75; Part II, May 1899, pp. 131–8. Father O'Donovan addresses the problems of economic and cultural poverty in Ireland and argues that they can be solved by national will, co-operation, and widespread education in up-to-date agricultural methods. He believes the Church must show more social conscience and that the clergy must provide leadership in secular affairs. He published many such articles in Irish periodicals at this time.

18. Gerald O'Donovan, *Father Ralph* (Macmillan, 1913), p. 484.

19. *Ibid.,* p. 494.

20. Beryl O'Donovan, 'Locusts Food', p. 75. All further quotations from Beryl O'Donovan are from 'Locusts Food'.

21. Brigid O'Donovan, speaking on 'O'Donovan Broadcast' and in personal interviews.

22. RM, 'Miss Anstruther's Letters', Chapter 14, *RM,* p. 167.

23. Brigid O'Donovan, personal interviews.

24. RM, *Non-Combatants,* p. 182.

25. Mary Agnes Hamilton, *Remembering My Good Friends* (Jonathan Cape, 1944), p. 133.

26. RM, *What Not,* pp. 156–7.

27. *Ibid.,* pp. 151–2.

28. *Ibid.,* p. 16.

29. Jean Macaulay, letter to Constance Babington Smith, 13 February 1962, Wren-Macaulay Archive.

30. Lance Sieveking, *The Eye of the Beholder* (Hulton Press, 1957), p. 293.

31. RM, *What Not,* p. 116.

32. *Ibid.,* p. 236.

33. Rose Macaulay, 'Problems of a Writer's Life', *CC,* pp. 50–1.

34. Unsigned review of *The Two Blind Countries, The Englishwoman*, 22 May 1914, p. 238.
35. RM, *Potterism*, p. 53.
36. RM, *What Not*, p. 164.
37. RM, 'People Who Should Not Marry', *Daily Mail*, 26 October 1929.
38. RM, *Letters*, 16 April 1951, p. 116.
39. RM, *Towers*, p. 185.
40. RM, *Letters*, 12 August 1951, p. 172.

10. Secrecy and Success

1. RM, 'To Thomas: An Easter Address', *Three Days* (Constable, 1919), p. 67.
2. Undocumented newspaper interview as quoted by Constance Babington Smith in *RM*, p. 95.
3. Storm Jameson, *Journey to the North*, Vol. I (Collins and Harvill Press, 1969), p. 161. Hereafter *Journey*.
4. *Ibid.*
5. RM, letter to Rosamond Lehmann, 11 September 1956, Modern Archives, King's College Library.
6. RM, *Towers*, p. 63.
7. RM, letter to unidentified recipient *re Potterism* [1920], Harry Ransom Humanities Research Center, University of Texas, Austin. Hereafter Humanities Research Center.
8. RM, *Potterism*, pp. 92–3.
9. *Ibid.*, p. 95.
10. Virginia Woolf, *VW Diary*, Vol. II, 10 August 1920, p. 57.
11. Virginia Woolf, letter to Hope Mirlees [end October 1920], *The Virginia Woolf Letters, Vol. VI, 1936–1941*, ed. Nigel Nicolson and Joanne Trautmann (Hogarth Press, 1980), Appendix B, Letters Found Too Late for Inclusion in the Earlier Volumes, p. 497. Hereafter *VW Letters*.
12. RM, letter to Rosamond Lehmann, 20 August 1942, Modern Archives, King's College Library.
13. Gerald O'Donovan, *The Holy Tree* (Macmillan, 1922), p. 302.
14. *Ibid.*
15. Father Hamilton Johnson, letter to his cousin, Mary Barham Johnson, 24 February 1952, as quoted by Constance Babington Smith, 'Introduction', *Letters*, p. 22.
16. RM, *What Not*, pp. 148–9.
17. RM, *Last Letters*, 6 October 1952, p. 37.
18. Evelyn Waugh, letter to Graham Greene, 26 October [1961], *The*

Letters of Evelyn Waugh, ed. Mark Amory (Weidenfeld & Nicolson, 1980), p. 576.

19. Alan Pryce-Jones, 'Knowing', p. 25.

20. RM, *Crewe Train* (Collins, 1926), p. 299.

21. *Ibid.*

22. Cesar Saerchinger, 'Rose Macaulay Satirical in Judging Persons and Art', New British Literary Horizons, *New York Evening Post,* 21 January 1929.

23. Constance Babington Smith, *RM,* p. 101.

24. Mary Agnes Hamilton, *Remembering My Good Friends* (Jonathan Cape, 1944), p. 137.

25. Storm Jameson, *Journey,* pp. 160–1.

26. Virginia Woolf, *VW Diary,* Vol. II, 5 June 1921, pp. 122–3.

27. Leonard Woolf, *Downhill All the Way: An Autobiography of the Years 1919–1939* (Hogarth Press, 1968), p. 80. Hereafter *Downhill.*

28. Virginia Woolf, *VW Diary,* Vol. II, 5 June 1921, p. 123.

29. Brigid O'Donovan, speaking on the 'O'Donovan Broadcast'.

30. Muriel Thomas, personal letter to author, 23 April 1990.

31. RM, *Towers,* p. 253.

32. RM, 'Miss Anstruther's Letters', *RM,* p. 168.

33. *Ibid.*

34. *Ibid.,* p. 169.

35. RM, *Towers,* p. 172.

36. RM, letter to Rosamond Lehmann, 20 August 1942, Modern Archives, King's College Library.

37. RM, 'Books Destroyed – and Indispensable', *Listener,* 14 July 1949, p. 63.

38. RM, 'Sources of Fiction', review of *Craft and Character in Modern Fiction* by Morton Dauwen Zabel (Gollancz, 1957), *Listener,* 3 October 1957, p. 530.

39. RM, 'Writing', *Pleasures,* p. 378.

40. *Ibid.,* pp. 378–9.

41. *Ibid.,* pp. 390–1.

42. RM, 'Venice Besieged: A Fragment of a Novel', *Sister,* p. 326.

43. RM, *Forster,* p. 7.

44. Virginia Woolf, *VW Diary,* Vol. III, 24 February 1926, p. 61.

45. RM, 'The New London Since 1914', *Current History* (periodical published by the *New York Times*), 9 May 1926, p. 171.

46. *Ibid.,* p. 174.

47. RM, *Life English,* p. 46.

48. RM, 'Writing', *Pleasures,* pp. 377–8.

49. Anonymous [probably RM] epigraph of *Ages,* p. [vi].

50. *Ibid.,* p. 269.

51. *Ibid.*

52. RM, *Idiot*, p. 237.
53. RM, 'Note', *Mystery*, p. [v.].
54. RM, *Idiot*, p. 313.
55. *Ibid.*, p. 93.
56. RM, letter to Neville Braybrooke, 1 October 1958.
57. Alan Pryce-Jones, 'Introduction', *Orphan Island* (Collins, 1960; originally published 1924), p. 10. Hereafter 'Introduction', *Orphan*.
58. RM, letter to E.M. Forster, 14 May 1945, Modern Archives, King's College Library.

11. New Friends

1. Storm Jameson, 'Learning from Experience', review of *RM, Spectator*, 21 October 1972.
2. Janet Adam Smith, 'Go, Happy Rose', *New Statesman*, 8 November 1958, p. 626.
3. John Betjeman, 'Rose Macaulay', Tribute, *Observer*, 2 November 1958.
4. Jacobine Sackville-West as quoted by Constance Babington Smith in *RM*, p. 213. She was referring specifically here to Rose at 76, seated on the floor, playing with the three Sackville-West children.
5. Jean Macaulay, letter to Constance Babington Smith, 1 April 1959. Jean Macaulay heavily edited RM's letters to her to exclude what seemed to her to be flippancy or irreverence. It is not surprising that RM kept her life with Jean quite separate from her social life as a writer. On 11 November 1960, Jean Macaulay wrote to Constance Babington Smith, 'I do think the literary world is more corrupt than other respectable worlds. I have only once heard a nurse say anything improper, and she was disapproved of by all the others. I was often shocked by things Rose quoted from her circle.' Of RM's letters to Father Johnson she wrote, 'I'm sure they would be much more discreet than her letters to me, which contained a lot of nonsense which wouldn't be understood by the public. She knew, of course, that I would not take them too seriously.'

There were other reasons than Jean's shockability for omissions from the letters: RM's troubled, sympathetic, and extended comments on the sad extra-marital love affair of a friend who was still living at the time of publication made radical deletion necessary in all three volumes of letters. In addition, RM's frank, amusing, and sometimes inaccurate statements about others posed problems of tact to Constance Babington Smith, the editor, and the possibility of legal liability to the publisher, Collins.

Those mentioned dismissively, humorously, or inaccurately were asked to choose one of four options: removal of any reference to them; selective deletion of RM's comments; insertion of a qualifying or clarifying footnote to the text; or the granting of permission to publish. Graham Greene, whom RM saw often at one period and whom she conversationally challenged on matters of religious doctrine, made the fourth choice; he did not edit the comments on himself. He believed they showed more about RM than about Graham Greene.

To read the Greene references in *Letters* and *Last Letters* is to recover the lively tone of much that was removed from the published correspondence. An example: 'On Tuesday I am bidden to a party at Graham Greene's. Wouldn't it be interesting if at that party I was surrounded by G. G. characters – evil men, racing touts, false clergymen, drunken priests and with G. G. in the middle of them talking about Sin?' *Letters,* 25 July 1952, p. 342.

6. RM, untitled, unsigned poem, 'Staying with Relations' (Collins, 1930), p. 5. Hereafter 'Relations'.

7. RM, letter to Grace Macaulay [early 1920s], quoted by Constance Babington Smith, *RM,* p. 99.

8. RM, *Appearances,* p. 27.

9. *Ibid.,* pp. 157–8.

10. Leonard Woolf, *Downhill,* p. 76.

11. Q.D. Leavis, *Fiction and the Reading Public* (Russell & Russell, 1965; originally published 1932), p. 37.

12. RM, 'Virginia Woolf', *Spectator,* 11 April 1941, p. 394.

13. Virginia Woolf, *VW Diary,* Vol. III, Wednesday, 24 February [1926], p. 61.

14. RM, *Appearances,* p. 69.

15. Virginia Woolf, *VW Diary,* Vol. II, 18 February 1921, p. 93.

16. *Ibid.,* Vol. III, Wednesday, 24 February [1926], p. 60.

17. Virginia Woolf, *VW Letters,* Vol. III, letter to Roger Fry, 16 September 1925, p. 209.

18. Leonard Woolf, *Downhill,* p. 108.

19. Virginia Woolf, *VW Diary,* Vol. III, Wednesday, 24 February [1926], p. 60.

20. Virginia Woolf, *VW Letters,* Vol. III, letter to V. Sackville-West, 16 March 1926, p. 249.

21. Leonard Woolf, *Downhill,* pp. 80–1.

22. Virginia Woolf as quoted by Jean Guiguet in the Preface to *Contemporary Writers,* ed. Jean Guiguet (Hogarth Press, 1965), p. 11.

23. Virginia Woolf, *VW Letters,* Vol. V, letter to Quentin Bell, 24 January [1934], p. 272.

24. Virginia Woolf, *VW Letters,* Vol. III, letter to Vanessa Bell, 25 May [1928], p. 501.

25. Virginia Woolf, *VW Diary,* Vol. III, February 1926, pp. 61–2.

26. *Ibid.,* 27 March 1926, pp. 70–1.

27. Virginia Woolf, *VW Letters,* Vol. III, letter to Vanessa Bell, 25 May 1928, p. 501.

28. Virginia Woolf, *VW Diary,* Vol. IV, 9 October 1934, p. 249.

29. Virginia Woolf, *VW Letters,* Vol. III, letter to V. Sackville-West, 27 May 1928, p. 503.

30. Virginia Woolf, *VW Diary,* Vol. IV, 9 October 1934, p. 250.

31. Virginia Woolf, *A Writer's Diary,* ed. Leonard Woolf (New York: Harcourt, 1953), 5 September 1925, p. 81.

32. Leonard Woolf, *Downhill,* p. 76.

33. Virginia Woolf, *VW Diary,* Vol. III, 24 February 1926, p. 61.

34. Virginia Woolf, *VW Diary,* Vol. V, 12 March 1938, p. 130. 'Running into the dirty drop' is a metaphor Virginia Woolf uses when Mr Ramsay says 'Damn you' to Mrs Ramsay in *To the Lighthouse*: '... without replying, dazed and blinded, she bent her head as if to let the pelt of jagged hail, the drench of dirty water, bespatter her unrebuked,' p. 51.

35. Harold Nicolson, 'Knowing', p. 23.

36. Elizabeth Bowen, adapted from an interview in the BBC television film, *A Night's Darkness, A Day's Sail,* reproduced in *Recollections of Virginia Woolf* (New York: William Morrow, 1972), p. 50. Hereafter *Recollections.*

37. Virginia Woolf, *VW Diary,* Vol. III, 31 May 1928, p. 185.

38. RM, *Catchwords,* p. 5. She meditates on the intense emotion a British orator can create by using such 'haloed' phrases and words as 'women and children' or 'cricket'.

39. *Ibid.,* p. 37.

40. Raymond Mortimer, 'Rose Macaulay', Obituary tribute, press clipping from *Sunday Times* [between 31 October and 6 November 1958].

41. RM, letter to Virginia Woolf, 10 October 1940.

42. RM, *Last Letters,* 15 January 1954, p. 141.

43. RM, letter to Leonard Woolf, 3 April [1941], University of Sussex Archives.

44. RM, 'Virginia Woolf', *Spectator,* 11 April 1941, p. 394.

45. RM, 'Virginia Woolf', *Encounter* article republished in *Recollections,* p. 166.

46. RM, *Crewe Train* (Collins, 1926), p. 307.

47. RM, *Appearances,* p. 303.

48. *Ibid.,* p. 126.

49. Jean Smith, letter to Constance Babington-Smith, 8 February 1972.

50. RM, *Sister,* 5 May 1929, p. 49.

51. RM, *Sister,* 23 January [1930], p. 53.

52. RM, *Relations,* p. 9.

53. *Ibid.,* pp. 38–9.

54. *Ibid.,* p. 39.

55. RM, *'A House and its Head'*, typescript for a review, [1935], [p. 1], Wren-Macaulay Archive.

56. Hilary Spurling, *Ivy*, p. 377.

57. Francis King, personal letter to author, 17 August 1990.

58. Elizabeth Sprigge, *The Life of Ivy Compton-Burnett* (Gollancz, 1973), p. 154.

59. Ivy Compton-Burnett as quoted by Kay Dick, *Ivy and Stevie*, p. 33.

60. Hilary Spurling, *Ivy*, p. 378.

61. *Ibid.*, p. 377.

62. *Ibid.*, pp. 377–8.

63. Richard Kennedy, *A Boy at the Hogarth Press* (Whittington, 1972), p. 69.

64. RM, *Last Letters*, 20 February 1955, p. 194.

65. RM as quoted by Hilary Spurling, *Ivy*, p. 377.

66. RM, typescript for review of *A House and its Head*, p. 4, Wren-Macaulay Archive.

67. Victor Gollancz, *Reminiscences*, p. 85.

68. Rose Macaulay, letter to Ruth and Victor Gollancz, December 1932, as quoted by Victor Gollancz, *Reminiscences*, p. 80.

69. RM, *Last Letters*, 13 December 1952, p. 58.

70. Victor Gollancz, *Reminiscences*, p. 83.

71. Compton Mackenzie as quoted by Constance Babington Smith in *RM*, pp. 133–4.

72. RM, 'Driving a Car', *Pleasures*, p. 168.

73. RM, *Towers*, p. 22.

74. Victor Gollancz, *Reminiscences*, p. 84.

75. Alan Pryce-Jones, 'Introduction', *Orphan*, p. 11.

76. John Betjeman, 'Rose Macaulay', *Observer*, 2 November 1958.

77. Alan Pryce-Jones, 'Introduction', *Orphan*, pp. 11–12.

12. New Directions

1. RM, *Letters*, 16 May 1952, p. 315.

2. RM, 'Note', *Some Religious Elements in English Literature* (Hogarth Press, 1931), p. 5. Hereafter *Religious Elements*.

3. *Ibid.*, p. 6.

4. *Ibid.*, p. 11.

5. *Ibid.*, p. 87; p. 120.

6. *Ibid.*, p. 102.

7. RM, *Letters*, 1 April 1952, pp. 299–300.

8. Unsigned review of *They Were Defeated*, *New Statesman and Nation*, 23 October 1932, p. 492.

9. Dr Roger Thompson, School of English and American Studies,

University of East Anglia, personal letter to author, 9 March 1980.

10. Unsigned review of *The Shadow Flies, Saturday Review of Literature,* 29 October 1932, p. 205.

11. Dr C. V. Wedgwood, personal letter to author, 2 April 1980.

12. Dr C. V. Wedgwood, 'Knowing', p. 28.

13. RM, *Letters,* 30 August 1950, p. 27; 27 November 1950, p. 35.

14. RM, letter to Jean Macaulay [May 1932], quoted by Constance Babington Smith in *RM,* p. 122. Not included in *Letters to a Sister.*

15. RM, *Defeated,* p. 344.

16. *Ibid.,* p. 386.

17. *Ibid.,* p. 348.

18. Ralph Strauss, *Sunday Times,* 16 October 1923, p. 7.

19. L. A. G. Strong, *Spectator,* 22 October 1932, p. 558.

20. Gerald O'Donovan, letter to Joseph Hone, 13 August 1935, Humanities Research Center.

21. RM, letter to Daniel George, 11 July [1939]. RM made this observation five years after the book's publication. Although she was not a bearer of grudges, she quoted this attack verbatim.

22. Basil de Selincourt, review of *Milton, Observer,* 28 January 1934, p. 5.

23. Unsigned review of *Milton, TLS,* 11 January 1934, p. 29.

24. RM, 'M. Saurat and Milton [To the editor of *The Spectator*]', 23 February 1934, p. 275.

25. RM, *Milton* (Duckworth, 1934), p. 80.

26. *Ibid.,* p. 10.

27. *Ibid.,* p. 140.

28. RM, undated letter to Elizabeth Bowen [written within seven days after de Selincourt's review on 28 January 1934], Humanities Research Center.

29. RM, letter to Mrs Stewart Roberts, 11 July [1934].

30. RM, letter to Mrs Stewart Roberts, 8 August [1934].

31. RM, 'Parties', *Pleasures,* p. 300.

32. *Ibid.,* 'Getting Rid', p. 237.

33. *Ibid.,* 'Departure of Visitors', p. 153.

34. Compton Mackenzie, *My Life and Times, Octave VII, 1931–1938* (Chatto & Windus, 1939), p. 157.

35. RM, letter to Rosamond Lehmann, undated [*c.* 1 October 1954].

36. RM, *Going Abroad* (Collins, 1941; originally published 1934), p. 256.

37. RM, *Appearances,* p. 29.

38. RM, *I Would Be Private* (Collins, 1937), p. [4].

39. RM, 'Marginal Comments', *Spectator,* 17 January 1936, p. 90.

40. W.A.R. Collins, letter to Spencer Curtis Brown, [n.d., 1937], as quoted by Constance Babington Smith, *RM,* p. 128.

41. RM, 'Marginal Comments', *Spectator*, 22 November 1935, p. 853.

42. RM, letter to Hugh Walpole, [n.d., 1932], Humanities Research Center.

43. RM, review of *Dangerous Ages, Time and Tide*, 5 June 1921, p. 534.

44. RM, *Crewe Train*, p. 145.

45. RM, *Appearances*, pp. 218–19.

46. RM, 'Reflection in a Mirror', review of *Hugh Walpole* by Rupert Hart-Davis (Macmillan, 1952), *Listener*, 20 March 1952.

47. RM, 'A New Aubrey', review of *Brief Lives and Other Selected Writings*, ed. Anthony Powell (undocumented clipping, 1949).

48. RM's reviews of travel books are a summation of her own method: 'Quest in Sicily', review of *The Golden Honeycomb* by Vincent Cronin, *Listener*, 11 March 1954, p. 447; 'Sicilian Diversion', review of *Spring in Sicily* by Peter Quennell, *Listener*, 29 May 1952, p. 883; 'Viva el Turismo!' review of *Places*, ed. Geoffrey Grigson and Charles Gibbs-Smith, *Listener*, 7 October 1954, p. 580; 'Pleasures of Travel', essay on travel books, *Listener*, 17 January 1957, p. 113.

49. RM, 'Great Argument', review of C.E.M. Joad's *Folly Farm*, undocumented clipping from *The Times*, Wren-Macaulay Archive.

50. E.M. Forster, letter to Leonard Woolf, 10 January 1938, *Selected Letters of E.M. Forster, Vol. 2, 1921–1970*, ed. Mary Lago and P.N. Furbank, p. 155.

51. Elizabeth Bowen, review of *The Writings of E.M. Forster*, *New Statesman and Nation*, 2 April 1938, p. 572.

52. M.L. Elting, review of *The Writings of E.M. Forster*, *Forum*, September 1938, p. iv.

53. Lionel Trilling, review of *The Writings of E.M. Forster*, *New Republic*, 5 October 1938, p. 247.

54. Lionel Trilling, *E.M. Forster* (New York: New Directions, 1943), p. 8.

55. RM, *Forster*, p. 100.

56. *Ibid.*, p. 225.

57. *Ibid.*, p. 247.

58. *Ibid.*, p. 268.

59. *Ibid.*, p. 300.

13. Politics and Escape

1. Alan Pryce-Jones, 'Introduction', *Orphan*, p. 11.

2. *Ibid.*

3. William Plomer, 'Knowing', p. 30.

4. RM, postcard to Daniel George, 10 April 1939.

5. Rose Macaulay, *Life English*, pp. 46–7.

6. Charles Loch Mowat, *Britain Between the Wars: 1918–1940* (Chicago: University of Chicago Press, 1963), p. 201.

7. RM, 'Marginal Comments', *Spectator,* 20 November 1936, p. 892.

8. *Ibid.*

9. C. L. Mowat, *Great Britain Since 1914* (Hodder & Stoughton, 1970), pp. 159–60.

10. RM, *Sister,* 10 November [1935], p. 69.

11. RM, *Non-Combatants,* pp. 181–2.

12. Noreen Branson and Margot Heinemann, *Britain in the Nineteen Thirties* (Panther, 1973; originally published Weidenfeld & Nicolson, 1971), p. 334.

13. Malcolm Muggeridge, 'Dear Rose – so earnest, so clever, so wrong!', review of *Sister, Evening Standard,* 14 April 1964. Malcolm Muggeridge was another of RM's verbal opponents, both on and off the air. Despite their disagreements, he bore her no ill will.

14. C. L. Mowat, *Britain Between the Wars,* p. 591.

15. RM, 'Marginal Comments', *Spectator,* 13 March 1936, p. 465.

16. RM, 'Marginal Comments', *Spectator,* 27 March 1936, p. 574.

17. RM, 'Marginal Comments', *Spectator,* 15 May 1936, p. 877.

18. RM, 'An Open Letter', pamphlet (Collins, 1937), p. 5.

19. *Ibid.,* pp. 7–8.

20. *Ibid.,* p. 8.

21. *Ibid.,* p. 3.

22. RM, *Sister,* [after 29 June 1940], p. 104.

23. *Ibid.,* 3 May [1926], p. 31.

24. *Ibid.,* p. 30.

25. *Ibid.,* p. 31.

26. RM, letter to Daniel George, 24 June 1936.

27. Unsigned, 'Daniel George Bunting', Obituary column, *Sunday Times,* undated item in the Wren-Macaulay Archive.

28. RM, letter to Daniel George, 14 February 1952.

29. RM, letter to Margaret Bunting, 13 July 1949.

30. Harold Nicolson, 'Knowing', p. 23.

31. RM, letter to Daniel George, 6 April 1938.

32. RM, letter to Daniel George, 19 April [1938].

33. RM, 'Introduction', *All in a Maze* (Collins, 1938), p. 7.

34. RM, letter to Daniel George, 13 June 1938.

35. RM, *Towers,* p. 248.

36. RM, postcard to Daniel George, 6 September 1938.

37. RM, postcard, 15 September 1938.

38. Brigid O'Donovan, personal interview, 1983.

39. RM as quoted by Constance Babington Smith from a news story in the *Penrith Observer,* August 1939, *RM,* p. 150.

40. RM as quoted by Jean Macaulay, *RM,* p. 151.

41. RM, *Towers*, p. 252.

42. RM, letter to Collins, 13 March 1940, Collins Archive.

43. RM, 'Moral Indignation', *English Genius: A Survey of the English Achievement and Character*, ed. Hugh K. Lund (Eyre and Spottiswood, 1938), pp. 173–90.

44. RM, *Sister*, 9 December [1934], p. 63.

45. Anthony West, 'New Novels', review of *And No Man's Wit*, *New Statesman and Nation*, 13 July 1940. RM had predicted in a letter to Daniel George that she would get a bad review from Anthony West.

46. RM, *And No Man's Wit* (Collins, 1940), p. 236. Hereafter *No Man's*.

47. *Ibid.*, p. 24.

48. *Ibid.*, p. 323.

49. *Ibid.*, p. 329.

50. RM, *Letters*, 9 February 1951, p. 68.

51. RM, letter to Daniel George, 5 October 1939.

52. RM, *No Man's*, pp. 33–4.

53. Robert Littell, review of *And No Man's Wit*, *Yale Review*, winter 1941.

14. War and Grief

1. David Wright, 'Pedals and Pluck', *Sunday Telegraph*, 5 November 1972.

2. RM, *Sister*, 3 May 1957, p. 219.

3. RM, postcard to Daniel George, 30 August 1939.

4. Virginia Woolf, *VW Diary*, Vol. V, 12 October [1940], p. 329.

5. RM, 'Notes on the Way', *Time and Tide*, 5 October 1940, pp. 981–2.

6. RM, *Last Letters*, 10 February 1953, p. 82.

7. RM, *Sister*, [3 October 1940], p. 115.

8. RM, *Life English*, p. 47.

9. RM, fragment of a typescript for a wartime article, n.d., p. 5, Wren-Macaulay Archive.

10. RM, *Sister*, [11 September 1940], pp. 110–11; letter to Daniel George, [mid-October], as quoted by Constance Babington Smith in *RM*, p. 155.

11. RM, letter to Daniel George, 25 October [1940].

12. RM, letter to Daniel George, 13 May [1941].

13. RM, letter to Storm Jameson as quoted in *Journey*, Vol. 2, p. 112.

14. *Ibid.*

15. RM, letter to Daniel George, 14 May [1941].

16. RM, letter to Daniel George, ? May [1941], as quoted by Constance Babington Smith, *RM*, p. 157.

17. RM, letter to Victor Gollancz as quoted in *Reminiscences,* p. 79.

18. RM, 'Books Destroyed – and Indispensable', *Listener,* 14 July 1949, p. 63. This library was RM's heritage from four generations of book-lovers.

19. RM, letter to Daniel George, 24 July [1941].

20. RM, typescript, Wren-Macaulay Archive.

21. RM, 'Frankly Speaking', BBC interview, July 1958.

22. Muriel Thomas [O'Donovan], personal letter to author, 12 December 1989.

23. RM as quoted by Storm Jameson in *Journey,* p. 112.

24. Brigid O'Donovan, personal interview, 1982.

25. Storm Jameson, *Journey,* p. 113.

26. RM, 'Miss Anstruther's Letters', as printed by Constance Babington Smith in *RM,* p. 161–70.

27. RM, letter to Rosamond Lehmann, 20 August 1942, Modern Archives, King's College Library.

28. RM, *Towers,* p. 253.

29. RM, letter to Rosamond Lehmann, 20 August 1942, Modern Archives, King's College Library.

30. RM, letter to Daniel George, 18 September 1942.

31. RM, *Wilderness,* p. 36.

32. RM, letter to Gilbert Murray, 2 December 1950.

33. RM, 'Notes on the Way', *Time and Tide,* 25 June 1932, pp. 709–10.

34. RM as quoted by Victor Gollancz, *Reminiscences,* p. 80.

35. One of Gilbert Murray's young friends, Margaret Cole, wrote to him after Christmas 1931, 'My Dear Monument'. Gilbert West says, 'Even in the 1930's he was coming to seem like a monument to the Victorian era, which she, in a younger generation, could respect but not wholly understand.' Francis West, *Gilbert Murray: A Life* (Croom Helm, 1984), p. 234. But RM could both respect and understand him. Her comment is found in a letter to him on 30 December 1953. On New Year's Day 1956, she wrote to him, 'One of the few things in my life that I am really proud of is that you have let me be your friend (if I may call it that), and sometimes have the immense pleasure of seeing and even of driving you.'

36. Alan Pryce-Jones, 'Knowing', p. 25.

37. Gilbert Murray, letter to RM, 13 January 1949, Department of Western Manuscripts, Bodleian Library, Oxford University.

38. RM, letter to Gilbert Murray, 30 January 1953.

39. RM, letter to Gilbert Murray, 23 November 1943.

40. T. S. Eliot, 'Euripides and Professor Murray' (1920), *Selected*

Essays of T.S. Eliot (New York: Harcourt, Brace and World, 1960; originally published 1932), p. 49.

41. RM, letter to Gilbert Murray, 16 October 1946.
42. RM, letter to Muriel Thomas, 13 August 1951. Lent to me by Muriel Thomas.
43. RM, letter to Gilbert Murray, 10 May 1943.
44. *Ibid.*
45. RM, letter to Lady Mary, 10 July 1944.
46. RM, letter to Gilbert Murray, 26 June 1944; 10 July 1944.
47. RM, letter to Gilbert Murray, 10 July 1944.
48. RM, *Letters,* 16 April 1951, p. 116.
49. House memo to RM, 23 March 1945, Collins Archive.
50. RM, letter to Collins, 25 March 1945, Collins Archive.
51. RM, letter to Daniel George, 15 June 1945.
52. RM, letter to David Ley as quoted by Constance Babington Smith, *RM,* p. 176.
53. RM, letter to Gilbert Murray, 24 May 1947.
54. RM, letter to Gilbert Murray, 12 June 1947.
55. RM, *Fabled Shore: From the Pyrenees to Portugal* (Hamish Hamilton, 1949), p. 26. Hereafter *Fabled Shore.*
56. *Ibid.,* p. 35.
57. *Ibid.,* p. 10.
58. *Ibid.,* p. 2.
59. *Ibid.,* p. 25.
60. *Ibid.,* p. 198.
61. Dr C. V. Wedgwood, *Time and Tide* review of *Fabled Shore* quoted on original book-jacket.
62. RM, letter to Gilbert Murray, 7 April 1948.
63 *Fabled Shore,* p. 2.
64. Elizabeth Bowen, *Tatler* review of *Fabled Shore* quoted on original book-jacket.
65. Virginia Woolf, 'Mr. Conrad; A Conversation', *Collected Essays,* Vol. I, p. 310.
66. Gilbert Murray, letter to Rose Macaulay as quoted by Constance Babington Smith, *RM,* p. 182.
67. Penelope Fitzgerald, 'Introduction', *The World My Wilderness* (Virago, 1982), p. xii.
68. Gilbert Murray, 'A Victorian Looks Back', BBC broadcast, 1947, as quoted by Francis West, *Gilbert Murray: A Life* (Beckenham, Kent: Croom Helm, 1984), p. 235.
69. RM, letter to Gilbert Murray, 13 February 1955.
70. RM, *Wilderness,* p. 152.
71. *Last Letters,* 7 November 1954, p. 176.
72. RM, 'T. S. Eliot', typescript of an article which appeared in *T. S.*

Eliot: A Symposium for His 70th Birthday (Hart-Davis, 1958), Wren-Macaulay Archive.

73. RM, *Wilderness,* p. 167.
74. *Ibid.,* p. 232.
75. RM, letter to Gilbert Murray, 2 May 1948.
76. RM, *Wilderness,* p. 21.
77. *Ibid.,* p. 50.

15. The Golden Fleece

1. RM, *Captives,* p. 219.
2. RM, *Letters,* 28 September 1950, p. 31.
3. RM, *Letters,* 28 October 1950, p. 32.
4. RM, letter to Gilbert Murray, 4 March 1945.
5. RM, letter to Daniel George, 31 July [1946]; postcard to Gilbert Murray, 15 May 1950.
6. RM, *Last Letters,* 10 November 1952, p. 49.
7. RM, letters to Gilbert Murray, 20 July 1948 and 11 August 1948.
8. RM, *Letters,* 14 June [1952], p. 324.
9. RM, *Letters,* 15 December 1951, p. 236.
10. RM, *Letters,* 1 March 1951, p. 90.
11. RM, *Last Letters,* 1 January 1954, p. 138.
12. *Ibid.*
13. RM, *Last Letters,* 25 September 1955, p. 209. Writing to Father Johnson about listening to a TV programme at Butlin's Holiday camp with Mary Anne and Jane O'Donovan, she says: 'One programme, which showed a panel of 4 famous people guessing "Who wrote that?" to my surprise quoted something from me (but I don't know where I said it) – something about "it is to the eccentrics that the world owes most of its knowledge." ... On the whole [most of them] agreed with me. The girls were delighted.'
14. RM, *Letters,* 6 December 1951, p. 231.
15. William Plomer, Anthony Powell, Mark Bonham Carter, 'Knowing', pp. 28–30.
16. C. David Ley, personal interview, February 1982.
17. Patrick Kinross, 'Knowing', pp. 26–7.
18. RM, *Letters,* 2 August 1952, p. 346.
19. RM, *Letters,* 15 December 1951, p. 238.
20. RM, *Letters,* 10 September 1951, p. 192. 'Yes, of course, gender must come into relationships; don't you think it does even between parents and children, and brothers and sisters? Certainly it does between friends. I don't think years make any difference to that; all they do is to get rid of *sex* in its strictly limited sense. I think it so happens that I have

more men friends than women; and I am sure their masculinity enhances the relationship.' Raymond Mortimer, editor of the *Sunday Times* Book Page, and three male friends, had an attractive home, Long Crichel, in Dorset where Rose was a frequent guest.

21. Rosamond Lehmann, 'Knowing', pp. 24–5.

22. V.S. Pritchett, 'Euodias and Syntechne', review of *Letters to a Sister* and *Last Letters to a Friend, New Statesman,* 17 April 1964.

23. RM, *Last Letters,* 18 November 1955, p. 212.

24. Raymond Mortimer, 'A Return to Faith', review of *Letters to a Friend: 1950–52, Sunday Times,* 17 April 1964.

25. Harold Nicolson, 'Knowing', pp. 23–4.

26. RM, *Last Letters,* 18 February 1953, p. 83.

27. RM, *Towers,* p. 7.

28. Alan Pryce-Jones, 'Knowing', pp. 25–6.

29. RM, *Letters,* Shrove Tuesday, February 1951, p. 67.

30. RM, *Letters,* 1 March 1951, p. 88.

31. RM, *Letters,* 9 January 1951, p. 51.

32. Father Johnson, letter to his English cousin, Mary Barham Johnson, 24 February 1952, quoted by Constance Babington Smith in the 'Introduction' to *Letters,* p. 22.

33. RM, *Letters,* 15 December 1950, p. 38.

34. RM, *Last Letters,* 8 January 1953, p. 71.

35. RM, *Sister,* [19 March 1953], p. 151.

36. RM, *Letters,* [22 January 1951], p. 60; 2 January 1951, p. 60.

37. RM, *Towers,* p. 256.

38. RM, *Last Letters,* 25 October 1953, p. 117.

39. RM, *Letters,* 30 August 1950, p. 28.

40. RM, *Letters,* Shrove Tuesday, February 1951, p. 67.

41. RM, *Letters,* 28 January [1951], p. 61.

42. RM, *Letters,* 11 July 1952, p. 338.

43. RM, as quoted by Harvey Curtis Webster in 'A Christian a Little Agnostic' in *After the Trauma* (Kentucky: University Press of Kentucky, 1970), p. 24. RM said she felt most at home with the Cambridge Platonists who believed that a good agnostic was in a better state of grace than a bad Christian. The work of Miguel de Unamuno also attracted her.

44. Rose Macaulay, *Sister,* 24 July 1958, p. 282.

45. RM, *Letters,* 27 April 1957, p. 218.

46. RM, *Letters,* 6 May 1952, p. 311.

47. RM, *Letters,* 15 August [1951], p. 175.

48. RM, *Last Letters,* 18 January 1953, p. 73.

49. RM, *Sister,* 22 February 1955, p. 169.

50. RM, *Letters,* 6 March 1952, p. 283.

51. Susanna Hodson, 'Rose Macaulay in the Courts of God', *Godly Mayfair* (Grosvenor Chapel, 1980), p. 37. Susanna Hodson, now the

Honourable Mrs Hodson, was at the time Rose knew her, Susan Lister. Rose dedicated *The Towers of Trebizond* to her.

52. RM, *Letters*, 25 May 1951, p. 135.

53. Sir John Betjeman, 'Introduction', *Godly Mayfair*, p. iv.

54. RM as quoted by Susanna Hodson, *Godly Mayfair*, p. 38.

55. RM, *Letters*, 22 March 1952, p. 292.

56. RM, *Last Letters*, 25 December 1952, p. 63.

57. RM, *Letters*, 24 April 1951, p. 119; 1 June 1951, p. 141.

58. William Plomer, 'Knowing', p. 31.

59. RM, *Letters*, 12 June 1951, pp. 144, 152; *Last Letters*, 20 November 1952, p. 53.

60. Victor Gollancz, *Reminiscences*, p. 84. Victor Gollancz's biographer, Ruth Dudley Edwards, attributes this rift to RM's integrity: 'As Victor's vanity grew, they [his friends] were constantly having to decide where to yield and where to assert their independence. Harold Rubenstein had long ago settled for acolyte status; Rose Macaulay played it the other way. She would not compromise her literary judgement by uncritical adulation of his published work. ... She died in 1958, their friendship but a shadow of what it had been in the 30's and 40's.' *Victor Gollancz* (Gollancz, 1987), p. 610.

61. RM, *Letters*, 19 January 1952, p. 255.

62. Revd Gerard Irvine, personal interview, February 1982.

63. Alan Pryce-Jones, 'Knowing', p. 25.

64. Mark Bonham Carter, personal interview, January 1979.

65. RM, *Sister*, 9 March 1954, p. 160.

66. RM, *Letters*, 27 March 1951, p. 107.

67. RM, *Sister*, 22 February [1955], p. 169.

68. RM, *Letters*, 5 March 1951, p. 91.

69. RM, *Letters*, 22 June 1951, p. 148.

70. RM, *Letters*, 15 February 1951, p. 75.

71. Patrick Kinross, 'Knowing', p. 26.

72. RM, *Letters*, 29 February 1952, p. 280.

73. RM, *Letters*, 29 August 1952, p. 355.

74. RM, *Letters*, 12 August 1952, p. 350.

75. Muriel Thomas, personal letter to the author, 20 September 1983.

76. RM, *Letters*, 14 January 1951, p. 56.

77. RM, *Pleasure of Ruins* (Weidenfeld & Nicolson, 1953), p. xv. Hereafter *Ruins*.

78. RM, letter to C. David Ley, [misdated 8 January 1952; should be 1953].

79. RM, *Last Letters*, 2 June 1953, pp. 101, 99.

80. *Ibid.*, p. 99.

81. RM, *Last Letters*, 11 July 1953, p. 102.

82. RM, *Last Letters*, 8 October 1953, p. 114.

83. RM, *Last Letters,* 1 March 1954, pp. 147–8.

84. RM, *Sister,* 9 March [1954], p. 161.

85. RM, unpublished letter to Susan Lister, Whitsuntide 1953, lent to me by Mrs Hodson.

86. RM as quoted by Alan Pryce-Jones, 'Knowing', p. 25.

87. RM, *Last Letters,* 3 November 1953, p. 119.

88. RM, letter to Gilbert Murray, 27 October 1955.

89. RM, *Towers,* [p. 6]. The epigraph, attributed to the non-existent *Dialogues of Mortality,* is by RM.

90. RM, *Towers,* p. 256.

91. RM, *Towers,* p. 255.

92. RM, typescript for 'Religious Writing', an article written for a *TLS* issue of 'The Frontiers of Literature', 17 August 1956, Wren-Macaulay Archives.

93. RM, *Sister,* [probably 24 September 1956], pp. 202–3.

94. RM, letter to 'Maisie', 23 July 1958.

95. RM, letter to Rosamond Lehmann, 11 September 1957, Lehmann Archives, King's College Library.

96. RM, *Sister,* 24 January [1958], p. 255.

97. RM, *Wilderness,* p. 198.

98. RM, letter to John Hayward, 11 September 1956.

99. RM, *Sister,* 24 July 1929, p. 50.

100. RM, *Sister,* 5 January 1958, p. 251.

101. Revd Patrick McLaughlin, information taken from a letter to Constance Babington Smith, 7 April 1974.

102. RM, 'The New Argonauts', *Queen,* 30 September 1958.

103. Patrick Kinross, 'Knowing', p. 25.

104. Diana Cooper, 'Knowing', p. 31.

105. Rose Macaulay, 'The New Argonauts'.

SELECTED BIBLIOGRAPHY

I. Books by Rose Macaulay (in chronological order)

Novels

Abbots Verney	John Murray, 1906
The Furnace	John Murray, 1907
The Secret River	John Murray, 1909
The Valley Captives	John Murray, 1911
Views and Vagabonds	John Murray, 1912
The Lee Shore	Hodder & Stoughton, 1912
The Making of a Bigot	Hodder & Stoughton, 1914
Non-Combatants and Others	Hodder & Stoughton, 1916
What Not: A Prophetic Comedy	Constable, 1918
Potterism: A Tragi-farcical Tract	Collins, 1920
Dangerous Ages	Collins, 1921
Mystery at Geneva	Collins, 1922
Told by an Idiot	Collins, 1923
Orphan Island	Collins, 1924
Crewe Train	Collins, 1926
Keeping Up Appearances	Collins, 1928
Staying with Relations	Collins, 1930
They Were Defeated	Collins, 1932
Going Abroad	Collins, 1934
I Would Be Private	Collins, 1937
And No Man's Wit	Collins, 1940
The World My Wilderness	Collins, 1950
The Towers of Trebizond	Collins, 1956

Selected Bibliography

Poetry

The Two Blind Countries	Sidgwick & Jackson, 1914
Three Days	Constable, 1919
Rose Macaulay: The Augustan Books of English Poetry, Second Series, No. 6, ed. Humbert Wolfe	Ernest Benn, 1927

Essays and Criticism

A Casual Commentary	Methuen, 1925
Catchwords and Claptrap	Hogarth Press, 1926
Some Religious Elements in English Literature	Hogarth Press, 1931
Milton	Duckworth, 1934
Personal Pleasures	Gollancz, 1935
The Writings of E.M. Forster	Hogarth Press, 1938

Anthology

The Minor Pleasures of Life	Gollancz, 1934

History and Travel

Life Among the English	Collins, 1942
They Went to Portugal	Jonathan Cape, 1946
Fabled Shore: From the Pyrenees to Portugal	Hamish Hamilton, 1949
Pleasure of Ruins	Weidenfeld & Nicolson, 1953
They Went to Portugal Too	Carcanet, 1990

Letters

Letters to a Friend: 1950–1952	Collins, 1961
Last Letters to a Friend	Collins, 1962
Letters to a Sister	Collins, 1964

II. Archival Sources

The chief source of unpublished family and personal papers, juvenilia, correspondence, diaries, typescripts, and ephemeral published material by and about Rose Macaulay is the E.R. Macaulay Archive of the Wren Library of Trinity College, Cambridge University. The Harry Ransom Humanities Research Center at the University of Texas, Austin, has all of Rose Macaulay's novels and many letters, chiefly professional rather than biographical in reference. Archives in the British Library, the Berg Collection of the New York Public Library, and the personal files of friends of Rose Macaulay hold unpublished primary materials. (Personal letters in RM's flat, with the exception of those from Gilbert Murray, were by her written directions, burned at the time of her death.) Both the BBC Archive of Written Records at Reading and the BBC Archives of Recorded Sound in London hold published and recorded Rose Macaulay broadcasts. The National Library of Ireland holds the many articles, speeches, and a number of short stories by Father Jeremiah O'Donovan.

III. Selected Writings by Rose Macaulay (in chronological order)

A full list of Rose Macaulay's journalistic comment (political, literary, linguistic, autobiographical) and her writing appearing in the essay collections would require a volume to itself. This brief bibliography is designed to show the variety of her interests and her expertise and the range of publications in which her work appeared between 1920 and 1958. All books were published in London unless otherwise specified.

Review of 'The Rescue', by Joseph Conrad, *Time and Tide*, 9 July 1920, p. 188.

Review of Arnold Bennett's *Our Women: Chapters on the Sex Discord*, *Time and Tide*, October 1920.

'Children's Books', *Time and Tide*, 31 December 1920, pp. 713–14.

Review of *Bliss and Other Stories*, *Time and Tide*, 14 January 1921, p. 41.

'Does Ancestry Matter?', *Daily Express*, 5 June 1928.

'A Church I Should Like', *St Paul's Review*, May 1929, p. 12.

'What I Believe', *Nation*, 16 December 1931, p. 666.

'Villa Macolai', *Little Innocents: Childhood Reminiscences* (Cobden-Sanderson, 1932), pp. 46–9.

'A Word on Family Life', *Spectator*, 20 February 1932, p. 246.

'Sir Thomas Browne', review of *The Works of Sir Thomas Browne*, Vols. V and VI, ed. Geoffrey Keynes, *Time and Tide*, 7 May 1932, pp. 520–1.

'The Return to Horridness in Literature', *Spectator*, 10 March 1933, p. 329.

'On Linguistic Changes', *Essays and Studies by Members of the English Association* (Oxford: Clarendon Press, 1935), Vol. 20, pp. 108–22.

'The Spice of Life, In Deep and Shallow Waters', *Listener*, 30 January 1936, p. 207.

'Marginal Comments' [anti-film censorship], *Spectator*, 29 May 1936, p. 976.

'Full Fathom Five', Auto-Obituary, *Listener*, 2 September 1936, p. 434.

'Marginal Comments' [anti-fascism; anti-police behaviour in Mosley riots], *Spectator*, 27 November 1936, p. 943.

'Lyly and Sidney', *English Novelists: A Survey of the Novel by Twenty*

Contemporary Novelists, ed. Derek Verschoyle (New York: Harcourt, Brace and Co., 1936), pp. 33–50.

'An Open Letter' for The Peace Pledge Union, pamphlet (Collins, 1937).

'Moral Indignation', *English Genius: A Survey of the English Achievement and Character,* ed. Hugh K. Lund (Eyre and Spottiswood, 1938), pp. 173–90.

'Consolations of the War', *Listener,* 16 January 1941, p. 75.

'Virginia Woolf', *Spectator,* 11 April 1941, p. 394.

'Virginia Woolf', *Horizon,* May 1941, pp. 316–18.

'The B.B.C. and War Moods: I', *Spectator,* 21 January 1944.

'Luther and Hitler', *Spectator,* 1 June 1945, p. 500.

'The Greatest Genius of his Age: Rose Macaulay on Jonathan Swift as letter-writer and diarist', *Listener,* 20 December 1945, pp. 738–9.

'The Future of Fiction', *New Writing and Daylight: By Various Writers,* ed. John Lehmann (Longmans, Green, & Co., 1946), pp. 71–5.

'Novels-Dead or Alive? A discussion between Rose Macaulay and James Stephens', *Listener,* (13 June 1946), pp. 782–3.

'Evelyn Waugh', *Horizon,* December 1946, pp. 360–76.

'The Age of Reason', *New Statesman and Nation,* 10 January 1948, pp. 27–8.

'A Very Mixed Party', review of *The Dictionary of National Biography 1931–40, Listener,* 8 December 1949, pp. 1011–12.

'Quest in Sicily', review of *The Golden Honeycombe* by Vincent Cronin, *Listener,* 11 March 1954, p. 447.

'Coming to London', *Coming to London* (Phoenix House, 1957), pp. 155–66.

'In Spain and Portugal', *Spectator,* 22 February 1957, p. 239.

'Sources of Fiction', review of *Craft and Character in Modern Fiction* by Morton Zabel, *Listener,* 3 October 1957, p. 530.

'The First Impact of *The Waste Land*', *T. S. Eliot, A Symposium for His 70th Birthday,* ed. Rupert Hart-Davis, 1958, pp. 29–31.

'The New Argonaut', *Queen,* 30 September 1958.

IV. Selected Books, Articles, and Unpublished Studies About or Referring to Rose Macaulay and Her Writings

All books were published in London unless otherwise specified.

Bensen, Alice R., *Rose Macaulay,* Twayne English Authors Series, No. 85 (New York: Twayne, 1950).

Braybrooke, Patrick, *Some Goddesses of the Pen* (C.W. Daniel Co., 1927).

Connolly, Cyril, *The Condemned Playground: Essays 1927–1944* (Macmillan, 1946).

—— *Ideas and Places* (New York: Harper and Brothers, 1953).

Selected Bibliography

Davenport, John, 'Talk with Rose Macaulay', *New York Times Book Review*, April 1957, p. 14.

Ellis, Geoffrey Uther, *Twilight on Parnassus: A Survey of Post War Fiction* (Michael Joseph, 1939).

Gould, Gerald, 'Some of Our Humorists', *Bookman*, October 1924, p. 3.

Howatch, Susan, 'Introduction' to *They Were Defeated* (Oxford: Oxford University Press, 1981).

Inglishman, John, 'Rose Macaulay', *Bookman*, May 1927, pp. 107–10.

Johnson, Reginald Brimley, *Some Contemporary Novelists* (Leonard Parsons Press, 1920).

Kuehn, Robert Earl, 'The Pleasures of Rose Macaulay: An Introduction to Her Novels', unpublished dissertation, University of Wisconsin, 1962.

Lawrence, Margaret, *The School of Femininity* (New York: F. Stokes Company, 1936).

Lockwood, William J., 'Rose Macaulay', *Minor British Novelists*, ed. Charles Alva Hoyt (Carbondale and Edwardsville: Southern Illinois University Press, 1967).

Marrocco, Maria Jane, 'The Novels of Rose Macaulay: A Literary Pilgrimage', unpublished dissertation, University of Toronto, 1978.

Nicolson, Harold; Lehmann, Rosamond; Pryce-Jones, Alan; MacDonald, Dwight; Kinross, Patrick; Wedgwood, C. V.; Bonham Carter, Mark; Powell, Anthony; Plomer, William; Cooper, Diana, 'The Pleasures of Knowing Rose Macaulay', *Encounter*, March 1959, pp. 23–31.

Passty, Josephine N., *Eros and Androgyny* (London and Toronto: Associated University Press, 1988).

Pryce-Jones, Alan, 'Introduction' to *Orphan Island* (Collins, 1960).

Rizzo, Philip Louis, 'Rose Macaulay: A Critical Survey', unpublished dissertation, University of Pennsylvania, 1959.

Sherman, Stuart, *Critical Woodcuts* (New York: Charles Scribner's and Sons, 1926).

Smith, Constance Babington, 'Rose Macaulay in her Writings', Marie Stopes Memorial Lecture in *Essays by Divers Hand: Being the Transactions of the Royal Society of Literature*, new series, Vol. 38, ed. John Guest (Oxford University Press, 1975), pp. 143–8.

Stewart, Douglas, *The Ark of God: Studies in Five Modern Novelists: James Joyce, Aldous Huxley, Graham Greene, Rose Macaulay, Joyce Carey* (Carey Kingsgate Press, 1961).

Swinnerton, Frank, *The Georgian Scene: A Literary Panorama* (William Heinemann, 1935).

Thomas, Susan, 'Embattled Women of the 1920s: May Sinclair, Rose Macaulay and Rebecca West', unpublished dissertation, University of Queensland, 1985.

Webster, Harvey Curtis, 'A Christian a Little Agnostic', *After the Trauma: Representative British Novelists after 1920* (Lexington: University Press of Kentucky, 1970).

Wedgwood, Cicely Veronica, 'Introduction' to *They Were Defeated* (Collins, 1960).

Wilson, A. N., 'Introduction' to *Told by an Idiot* (Virago, 1983).

V. Selected Background Reading

All books were published in London unless otherwise specified.

Annan, Noel, 'The Intellectual Aristocracy', in *Studies in Social History,* ed. J. H. Plumb (Longmans, Green, and Co., 1955), pp. 254–5, 258.

Armstrong, Judy, *The Novel of Adultery* (London & Basingstoke: Macmillan, 1976).

Boose, Lynda E., and Flowers, Betty S. (eds.), *Daughters and Fathers* (Baltimore: Johns Hopkins Press, 1989).

Bowen, Elizabeth, *Collected Impressions* (Longmans, Green, & Co., 1950).

Boyne, Don (pseud.), *I Remember Maynooth* (Longmans, Green, & Co., 1937).

Branson, Noreen, and Heinemann, Margot, *Britain in the Nineteen Thirties* (Weidenfeld & Nicolson, reissued by Panther, 1973).

Braybon, Barbara, and Summerfield, Penny, *Out of the Cage: Women's Experiences in Two World Wars* (Pandora, 1987).

Braybon, Gail, *Women Workers in the First World War: The British Experience* (Croom Helm, 1981).

Briggs, Asa, and Macartney, Anne, *Toynbee Hall: The First Hundred Years* (Routledge and Kegan Hall, 1984).

Brittain, Vera, *Chronicles of Friendship: Vera Brittain's Diary of the Thirties: 1932–1939,* ed. Alan Bishop (Gollancz, 1986).

—— and Holtby, Winifred, *Testament of a Generation: The Journalism of Vera Brittain and Winifred Holtby,* ed. Paul Berry and Alan Bishop (Virago, 1985).

—— *The Women at Oxford: A Fragment of History* (George Harrap and Co., 1960).

Brooke, Rupert, *Rupert Brooke: The Collected Poems,* with a Memoir by Edward Marsh (third edition, revised November 1942) (Sidgwick & Jackson, 1942).

—— *The Letters of Rupert Brooke,* chosen and edited by Geoffrey Keynes (New York: Harcourt, Brace & World, 1986).

Brumberg, Joan Jacobs, *Fasting Girls: The Emergence of Anorexia Nervosa as a Modern Disease* (Cambridge, Mass. and London: Harvard University Press, 1988).

Byrne, Muriel St. Clare, and Mansfield, Catherine Hope, *Somerville College* (Oxford: Oxford University Press [1920?]).

Cadogan, Mary, and Craig, Patricia, *Women and Children First: The Fiction of Two World Wars* (Gollancz, 1978).

Delany, Paul, *The Neo-pagans: Rupert Brooke and the Ordeal of Youth* (New York: The Free Press, 1987).

Dick, Kay, *Ivy and Stevie: Conversations and Reflections* (Duckworth, 1971).

Drew, Elizabeth, *The Modern Novel: Some Aspects of Contemporary Fiction* (New York: Harcourt, Brace and Company, 1926).

Dyhouse, Carol, *Girls Growing Up in Late Victorian and Edwardian England* (Routledge & Kegan Paul, 1981).

Edwards, Ruth Dudley, *Victor Gollancz* (Gollancz, 1987).

Farnell, Vera, *A Somervillian Looks Back* (Oxford: privately printed at the University Press, 1948).

Forster, E. M., *Selected Letters of E.M. Forster, Vol. 2, 1921–1970*, ed. Mary Lago and P. N. Furbank (Cambridge, Mass.: Belknap Press, 1985).

Furbank, P. N., *E. M. Forster: A Life* (Secker & Warburg, 1977–9).

Fussell, Paul, *Abroad: British Literary Traveling between the Wars* (Oxford: Oxford University Press, 1980).

Gilbert, Sandra M., and Gubar, Susan, *No Man's Land: The Place of the Woman Writer in the Twentieth Century*, Vol. I (New Haven and London: Yale University Press, 1987).

—— ' "Soldier's Heart": Literary Women and the Great War', *Signs: Journal of Women in Culture and Society*, Spring 1983, pp. 422–50.

Glendinning, Victoria, *Vita: The Life of V. Sackville-West* (New York: Alfred A. Knopf, 1983).

Gollancz, Victor (ed.), *The Making of Women: Oxford Essays in Feminism* (George Allen & Unwin, 1917).

—— *Reminiscences of Affection* (Gollancz, 1968).

Hamilton, Mary Agnes, *Remembering My Good Friends* (Jonathan Cape, 1944).

Hassell, Christopher, *Edward Marsh* (Longmans, Green, & Co., 1959).

—— *Rupert Brooke: A Biography* (New York: Harcourt, Brace & World, 1964).

Heilbrun, Carolyn, *Hamlet's Mother* (New York and London: Columbia University Press, 1990).

—— *Reinventing Womanhood* (New York: Norton, 1979).

—— *Towards a Recognition of Androgyny* (New York: Knopf, 1964).

Hodges, Sheila, *Gollancz: The Story of a Publishing House, 1928–1978* (Gollancz, 1978).

Jameson, Storm, *Journey from the North,* Vols. I and II (Collins & Haverhill Press, 1969, 1970).

Leavis, Q. D., *Fiction and the Reading Public* (Russell & Russell, 1965).

Lehmann, John, *The Strange Destiny of Rupert Brooke* (New York: Holt, Rinehart and Winston, 1980).

Leonardi, Susan J., *Dangerous by Degrees: Women at Oxford and the Somerville College Novelists* (New Brunswick and London: Rutgers University Press, 1989).

Macaulay, George, *The History of Herodotus,* Book I (Macmillan, 1904).

—— 'Preface' to *The Chronicles of Froissart* (Macmillan, 1895).

Macaulay, Margaret (Sister Margaret), *The Deaconess* (The Faith Press, 1919).

—— *The Sentence Absolute* (James Nisbet, 1914).

McCrosson, Doris Ross, *Walter de la Mare* (New York: Twayne Publishers, 1966).

Mackenzie, Compton, *My Life and Times: Octaves VII and VIII* (Chatto & Windus, 1969).

Markham, Violet, *Return Passage: The Autobiography of Violet R. Markham, C. H.* (London, New York, Toronto: Oxford University Press, 1953).

Marwick, Arthur, *The Deluge: British Society and the First World War* (Macmillan, 1965).

Meacham, Standish, *Toynbee Hall and Social Reform: 1880–1914* (New Haven and London: Yale University Press, 1987).

Moorman, F. W., *Robert Herrick: A Biographical and Critical Study* (1910, reissued New York: Russell and Russell, 1962).

Mowat, Charles Loch, *Britain Between the Wars, 1918–1940* (Chicago: University of Chicago Press, 1955).

—— *Great Britain Since 1914: The Sources of History* (Hodder & Stoughton, 1970).

Noble, Joan Russell (ed.), *Recollections of Virginia Woolf* (New York: William Morrow and Co., 1972).

O'Donovan, Beryl, 'Locusts Food', unpublished memoir, n.d.

O'Donovan, Gerald, *Conquest* (London: Constable, 1921; New York: Putnam's, 1921).

—— *Father Ralph* (London: Macmillan, 1913; New York: Mitchell Kennerley, 1914).

—— *The Holy Tree* (London: Heinemann, 1922; New York: Boni & Liveright, 1923).

—— *How They Did It* (Methuen, 1920).

—— *Vocations* (London: Martin Secker, 1921; New York: Boni & Liveright, 1922).

—— *Waiting* (London: Macmillan, 1914; New York: Mitchell Kennerley, 1915).

Paget, Francis D. D., *The Spirit of Discipline, together with an Introductory Essay on Accidie* (Longmans, Green, & Co., 1903).

Pimlott, J. A. R., *Toynbee Hall* (J. M. Dent & Sons, 1935).

Powicke, Fredericke J., *The Cambridge Platonists: A Study* (Cambridge, Mass.: Harvard University Press, 1926).

Raverat, Gwen, *Period Piece* (Faber & Faber, 1952).

Rhondda, The Viscountess [Margaret Haig], *This Was My World* (Macmillan, 1933).

Ridler, Anne, *Olive Willis and Downe House: An Adventure in Education* (John Murray, 1967).

Rogers, Annie M. A. H., *Degrees by Degrees* (Oxford: Oxford University Press, 1938).

Ryan, John, 'Gerald O'Donovan, Priest, Novelist and Intellectual: A Forgotten Leader of the Irish Revival', unpublished thesis presented for the degree of MA at University College, Galway.

Sievking, Lance, *The Eye of the Beholder* (Hulton Press, 1957).

Smith, Naomi Royde, *The Double Heart: A Study of Julie de Lespinasse* (New York and London: Harper and Brothers, 1931).

Soulsby, Lucy, *Stray Thoughts on Reading*, fifth impression (Longmans, Green, & Co, 1904).

—— *A Woman's Movement* (Longmans, Green, & Co, 1913).

Spender, Dale, *Time and Tide Waits for No Man* (Pandora Press, 1984).

Spender, Stephen, *World within World* (New York: Harcourt, Brace & Co., 1948).

—— *The 30s and After: Poetry, Politics, People, 1930s–1970s* (New York: Random House, 1978).

—— *Journals 1939–1983*, ed. John Goldsmith (Faber and Faber, 1985).

Sprigge, Elizabeth, *The Life of Ivy Compton-Burnett* (New York: George Braziller, 1973).

Spurling, Hilary, *Ivy: The Life of Ivy Compton-Burnett* (New York: Knopf, 1977).

Strachey, Ray, '*The Cause*': *A Short History of the Women's Movement in Great Britain* (Port Washington, NY: Kennikat Press, 1928).

Swinnerton, Frank, *The Georgian Scene: A Literary Panorama* (New York: Farrar, Rinehart, 1934).

Villari, L., *Italian Life in Town and Country* (George Newnes, 1902).

Waugh, Evelyn, *The Letters of Evelyn Waugh*, ed. Mark Amory (Weidenfeld & Nicolson, 1980).

West, Francis, *Gilbert Murray: A Life* (Croom Helm, 1984).

West, Rebecca, *1900* (Weidenfeld & Nicolson, 1982).

Wheelwright, Julie, *Amazons and Military Maids* (Pandora, 1989).

Woolf, Leonard, *Downhill All the Way: An Autobiography of the Years 1919–1939* (Hogarth Press, 1968).

Woolf, Virginia, *Contemporary Fiction*, ed. Jean Guiguet (Hogarth Press, 1965).

—— *The Diary of Virginia Woolf,* ed. Anne Olivier Bell, 5 vols. (Hogarth Press, 1977–84).

—— *The Letters of Virginia Woolf,* ed. Nigel Nicolson and Joanne Trautmann, 6 vols. (Hogarth Press, 1975–80).

Index

Note: Works by Rose Macaulay appear under title; works by others under author's name

Index

Index

Macaulay, Jean Babington (*cont.*)
  religious beliefs and practices, 300, 302–3, 306–7; holidays in Isle of Wight with RM, 310; and RM's intruders, 313; and success of *Towers of Trebizond*, 317; CBE, 318; and RM's prediction of death, 320; editing RM's letters, 344–55
Macaulay, Kenneth (RM's uncle), 12, 26, 46–7, 94, 110, 201
Macaulay, Margaret Campbell (RM's sister): born, 18; childhood, 19; character, 34; relations with mother, 37, 60, 90, 104, 118, 127–8, 158; school in Oxford, 45, 52, 60; social life, 60; career, 87, 98; relations with RM, 88, 125; edits *Canterbury Tales*, 90; on arguments between RM and mother, 92; Italian holidays with uncles, 94, 110; and Dick Brooke, 107; enters religious community as deaconess, 127–9, 132, 138; attends father's funeral, 153; stays at Regi's Scottish lodge, 179; travels in USA with RM, 207, 218; buys house at Liss, 226; and writing of *They Were Defeated*, 229; RM visits, 253; cancer and death, 266–7, 271; *The Deaconess*, 128; *The Sentence Absolute*, 85–6
Macaulay, Mary (RM's aunt), 47
Macaulay, Reginald Heber (RM's Uncle Regi and godfather): visits Macaulays in Italy, 26; influence on RM, 31, 78; helps Uncle Harry, 40; supports RM at Oxford University, 61, 83; qualities, 61–2; RM visits in Scotland, 89–90; and death of Aulay, 116; receives RM's books, 133; gives London flat to RM, 138; death and legacies, 238–9
Macaulay, Dame Rose (Emilie Rose): tributes at death, 1–4; energy, 4; literary output, 4; family background, 9–12; questions dogma, 15, 302–3; born, 18; childhood, 19; growing up in Italy, 23–9, 33–5, 41–3; home education, 26–7; parental influences on, 30–1, 156; desires maleness, 31–3, 45–6, 48–9; relations with brothers and sisters, 33–5; schooling in Italy, 40–1; swimming, 42–3, 253, 261, 278, 281, 296, 310–11; return to England, 44–7; school at Oxford, 45, 49–53, 60; visits Italy with mother, 47, 60–1; appearance, 48, 66, 162, 182–3, 206, 271, 297; dress, 52–3, 67, 162, 206, 212, 263,

296; early innocence of sex, 54–6, 59; influenced by à Kempis, 55–7; adolescent loss of faith, 57–8; confirmation, 58–9; uninterested in social life, 60; at Somerville College, Oxford, 61–70; debating, 63, 68, 71, 78; voice and speech, 63, 68, 99, 222, 278; eating habits, 66; studies history, 70–1, 80; on position of women, 72–7, 202; social manner, 78–9; awarded Oxford Aegrotat, 79–80, 136; self doubts and sense of failure, 79, 82; begins writing, 85, 91; on career, 86–7; and family life, 87–9, 103–4; in Wales, 90–1; disputes with mother, 91–4; visits Italy with uncles, 94, 110–11; at Chesterfield House, 97–9; sensitivity to suffering and pain, 98–9, 152–3; attempts to obliterate early books, 101–2; relations with father, 29–30, 103, 111, 188; friendship with Rupert Brooke, 107–9, 113, 125–7, 129–30, 141–2, 148; nude bathing, 108–9; visits Venice, 110; and Aulay's death, 117, 154; serious churchgoing, 119–21; visits to London, 129–30, 138; view of the poor, 132–4; wins literary prize, 136; on Greek cruise with father, 136–8; friendship with Ronald Ross, 136–7; vocabulary, 141; poetry, 141–2, 155–6, 158, 178–9, 182, 196, 207, 218; London literary circle, 141–2, 144–8, 161–2, 188; conversation and talk, 142–3, 318; described, 143, 151–2, 182–3, 263, 296–7; visits and confesses to Cowley Fathers, 146–7, 158; gives London party, 147–8; visit to Canada, 148; and outbreak of First World War, 148–50; and Rupert Brooke's death, 150–2; as VAD in war, 152, 154; and father's death, 153–4, 156; works on land in war, 155–6; in love with and relations with Gerald O'Donovan ('secret life'), 159–60, 175–9, 183–4, 188–91, 193–5, 206, 217, 220, 264, 295, 302, 307; as wartime civil servant, 159–61; relations with mother, 93–4, 161, 295; published by Collins, 173, 179; adventurousness, 176, 183; privacy, 5, 177, 207, 251; dog, 178–9; views on marriage and love, 85–6, 180–1, 185–6, 189–90, 230–1; and Gerald's move to Rome, 181; weekly salons, 182–3; loses faith, 183; ceases confession and communion, 186;

Index

Index

Roberts, Mrs Ernest Stewart, 233–4
Rogers, Annie M. A. H., 71
Roman Catholicism: RM's views on, 41, 305–6, 312
Rome, 94–5, 181, 183–4
Ross, Ronald, 136–7, 144
Royde-Smith, Naomi: friendship with RM, 91, 148, 161, 191, 210; as literary editor of *Westminster Gazette*, 142; on RM's talk, 142–4; friendship with de la Mare, 146; and O'Donovan, 175, 191–2; entertaining, 175, 182, 183, 191–2; character, 191; depicted in RM novels, 192, 216; *The Double Heart*, 192–3
Ruskin, John, 77, 97, 98
Russell, Bertrand, 249
Russell, George *see* A.E.
Ryan, John P., 164, 341 n. 14
Rysselburgh, Elisabeth van, 109

Sackville-West, Josephine, Lady, 207
Sackville-West, Vita, 3, 210–11, 213, 222
Saerchinger, Cesar, 190
St Edward's House, Westminster, 146, 158, 186, 298, 301
St Paul's, Knightsbridge (church), 303–4, 306
St Thomas's, Regent Street (church), 306
Sassoon, Siegfried, 249
Saturday Westminster Gazette, 91
Saurat, Denis, 232
Sawston, Cambridgeshire, 121–2
Sayers, Dorothy L., 67, 306
Schrijvfer, Herman, 222
'Sea, The' (RM: juvenile poem), 47
Secret River, The (RM: novel): mysticism in, 42, 119; themes, 102, 111–14, 121–2; modernism, 106; Rupert Brooke depicted in, 110, 114; publication, 117; depression in, 120; love in, 151; and RM's father, 156
Shadow Flies, The see They Were Defeated
Shaw, George Bernard, 133, 170
Shaw Lefevre, Madeleine, 77–8
Sheppard, Revd Dick, 249–50
Sicily, 227
Sidgwick, Frank, 148
Sieveking, Lance, 176
Sitwell, Dame Edith, 191, 309
Skyros (island), 150, 320
Smith, Alice, 238
Smith, Constance Babington (RM's third

cousin): on Macaulays' life in Italy, 35; on Eleanor, 37; on RM's adolescent last will, 57; on de la Mare, 146; and RM's trip to Canada, 148; on RM as VAD, 153; and effect of father's death on RM, 158; and RM's trip down West Coast of America, 218; refutes charge of RM being uncaring, 236; on O'Donovan's road accident injury, 257; meets RM at St Paul's, Knightsbridge, 304
Smith, Daisy (RM's cousin), 26
Smith, Jean (RM's cousin), 217
Smith, Logan Pearsall, 136
Smythe, Dame Ethel, 265
'Solitude' (RM: essay), 42
Some Religious Elements in English Literature (RM), 208, 226–7
Somerville College, Oxford: RM attends, 61–71; ethos, values and style, 63–71, 77; and women's suffrage, 73
Somerville, Mary, 64
Soulsby, Lucy, 49–52, 56, 58; praises *Abbots Verney*, 96
'Sources of Fiction' (RM: review), 196
Southernwood, Great Shelford (house), 103
Southey, Robert, 277
Spain, 280–2, 294
Spanish Civil War, 243, 245–6, 256–8
Spectator (journal): RM writes for, 69, 80, 87, 207, 209, 215, 239, 244–7, 268; praises *The Lee Shore*, 136; RM defends *Milton* in, 232; loses de Clifford libel action, 237–8
Spender, Natasha (Lady), 296
Spender, (Sir) Stephen, 225, 246, 256, 261, 296
'Spreading Manure' (RM: poem), 155
Sprigge, Elizabeth, 221
Spurling, Hilary, 221
Staying with Relations (RM: novel), 207, 219–20
Steed, Wickham, 161
Stewart-Roberts, Margaret, 155
Strachey, Julian, 110
Strachey, Lytton, 232
Strauss, Ralph, 231
Suckling, Sir John, 229
Sunday Times, 286
Swinnerton, Frank, 143, 283, 285

Taylor, Margerie Venables, 95, 99, 104, 110, 112–13, 117

Index

'What People Want' (RM: lecture), 188
Whiteman, Father Harry, 304
'Why I Dislike Cats, Clothes and Visits'
  (RM: article), 67, 206
Wight, Isle of, 310
Wilkins, Father George Percy, 301
Willetts, Nancy, 138, 148, 310
Williams, Revd F. H. A., 121
Williams, Iolo, 148
Willis, Elsie, 97
Willis, Olive: friendship with RM at
  Somerville, 63, 66, 68, 79–80; teaching,
  86; depicted in *Abbots Verney*, 96; and
  RM's sense of failure, 136; on RM's
  confidence of own opinion, 157
Wilson, A. N., 78
Wolfe, Humbert, 142, 158, 223, 230
women: at Oxford, 63–72; votes for, 72–3;
  RM's views on position of, 73–7
Woolf, Leonard: on Rupert Brooke, 110;
  on Virginia's snobbery, 192; on best-
  sellers, 209; in Bloomsbury Group, 209;
  on Eliot, 210; on Virginia's common
  sense, 211; fondness for RM, 213; and
  Virginia's suicide, 215; dismisses Ivy
  Compton-Burnett, 222; on reviewing,
  240; letter from Forster on RM's book
  on writings, 241, 243; RM borrows book
  from, 254
Woolf, Virginia: on RM's 'donnishness',
  76, 186, 213–14; nude bathing with
  Rupert Brooke, 108; on RM's mysticism,
  112, 210; receives copy of *Georgian
  Poetry*, 142; reads *Potterism*, 186;
  mistaken view of RM's sexlessness, 189;
  despises Royde-Smith's parties, 191–2;
  criticizes RM's writing on contemporary
  history, 199; highbrow reputation, 209;

RM's obituary tributes to, 209, 215;
criticizes RM as 'Cambridge', 209;
discomfits RM, 210; relations with and
descriptions of RM, 210–15, 226; suicide,
215; and Ivy Compton-Burnett, 222; and
RM in *Spectator* libel action, 238; writing
on Forster, 241; RM visits during war,
264; praises RM's ambulance driving,
265; on writers' complex selves, 283;
refuses honorary doctorate, 309; *Jacob's
Room*, 212; *Orlando*, 214; 'Reviewing'
(essay), 240; *A Room of One's Own*, 209,
231; *To the Lighthouse*, 4, 199; *The
Voyage Out*, 56, 85; *The Years*, 199
Wordsworth, Dame Elizabeth, 78
World My Wilderness, The (RM: novel):
kept in print, 4; three voices in, 5, 283,
288–9; and sexual ignorance, 56; on
parents, 103–4; on O'Donovans, 170;
writing, 179, 264, 283, 294; on solitary
mourning, 273; and post-war morals,
274, 284, 287, 289; reception, 283–4;
structure, 284; plot and themes, 284–90,
293, 311; and spiritual quest, 297, 301;
on friends, 318
Wright, David, 143, 263
Writers' Anti-Fascist Meeting, 1938, 254
'Writing' (RM: essay), 196–7
Writings of E. M. Forster, The (RM), 91,
  197, 208, 213, 239, 241–3

Yeats, Jack B., 166
Yeats, Lilly (Susan Mary), 166
Yeats, Lolly (Elizabeth Corbet), 166
Yeats, W. B., 111, 165, 168; 'The Two
  Trees', 187

Zabel, Morton, 196